THE MAGILL BIBLIOGRAPHIES

The American Presidents, by Norman S. Cohen, 1989
Black American Women Novelists, by Craig Werner, 1989
Classical Greek and Roman Drama, by Robert J. Forman, 1989
Contemporary Latin American Fiction, by Keith H. Brower, 1989
Masters of Mystery and Detective Fiction, by J. Randolph Cox, 1989
Nineteenth Century American Poetry, by Philip K. Jason, 1989
Restoration Drama, by Thomas J. Taylor, 1989
Twentieth Century European Short Story, by Charles E. May, 1989
The Victorian Novel, by Laurence W. Mazzeno, 1989
Women's Issues, by Laura Stempel Mumford, 1989
America in Space, by Russell R. Tobias, 1991
The American Constitution, by Robert J. Janosik, 1991
The Classic Epic, by Thomas J. Sienkewicz, 1991
English Romantic Poetry, by Brian Aubrey, 1991
Ethics, by John K. Roth, 1991
The Immigrant Experience, by Paul D. Mageli, 1991
The Modern American Novel, by Steven G. Kellman, 1991
Native Americans, by Frederick E. Hoxie and Harvey Markowitz,
  1991
American Drama: 1918-1960, by R. Baird Shuman, 1992
American Ethnic Literatures, by David R. Peck, 1992
American Theater History, by Thomas J. Taylor, 1992
The Atomic Bomb, by Hans G. Graetzer and Larry M. Browning, 1992
Biography, by Carl Rollyson, 1992
The History of Science, by Gordon L. Miller, 1992
The Origin and Evolution of Life on Earth, by David W. Hollar, Jr.,
  1992
Pan-Africanism, by Michael W. Williams, 1992
Resources for Writers, by R. Baird Shuman, 1992
Shakespeare, by Joseph Rosenblum, 1992
The Vietnam War in Literature, by Philip K. Jason, 1992
Contemporary Southern Women Fiction Writers, by Rosemary M.
  Canfield Reisman and Christopher J. Canfield, 1994
Cycles in Humans and Nature, by John T. Burns, 1994
Environmental Studies, by Diane M. Fortner, 1994
Poverty in America, by Steven Pressman, 1994
The Short Story in English: Britain and North America, by Dean

Baldwin and Gregory L. Morris, 1994
Victorian Poetry, by Laurence W. Mazzeno, 1995
Human Rights in Theory and Practice, by Gregory J. Walters, 1995
Energy, by Joseph R. Rudolph, Jr., 1995
The History of the Book, by Joseph Rosenblum, 1995
Psychology, by The Editors of Salem Press, 1996
The Search for Economics as a Science, by The Editors of Salem Press, 1996

The Search for Economics as a Science

An Annotated Bibliography

Lynn Turgeon,
Consulting Editor

Magill Bibliographies

The Scarecrow Press, Inc.
Lanham, Md., & London
and Salem Press
Pasedena, Calif. / Englewood Cliffs, N.J.

SCARECROW PRESS, INC.

Published in the United States of America
by Scarecrow Press, Inc.
4720 Boston Way
Lanham, Maryland 20706

4 Pleydell Gardens, Folkestone
Kent CT20 2DN, England

British Cataloguing-in-Publication Information Available

Library of Congress Cataloging-in-Publication Data

The search for economics as a science : an annotated bibliography / the editors
of Salem Press ; consulting editor, Lynn Turgeon.
p. cm. — (Magill bibliographies)
Includes bibliographical references and index.
1. Economics—History—Bibliography. 2. Economics—Bibliography. I.
Turgeon, Lynn, 1920– . II. Salem Press. III. Series.
Z7164.E2S39 1996 [HB75] 016.33—dc20 95–48937 CIP

ISBN 0-8108-3120-1 (cloth : alk paper)

⊖™ The paper used in this publication meets the minimum requirements of
American National Standard for Information Sciences—Permanence of
Paper for Printed Library Materials, ANSI Z39.48–1984.
Manufactured in the United States of America.

CONTENTS

INTRODUCTION

This annotated bibliography represents a collection of the best in worldwide economic thinking of the past three centuries. It is divided into five chapters comprising fourteen sections. Each section corresponds more or less to a course frequently taught in departments of economics and business in U.S. universities. In some cases, there is an overlap of subject matter into at least two sections. In such instances, the book or article is annotated only once, in the section most relevant.

Although the collection emanates from many countries, only English translations of non-English sources are included. There is also a very high concentration of sources from two English-speaking countries: Great Britain, from Adam Smith's *Wealth of Nations* until World War II, and the United States for the postwar years. Germany is represented by the great nineteenth century political economist Karl Marx, and France provides Léon Walras, the father of general equilibrium theory, which came to dominate neoclassical economics after 1871. Important French economists preceded Smith, particularly the Physiocrats, who considered land as the source of all value, and mercantilists, among them French finance minister Jean-Baptiste Colbert. Mercantilists were found in all trading countries. They had a high regard for gold and silver and for the so-called "favorable" balance of trade that permitted countries to acquire these forms of commodity money.

The classical economists, beginning with Smith and ending with Marx, tended to emphasize labor as a basis for value or surplus value. They also tended to look at economics as a whole for the nation, rather than at the economics of a nation's component parts. Both Smith and David Ricardo considered capital accumulation to be important for growth. Ricardo championed the repeal of the British Corn Laws and the importation of cheaper foreign grain, thus shifting domestic resources and income away from agriculture into the nascent manufacturing sector.

The early economists began to pursue what seemed to be two contradictory goals: the moral philosophical goals of the early Adam Smith and the later, more materialistic thinking found in Smith's *Wealth of Nations*. Subsequently, Milton Friedman would christen these two strands as normative and positive thinking. Still later, Alan Blinder would distinguish between "soft hearts" and "hard heads." Arthur Okun also popularized the supposed conflict between the goals of equity and efficiency. As Robert Solow has said, most economic discussion involves the distribution of income.

There is an important dialectical relationship between these two broad types of economists, beginning with the optimistic William Godwin and his adversary, the pessimistic Thomas Malthus. More recently, the argument has surfaced between optimists, who value the growing role of the state as a stabilizer of economic activity, and pessimists, who believe that only the unfettered market can solve most economic problems.

Until World War II, U.S. economists made few lasting contributions to global economic thinking. Henry George's ideas on rent and a "single tax" survive in the writings of Harold Hotelling and William Vickrey. Likewise, the approach of the founder of the early twentieth century institutionalists, Thorstein Veblen, has been continued by John Kenneth Galbraith. U.S. economists also attempted to interpret John Maynard Keynes, who frequently tended to obfuscate what he really meant. The addition of Alvin Hansen's ideas on secular stagnation and Abba Lerner's function finance represented logical extensions of Keynes's *General Theory*.

Lord Keynes's magnum opus came to dominate economic thinking of the mid-twentieth century. His primary contribution was a rejection of Say's Law, a denial of Malthus' general glut. Say's Law had dominated economic thought since the early nineteenth century, when Malthus conceded victory to French economist Jean-Baptiste Say. Keynes also produced a return to the classical school's emphasis on the economy as a whole, which the neoclassical school of his mentor, Alfred Marshall, downplayed in favor of a partial equilibrium analysis of the firm or the consumer.

From Marshall until Keynes, all economics was microeconomics, and the whole was simply the sum of its parts. Keynes's great insight, arising out of the Great Depression, was that what was good for the part might be harmful for the whole. Thus, according to his paradox of thrift, saving might be helpful for individuals but harmful for an economy mired in unemployment. It is interesting to note that Keynes, in his own writings, failed to distinguish between neoclassical and classical economics, instead lumping the former into the latter. Thus, he blurred the distinction between the classical school, based on labor as a source of value, and the neoclassicals, who recognized the productivity of capital.

Although Keynes should receive credit for what is now referred to as macroeconomics—which itself gave rise to Simon Kuznets' national income and product accounting—other world economists and policymakers were practicing antideflationary policies and saying virtually the same thing as Keynes in other languages: Michal Kalecki in Polish, Bertil Ohlin in Swedish, Hjalmar Schacht in German, and Korekiyo Takahashi in Japanese. The economic prosperity of the United States during World War II seemed to confirm the validity of the *General Theory*. Milton Friedman, who would later father monetarism (the counterrevolution to Keynesian thinking), became disillusioned during the war, and Arthur Burns held out for the optimistic belief, correctly as it turned out, that the postwar period would produce prosperity rather than the depression that most Keynesians feared would appear without the stimulus of increased government spending.

Among the converts to Keynesian thinking at Harvard University in the 1930's was the young Paul Samuelson, who later admitted that one of the things he would have to answer for at the "pearly gates" would be the increased mathematization of economics. By the 1950's—the decade of McCarthyism in the United States—all certified economists were expected to be able to express themselves in mathematical terms. The study of economics would resemble that of physics, so that predicting future economic developments seemed possible. The other side of this coin was a deemphasis on the study of history. Lord Keynes, Gunnar Myrdal, and Joseph Schumpeter all warned against the substitution of mathematics and its preciseness for the study of history.

Another branch of economics after World War II developed around the growth problems of the Third World. Conflict arose between the International Monetary Fund (IMF) and the so-called "structuralists," who tended to reject the international division of labor and favor import substitution by the developing countries. Gradually, the IMF convinced policymakers in the Third World that they should adopt monetarist free market thinking and rely on export-driven growth policies. Global economic policies based on international specialization and a worldwide market for both direct and portfolio capital would henceforth ensure development in poorer countries. In carrying out IMF policy directives, which usually involved currency devaluation, the recipients of foreign investment would be expected to carry out structural adjustment programs, relying on the market with a minimum of government interference.

The economic principles textbook by Paul Samuelson published in 1947 represented an attempt to develop a Keynesian neoclassical synthesis. Keynesian macroeconomic tools would be used by the state to achieve full employment, and thereafter the microeconomic principles of neoclassical Marshallian economics would be applicable. Market reactions and revealed preferences led to all best-selling textbooks at the introductory level being clones of Samuelson's *Economics*. Samuelson rejected the deflationary prescriptions encouraged by believers in the international gold standard, and in his first edition he was willing to concede that inflation rates of as high as 5 percent might be required to maintain full employment. Samuelson also welcomed the March, 1951, accord between the U.S. Treasury and the Federal Reserve Board that ended almost a decade of neutralized monetary policy. Samuelson believed that an active monetary policy could be a useful tool in stabilizing the trade-off between inflation and unemployment. By 1957, John Kenneth Galbraith, in *The Affluent Society*, recognized that 7 percent unemployment might be required to control inflation. Australian A. W. Phillips depicted graphically the supposed trade-off between inflation (or increases in money wages) and unemployment.

The first two postwar decades are sometimes pictured as the "golden age" of the advanced capitalist system. Productivity and gross domestic product in both advanced and less developed countries were growing at rates that exceeded those for previous periods. By 1960, however, it seemed possible that the rapidly growing Soviet-type economy might actually overtake Western capitalism, as Nikita Khrushchev had predicted. In response, Walter Heller, as chairman of John F. Kennedy's Council of Economic Advisers, carried out a "New Economics" program that produced—as a result of increased military expenditures and cuts in tax rates—a continuation of rapid growth in the U.S. economy.

In the late 1960's, however, there was a sharp decline in the rate of increase in labor productivity in the United States, along with an acceleration of inflation. The combination, present at the time, of rising unemployment and a high rate of inflation was labeled "stagflation." At the same time, the ideas of Milton Friedman, which Karl Brunner had labeled "monetarism" in 1968, were gaining adherents. One key position of monetarism was that fixed rates of exchange lay behind the so-called "balance of payments problem." The Richard Nixon Administration was receptive to the Friedman solution of floating exchange rates, and the Paul Volcker group working in the Treasury Department came up with Nixon's New Economic Policy: a devaluation of the dollar euphemistically known as a "closing of the gold window" and the beginning of the end of fixed rates of exchange supervised by the International Monetary Fund.

The members of the Organization of Petroleum Exporting Countries (OPEC) eventually retaliated for the sudden deterioration in their terms of trade. In November, 1973, they administered a huge increase in oil prices, which Charles Schultze recognized to be the equivalent of a large excise tax imposed on the advanced capitalist countries that imported oil. This increase in oil prices coincided with the recession of 1974-1975.

INTRODUCTION

Economists came to accept that by the mid-1970's, the Phillips curve—now representing a lack of trade-off between inflation and unemployment—was in crisis.

The crisis in post-Keynesian thinking gave stimulus to monetarism as an alternative to Keynesian demand management and fueled the development of supply-side economics. The pioneer article by Robert Mundell appeared in *The Wall Street Journal* in 1974, and by the late 1970's, the Kemp-Roth bill was floated in Congress, calling for three successive 10 percent annual cuts in the rates of income taxation. What was lacking was a frank admission that the Republican Party was building its program on the basis of the Democratic tax cut of 1964. If the earlier tax cut could almost balance the budget in 1965, it seemed logical that three successive tax cuts in the Ronald Reagan years would produce a balanced budget by 1984. The problem was that by the early 1980's real interest rates had skyrocketed to postwar heights, offsetting some of the potential stimulation coming from increased military spending and the tax cuts.

Although Reaganomics produced an upturn in growth and profit rates—both of which had become sluggish after 1966—the monetarist paradigm began to experience problems in explaining the erratic behavior of the velocity of money. Milton Friedman's theories came into question in the face of problems in predicting inflation based on changes in the supply of money. In early 1984, Friedman predicted double-digit inflation by the end of the year, based on the large expansion of the monetary aggregates in 1983. Instead, the rate of inflation continued to fall.

Out of this impasse, a number of deviations from both Samuelsonian post-Keynesian and monetarist schools of thought blossomed: rational expectations, New Classical, and New Keynesian. In addition, the non-Samuelson Post Keynesians (without a hyphen), coming out of the Vietnam War, were still gaining adherents under the leadership of Paul Davidson. Even the Austrian school, based on the writings of Friedrich von Hayek and Ludwig von Mises, experienced a revival. What had begun as a search for economics as a science was now best described as many flowers blooming in the field of economics.

Along with the continuity of the search for scientific economics, there seem to have been changes in the relative strengths of global versus nationalist approaches to economics. Within U.S. economic thinking, this produced a declining interest in both antitrust prosecution and the non-competitive activities of trade unions. Some economists have argued that international competition will overcome national monopoly power. By 1995, a consensus seemed to be developing that global planning for freer trade represented the wave of the future. The creation in 1994 of the World

Trade Organization, an entity planned at Bretton Woods fifty years earlier, represented what appeared to be a defeat for national protectionism.

Another trend is a secular worldwide increase in unemployment rates, which according to the International Labour Organization are higher than at any time since the Great Depression. Protectionist sentiment naturally thrives in this environment. Unless unemployment trends are reversed, the flowering of freer trade seems at best to be problematic in the long run.

Mercantilist thinking, which Adam Smith hoped to eliminate, also gained strength. Although export surpluses do help individual parts of an economy, for the nation as a whole, the fruits of international trade are still found in its imports, a point well made by Paul Krugman in his critique of industrial policy. In contrast to early mercantilists, however, later counterparts virtually abandoned gold as a basis for economic institutions.

Optimists will tend to minimize the birth pangs of the increased globalization of economics: the internationalization of finance, the rise of international currency speculation and associated fluctuations in exchange rates, the loss of control over domestic policy by central banks, the decline of national sovereignty, the universal worry concerning deficit financing, and the high real interest rates administered by the Bundesbank and the Federal Reserve System. Pessimists will predict and even work for a return to the national economics of the 1920's that led to the Great Depression. In the meantime, the search for scientific economics continues.

Lynn Turgeon

HISTORY

History of Economic Thought and General Concepts

Allais, Maurice. "Vilfredo Pareto." In *International Encyclopedia of the Social Sciences*, edited by David D. Sills. Vol. 11. New York: Macmillan, 1968.
An analysis of Pareto's contribution by a leading French follower.

Anikin, Andre. *A Science in Its Youth*. Moscow: Progress, 1975.
Anikin takes an encyclopedic look at the "precursors of Marx." In addition to mentioning early contributions of Russian economic thinkers, such as Chernyshevsky, he looks at the mercantilist and classical schools, and even Benjamin Franklin's economic writings. There are also interesting comments on the early roots of Keynesian thinking.

Barber, William J. *A History of Economic Thought*. New York: Penguin Books, 1967.
Provides an excellent description of the major classical and neoclassical economists, with emphasis on the importance of their writings. David Hume and his attack on mercantilism and its policies are discussed on pages 48 and 49.

Becker, Howard, and Harry Elmer Barnes. *Social Thought from Lore to Science: A History and Interpretation of Man's Ideas About Life with His Fellows to Times When His Study of the Past Is Linked with That of the Present for the Sake of the Future*. Vol. 2. 3d ed. New York: Dover, 1961.
Reviews the structural conditions influencing Smith's belief that competitive market forces would act as an invisible hand. Unlike some scholars, the authors dismiss the supposed "Adam Smith problem," a contradiction between the altruism of his first book, *A Theory of Moral Sentiments* (1759), and the egoism of his second book, *An Inquiry into the Nature and Causes of the Wealth of Nations* (1776).

Blaug, Mark. *Economic Theory in Retrospect*. 4th ed. New York: Cambridge University Press, 1985.

Blaug's work is technically demanding, particularly for those with no background in economics. For those with some understanding of economic theory and mathematics, chapters 8, 9, 10, and 15 are excellent. The "reader's guides" to Alfred Marshall's *Principles of Economics* are especially useful for those who wish to tackle Marshall directly. Chapters 3-5 of this outstanding text develop the Ricardian system. Chapter 4, "Ricardo's System," is devoted to David Ricardo and contains a high-level interpretation of the Bullionism controversy. The following chapter, "Say's Law and Classical Monetary Theory," provides a setting for both the Bullionist and Antibullionist positions in the controversy. Chapter 6, "John Stuart Mill," presents the Currency-Banking controversy in the context of classical (1800-1850) English political economy and thus gives an accurate historical picture of the conclusions of John Stuart Mill and his contemporaries in relation to such issues of the day as the Bullion Report and the Bank Act of 1844.

_____ . *The Methodology of Economics*. Cambridge, England: Cambridge University Press, 1980.

A historical survey of economic methodology of economics, including positivism, from a related but somewhat different viewpoint which stresses the ideas of the post-Popperian philosopher of science Imre Lakatos. Accessible to the general reader.

_____ . *Ricardian Economics*. New Haven, Conn.: Yale University Press, 1958.

An interpretation of David Ricardo's work based on his publications and correspondence. Emphasizes the abstract nature of Ricardo's theory.

Cannan, Edwin. *A History of the Theories of Production and Distribution in English Political Economy from 1776 to 1848*. 3d ed. London: P. S. King & Son, 1924.

Probably the most important work for the nineteenth century development of diminishing returns. Cannan, a specialist in the history of doctrine, did extensive research on diminishing returns. His account is not merely descriptive but includes a careful logical analysis, often highly critical in tone, of the views discussed.

Canterbery, E. Ray. *The Making of Economics*. 3d ed. Belmont, Calif.: Wadsworth, 1987.

An excellent introduction to the history of economics, placing the ideas in the intellectual and political climate from which they came. Provides a very good history of the concept of utility and its role in economic theory. Discussion ranges from Jeremy Bentham and the early utilitarians to the marginalists to modern theorists.

Cantillon, Richard. *Essay on the Nature of Trade in General.* 1755. Reprint. New York: Augustus M. Kelley, 1964.

Well known to historians of economic thought as the first systematic treatise on economic theory. Cantillon, a wealthy Paris banker of Irish descent, concentrates on issues such as money, prices, and international trade. Chapter 4 includes an excellent discussion, with examples, ofGresham's law. This work, although burdened by an archaic style, is suitable for all readers.

Chamberlin, Edward H. *The Theory of Monopolistic Competition.* 8th ed. Cambridge, Mass.: Harvard University Press, 1962.

Chapter 3 contains a brief historical summary of Antoine Augustin Cournot, Joseph Bertrand, Francis Ysidro Edgeworth, A. C. Pigou, and Alfred Marshall on duopoly, as well as Chamberlin's own analysis of duopoly. There is some technical economics, and Chamberlin's style is sometimes difficult.

Clark, John Bates. *The Distribution of Wealth.* New York: Macmillan, 1899.

This reference is included as a representative of an early definitive study on the relation between wages and worker productivity. It should be read from the standpoint of the history of ideas rather than as a technical treatise on economic theory, as a good example of the nature of economic analysis of an earlier time, when rigorous analysis was developed without the use of either graphs or equations.

Cole, G. D. H. *A History of Socialist Thought.* 5 vols. London: Macmillan, 1953-1960.

A classic general study of the development of socialist movements throughout the world and of the development of socialist thought. An accessible, clear, well-researched survey that is particularly strong on the growth of socialism and laborism in Great Britain and on socialist political thought in Western Europe.

Davidson, Greg, and Paul Davidson. *Economics for a Civilized Society.* New York: W. W. Norton, 1988.

Argues that economic policies can be successful only if they appeal to civic duties, as well as to individual self-interest. The authors then demonstrate how post-Keynesian policies satisfy this condition.

De Vivo, G. "David Ricardo (1772-1823)." In *The New Palgrave: A Dictionary of Economics*, edited by John Eatwell, Murray Milgate, and Peter Newman. Vol. 4. New York: Stockton Press, 1987.
An excellent and remarkably detailed short summary of Ricardo's economic ideas and their development. Written for economists, but accessible to those with modest backgrounds in formal economics. Extensive bibliography.

Dobb, Maurice H. *Theories of Value and Distribution Since Adam Smith.* Cambridge, England: Cambridge University Press, 1973.
Dobb, a leading British Marxist, argues that Piero Sraffa's system strongly supports Karl Marx and shows that profits are not determined by prices: It is prices that are, instead, determined by the distribution of income. This supports Marx's view that the struggle between capital and labor underlies capitalism. Dobb traces the development of the two competing theories of value (the labor theory of value and the utility theory of value).

Eatwell, John, Murray Milgate, and Peter Newman, eds. *The New Palgrave: The Invisible Hand.* New York: W. W. Norton, 1989.
This high-quality paperback includes an essay on Smith, as well as David Hume's letter to Smith, reminding him of the futility of writing for fame and public approval. Notes that institutions of the exchange economy are not sufficient to establish Smith's "system of natural liberty."

Eichner, Alfred S. *A Guide to Post-Keynesian Economics.* Armonk, N.Y.: M. E. Sharpe, 1978.
A collection of essays by leading post-Keynesian economists. Each applies post-Keynesian theory to a different topic area and each discusses the policy implications of post-Keynesian theory. All the essays are of high quality and all are accessible to undergraduate students. Together they constitute the best introduction to post-Keynesian economics.

Ekelund, Robert B., and Robert H. Hebert. *A History of Economic Theory and Method.* New York: McGraw-Hill, 1975.

Parts 4 and 5 of this standard undergraduate text cover the marginal revolution, William Stanley Jevons, the Austrians, Léon Walras, and Marshallian economics. Interprets past contributions through a very defined positivist viewpoint. There are some fairly technical sections, but the book is generally accessible to those without an extensive background in formal economics.

Feiwel, George R., ed. *Arrow and the Ascent of Modern Economic Theory.* London: Macmillan, 1987.
An anthology that presents the developments in modern economic theory. Chapter 1 discusses the developments in general equilibrium theory and contrasts them with the Marshallian and other modes of thought.

Fink, Richard H., and Jack C. High, eds. *A Nation in Debt.* Frederick, Md.: University Publications of America, 1987.
This collection of essays by noted economists, both past and present, surveys the alternate viewpoints economists have had concerning the impact of the national debt. Included in its three hundred pages are essays by Adam Smith, Karl Marx, and John Maynard Keynes, as well as Nobel laureates James Tobin, James M. Buchanan, Jr., and Milton Friedman.

Fitzgibbons, Athol. *Keynes's Vision: A New Political Economy.* New York: Oxford University Press, 1988.
This 216-page book focuses on the thinking of Keynes in economic and political matters, as well as his approach to economic policy. Written for noneconomists who are interested in the Keynesian philosophical writings.

Fox-Genovese, Elizabeth. *The Origins of Physiocracy.* Ithaca, N.Y.: Cornell University Press, 1976.
Tends to focus primarily on the biographies and innovative contributions of two men: François Quesnay and Victor Riqueti, the Marquis de Mirabeau. Includes a full chapter (chapter 7) on Quesnay's major work, the *Tableau économique* (1758).

Fusfeld, Daniel R. *The Age of the Economist.* Glenview, Ill.: Scott, Foresman, 1977.
A very readable history of the development of economics from the 1700's to the 1970's. The emphasis is on important economists who

influenced the development of the field and on macroeconomic ideas. The suggested readings section at the end of the book is very good and contains descriptions of other readings that are specific to the classical and Keynesian models.

Garraty, John A. *Unemployment in History: Economic Thought and Public Policy*. New York: Harper & Row, 1978.

A historical account of public perceptions and the views of economists about the unemployed, beginning in ancient and medieval times and continuing up to the 1970's. Also discusses the different economic policies that have been designed over time in order to deal with the problem of joblessness.

George, Henry. *Progress and Poverty*. New York: Doubleday, 1912.

George attributes low wages and unemployment—despite increases in wealth—to the artificial scarcity of land and to barriers to free exchange. He proposed to raise ad valorem property tax rates on bare land, thus socializing rent without an excess burden. His tax would force land into full use. He sought to remove taxes on capital and commerce for the benefit of labor. Harold Hotelling and William Vickrey, among contemporary economists, have been influenced by George in calling for social dividends, the free provision of public goods, and marginal cost pricing for urban mass transit and utilities.

Gide, Charles, and Charles Rist. *A History of Economic Doctrines*. Translated by R. Richards. Boston: D. C. Heath, 1948.

An authoritative, still eminently useful book. Not written for popular audiences, it is nevertheless clear, insightful, and authoritative, particularly in book 1, which deals with the Physiocrats, Adam Smith, Thomas Robert Malthus, and David Ricardo. There are no illustrative materials; the end-of-page footnotes are a rich source and an adequate replacement for a bibliography. Extensive index.

Gray, Alexander. *The Development of Economic Doctrine*. London: Longmans, Green, 1961.

An excellent survey of the history of economic thought; long considered the standard text in the field. Particularly interesting is Gray's discussion of economic theorizing in the Middle Ages. He points out, for example, that the principle known today as Gresham's law was described in detail by Nicholas Oresme, Bishop of Lisieux, in the fourteenth century.

Gruchy, Allan G. *Contemporary Economic Thought: The Contribution of Neo-Institutional Economics.* Clifton, N.J.: Augustus M. Kelley, 1972.

This sequel to Gruchy's *Modern Economic Thought* emphasizes institutionalist research since 1939. Includes chapters on Clarence E. Ayres, John Kenneth Galbraith, Gunnar Myrdal (the only institutionalist to win a Nobel Prize in Economics), and Gerhard Colm.

_____. *Modern Economic Thought: The American Contribution.* Englewood Cliffs, N.J.: Prentice-Hall, 1947.

An important early effort to describe and assess the contributions of institutionalism's founders. Includes long, but clear, chapters on Thorstein Veblen, John R. Commons, Wesley Mitchell, John M. Clark, Rexford Tugwell, and Gardiner Means.

Hansen, Bent. *A Survey of General Equilibrium Models.* New York: McGraw-Hill, 1970.

Presents a summary of each of the systems of equations that are used by well-known economists to model the evolution of the entire economy. Included are descriptions of the systems of equations created by Léon Walras, Gustav Cassel, John Maynard Keynes, Sir John R. Hicks, Paul A. Samuelson, Don Patinkin, Wassily Leontief, John von Neumann, and Robert M. Solow.

Hanusch, Horst. *Evolutionary Economics: Applications of Schumpeter's Ideas.* Cambridge, England: Cambridge University Press, 1989.

Represents a composite of papers commemorating the foundation of the International Joseph A. Schumpeter Society (ISS). The weaknesses of neoclassical theory and the need for evolutionary theory are stressed.

Hausman, Daniel M., ed. *The Philosophy of Economics: An Anthology.* Cambridge, England: Cambridge University Press, 1984.

A survey of economic methodology, including positivism, by an avowed eclectic who finds something of value in most schools of thought on the nature and methods of economics.

Heilbroner, Robert L. *The Essential Adam Smith.* New York: W. W. Norton, 1986.

An excellent introduction to the basic works of Adam Smith. Very readable.

_____. *The Quest for Wealth.* New York: Simon & Schuster, 1956.

A well-written and entertaining history of the acquisitive nature of Western culture. Delightful insights.

_____ . *The Worldly Philosophers*. 6th ed. New York: Simon & Schuster, 1987.

An entertaining and informative history of the great economists, their lives, and their ideas. There is no better starting point for the history of economics, as well as for an understanding of economics. Provides the easiest and most painless sketches of these economists for those with little or no background in formal economics. Nontechnical and highly readable, but very thin for anything but a cursory view.

Heiman, Eduard. *A History of Economic Doctrines*. New York: Oxford University Press, 1945.

A lively, scholarly account of the subject. Chapters 1-4, dealing with the Physiocrats, the classical economists, and their historical environments, are especially useful. There are no footnotes or illustrative materials, and the select bibliography is useless; the index is useful. With these minor exceptions, an excellent study.

Hicks, John R. *Value and Capital*. Oxford, England: Clarendon Press, 1979.

Presents an exposition of modern marginalist economics that is clear and accessible. Suitable for college students. The appendices contain mathematical expositions for more advanced readers.

Hont, Istvan, and Michael Ignatieff, eds. *Wealth and Virtue: The Shaping of Political Economy in the Scottish Enlightenment*. Cambridge, England: Cambridge University Press, 1983.

A collection of essays on the origin of classical political economy.

Humphrey, Thomas M. "The Concept of Indexation in the History of Economic Thought." In *Essays on Inflation*. 3d ed. Richmond, Va.: Federal Reserve Bank of Richmond, 1974.

The history of indexation and its application to wages and debts.

Hunt, E. K., and Howard J. Sherman. *Economics: An Introduction to Traditional and Radical Views*. 6th ed. New York: Harper & Row, 1990.

Written from a Marxist historical perspective, this book is very readable, starting with economic evolution in ancient Greece, moving on to mercantilism, the corporate rise of capitalism, monopoly power, income distribution, and economic theories, and ending with comparative economic systems, such as market socialism and central planning in the Soviet Union. Fine for the general reader.

Kahn, R. F. "The Relation of Home Investment to Unemployment." *Economic Journal* 41 (June, 1931): 173-198.

This article contains the first exposition of the multiplier and was used by John Maynard Keynes as the basis for the development of his theory. Of interest mainly to those who are interested in history of thought.

Katzner, Donald W. *Static Demand Theory*. New York: Macmillan, 1970.

Modern axiomatic demand theory is presented in this highly mathematical volume, which represents a distillation of hundreds of years of thought on the concept of utility and its implications. The introduction contains a very good brief history of the development of utility theory.

Kolakowski, Leszek. *Main Currents of Marxism*. 3 vols. New York: Oxford University Press, 1978.

Considered by many a modern classic in the critical exposition of the development of Marxist thought. Surveys the origins of Marxism, distinguishes it from other forms of socialism, examines the controversies among various Marxist theorists, and traces the developments in socialism and Marxism since World War II.

Lange, Oscar. "Say's Law: A Restatement and Criticism." In *Mathematical Economics and Econometrics*, edited by Oscar Lange, F. McIntyre, and T. O. Yntema. Chicago: University of Chicago Press, 1942.

This paper began something of a revolution in monetary theory. Not easy to read, as graduate students can attest.

Lekachman, Robert. *A History of Economic Ideas*. New York: McGraw-Hill, 1959.

The chapter on John Maynard Keynes and Keynesian economics is an excellently written summary of the revolutionary impact of his ideas. The book provides the reader with the economic reasoning of the mercantilist view within the framework of the development of economic ideas. It does not, however, attempt to treat applications, but instead analyzes the contributions of the economists and focuses on regulations affecting the economic life and setting of the period.

_____ . *Varieties of Economics*. New York: Meridian, 1962.

The early chapters are a valuable survey, which includes the classical economists' works in critical, summary fashion. Few notes; spare bibliography and index.

List, Georg Friedrich. *National System of Political Economy*. Translated by S. S. Lloyd. London: Longmans, Green, 1904.
List's first major work, in which he clearly states the methodological basis for historicism and its superiority as an analytical technique over classical principles. List's advocacy of tariffs was used by American protectionists in support of their own interests.

Machlup, Fritz. *A History of Thought on Economic Integration*. New York: Columbia University Press, 1977.
A broad discussion of economic integration including free trade areas, customs unions, and the formation of nation-states.

McNally, David. *Political Economy and the Rise of Capitalism*. Berkeley: University of California Press, 1988.
A revisionist account of the rise of political economy.

Marx, Karl. *Capital*. 3 vols. Moscow: Foreign Languages Publishing House, 1957-1959.
The major economic work of Marx in which he presents his analyses of capitalism as a mode of production and of the contradictions, inherent in the social relations of capitalism, which he argues will lead to its transformation by socialism.

Meek, Ronald L. *The Economics of Physiocracy*. Cambridge, Mass.: Harvard University Press, 1963.
Although some of the ideas presented by Meek are contested by other scholars (specifically by Gianni Vaggi, below), Meek is frequently cited as the most comprehensive scholar writing in English on Physiocracy.

_____ . *Studies in the Labor Theory of Value*. New York: Monthly Review Press, 1956.
A classic in the field of the history of economic thought. Meek provides an excellent analysis of the development of the labor theory of value from Adam Smith through David Ricardo to Karl Marx and the contributions made by the neoclassicals and Piero Sraffa to value theory. Should serve as background material for Marx's *Capital*.

Menger, Carl. *Principles of Economics*. Glencoe, Ill.: Free Press, 1950.
A key work of the 1870's marginalist revolution. It breaks with the objective cost-of-production approach to value of classical economics. Price is accounted for as the outcome of preference. The ability of the market to coordinate the activity of economic agents without central

direction is stressed. Menger is critical of external standards of appraisal of the market that do not stem from its natural development.

Miernyk, William H. *The Elements of Input-Output Analysis.* New York: Random House, 1965.
This clear and concise introduction to input-output analysisis well suited for the nonspecialist. Miernyk relates the input-output model to its roots in the history of economic thought. The structure of the model and its uses are verbally expressed, with a minimum of mathematics.

Miliband, Ralph. *Marxism and Politics.* New York: Oxford University Press, 1977.
An excellent, very readable, nonsectarian introduction to the politics of Marxism. Reconstructs the main elements of the political theory and actual politics that are specific to Marxism. Also discusses some of the problems and contradictions that are found in the Marxist political tradition.

Miller, H. Laurence. "On the 'Chicago School of Economics.'" *Journal of Political Economy* 70 (1962): 64-69.
This specialized journal article is purposely written for easy understanding by generalists. It reviews the main phases of the Chicago School from its origins in the 1930's to the "new generation" symbolized by the work in the 1960's and 1970's of Milton Friedman.

Morgan, Mary S. *The History of Econometric Ideas.* Cambridge, England: Cambridge University Press, 1990.
One of the least mathematical texts on econometrics. Provides a good insight into the importance of least squares in the development of mathematical economics. Although this is an academic history, it is well written and gives a good insight into how ideas develop.

Myrdal, Gunnar. *The Political Element in the Development of Economic Theory.* Cambridge, Mass.: Harvard University Press, 1954.
A history of political economy and economics which stresses the political and ideological element.

Nickerson, Jane Soames. *Homage to Malthus.* Port Washington, N.Y.: Kennikat Press, 1975.
In less than 150 pages, this readable study tells the important things about Thomas Malthus' life and work. For the general reader.

Niehans, Jurg. *A History of Economic Theory: Classic Contributions, 1720-1980.* Baltimore: The Johns Hopkins University Press, 1990.
    An excellent treatment of the ideas and policies of John Law can be found on pages 48-51. Written at a level understandable by high school students.

Norton, Hugh. *The Role of the Economist in Government: A Study of Economic Advice Since 1920.* Berkeley, Calif.: McCutchan, 1969.
    Provides a unique description of the American economic thought and advisership in the Presidency, especially during the post-World War II period. Suitable for a general reader who is interested in understanding the role of economists in governmental policy-making.

Oser, Jacob, and Stanley L. Brue. *The Evolution of Economic Thought.* 4th ed. New York: Harcourt Brace Jovanovich, 1988.
    A history of economic thought that gives the background to the development of the marginalist school and welfare economics.

Patinkin, Don. *Money, Interest, and Prices.* 2d ed. New York: Harper & Row, 1965.
    A classic theoretical treatise that integrates monetary theory with microeconomic analysis. Contains extensive material on the history of ideas, but not much on empirical or policy questions. For the advanced reader.

Pigou, Arthur C., ed. *Memorials of Alfred Marshall.* London: Macmillan, 1925.
    Pigou was Alfred Marshall's student, his successor to the chair in political economy at Cambridge and himself a major figure in the development of neoclassical economics. This volume, compiled after Marshall's death, contains obituaries of Marshall (including John Maynard Keynes's magnificent biographical obituary), selections from Marshall's writings, and correspondence.

Ricardo, David. *The Principles of Political Economy and Taxation.* 1817. Reprint. Baltimore: Penguin Books, 1971.
    The original, classic work on comparative advantage. Suitable for beginning students.

Rima, Ingrid Hahne. *Development of Economic Analysis.* 4th ed. Homewood, Ill.: Richard D. Irwin, 1986.

Part 4 in this established text in history of economic thought provides a very good brief summary of nearly all aspects of neoclassical economics. Some background in elementary economics is required, but the technical demands are modest.

Robbins, Lionel. *The Theory of Economic Policy in English Classical Political Economy.* New York: Macmillan, 1952.
Stresses the political aspects of classical theory. Uses numerous quotations to support the claim that classical economists did not advocate pure laissez-faire.

Roll, Eric. *A History of Economic Thought.* Homewood, Ill.: Richard D. Irwin, 1974.
Gives a particularly sympathetic treatment of the mid-nineteenth century reaction to classical macroeconomic conclusions, mostly in chapters 4, 5, and 6.

Roscher, Wilhelm. *Principles of Political Economy.* Translated by John J. Lalor. 2 vols. Chicago: Callaghan, 1882.
Roscher offers in this voluminous work a complete exposition of the same topics John Stuart Mill covered in his own work on economics. Although Roscher promises, he does not deliver on the establishment of the laws of economic development, derived from the investigation of national histories.

Samuels, Warren J., ed. *The Chicago School of Political Economy.* East Lansing: Michigan State University Press, 1976.
A technical work. Although several of the contributors address the question of the evolution of the Chicago School itself, the majority deal, more or less in Chicagoan fashion, with some of the major economic theory issues of the day, including the phenomenon of structuralism, price theory, and jurisprudence.

Schapiro, J. Salwyn. *Condorcet and the Rise of Liberalism.* New York: Harcourt, Brace & World, 1934.
An excellent reading to understand the conventional wisdom of the last quarter of the eighteenth century that provoked Thomas Robert Malthus to write his essay on population. If the views of the Marquis de Condorcet and William Godwin had not gained such a great influence and popular acceptance at that time, Malthus' essay might never have been written.

Schmoller, Gustav. *The Mercantile System and Its Historical Signifi-cance: Illustrated Chiefly from Prussian History.* New York: Macmillan, 1897.
Little of Schmoller's work has been translated into English, and although this is not a principal work, it illustrates his approach. He was a historian and well prepared to argue against the laissez-faire econom-ics of England. He advocated a policy approach much more like mercantilism, the predecessor of liberalism.

Schmukler, Nathan, and Edward Marcus, eds. *Inflation Through the Ages: Economic, Social, Psychological, and Historical Aspects.* New York: Columbia University Press, 1983.
Contains fifty-four papers extending over nearly nine hundred pages and providing a treasure trove of material. Papers by Tobin, Wilson, Dewald, Selden, Tracy, and Trescott, and most of the case studies in parts 4 and 5, bear particularly on demand-pull analysis.

Schumpeter, Joseph A. *A History of Economic Analysis.* New York: Oxford University Press, 1963.
Contains a comprehensive discussion of the growth of economics as a discipline. The intertwining of practical, theoretical positions and normative topics throughout the history of economics is a marked feature of Schumpeter's account. Schumpeter evaluates the contribu-tions to returns to scale concepts and their application by David Ricardo, Thomas Robert Malthus, Karl Marx, Alfred Marshall, and others. Chapter 7 contains a good nonmathematical, but demanding, critique of the Cournot model. Contains an excellent discussion of the law of diminishing returns, its historical evolution, and its impact on the development of economic theory. Tough reading, but worth the effort. Schumpeter's is the best advanced text in this general area, covering many details left out of more popular works.

_____. *Ten Great Economists.* New York: Oxford University Press, 1965.
Reflections on master economists by a leading historian of economic analysis. Chapters 3 and 6 provide insights on the development of opportunity cost theory. Chapter 4 is on Vilfredo Pareto's contributions to economics and sociology.

Smith, Adam. *An Inquiry into the Nature and Causes of the Wealth of Nations.* Reprint. New York: Modern Library, 1937.
The original work on absolute advantage. Suitable for college students.

Soule, George. *Ideas of Great Economists*. New York: Viking Press, 1952.
A well-written book, easy to read. It presents the salient features of the
history of economic ideas in a contextual setting. Chapter 3, on the
classical economists, shows the developing ideas that provided the
setting for later analysis.

Spiegel, Henry W. *The Growth of Economic Thought*. Durham, N.C.:
Duke University Press, 1983.
A comprehensive description of the history of economic thought.
David Hume's specie-flow theory, as well as his other contributions to
economic thought, is discussed in the two chapters on the founders of
political economy, chapters 7 and 9. Provides an excellent description
of the world historical setting within which the movement of historicism arose (see chapter 18).

Stark, Werner. *History of Economics and Its Relations to Social Development*. Oxford, England: Oxford University Press, 1944.
Stark applies the sociology of knowledge approach of analysis to the
history of economics in this very short (less than one-hundred-page)
book.

Stigler, George J. *Essays in the History of Economics*. Chicago: University
of Chicago Press, 1965.
The article on "The Development of Utility Theory" is particularly
relevant to complements and substitutes. Utility theory is behind the
theory of choice and indifference curves as consumers select among
different goods. Contains two of the best historical synopses of demand
theory and empirical demand studies, respectively, in Stigler's "The
Development of Utility Theory" (chapter 5) and "The Early History of
Empirical Studies of Consumer Behavior" (chapter 7). Given their
readability and insight, these writings should be the first that are
consulted by the novice.

_____ . *Production and Distribution Theories: The Formative
Period*. New York: Macmillan, 1941.
Developed from Stigler's Ph.D. thesis, this critical survey chronicles
the development of the marginal productivity theory and its relationship to a cohesive theory of distribution. The coverage spans the work
of ten primary economists from 1870 to 1895.

Theocharis, Reghinos D. *Early Developments in Mathematical Econom-ics.* 2d ed. Philadelphia: Porcupine Press, 1983.
> A very readable survey of the work in mathematical economics up to, and including, Antoine Augustin Cournot.

Tool, Marc R. *The Discretionary Economy: A Normative Theory of Political Economy.* Glenview, Ill.: Scott, Foresman, 1979.
> From a perspective sympathetic to institutionalism, Tool compares how institutionalists, neoclassicals, and Marxists address each of the following: the preconceptions of economics; normative questions of economic policy and decision making; and the meaning of freedom, equality, and justice. His treatment of political processes—which links institutionalism and participatory democracy—is especially signifi-cant.

Vaggi, Gianni. *The Economics of François Quesnay.* Durham, N.C.: Duke University Press, 1987.
> Less biographical or political than other works, Vaggi's study focuses on an analysis of specific subcategories of Physiocratic thought. These include "fundamental prices of commodities," "profits as a temporary share of the surplus," and others.

Weulersse, Georges. *La Physiocratie a la fin du regne de Louis XV, 1770-1774.* Paris: Presses Universitaires de France, 1959.
> Somewhat more general than the specific study of ministerial politics under the Physiocrat Anne Robert Jacques Turgot, this book provides more background on the principles of Physiocracy and the economic dilemmas which France faced at the time that Louis XVI appointed Turgot to head his faltering ministry of finance.

_____ . *La Physiocratie sous les ministères de Turgot et de Necker, 1774-1781.* Paris: Presses Universitaires de France, 1950.
> Weulersse is frequently cited as the most accomplished and meticulous French scholar of the Physiocratic movement. This monograph exam-ines the practical political side of application of Physiocratic programs under two prominent ministers of state only a few years before the French Revolution.

Whittaker, E. *Schools and Streams of Economic Thought.* Chicago: Rand McNally, 1960.
> Whittaker traces the concept of opportunity costin the history of economic ideas.

Wright, A. L. "The Genesis of the Multiplier Theory." *Oxford Economic Papers* 8, no. 2 (1956): 181-193.

Traces of the origins of the multiplier theory to Walter Bagehot in the 1870's. Although R. F. Kahn is usually given credit for the formulation of the multiplier theory, Wright argues that he never actually used the term "multiplier." Others, including John Maynard Keynes, however, had used the term before 1936.

Economic History

Abramovitz, Moses. *Inventories and Business Cycles*. New York: National Bureau of Economic Research, 1950.

This classic book explains the role of inventories in forecasting and explaining business cycles. Nontechnical and accessible to the lay reader.

Anderson, Benjamin M. *Economics and the Public Welfare: A Financial and Economic History of the United States, 1914-1946*. Indianpolis: Liberty Press, 1979.

This is a lengthy (almost six hundred pages) and thorough review of American economic history from World War I through World War II. The prime concern is with monetary and financial matters, both domestic and those of foreign origin, that had repercussions in the United States. Anderson also offers a brief theoretical discussion of Say's Law and John Maynard Keynes's critique of it.

Ashton, Thomas S. *The Industrial Revolution: 1760-1830*. Rev. ed. New York: Oxford University Press, 1969.

A classic synthesis of Britain's initial industrialization. Clearly written, pithy, descriptive, and analytical. Scholars who are less sure about the immediate benefits of industrialization have disagreed with Ashton's interpretations, and fresh research lends credibility to some of their exceptions. Nevertheless, Ashton remains invaluable. A brief, revised bibliography and an adequate index.

Aydelotte, William O. "The Country Gentlemen and the Repeal of the Corn Laws." *English Historical Review* 82 (January, 1967): 47-60.

An extremely important article in which the author shows that despite the common assumption that the Corn Law vote was based on class, it was in fact much more strongly related to party affiliation and constituency than on any social or economic factor.

Bailey, Stephen K. *Congress Makes a Law*. New York: Columbia University Press, 1950.

Although Bailey's main interest is the legislative process, his example is the Employment Act of 1946, and he discusses the origins and nature of the act in some detail.

Baker, Stephen A. *An Introduction to International Economics*. New York: Harcourt Brace Jovanovich, 1990.

While providing expositions of traditional theories of international trade and finance, this book devotes much attention to the consideration of the history of trade and exchange rates. A knowledge of basic economic concepts is assumed.

Basalla, George. *The Evolution of Technology*. Cambridge, England: Cambridge University Press, 1988.

A historian describes the evolution of technology from the perspective of some of its characteristics, such as diversity, necessity, continuity and discontinuity, novelty, and selection. This relatively short but clearly written paperback (248 pages) includes illustrations together with a good bibliography and index.

Benoit, Emile. *Europe at Sixes and Sevens: The Common Market, the Free Trade Association, and the United States*. New York: Columbia University Press, 1961.

An early book comparing the original six Common Market countries with the European Free Trade Association.

Benston, George J., ed. *Financial Services: The Changing Institutions and Government Policy*. Englewood Cliffs, N.J.: Prentice-Hall, 1983.

An excellent overview of the historical development of U.S. public policy toward banks, thrift institutions, and other financial institutions.

Bernstein, Michael A. *The Great Depression*. New York: Cambridge University Press, 1987.

This excellent book focuses primarily on the reasons that the Great Depression and accompanying cyclical unemployment lasted during the entire decade of the 1930's. Also considers contemporary problems of unemployment and economic growth from a historical perspective. Written for a varied audience.

Bigman, David, and Teizo Taya, eds. *Floating Exchange Rates and the State of World Trade and Payments*. Cambridge, Mass.: Ballinger, 1984.

This set of technical essays considers the role of central banks and capital controls in the process of the adjustment of exchange rates toward equilibrium. The essays analyze and draw on the actual history of exchange-rate movements to support or negate theories in this area.

Blinder, Alan S. *Economic Policy and the Great Stagflation.* New York: Academic Press, 1979

A perceptive history lesson and in-depth analysis of governmental economic policy in the 1970's. Carefully discusses the dilemma of policy-making in that period and the effects of inappropriate policy decisions. This concise and well-written book is suitable for the general reader. Illustrated with figures and economic data.

Boaz, David, ed. *Assessing the Reagan Years.* New York: Cato Institute, 1988.

This 430-page book provides a good guide to the development of government fiscal policies in the 1980's. Reviews of the Reagan Administration's economic programs on taxation, spending, and transfer payment policies are given by various contributors, including Malcolm Forbes, Jr., and Robert W. Crandall. Well suited to a general audience.

Box, George E. P., and Gwilym M. Jenkins. *Time Series Analysis: Forecasting and Control.* San Francisco: Holden-Day, 1970.

The best book on the Box-Jenkins technique of time series analysis, which involves the identification of trends within a time series. These trends, which include autoregressive, moving-average, and seasonal components, can be identified by examining the correlations of the elements of a time series with its past values, leaving a residual series that is truly random. Presupposes that the reader has advanced mathematical training.

Braeman, John, Robert H. Bremmer, and David Brody, eds. *The New Deal: State and Local Levels.* Columbus: Ohio State University Press, 1975.

This book is not necessarily more specialized in its technical treatment of New Deal policies to fight the depression but is in its geographical level of focus. Diverse authors study the effects of New Deal legislation not only at the state and local levels but also in different regions of the United States.

Braudel, Fernand. *The Perspective of the World.* Translated by Sian Reynolds. Vol. 3 in *Civilization and Capitalism, Fifteenth-Eighteenth Century.* New York: Harper & Row, 1979.

A brilliant, sweeping, interpretive synthesis of events and personalities important to the origins of modern commercial and industrial capitalism. As one of France's *Annaliste* historians, concerned with melding a broad range of interdisciplinary materials into historical writing as well as adopting both long-term and short-term explanations for the origins of international capitalism and the deep roots of European industrialization, Braudel has few peers. Although at times argumentative, he founds his positions on a profound scholarship, which is well expressed. There are many reproductions, maps, charts, tables, and graphs and fine, double-columned endnotes that substitute for a bibliography. The index is voluminous.

_____. *The Wheels of Commerce.* Vol. 2 in *Civilization and Capitalism, Fifteenth-Eighteenth Century.* Translated by Sian Reynolds. New York: Harper & Row, 1982.

Excellently presented both interpretively and substantively by a leading exponent of the French *Annales* school. While not concentrating its six hundred pages on Colbertism, it illuminates the context in which mercantilism, Colbertism, and nascent capitalism were developing. Included are 150 illustrations, maps, charts, and splendid double-columned chapter footnotes that supplant a bibliography.

Braun, Ernst. *Wayward Technology.* Westport, Conn.: Greenwood Press, 1984.

A very good description of the rise and future of industrial society from the perspective of its technical, social, economic, and political aspects, with specific references mostly to the British case. Helpful tables and diagrams, but a skimpy one-page index.

Braunthal, Gerard. *The West German Social Democrats, 1969-1982.* Boulder, Colo.: Westview Press, 1983.

A very detailed analysis of the West German Social Democratic Party during its thirteen years in office as the senior member of coalition cabinets. This book is replete with historical details and political analyses of the German Social Democratic movement. Suitable for both specialists and nonspecialists.

Brownlee, W. Elliot. *The Dynamics of Ascent: A History of the American Economy.* New York: Alfred A. Knopf, 1974.

In this concise study, intended for nonspecialists, of American industrialization from A.D. 1000 (for European background) to the 1970's, Brownlee accurately describes American imitations of, and variations on, Britain's industrializing experiences. For an overview of the world's second experimenter with industrialization, this is a specific useful work. Numerous photographs, maps, tables, and charts. Notes and suggested readings close each chapter, and there is an excellent double-columned index.

Burns, Arthur F. *The Business Cycle in a Changing World.* New York: National Bureau of Economic Research, 1969.

This 352-page book contains Burns's essays reprinted to honor his involvement in the business cycle research of the National Bureau of Economic Research. Topics cover the nature, causes, and old and new facts of business cycles. The essays provide descriptive analysis of the U.S. economic history since the 1920's. Tables, charts, and an index are included. Suitable for a general audience.

Burns, Arthur F., and Wesley C. Mitchell. *Measuring Business Cycles.* New York: National Bureau of Economic Research, 1946.

The standard reference work on the NBER method. Explains how the NBER dates recessions and how different parts of the economy behave during a recession. Also includes international comparisons. One of the most important contributions to the study of business cycles. Charts and illustrations included.

Campbell, Colin D., ed. *Wage-Price Controls in World War II: United States and Germany.* Washington, D.C.: American Enterprise Institute, 1971.

This collection of readings on wartime economies contains two excellent articles on rationing: "The Rationing of Consumer Goods," by Harvey Mansfield and associates, and "America's Black Markets," by Leo M. Cherne.

Chaloner, W. H. "The Anti-Corn Law League." *History Today* 18 (March, 1968): 196-204.

An excellent popular article providing background about the organization that led the fight against the Corn Laws. A good introduction to the subject.

Chandler, Lester V. *America's Greatest Depression, 1929-1941.* New York: Harper & Row, 1970.

An excellent overview of the conditions leading to the Great Depression and of governmental policy responses. Descriptive and factual with emphasis on the events and institutional structure of the period.

Clark, Ronald C. *Works of Man: A History of Invention and Engineering from the Pyramids to the Space Shuttle.* New York: Viking Press, 1985. Well illustrated, this popularly written survey is especially useful for contextual as well as functional understanding of inventions that were integral to Great Britain's Industrial Revolution. Chapters are titled, not numbered. Pages 58-141, dealing with the coming of steam, the engineering of artificial waterways, the advent of the railroad, and new metals and better bridges, are pertinent to eighteenth and nineteenth century industrial developments in Great Britain, though Clark covers seminal events elsewhere. Contains an excellent, double-columned bibliography, mostly of readily available books, and an extremely useful, four-columned index.

Cole, Charles Woosley. *Colbert and a Century of French Mercantilism.* 2 vols. New York: Columbia University Press, 1939. Despite their age, these volumes constitute one of the most thoroughly documented and objective historical analyses of the subject. Each volume is dense, but an excellent, double-columned index closing volume 2 allows for informative selective reading. The writing, directed toward interested yet not necessarily specialized readers, is clear, if professionally inelegant. Still, this is an essential source on the subject. There are no illustrations; footnoting, page by page, is rich and ample in sources. Except for documents cited, many other bibliographical entries are outdated.

Colm, Gerhard, ed. *The Employment Act Past and Present: A Tenth Anniversary Symposium.* Washington, D.C.: National Planning Association, 1956. A collection of short comments by individuals who are prominent in politics, business, unions, and academia. More useful for getting a sense of how various groups feel about the Employment Act of 1946 than for specific information.

Colton, Joel, and Stuart Bruchey, eds. *Technology, the Economy, and Society.* New York: Columbia University Press, 1987. A collection of papers by distinguished academics examines the question of how technological, economic, and social changes interrelate, with specific reference to the American experience.

Commons, John R., et al. *History of Labor in the United States*. 2 vols. New York: Macmillan, 1918.

A history of the labor movement in the United States during the nineteenth century. It is written by one of the leading labor economists and reformers of the early twentieth century and a major figure in the development of the Wisconsin school of labor history. Commons' approach views the U.S. labor movement as lacking the class consciousness of the European labor movement and characterizes it as a nonantagonistic interest group competing for limited goals in a pluralist society.

Corn, Joseph J., ed. *Imagining Tomorrow: History, Technology, and the American Future*. Cambridge, Mass.: MIT Press, 1986.

A series of essays by academics and specialists about the American technological culture in various areas, the reasons behind some predictions of technological utopias, and why many of these failed to materialize. This short work (237 pages) is clearly, tantalizingly written and attractively illustrated to depict various, not-so-accurate visions of the future.

Cornwall, John *After Stagflation*. Armonk, N.Y.: M. E. Sharpe, 1984.

A series of seven papers that deal with the issue of stagflation from a number of different perspectives. The introduction is especially helpful in setting a recent historical context and outlining alternative explanations and policy implications.

Crafts, N. F. R. *British Economic Growth During the Industrial Revolution*. New York: Oxford University Press, 1985.

Brief and clear, eminently suitable for nonspecialists, this interpretive volume updates, though it does not significantly alter, the conclusions of T. S. Ashton's work. There are numerous tables and a few graphs. The bibliography is selective but valuable.

Crump, Thomas. *The Phenomenon of Money*. London: Routledge & Kegan Paul, 1981.

Examines the history of money and monetary institutions. Chapter 17 is devoted to inflation and contains a good discussion of hyperinflations.

Daltrop, Anne. *Politics and the European Community*. 2d ed. New York: Longman, 1990.

An excellent introduction to the EEC, with a good treatment of the history of the EEC. This book makes particular references to the many debates concerning the relative powers of the Community over individual member nations. Particularly emphasizes the British experience in the Common Market.

Daumas, Maurice, ed. *A History of Technology and Invention: Progress Through the Ages*. Translated by Eileen B. Hennessy. 2 vols. New York: Crown, 1969.
An authoritative account by a panel of mostly French scholars of the methods that humankind has discovered and used to improve the conditions of existence. Attractively illustrated, with a useful bibliography and index.

David, Paul, Herbert Gutman, Richard Sutch, and Gavin Wright. *Reckoning with Slavery: A Critical Study in the Quantitative History of American Negro Slavery*. New York: Oxford University Press, 1976.
Consists of a collection of essays that critically examine the arguments and conclusions of Robert Fogel and Stanley Engerman's *Time on the Cross* (1974).

Davis, John P. *Corporations: A Study of the Origin and Development of Great Business Combinations and of Their Relation to the Authority of the State*. New York: Capricorn Books, 1961.
An exhaustive essay on the historical development of the corporation in all its forms, from the feudal period to the modern age. This survey effectively sets the historic stage for many of the modern issues surrounding the corporation, the individual, and the state.

Deane, Phyllis. *The First Industrial Revolution*. Cambridge, England: Cambridge University Press, 1965.
A highly respected authority on British economic growth, particularly on statistical evidence, Deane gives an excellent, clearly written overview of the historical antecedents of Great Britain's Industrial Revolution, placing it in a continuum of economic, political, and social developments of preceding centuries. Good bibliography and a useful index.

Dillard, Dudley. *Economic Development of the North Atlantic Community*. Englewood Cliffs, N.J.: Prentice-Hall, 1967.
Chapters 2, 4, and 8 are valuable summaries of the decline of the manorial system and the enclosures in England.

Eichengreen, Barry, and Peter H. Linhert, eds. *The International Debt Crisis in Historical Perspective.* Cambridge, Mass.: MIT Press, 1989.
Examines the Latin American debt crisis of the 1980's in light of prior Latin American and other international debt crises.

Elliot, John E. *Marx and Engels on Economics, Politics, and Society.* Santa Monica, Calif.: Goodyear, 1981.
This book compiles the representative writings by Karl Marx and Friedrich Engels on economics, politics, and society into topical themes. Chapter 5 deals with exploitation. This book is especially helpful since it first explains the basic concepts.

Ellsworth, Paul Theodore, and J. Clark Leith. *The International Economy.* New York: Macmillan, 1987.
Presents mercantilist theories and their applications to economic policy and practice in an excellent narrative. The first edition provides more historical data than the later editions. The information is well documented and is reported in a manner that will interest the reader. The shortcomings of the mercantilist system are also noted.

Fabritius, M. Manfred, and William Borges. *Saving the Savings and Loan: The U.S. Thrift Industry and the Texas Experience, 1950-1988.* New York: Praeger, 1989.
One of the best books on the history of the S&L industry. The authors highlight, in a chronological order, the behavior of the S&L industry under various economic conditions. The authors also use the state-chartered Texas S&L reform model to demonstrate how it reformed and reshaped the Texas S&L industry as well as the national industry.

Feis, Herbert. *1933: Characters in Crisis.* Boston: Little, Brown, 1966.
A well-written narrative account of the repercussions of abandonment of the gold standard, including a detailed review of the conflicting interests of the parties who participated in the 1933 World Monetary and Economic Conference.

Fels, Rendigs, and C. Elton Hinshaw. *Forecasting and Recognizing Business Cycle Turning Points.* New York: National Bureau of Economic Research, 1968.
Evaluates the comparative performance of recognizing business cycle turning points by the National Bureau of Economic Research and the Federal Reserve Board, the government monetary agency. This 131-

page book provides qualifications for government agencies for monitoring the overall economy. Suitable for a general audience.

Fetter, Frank W. *Development of British Monetary Orthodoxy, 1797-1875.* Cambridge, Mass.: Harvard University Press, 1965. Reprint. Fairfield, N.J.: Augustus M. Kelley, 1978.

The classic historical treatment of the development of British monetary thought and policy. The chapters on the Bullionist controversy and the Banking School-Currency School controversy provide many examples of the arguments made by both proponents and opponents of the real bills doctrine. Suitable for college students.

Fogel, Robert W., and Stanley L. Engerman. *Time on the Cross: The Economics of American Negro Slavery.* 2 vols. Boston: Little, Brown, 1974.

One of the most comprehensive and controversial examinations of slavery in the United States. Using cliometric techniques, Fogel and Engerman present a revisionist view of slavery that resulted in a substantial increase in the research on the subject. The second volume contains the theoretical and statistical techniques that they utilized in order to reach their conclusions.

Friedman, Milton. *Adam Smith's Relevance for 1976.* Los Angeles: International Institute for Economic Research, University of California at Los Angeles, 1976.

As the title suggests, this commemorative lecture reexamines the basic tenets of Adam Smith's 1776 book, *The Wealth of Nations*, and compares them to (then) currently observable political and economic issues, including rising interest rates and taxation policies.

Friedman, Milton, and Anna J. Schwartz. *A Monetary History of the United States, 1867-1960.* Princeton, N.J.: Princeton University Press, 1963.

Written by two eminent economists (Friedman is a Nobel Prize winner), this book is a fascinating historical narrative of nearly a century of changes in the U.S. money stock. The history, development, and policies of the Federal Reserve System are examined in detail. The discussion of the banking collapse during the Great Depression—a massive liquidity crisis—is classic. Friedman and Schwartz argue that, contrary to prevailing wisdom, the Federal Reserve was to blame for the severity of the Great Depression of the 1930's because it failed to expand reserves and prevent the money supply from falling.

Galbraith, John Kenneth. *The Age of Uncertainty*. Boston: Houghton Mifflin, 1977.
> The well-written 365-page book by Galbraith provides a historical review of how different political and economic events have shaped modern life and expectations under uncertainty in both capitalistic and socialist economies since the beginning of the twentieth century. The stories are based on a television series produced by the British Broadcasting Corporation. Numerous illustrations are included. Suitable for a general audience.

_____. *Economics in Perspective: A Critical History*. Boston: Houghton Mifflin, 1987.
> Reviews the history of economics, the power of corporations over their prices, the weakness of military aggression as a path to national greatness, how farm subsidies are a failure of capitalism, how economics masks the reality of economic power and motivation, and the need for public planning.

_____. *The Great Crash: 1929*. New York: Time, 1961.
> Galbraith examines the causes of the Great Depression. This highly readable account will introduce the reader to modern employment theory through its analysis of the Depression.

_____. *A Life in Our Times*. Boston: Houghton Mifflin, 1981.
> These memoirs of one of the chief Office of Price Administration managers give many interesting insights into the whole process of administering economic controls in wartime. Chapters 8-12 are devoted to this process, providing a very readable and interesting account of the political and managerial problems of these controls.

_____. *Money: Whence It Came, Where It Went*. Boston: Houghton Mifflin, 1975.
> Galbraith, in his best style, gives an excellent history of the development of money, including currency. Primarily an account of the development of money in the United States, the first six chapters are especially rich in their discussion of currency.

Garraty, John A. *The Great Depression*. San Diego: Harcourt Brace Jovanovich, 1986.
> An overview of the effects of the Great Depression not only in the United States but in other key countries mainly in Europe. Garraty's

treatment is particularly useful for its breakdown of effects for agricultural, labor, and other interests.

Garrett, Garet, and Murray Rothbard. *The Great Depression and New Deal Monetary Policy.* San Francisco: Cato Institute, 1980.

The authors survey the impact, in international terms, of changing monetarist policies practiced by the United States both before and during the Great Depression.

George, Stephen. *Politics and Policy in the European Community.* 2d ed. New York: Oxford University Press, 1990.

Excellent introduction to the Community, its origins, and its programs. Considers the European Economic Community in a wider context of general economic theories about planning and neofunctionalism. The analysis is particularly worthwhile in its revelation of the important connections between economics and politics in the development and current policies of the Community.

Goldin, Claudia. *Understanding the Gender Gap: An Economic History of American Women.* New York: Oxford University Press, 1990.

This comprehensive book examines women's labor supply and labor force participation in the United States from the late 1800's to the 1980's. Topics covered include the differences between nonwhite and white women and between single and married women in their labor force participation; the laws and customs that discouraged the employment of married women (the marriage bar); and the effects of education and child rearing on women's employment. Contains 287 pages, figures, tables, and an index.

Goodfriend, Marvin, and Monica Hargraves. "A Historical Assessment of the Rationales and Functions of Reserve Requirements." *Economic Review* 9 (March/April, 1983): 3-21.

Goodfriend and Hargraves offer a detailed historical account of the rationales for reserves. Some economic knowledge is assumed.

Goodhart, Charles A. E. *The Evolution of Central Banks.* Cambridge, Mass.: MIT Press, 1988.

A spirited defense of central banking by a former adviser to the Bank of England. Particularly interesting are the author's discussions of free banking(chapter 2) and private deposit insurance (chapter 6). Strongly advocates the importance of the lender-of-last-resort function of a central bank. Includes a bibliography and an index. Nontechnical; can be understood by the nonspecialist.

Gordon, Robert A. *Business Fluctuations*. 2d ed. New York: Harper & Brothers, 1961.
Long the leading text on business cycles, this book, unfortunately out of print, is still available in many libraries. Both the causes of recessions and their nature are covered in exemplary fashion.

Gregg, Pauline. *Modern Britain: A Social and Economic History*. New York: Pegasus, 1967.
An excellent survey with good coverage of the creation and repeal of the Corn Laws.

Gregory, Paul R., and Robert C. Stuart. *Soviet Economic Structure and Performance*. 3d ed. New York: Harper & Row, 1986.
Chapter 7 is a good summary of the theory of central planning in the U.S.S.R. Chapter 13 analyzes attempts at economic reform of system in the early 1980's.

Greider, William. *Secrets of the Temple: How the Federal Reserve Runs the Country*. New York: Simon & Schuster, 1987.
Provides a fascinating and detailed picture of how monetary policy was conducted under Paul A. Volcker, Federal Reserve chairman from 1979 to 1987. Most of the 700-plus pages are devoted to Federal Reserve policies from 1979 through 1982. A valuable source of what happened and why, but the reader should be wary of how Greider's opinions creep into his discussion of the facts. The author has virtually no appreciation for the dangers of inflation and is convinced the Federal Reserve is run in an "undemocratic" fashion. The rise of monetarism is viewed through its political overtones. The difficulty of controlling the money supply in an era of financial deregulation, and the failure of "fine-tuning" the money supply, are discussed in an informal tone.

Habakkuk, H. J. *American and British Technology in the Nineteenth Century: The Search for Labour-Saving Inventions*. Cambridge, England: Cambridge, University Press, 1962.
Explains why some countries invent and innovate faster than others, with reference to the different industrialization experiences of the United States and Great Britain in the nineteenth century. Habakkuk, an economic historian at the University of Oxford, is a major proponent of the thesis that economic forces underlie technological novelties.

Haberler, Gottfried. *Prosperity and Depression*. Lake Success, N.Y.: United Nations, 1946.
A famous study of prewar business cycle theories. Haberler explains the various theories and attempts to synthesize them.

Hansen, Niles M. *French Regional Planning*. Bloomington: Indiana University Press, 1968.
A detailed and advanced analysis of regional planning that concentrates on growth pole analysis.

Harris, Seymour E. *Price and Related Controls in the United States*. New York: Da Capo Press, 1976.
This analysis of World War II economic controls provides many examples of how rationing lends support to price control programs. Chapter 21, "Rationing and Prices," is a detailed and somewhat technical discussion of this relationship.

Hays, Samuel P. *The Response to Industrialization, 1885-1914*. Chicago: University of Chicago Press, 1961.
This book is written for college-level reading and provides a good historical account of how the American economic system responded to the same pressures that stimulated Marxism in other parts of the world.

Hicks, John R. *A Theory of Economic History*. Oxford: England: Clarendon Press, 1969.
A theoretical essay of economic history in general and the market in particular.

Hobsbawm, Eric J. "The British Standard of Living." *The Economic History Review* 10 (August, 1957): 46-61.
The historian author controverts the widely held view that the Industrial Revolution raised living standards in Great Britain. This article preceded a barrage of scholarly debates about the general impact of industrialization. It is lively, well researched, and, though intended for other scholars, readily understandable by nonspecialists. Essential reading for an open-minded perspective on the first Industrial Revolution.

Hodges, Richard. *Primitive and Peasant Markets*. Oxford, England: Basil Blackwell, 1988.
An overview of different types of markets prior to industrialization.

Hollander, Samuel. *The Economics of David Ricardo.* Toronto: University of Toronto Press, 1979.
This is a rather lengthy book that summarizes Ricardo's contribution to economics. Particular emphasis is placed on distinguishing Ricardo's work from Adam Smith's, and illustrating the similarities between Ricardo's theories and Alfred Marshall's theories.

_____. *The Economics of John Stuart Mill.* Toronto: University of Toronto Press, 1985.
This two-volume set summarizes Mill's contributions to the classical school. Particular emphasis is placed on how Mill extends Ricardian theory.

Homer, Sidney. *A History of Interest Rates.* 3d ed. New Brunswick, N.J.: Rutgers University Press, 1991.
Worldwide interest-rate trends from ancient times to the 1970's are described. Chapter 17, "The United States in the Twentieth Century," provides a chronological description of the major trends in U.S. interest rates and their causal forces from 1900 to 1975. The third edition is the first to contain series on "real," or inflation-adjusted, interest rates.

Horsman, George. *Inflation in the Twentieth Century: Evidence from Europe and North America.* New York: St. Martin's Press, 1988.
Provides an historical survey and discussion of inflation. Horsman concludes that the disparity of income levels and the resulting conflict explains the reason that inflation has been a persistent problem. Both interesting and accessible.

Hudson, Ray, David Rhind, and Helen Mounsey. *An Atlas of EEC Affairs.* New York: Methuen, 1984.
Perhaps the most accessible of all introductions to the Common Market, this atlas includes brief policies of the EEC. It also considers European demography, social development, economic resources, patterns of consumption, and the labor market in the member nations. Many helpful maps and charts.

Hunt, E. K. *Property and Prophets: The Evolution of Economic Institutions and Ideologies.* New York: Harper & Row, 1972.
A comprehensive overview of the evolution of the concept of property and individual property rights from European feudalism to the present day. Summarizes the various, sometimes conflicting views of property, the individual, and society from a number of perspectives.

Hunt, E. K., and Howard J. Sherman. *Economics: An Introduction to Traditional and Radical Views*. 6th ed. New York: Harper & Row, 1990.
   Written from a Marxist historical perspective, this book is very readable, starting with economic evolution in ancient Greece, moving on to mercantilism, the corporate rise of capitalism, monopoly power, income distribution, and economic theories, and ending with comparative economic systems, such as market socialism and central planning in the Soviet Union. Fine for the general reader.

Jevons, William Stanley. *Investigations in Currency and Finance*. London: Macmillan, 1884. Reprint. New York: A. M. Kelley, 1964.
   This classic book contains one of the first attempts to identify business cycles. A ten-to-eleven-year periodicity in certain time series is attributed to fluctuations in crop yields which, in turn, are attributed to a similar periodicity in sun spots.

Jones, David M. *Fed Watching and Interest Rate Projections: A Practical Guide*. 2d ed. New York: New York Institute of Finance, 1989.
   Intended for the serious investor, this concise two hundred-page book presents the basic rules for predicting Federal Reserve policy changes. Jones does an excellent job of explaining difficult concepts in an understandable fashion. Includes a glossary, and the more technical material is placed in appendices.

Kalecki, Michal. *Selected Essays on the Dynamics of the Capitalist Economy, 1933-1970*. Cambridge, England: Cambridge University Press, 1971.
   This compilation presents Kalecki's version of the theory of effective demand, his own policy implications, and refinements of the theory over more than thirty years.

Keller, Robert R., and Ann Mari May. "The Presidential Political Business Cycle of 1972." *Journal of Economic History* 44 (June, 1984): 265-271.
   The authors analyze whether President Richard M. Nixon used his office to manipulate the economy to facilitate his reelection. Despite some data that suggest the existence of the political cycle, this article illustrates how difficult it is to analyze motivation empirically.

Kemmerer, Donald L., and Clyde C. Jones. *American Economic History*. New York: McGraw-Hill, 1959.
   One of many textbooks in the field of U.S. economic history that provides basic background information on U.S. depressions.

Kettl, Donald F. *Leadership at the Fed.* New Haven, Conn.: Yale University Press, 1986.

Kettl, a political scientist, provides a concise and very readable account of the history of Federal Reserve policy-making. The central argument of the book is that the growth in the power and prestige of the Federal Reserve is largely the result of strong leadership by its chairmen.

Keynes, John Maynard. *Essays In Biography.* New York: W. W. Norton, 1963.

Offers biographies that touch on economic debates and development of theory. David Ricardo is always identified as the principal Bullionist, but the intellectual help that he received from Thomas Robert Malthus may eventually have had more impact on modern monetary theory and policy. Malthus wrote little beyond the *Essay on Population*, but his influence on Ricardo must have been immense.

_____. *The General Theory of Employment, Interest, and Money.* New York: Harcourt, Brace, 1935.

Chapter 22, on business cycles, is one of the most readable chapters in this famous work, one of the classic works of theory.

Kindleberger, Charles P. *The World in Depression, 1929-1939.* Rev. ed. Berkeley: University of California Press, 1986.

One of the best explanations of international economic developments in the 1930's, with emphasis on how the Great Depression spread worldwide through such international linkages as exchange rates, financial markets, and commodity price deflation.

Klein, Phillip A., ed. *Analyzing Modern Business Cycles.* Armonk, N.Y.: M. E. Sharpe, 1990.

Chapter 2, "Plan of the Book," gives the reader many excellent ideas for further study. The included articles take various points of view.

Kolko, Gabriel. *Wealth and Power in America.* New York: Praeger, 1962.

A challenging assertion that neither alterations in the tax structure nor other government policies have redistributed wealth in the twentieth century United States. Overall, a provocative thesis. The notes are full, the select bibliography is adequate, and the index is helpful.

Kondratieff, Nikolai. *The Long Wave Cycle.* Translated by Guy Daniels. New York: Richardson and Snyder, 1984.

A translation (from Russian) of a 1926 paper read by Kondratieff at the Russian Economics Institution. This lengthy paper fully develops his theory of business cycles and provides empirical evidence supporting his long-wave theory. An extensive introduction is provided by Julian Snyder and a summary of Kondratieff's main points is also presented.

Krooss, Herman E., and Martin R. Blyn. *A History of Financial Intermediaries*. New York: Random House, 1971.
Covers the history and development of all types of financial institutions from colonial times to 1970. Information is presented in a chronological format, and material on the thrifts is interspersed with discussion of commercial banks, investment banking, life insurance companies, and their relationships to one another and the national credit market.

Leijonhufvud, Axel. "Capitalism and the Factory System." In *Economics as a Process*, edited by Richard Langlois. Cambridge, England: Cambridge University Press, 1986.
A brief (eighteen-page), thought-provoking examination of Adam Smith's theory from the angle of economic history. Leijonhufvud explains the linkages between the division of labor and the extent of the market and traces some implications for the social and economic consequences of industrial development. A wide-ranging, twenty-eight-item bibliography is included.

Lodge, Eleanor C. *Sully, Colbert, and Turgot*. London: Methuen, 1931.
Written for nonspecialists, this modest work, while dated in some respects, remains an excellent introduction to these three eminent champions of seventeenth and eighteenth century mercantilist policies. Appreciative of Colbert's extraordinary abilities, the author frankly deals with weaknesses in Colbert's personality and policies. There are no footnotes, illustrations, or bibliography. The double-columned index, however, is very useful.

McCord, Norman. *The Anti-Corn Law League, 1838-1846*. London: Allen & Unwin, 1958.
A very good and scholarly account of the topic. The coverage is thorough and conclusions judicious. Recommended to anyone needing a book-length study of the subject.

Mager, Nathan. *The Kondratieff Waves*. New York: Praeger, 1987.
Considers the evidence for the Kondratieff cycle within the context of U.S. business cycle history. One of the very few contemporary books to provide a considerable degree of biographical information on Kon-

dratieff, this work is not highly technical and thus has appeal to a general audience.

Malthus, Thomas Robert. *An Essay on the Principle of Population*, edited by Philip Appleman. New York: W. W. Norton, 1976.
In addition to containing the original and revised editions of Malthus' *Essay*, this volume includes the writings of individuals who influenced Malthus, commented on Malthus, and discussed the relevance of Malthus' theory in the twentieth century.

Marglin, Stephen, and Juliet Schor. *The Golden Age of Capitalism*. Oxford: Oxford University Press, 1990.
On the cutting edge of a new brand of economics that is neither Marxian nor Keynesian. The authors reach for an alternative to pure laissez-faire. Several essays attempt to integrate the seemingly contradictory analysis of John Maynard Keynes (stressing the importance of wages as a source of aggregate demand) and Karl Marx (emphasizing how wages cut into profits). An antidote to ahistorical and vacuous historical descriptions.

Marx, Karl, and Friedrich Engels. *The Communist Manifesto*. 1848. Reprint. New York: W. W. Norton, 1988.
The most famous document in the history of the socialist movement. It announced to the world, in brief and brilliant prose, the new synthesis of socialist ideas that was worked out by Marx and Engels in the early 1840's.

Matthaei, Julie A. *An Economic History of Women in America: Women's Work, the Sexual Division of Labor and the Development of Capitalism*. New York: Schocken Books, 1982.
Provides much useful information on the economic status of women in America in the pre-World War II stages. Analysis is carried out in the Marxist tradition, stressing class considerations and worker exploitation. For advanced undergraduates.

Mill, John Stuart. *Principles of Political Economy*. Edited by W. J. Ashley. 1909. Reprint. New York: Augustus M. Kelley, 1961.
Like other classical economists, Mill advocated a minimal role for government and a maximum role for private markets. Nevertheless, his analysis of public education in book 5, chapter 11 treats public education as a public good.

Mints, Lloyd W. *A History of Banking Theory in Great Britain and the United States.* Chicago: University of Chicago Press, 1945.
The classic study of the real bills doctrine. Mints's antagonism to the real bills doctrine pervades his entire study. Suitable for college students.

Mitchell, Wesley C. *Business Cycles.* Berkeley, Calif.: University of California Press, 1913.
The first of a series of books by this great business-cycle-indicator analyst. In this book, Mitchell searches for systematic leading, lagging, and coincident relationships among economic time series. Wile some intuition is used, Mitchell mainly relies on the numbers themselves for these patterns. A later work based on this method is Arthur F. Burns and Mitchell's *Measuring Business Cycles* (New York: National Bureau of Economic Research, 1946).

Moore, Geoffrey H. *Business Cycles, Inflation, and Forecasting.* 2d ed. Cambridge, Mass.: Ballinger, 1983.
Discusses the definition of a recession, the difference from a depression, growth cycles, the method used by the National Bureau of Economic Research, forecasting, the cyclical behavior of prices, and more.

Moore, Geoffrey H., and Melita H. Moore. *International Economic Indicators.* Westport, Conn.: Greenwood Press, 1985.
Describes and gives sources of data for predicting and analyzing recessions in seven important countries. Very little analysis is included.

Morazé, Charles. *The Triumph of the Middle Classes.* Garden City, N.Y.: Doubleday, 1968.
A sweeping survey of the "class" that figured most prominently throughout the world in the emergence of capitalism and the launching of industrialization by another French *Annaliste* historian. Unfortunately no longer in print, but still available on library shelves, this is an invaluable, clearheaded synthesis intended for laypersons. Morazé correctly perceives the middle classes (the bourgeoisie) as revolutionary forces—intellectually, politically, and economically. Required reading for a sound understanding of industrialization's varied social transformations. Although there are no footnotes, there is a brief, unannotated bibliography and a lengthy, double-columned, useful index. Essential and intriguing reading.

Murat, Ines. *Colbert*. Translated by Robert Francis Cook and Jeannie Van Asselt. Charlottesville: University Press of Virginia, 1984.
A survey of Colbert's life, of its setting and of Colbertism. Murat, a descendant of Colbert, presents unpublished information on the man and his ministry. The book is well-crafted, easily read, and in many areas, despite its brevity, authoritative. Like most Colbert studies, this one necessarily relies heavily upon Pierre Clement's untranslated multivolume masterpieces, published between 1846 and 1882. There are no maps, charts, or illustrations, but the bibliography and index are excellent.

Myrdal, Gunnar. *American Dilemma: The Negro Problem and Modern Democracy*. New York: Harper and Row, 1962.
This magnum opus, completed during World War II, is a definitive study of the conditions of African Americans in the South as of that time. Myrdal pointed out the inconsistency between United States ideology and treatment of the black population. In later studies, Myrdal expressed a preference for genuine full employment as opposed to affirmative action as a means of aiding African Americans economically.

Nelson, Donald M. *Arsenal of Democracy*. New York: Harcourt, Brace, 1946.
During World War II, Nelson headed the War Production Board, which planned and carried out the production of immense quantities of war materials for the United States and its allies. Written as a personal memoir, the book is an interesting, nontechnical description of the sorts of real-world planning decisions that frequently involved considerations of the relationship between time and supply elasticity. Although based on government planning, many of the ideas and approaches are used by private businesses for their own internal planning.

Nicholson, Francis, and Roger East. *From the Six to the Twelve: The Enlargement of the European Communities*. Chicago: St. James Press, 1987.
A detailed account of the expansion of the European Economic Community from the 1960's through 1986, with separate sections for the entry of each of the newer member nations. Also has valuable discussions of both the Norwegian decision not to take up membership and Greenland's withdrawal. A description of the trade policies between the EEC and other European nations is included.

North, Douglass C. *Structure and Change in Economic History.* New York: W. W. Norton, 1981.

North concentrates on economic forces that have created, altered, or destroyed the institutional structures (including those of economic thought) and that have channeled economic activities, none of them more important than modern industrialization. The book's chronological scope ranges from the late eighteenth century to the late 1970's, while its geographical coverage is international. Economic theories, in simplified fashion, are explored, but not to the detriment of nonspecialist readers. Few footnotes; brief bibliography, unannotated but current; and a valuable double-columned index.

Norton, Hugh S. *The Employment Act and the Council of Economic Advisers, 1946-1976.* Columbia: University of South Carolina Press, 1977.

A scholarly but readable study of the CEA. Chapter 4 is particularly focused on the Employment Act of 1946. An excellent source for a study of the long-term results of the Employment Act.

Nourse, Edwin G. "Early Flowering of the Employment Act." *Virginia Quarterly Review* 43 (Spring, 1967): 233-247.

Although sometimes defensive, Nourse's comments about the early period of the life of the Employment Act are important because of his intimate involvement with it.

_____ . *Economics in the Public Service; Administrative Aspects of the Employment Act.* New York: Harcourt, Brace, 1953.

An autobiographical account by the first chairman of the Council of Economic Advisers, this book suffers from the author's inclination to defend his own actions, but it is a valuable and useful firsthand account of the first years of the Employment Act of 1946.

_____ , ed. "The Employment Act in the Economic Thinking of Our Times: A Symposium." *American Economic Review, Papers and Proceedings* 47 (May, 1957): 96-144.

Contains six papers that were presented at the sixty-ninth meeting of the American Economic Association. Although more scholarly than many general readers will want, these papers provide a solid academic assessment of the workings and effects of the Employment Act.

O'Brien, D. P. *The Classical Economists.* Oxford, England: Clarendon Press, 1975.

Provides a summary of the major theories developed by the classical economists. Chapters are organized by area of economic theory rather than by individuals.

Okun, Arthur. *The Political Economy of Prosperity.* New York: W. W. Norton, 1970.
This well-written book presents a background study on economic policy-making in clear, understandable terms. Okun expressed a more realistic view of Keynesian policy than that generally held in the 1960's. The topics include consensus, controversy, and implementation in the political arena. Suitable for a general audience.

Paterson, William E., and Alastair H. Thomas, eds. *The Future of Social Democracy.* Oxford, England: Oxford University Press, 1986.
A collection of articles on the British, German, Austrian, French, and Scandinavian socialist parties. All the articles emphasize the circumstances under which social democratic parties had come to operate by the mid-1980's. Suitable for a general audience.

Pechman, Joseph A. *Who Paid the Taxes, 1966-1985.* Washington, D.C.: Brookings Institution, 1986.
Only eighty-three pages, but an excellent overview at an introductory level of tax revenue issues. The book looks at tax incidence and tax burden of various tax revenue schemes, including individual and corporate income, general sales, excise, and property taxes. Contains several tables, no equations. The payroll tax, or social security tax, is also featured.

Pelinka, Anton. *Social Democratic Parties in Europe.* New York: Praeger, 1983.
A seminal study of European social democracy. Examines the nature of social democratic ideology and gives a very detailed analysis of the organizational structures of social democratic parties in Europe. Both specialists and nonspecialists may benefit from this book.

Prentice, Archibald. *History of the Anti-Corn-Law League.* 2 vols. 2d ed. London: Frank Cass, 1968.
Originally published in 1853, Prentice's eyewitness account of the Corn Law controversy is very valuable.

Przeworski, Adam, and John Sprague. *Paper Stones: A History of Electoral Socialism.* Chicago: University of Chicago Press, 1986.

Probably the most sophisticated and original study of social democracy. Concentrates on the relationship between social goals and electoralism and strives to demonstrate why socialist parties had so far never been able to win the absolute electoral majority in advanced capitalist countries. Combines historical analysis with abstract (mathematical) modeling. Suitable for advanced graduate students and specialists.

Ransom, Roger L., and Richard Sutch. *One Kind of Freedom: The Economic Consequences of Emancipation.* Cambridge, England: Cambridge University Press, 1977.

Written in response to *Time on the Cross* (1974), this book provides a detailed criticism of some of the techniques and conclusions of Robert Fogel and Stanley Engerman.

Roll, Eric. *A History of Economic Thought.* Englewood Cliffs, N.J.: Prentice-Hall, 1954.

Presents the ideas of premercantilists along with the central policies of the period. The quality of mercantilism is examined, and there is a special section on Bullionism and its relation to the mercantilist philosophy. Contains a further analysis of the major writings of the period, and significant legislative policies are identified.

Rosenberg, Nathan, and L. E. Birdzell, Jr. *How the West Grew Rich.* New York: Basic Books, 1986.

This concise synthesis of economic history argues that the underlying source of the West's ability to attract economic revolution was a unique use of experiment in technology and organization to harness resources to the satisfaction of human wants. See especially chapter 8, which examines the connection between science and Western wealth.

Rostow, Walt W. *Politics and the Stages of Economic Growth.* Cambridge, England: Cambridge University Press, 1971.

A noted political scientist, public servant, and economist, Rostow coined the phrase "takeoff" to describe the political economy of industrialization. Broad-gauged and clearly written, this provocative book received wide readership. Its scope ranges from pre-Newtonian political thought (as it affected industrialization) to the nation-building, industrializing efforts in the Third World following 1945. Essential reading, although it concentrates on the primacy of politics as a background to economic development. There are numerous useful tables and a few graphs. Instructive notes for each chapter close the book, supplanting the need for a bibliography. The index is double-columned, extensive, and valuable.

_____. *The World Economy: History and Prospect.* Austin: University of Texas Press, 1978.

In Rostow's view, an economy reaches a "take-off point" when a critical mass is reached in industry, particularly in factory industry.

Rothbard, Murray N. *America's Great Depression.* Kansas City, Mo.: Sheed & Ward, 1975.

Presents an excellent overview of the events from 1921 to 1932, from an Austrian perspective. In order to establish a sound framework within which to analyze those events, the author first offers his theory regarding the causes of business cycles. There is a wealth of historical detail; yet the relationships between events are lucidly explained. Suitable for both college students and the layperson.

Schuettinger, Robert L., and Eamonn F. Butler. *Forty Centuries of Wage and Price Controls: How Not to Fight Inflation.* Washington, D.C.: Heritage Foundation, 1979.

An interesting look at how wage and price controls have been repeatedly (and unsuccessfully) used to try to stop inflation. Suitable for advanced high school and college students.

Schumpeter, Joseph A. *Business Cycles.* New York: McGraw-Hill, 1939.

Provides a detailed account of the Hayek effect, stressing the way in which differences in factor prices between labor and machinery influence the choice of a method of production. Schumpeter supports the effect but rejects Austrian business cycle theory. Schumpeter was a leading authority on business cycles. Although of Austrian nationality, he was a Walrasian rather than a supporter of the Austrian school and often differed with Hayek. Schumpeter identifies three business cycles, each superimposed on the other: a long cycle of approximately fifty years, referred to as the Kondratieff cycle; an intermediate cycle of approximately ten years, referred to as the Juglar cycle; and a short cycle of three to four years, referred to as the Kitchin cycle.

_____. *History of Economic Analysis.* New York: Oxford University Press, 1954.

Schumpeter provides a critique of the theory underpinning virtually all of the historical schemes for supplying money.

Shapiro, Max. *The Penniless Billionaires.* New York: Times Books, 1980.
   A book about inflation that is intended for the general reader. Chapter 5
   is a long analysis of the German hyperinflation of the 1920's.

Shaw, W. A. *The History of Currency, 1252 to 1896.* Reprint. New York:
Augustus M. Kelley, 1967.
   Originally published in 1896, this work exclusively studies the minting
   of coins by various Western nations, with a wealth of data for anyone
   interested in monetary history. Those investigating Gresham's law
   should pay particular attention to the tables that record the annual
   market fluctuations in the exchange rate between gold and silver for
   the period 1687 to 1893.

Shniderman, Harry, and Bingham Leverich. *Price Discrimination in
Perspective.* 2d ed. Philadelphia: American Law Institute-American Bar
Association, 1987.
   An analysis of the 1936 Robinson-Patman Act, which amended the
   price discrimination provisions of the 1914 Clayton Act. Various court
   decisions are covered in the volume. A reference for the generalist and
   antitrust specialists as well.

Shonfield, Andrew. *Modern Capitalism.* New York: Oxford University
Press, 1965.
   Though it requires some updating, this is an ambitious, authoritative,
   and easily read survey of the changing balance between public and
   private power. Excellent on the restructuring of tax systems in France,
   Great Britain, the United States, West Germany, and other capitalist
   states of Western Europe. The closing essay on the political implications of active governments is splendid. Requires reading for substance
   as well as context. Liberally footnoted, and contains five appendices
   and a fine index.

Sklar, Martin J. *The Corporate Reconstruction of American Capitalism,
1890-1916.* Cambridge, England: Cambridge University Press, 1988.
   The examination of the gulf between the ideal and reality of the market
   in a crucial period of the development of American capitalism.

Slawson, W. David. *The New Inflation.* Princeton, N.J.: Princeton University Press, 1981.
   Although slightly dated, this book is interesting for its solution to the
   problem of persistent inflation. Slawson, after detailing the causes of
   this "new inflation," argues for a system of wage and price controls.

Solomou, Solomos. *Phases of Economic Growth, 1850-1973.* Cambridge, England: Cambridge University Press, 1987.
Focusing on an empirical verification of Kondratieff's business cycle theory, this well-written treatise is one of the best published studies available on the topic. The author concludes, after an exhaustive investigation, that there is little support for the existence of Kondratieff cycles in industrialized countries for the period examined.

Sowell, Thomas. *Say's Law: An Historical Analysis.* Princeton, N.J.: Princeton University Press, 1972.
The definitive, modern study of Say's law. Sowell makes abundantly clear the conditional nature of the law. The principal focus of the work is on the nineteenth century controversies between the defenders of Say's law and their critics. Addressed to specialists, but useful to college students.

Spellman, Lewis J. *The Depository Firm and Industry.* New York: Academic Press, 1982.
An advanced text that examines financial isntitutions and their role in the economy. Begins with a good historical perspective of depository firms and institutions from the 1800's to the Banking Act of 1980. Examines the economic theory of the financial firm in detail, alternative goals of the firm (including deposit rather than profit maximization), the effects of disintermediation on the financial firm, the difficulties of deposit ceilings, and empirical studies of implicit deposit rates and average production costs. Also discusses the role of capital accumulation in the financial system, financial policy, and the aggregate economy and an aggregate growth model with a financial-sector emphasis. Primarily for the specialist, but the nonspecialist will also find many of the topics interesting. Each chapter has a good bibliography. Also contains an index.

Stampp, Kenneth. *The Peculiar Institution: Slavery in the Ante-Bellum South.* New York: Alfred A. Knopf, 1956.
Contains an easily understood overview of .

Stein, Herbert. *Presidential Economics: The Making of Economic Policy from Roosevelt to Reagan and Beyond.* 2d ed. New York: Simon & Schuster, 1988.
Stein makes the subject of economic writing understandable to the general reader. This 450-page book integrates the development of economic theory with the history of policy-making. A careful overview

of fiscal policies in practice from the Great Depression of the 1930's to the Reagan period. Contains figures and data on major economic indexes from 1930 to 1982.

Stocking, George W., and Myron W. Watkins. *Cartels in Action.* New York: Twentieth Century Fund, 1946.

An in-depth analysis of cartel formation and objectives, establishing important historical evidence as to when and why certain cartels have pursued price-fixing objectives.

Survey of Current Business. 1920-

A monthly publication from the Bureau of Economic Analysis of the Department of Commerce that contains recent estimates of items in the national incomes and product accounts and related articles.

Thompson, E. P. *The Making of the English Working Class.* New York: Vintage Books, 1963.

One of the classic works on the origins of the labor movement in England during the Industrial Revolution of the late eighteenth and early nineteenth centuries. The book emphasizes the interrelationships among social, cultural, political, and workplace issues in explaining the development of the consciousness and organization of the English working class.

Thornton, Henry. *An Enquiry into the Nature and Effects of the Paper Credit of Great Britain.* London: Allen & Unwin, 1939. Reprint. Fairfield, N.J.: Augustus M. Kelley, 1978.

Thornton's book, written in 1802, was perhaps the best book on monetary theory of the nineteenth century. Unfortunately, it is poorly organized and at times difficult to read.

Timberlake, Richard H., Jr. *The Origins of Central Banking in the United States.* Cambridge, Mass.: Harvard University Press, 1978.

Examines the historical forces that led to the creation of the Federal Reserve System, including the banking crises of the late nineteenth century. Suitable for college students.

Tobin, James. *The New Economics One Decade Older.* Princeton, N.J.: Princeton University Press, 1974.

A Nobel Prize-winning Keynesian economist, Tobin describes, in simple and clear language, how the ideas of Keynesian economics came to the United States and how they were used in the 1960's in order to fight cyclical unemployment.

Triffin, Robert. *Gold and the Dollar Crisis*. New Haven, Conn.: Yale University Press, 1960.

This classic book on the failings of the Bretton Woods system addresses the question of liquidity constraints imposed by the use of a relatively slow-growing international reserve asset (gold) in the face of rapid world growth. The Triffin dilemma is discussed succinctly.

U.S. Chamber of Commerce. *The Bretton Woods Program: International Monetary Fund and International Bank for Reconstruction and Development—Report of the Finance Committee Approved by the Board of Directors*. Washington, D.C.: Author, April, 1945.

This report examines the pros and cons of U.S. involvement in the two proposed international agencies that came out of late-World War II financial talks. It advises considerable caution before considering U.S. participation in the International Monetary Fund.

U.S. Congress. Congressional Budget Office. *The Changing Distribution of Federal Taxes: 1975-1990*. Washington, D.C.: Government Printing Office, 1987.

Measures changes in the distribution of major federal taxes (combined and separately) for three representative years: 1977, 1984, and 1988. Concludes that between 1977 and 1984, federal taxes became less progressive, but between 1984 and 1988, the distribution of taxes (subsequent to the 1986 Tax Reform Act) became more progressive but less than in 1977. Numerous tables on tax-burden distribution by income levels. Well written; any interested reader can benefit. No index.

U.S. Department of Commerce. Bureau of Economic Analysis. *Business Conditions Digest*. Washington, D.C.: Author.

This monthly publication contains many valuable charts showing how various sectors of the economy behave during recessions. Unfortunately, publication was discontinued after the March, 1990, issue as an economy measure, but past issues are very useful in studying past recessions.

_____. *Survey of Current Business*. Washington, D.C.: Author.

Another monthly publication. Contains much data and some of the charts formerly carried in the *Business Conditions Digest*. Blow-by-blow accounts of past recessions can be found in issues current at the time of the recession.

Valentine, Lloyd M. *Business Cycles and Forecasting.* 7th ed. Cincinnati: South-Western, 1987.

A popular text on business cycles. Chapter 4 contains a worthwhile description of what happens during recessions, described in a manner that is relatively easy to understand. Lists the National Bureau of Economic Research dates for all recessions since 1854.

Vasko, Tibor, ed. *The Long Wave Debate.* Berlin: Springer-Verlag, 1987.

Contains thirty papers presented at a major conference on "Long-term Fluctuations and Economic Growth" held in Weimar, German Democratic Republic. These papers reflect the contributions of both Marxist and non-Marxist economists to the long-wave debate. The existence or nonexistence of Kondratieff cycles in countries at varying stages of economic development is considered. The quality of the papers varies, but they are all generally good.

Volin, Lazar. *A Century of Russian Agriculture from Alexander II to Khrushchev.* Cambridge, Mass.: Harvard University Press, 1970.

A masterly economic history of Russian and Soviet agriculture. The early chapters contain a wealth of information on land tenure arrangements before the emancipation of the serfs, the post-emancipation peasantry, Tsarist attempts at land reform, and Stalinist collectivization.

Walton, Gary M., and Hugh Rockoff. *History of the American Economy.* 6th ed. Orlando, Fla.: Harcourt Brace Jovanovich, 1990.

A textbook on U.S. economic history, chapters 2-6 are devoted to colonial history. These chapters contain the most complete, succinct description and analysis of the American colonial economy. Bibliographic listings at the end of each chapter are an adequate introduction to more specialized literature.

Ware, Susan. *Holding Their Own: American Women in the 1930's.* Boston: Twayne, 1982.

An interesting discussion of how women fared relative to men both economically and in other areas. Includes a description of women's roles in politics, social reforms, and the popular culture of the 1930's.

Webb, Sidney, and Beatrice Webb. *The History of Trade Unionism.* New York: Longmans, Green, 1920.

A classic study of British trade unionism, written by two leading supporters of British industrial reform who were influential members of the Fabian Society, a socialist group that advocated an evolutionary road to socialism. While they saw the rise of labor unions as rooted in class struggle, they believed unions primarily were evolutionary economic institutions, not revolutionary ones, whose main goal was improving the conditions of lives of wage earners.

Weber, Carolyn, and Aaron Wildavsky. *A History of Taxation and Expenditure in the Western World.* New York: Simon & Schuster, 1986.

An excellent history of the role of the public sector, including both tax and expenditure issues. In 734 pages, covers the history of Western civilization and the role of taxes within that history. Includes an index and an exhaustive bibliography.

Weintraub, Sidney, and Marvin Goodstein, eds. *Reaganomics in the Stagflation Economy.* Philadelphia: University of Pennsylvania Press, 1983.

A series of essays that were presented at an economics symposium in 1981. They are all accessible and deal with a variety of issues surrounding stagflation, in particular, how the Reagan Administration planned to deal with it.

Willett, Thomas D. *Political Business Cycles: The Political Economy of Money, Inflation, and Unemployment.* Durham, N.C.: Duke University Press, 1988.

This book has mostly a monetarist bent and so is unsupportive of solutions that include managing the economy. Despite this bias, it is interesting for the political aspects of inflation and unemployment.

Williams, Trevor I. *A Short History of Twentieth-Century Technology c. 1900-1950.* New York: Oxford University Press, 1982.

An excellent, easy-to-understand, sector-by-sector survey of the topic's technological aspects ranging from agriculture, fishing, and mining to medicine and warfare. Generously illustrated with mostly period photographs.

Williamson, Jeffrey G., and Peter H. Lindert. *American Inequality: A Macroeconomic History.* New York: Academic Press, 1980.

This 362-page book utilizes Gini coefficients rather than Lorenz curves but has extensive sources and references to historical data on American wealth and income distribution since colonial times, which would allow one to construct Lorenz curves. For advanced undergraduates.

Wright, Gavin. *The Political Economy of the Cotton South.* New York: W. W. Norton, 1978.
Provides an excellent description of the roles of cotton and slavery in the economic development of the Southern economy.

CONCEPTS

Basic Concepts of Economic Theory

Abel, Andrew B. "Ricardian Equivalence Theorem." In *The New Palgrave: A Dictionary of Economics*, edited by John Eatwell, Murray Milgate, and Peter Newman. Vol. 4. New York: Stockton Press, 1987.
A brief summary of the equivalence theorem. Although it is essentially nontechnical, it is written for readers with backgrounds in economics and familiarity with economic literature. Contains an extensive bibliography.

Adams, F. Gerard, and Susan M. Wachter. *Savings and Capital Formation*. Lexington, Mass.: Lexington Books, 1986.
An orthodox examination of the relation between savings and investment, with special focus on capital accumulation.

After the Phillips Curve: Persistence of High Inflation and High Unemployment. Boston: Federal Reserve Bank of Boston, 1978.
A series of essays by leading proponents of both the classical and Keynesian views that tries to explain why inflation remained so high in the 1970's in spite of high unemployment. This collection is appropriate for undergraduates and graduate students, as the essays contain a modest amount of theoretical and empirical discussion.

Alchian, Armen A. "Costs and Outputs." In *Allocation of Economic Resources*, edited by Moses Abramovitz. Stanford, Calif.: Stanford University Press, 1959.
An important article that resolved certain ambiguities in cost theory which had surfaced in the literature.

Aldrich, Mark, and Robert Buchele. *The Economics of Comparable Worth*. Cambridge, Mass.: Ballinger, 1986.
This volume discusses the history of antidiscrimination actions from World War I until the 1980's. Provides a detailed theoretical and empirical analysis of comparable worth. Focuses on comparable worth

as a remedy for occupational segregation and estimates the economy-wide impact of an extensive comparable worth program.

Allen, R. G. D. *Mathematical Analysis for Economics.* New York: St. Martin's Press, 1938.

A classic text of the use of mathematics in economics. For those interested in the mathematics that underlies economics, Allen's work provides a lucid presentation of the mathematical analysis of time and supply elasticity, as well as much of the rest of economic theory. Some familiarity with differential calculus is necessary.

Allingham, Michael. *General Equilibrium.* London: Macmillan, 1975.

One of the best short, intuitive introductions to modern general equilibrium theory, this book assumes very little previous exposure yet covers most of the major topics.

Anderson, Frederick, et al. *Environmental Improvement Through Economic Incentives.* Baltimore: The Johns Hopkins University Press, 1977.

A very complete presentation of the theory and practice of the use of pricing for environmental effects. Easily accessible to the nonspecialist.

Andrews, Philip W. S. *On Competition in Economic Theory.* London: Macmillan, 1964.

A summary of the cost-plus pricing controversies, presented from the vantage point of a leading representative of the Oxford "empirical school."

Aoki, Masanao. *Optimal Control and System Theory in Dynamic Economic Analysis.* Amsterdam: North-Holland, 1976.

Introduces the reader to the general properties (such as stability or instability) of dynamic systems of equations and examines the economic models that comprised systems of nonstochastic equations (in both discrete time and continuous time). Aoki carries out stability analysis and shows the impact of attempts to control the system of equations (and thus the economy) by using monetary and/or fiscal policy. Also examines the economic models that comprised systems of stochastic equations (in both discrete time and continuous time), and this section will be of primary interest to readers of this article.

Apgar, William C., and H. James Brown. *Microeconomics and Public Policy.* Glenview, Ill.: Scott, Foresman, 1987.

Most applied microeconomic texts contain chapters on the concept of externalities. This book provides an excellent treatment of the subject in terms of economic theory and provides a framework for analysis including an evaluation of alternative government intervention strategies.

Arnott, Richard. "Economic Theory and Housing." In *The Handbook of Regional and Urban Economics*. Vol. 2, edited by Edwin Mills. New York: Elsevier Science, 1987.

An excellent review of the state of the art in the microeconomic modeling of the housing sector.

Aronson, J. Richard. *Public Finance*. New York: McGraw-Hill, 1985.

Chapter 2 contains a fairly simple and quite clear introduction to public goods. The formal economics that is required is minimal and the chapter is well summarized.

Arrow, Kenneth J. *Aspects of the Theory of Risk-Bearing*. Helsinki: Yrjo Jahnssonin Saatio, 1965.

One of the seminal works formally incorporating uncertainty into economic models. This pamphlet was originally given in lecture form, so it is quite accessible and covers many of the important topics in uncertainty analysis: risk taking and risk aversion, insurance, and the role of uncertainty in resource allocation.

_____ . *Essays in the Theory of Risk Bearing*. San Francisco: Holden-Day, 1970.

This book extends Arrow's earlier work on uncertainty by applying the analysis to financial securities, inventive research, public investments, welfare economics, and the value and demand for information. It is more formal and theoretical than his first piece.

_____ . *The Limits of Organization*. New York: W. W. Norton, 1974.

A series of lectures in which a leading theoretician explains for the lay reader the strengths and weaknesses of both market and nonmarket allocations of resources.

_____ . *Social Choice and Individual Values*. New York: John Wiley & Sons, 1951.

The seminal work in which Arrow presents his famous impossibility theorem. The introductory and concluding sections are largely verbal, but the core of the book is a series of rigorous mathematical proofs.

Readers who have no training in symbolic logic will find most of this book to be incomprehensible.

Arrow, Kenneth J., and Gerard Debreu. "Existence of an Equilibrium for a Competitive Economy." *Econometrica* 22 (1954): 265-290.
The first appearance of the Arrow-Debreu model. This paper revolutionized the manner in which economists approached general equilibrium analysis. Contains two existence proofs of equilibrium under slightly different sets of assumptions.

Arrow, Kenneth J., and Frank Hahn. *General Competitive Analysis.* San Francisco: Holden-Day, 1971.
An outstanding survey of general equilibrium theory, this book begins with a historical introduction, explains how producer and consumer decisions interact in market equilibrium, and addresses the existence, uniqueness, and stability properties of general equilibrium. The importance of the various assumptions are examined. The core and a Keynesian model are also included.

Arrow, Kenneth J., and Seppo Honkapohja, eds. *Frontiers of Economics.* Oxford, England: Basil Blackwell, 1985.
In chapter 1, Robert J. Aumann, one of the most eminent practitioners of game theory, provides philosophical reflections on its nature, uses, and limits.

Arrow, Kenneth J., and Michael D. Intriligator, eds. *Handbook of Mathematical Economics.* 3 vols. Amsterdam: North-Holland, 1981-1986.
A veritable, and somewhat imposing, encyclopedia of mathematical economics. This set consists of essays written on the major themes by several prominent mathematical economists. Not for the novice.

Arrow, Kenneth J., Samuel Karlin, and Herbert Scarf. *Studies in the Mathematical Theory of Inventory and Production.* Stanford, Calif.: Stanford University Press, 1958.
A very technical, advanced treatment of the theory of the firm and inventories. Knowledge of advanced mathematics is required.

Athanasion, L. "Some Notes on the Theory of Second Best." *Oxford Economic Papers* 18 (March, 1966): 83-87.
Explores some special aspects of the theory of the second best, but presented in rather technical terms.

Atkinson, A. B. *The Economics of Inequality*. 2d ed. Oxford, England: Clarendon Press, 1983.

Designed to be used as a textbook for the advanced undergraduate and is an excellent survey of the topic. Covers the measurement of inequality using various indexes, as well as the Lorenz curve, and compares the outcomes from the various measures.

Attfield, C. L. F., David Demery, and N. W. Duck. *Rational Expectations in Macroeconomics*. Oxford: Basil Blackwell, 1985.

An excellent textbook approach to using rational expectations in the analysis of macroeconomic issues. Suitable for undergraduates.

Avedon, Elliot M., and Brian Sutton-Smith. *The Study of Games*. New York: John Wiley & Sons, 1971.

The chapter entitled "Games in Social Science" does not discuss John von Neumann's theory in much detail, but Avedon clarifies some of the most difficult points by comparing it to other examples of game theory.

Averch, Harvey, and Leland L. Johnson. "Behavior of the Firm Under Regulatory Constraint." *American Economic Review* 52 (December, 1962): 1052-1069.

This is the original article that set forth the Averch-Johnson effect. Some of the parts are technical, but the discussion can still be understood if those technical sections are ignored. Gives the reader the best picture of the various Averch-Johnson concepts.

Ayer, A. J. *Language, Truth, and Logic*. London: Gollanez, 1936.

A statement of the main views of the logical positivists in the form of a critical manifesto, this work has exercised enormous influence on twentieth century economists. Ayer contends that ethical statements do not state matters of fact. They instead express approval or aversion and, as such, are incapable of being proved or disproved. Those inclined to their view will not look with favor on the exclusion of normative statements in scientific economic treatises.

Ayres, C. E. *The Theory of Economic Progress*. 2d ed. New York: Schocken Books, 1962.

Ayres's attempt to present a theory of economic progress is also an effort to outline an institutionalist's conception of economics. While the first four chapters contain a critical examination of conventional economics, the rest of the volume develops an institutional approach to economic analysis, values, and progress. The second edition is superior to the first (1944) because it contains an excellent new foreword by the author.

_____ . *The Theory of Economic Progress: A Study of the Fundamentals of Economic Development and Cultural Change.* Chapel Hill: University of North Carolina Press, 1944.

A pioneering work that relates technology to resource creation and economic development. A work of immense scholarship that places "natural" resources and economics in a broader historical and multicultural context. This is a classic statement of the institutional economics concept of growth as transformation in which technological progress is a key element.

Bacon, Robert. *A First Course in Econometric Theory.* Oxford, England: Oxford University Press, 1988.

A textbook on econometric methods and models, with emphasis on the applications and the use of models and on the methods of intermediate levels of difficulty. Assumes a knowledge of basic economics and mathematics.

Baily, Martin Neil, and Alok K. Charkrabarti. *Innovation and the Productivity Crisis.* Washington, D.C.: Brookings Institution, 1988.

Deals with the problem of sagging productivity. The authors explore commonly mentioned causes, such as escalating fuel prices, but find that the decline in productivity is better explained by a slowing of innovation. Includes industry studies and is not very technical.

Baker, Samuel, and Catherine Elliott, eds. *Readings in Public Sector Economics.* Lexington, Mass.: D. C. Heath, 1990.

Section 2, "Economics of Externalities," contains several significant articles, including Ronald Coase's "The Problem of Social Cost," reprinted from *Journal of Law and Economics* 3 (October, 1960), and Garrett Hardin's "The Tragedy of the Commons," reprinted from *Science* 162 (December 13, 1968).

Baran, Paul. *The Political Economy of Growth.* New York: Monthly Review Press, 1957.

A pioneering survey of the major problems inherent in economic development, emphasizing the need for the creation of a surplus. The author worked for the Federal Reserve Bank of New York.

Baran, Paul, and Paul M. Sweezy. *Monopoly Capital: An Essay on the American Economic and Social Order*. New York: Monthly Review Press, 1966.

The first serious attempt to extend Marx's model of competitive capitalism to the new conditions of monopoly capitalism. It presents what are often quite difficult problems in terms accessible to nonspecialist readers. Contains an appendix purporting to measure the surplus as of the mid-1960's. This book was influential on the "New Left" economics that developed out of the Vietnam War.

Barone, Enrico. "The Ministry of Production in a Collectivist State." In *Collectivist Economic Planning*, edited and translated by F. A. von Hayek. London: Routledge & Kegan Paul, 1935.

The seminal article in debate over central planning and the role of markets. Most of the article is mathematical and tough sledding, especially for those without extensive backgrounds; however, Barone's conclusions and arguments are interesting.

Barrere, Alain, ed. *Keynesian Economic Policies*. New York: St. Martin's Press, 1990.

The proceedings of a conference held at the University of Paris I-Pantheon-Sorbonne, September 12-15, 1983. This 206-page book provides a good discussion of developments in economic theory and the challenges of economic policies on the basis of Keynesian theories. Current issues of unemployment and international monetary economy are also emphasized. Suitable for college students with economics background.

Barro, Robert J. *Macroeconomics*. 3d ed. New York: John Wiley & Sons, 1990.

Chapter 14 presents Barro's analysis of the effects of budget deficits including his "deficits neutrality theorem." Chapter 15 is a discussion of the Ricardian equivalence implications by the modern economist who popularized David Ricardo's idea.

Barry, Brian, and Russell Hardin, eds. *Rational Man and Irrational Society? An Introduction and Sourcebook*. Beverly Hills, Calif.: Sage Publications, 1982.

A handy compilation of many of the more important contributions to public choice theory, with accompanying contextual and explanatory commentary by the editors. The bulk of the selections are reprints of articles, such as William Vickrey's "Utility, Strategy, and Social Decision Rules" (1960), Allan Gibbard's "Manipulation of Voting Schemes: A General Result" (1973), and Kenneth J. Arrow's "Current Developments in the Theory of Social Choice" (1977). There are also extracts from books, most notably from Olson's *The Logic of Collective Action; Public Goods and the Theory of Groups* (1965) and Thomas C. Schelling's *Micromotives and Macrobehavior* (1978).

Barten, A. P. "Family Composition, Prices, and Expenditure Patterns." In *Econometric Analysis for National Economic Planning*, edited by P. E. Hart et al. London: Butterworths, 1964.
Presents data from studies on the impact of family size and composition and prices on consumption patterns. A somewhat technical book, but Barten's data give a clear idea as to the impact of family composition and prices on typical Engel curve data.

Baumol, William J. *Economic Dynamics*. London: Macmillan, 1970.
Relying heavily on the language of mathematics, Baumol presents a lengthy overview of John von Neumann's principle of balanced growth. Like von Neumann's book, this work is especially suitable for those readers with a solid background in mathematics.

_____. *Economic Theory and Operations Analysis*. 4th ed. Englewood Cliffs, N.J.: Prentice-Hall, 1977.
Baumol covers many topics in microeconomic theory and presents a very readable introduction to duality in the context of linear programming in chapter 6 and a wonderful introduction to the more general duality results in chapter 14. The book contains an often-cited explanation of the economic order quantity approach to inventory management. Baumol was the first to extend this theory to the demand for money.

_____. *Superfairness*. Cambridge, Mass.: MIT Press, 1986.
This award-winning book is a very readable presentation of fairness theory and includes several applications. Particularly strong regarding equity and rationing.

Baumol, William J., and Alan S. Blinder. *Economics: Principles and Policy*. 5th ed. New York: Harcourt Brace Jovanovich, 1991.
A basic textbook covering microeconomic and macroeconomic theory. Introduces the concept of "crowding in" as opposed to "crowding out,"

as popularized by monetarists. The authors are Keynesian economists, and Blinder served as deputy chairman of the Federal Reserve Board. Suitable for college students.

Becker, Gary S. *The Economic Approach to Human Behavior.* Chicago: Ill.: University of Chicago Press, 1976.
Gives a unique viewpoint to the choice-among-substitutes problems that are faced by humanity. Becker has spent most of his professional career applying economic methods and models to a wide range of noneconomic applications, from the choice of a spouse to crime. This book is a condensation of Becker's previous work, rewritten for the general reader.

_____. *Economic Theory.* New York: Alfred A. Knopf, 1971.
A book based on Becker's lectures in price theory to graduate students. Includes calculus, but this part of the material can be skimmed. Much of the book provides an excellent description of some of the most important developments in consumer theory since World War II. Appropriate for college students, or those with some background in microeconomic theory.

_____. *The Economics of Discrimination.* Chicago: University of Chicago Press, 1957.
In the first comprehensive book on the economics of discrimination, Becker developed almost all the neoclassical discrimination theories in use through the 1980's. Readers will find the presentation somewhat dated, but any serious further research into discrimination requires a look at this classic. Becker was the first economist to consider discrimination systematically from an economic perspective. Particularly recommended for those with a background in economics.

_____. *Human Capital: A Theoretical and Empirical Analysis with Special Reference to Education.* 2d ed. New York: Columbia University Press, 1975.
The classic work on human capital theory. Investigates the theoretical effects of on-the-job training and education on wages in great detail, as well as introducing, with simple mathematics, the concept of the rate of return on human capital. Becker starts with the premise that productivity is a (if not the) major determinant of wages. Although the presentation can be somewhat technical, the main points of the book are easily accessible to the lay reader.

Begg, D. K. H. *The Rational Expectations Revolution in Macroeconomics.* Oxford, England: Phillip Allan, 1982.
    This book can be recommended on the grounds that it explores the role of rational expectations in economic theory. Quite theoretical and not suitable for a general audience, but would be recommended for advanced undergraduates and graduate students.

Bell, Daniel. "Socialism." In *International Encyclopedia of the Social Sciences.* Vol. 14, edited by David L. Sills. New York: Macmillan, 1968.
    One of the best available short surveys of socialism. Bell discusses the formulation of early socialist doctrines, the development of and differences in socialist political movements, the role of socialist political parties, and the variations in socialist thought since Karl Marx.

Berg, Sanford V., and John Tschirhart. *Natural Monopoly Regulation.* Cambridge, England: Cambridge University Press, 1988.
    This book devotes part of a chapter to the Averch-Johnson effect. Contains a particularly good section on the search for the Averch-Johnson effect.

Bergson, Abram. *Essays in Normative Economics.* Cambridge, Mass.: Harvard University Press, 1966.
    A collection of ten essays on the foundations of welfare economics, including Bergson's 1938 paper, which began the modern mathematical approach. Somewhat technical.

Berlin, Isaiah. *Karl Marx: His Life and Environment.* 3d ed. New York: Oxford University Press, 1963.
    A very complete biography of Marx which places his work as an economic theorist in a wider context. Examines not only his career as a journalist and researcher, but also the mid-nineteenth century political organizations under which he lived, both in Germany and in England.

Berndt, Ernst. *The Practice of Econometrics: Classic and Contemporary.* Reading, Mass.: Addison-Wesley, 1991.
    An advanced undergraduate or beginning graduate text in applied econometrics. While the coverage is quite broad, the treatment of maximum likelihood in the context of specific examples, which the reader may duplicate, is very helpful.

Blackorby, Charles, Daniel Primont, and R. Robert Russell. *Duality, Separability, and Functional Structure: Theory and Economic Applications.* New York: Elsevier, 1978.
Among the best modern references on general duality results, the level of presentation in this book is quite sophisticated. Includes an appendix with many duality theorems and their proofs.

Blecker, Robert A. *Are Americans on a Consumption Binge? The Evidence Reconsidered.* Washington, D.C.: Economic Policy Institute, 1990.
The most complete examination of saving in the United States for the two decades prior to 1990. The author finds that the national saving rate did decline, but he attributes most of the decline to accelerated depreciation of plant and equipment by firms and to the trade deficit.

Blinder, Alan S. "Retail Inventory Behavior and Business Fluctuations." *Brookings Papers on Economic Activity* 11 (1981): 431-453.
In this paper, which is accessible to the lay reader, Blinder carefully explains the theory of retail inventory accumulation and the role that it plays in propagating business cycles.

Blinder, Alan S., and Angus S. Deaton. "The Time Series Consumption Function Revisited." *Brookings Papers on Economic Activity* 2 (1985): 465-521.
Blinder and Deaton examine the impact of transitory tax changes including the temporary tax surcharge of 1968 and the temporary tax reduction of 1975. They found that neither affected consumption much, which finding supports the permanent income hypothesis.

Bluestone, Barry, Bennett Harrison, and Lawrence Baker. *Corporate Flight: The Causes and Consequences of Economic Dislocation.* Washington, D.C.: Progressive Alliance, 1981.
A very short and readable first approach to the problems of plant closings, corporate flight, and industrial policy. This short book should be the first reading that a novice does in this area.

Boeke, J. H. *Economics and Economic Policy of Dual Societies.* Homewood, Ill.: Richard D. Irwin, 1953.
The book that popularized the concept of dualism. The analysis, however, is more sociological in nature than economic. For readers interested in sociology and anthropology, this is a good book for understanding the broad nature of a dual economy.

Bohi, Douglas R. *Analyzing Demand Behavior: A Study of Energy Elasticities*. Baltimore: The Johns Hopkins University Press, 1981.

A somewhat technical but readable detailed analysis of demand for energy, including empirical estimates of price and income elasticities.

Böhm-Bawerk, Eugen von. *Capital and Interest*. Translated by G. D. Hunkle and H. F. Sennholz. 1884. Reprint. South Holland, Ill.: Libertarian Press, 1959.

Develops the first statement of the Austrian theory of capital and interest. The first word on time preference. Although there are certain errors, corrected by Ludwig von Mises in *Human Action* (1949), Böhm-Bawerk brilliantly demolishes the former abstinence justification of interest and the Marxist exploitation theory of interest.

Borch, Karl. *The Economics of Uncertainty*. Princeton, N.J.: Princeton University Press, 1968.

An outstanding general presentation of many of the facets of uncertainty as they pertain to economics. Topics include expected utility maximization, portfolio selection, market equilibrium under uncertainty, and game theory. An excellent primer for the interested reader.

Bornstein, Morris. *Comparative Economic Systems: Models and Cases*. 6th ed. Homewood, Ill.: Richard D. Irwin, 1989.

The best and most accessible edited collection on comparative economic systems available. Part 4 deals with central planning and command economies. Earlier editions of this book are also valuable sources.

Bosworth, Barry P. "There's No Simple Explanation for the Collapse in Saving." *Challenge* 32 (July/August, 1989): 27-32.

One of a series of articles in *Challenge* that examine the fall of the U.S. saving rate during the 1980's. Unfortunately, Bosworth (like most noneconomists) falls into the trap of confusing individual behavior with that of the economy (the "fallacy of composition") and so blames the lack of saving on "overspending."

Boulding, Kenneth E. *Macroeconomics*. Vol. 2 in *Economic Analysis*. 4th ed. New York: Harper & Row, 1966.

Presents an unusual analysis of the multiplier principle, incorporating induced investment (as well as induced consumption) within the multiplier. Boulding also explicitly relates the multiplier principle to his analysis of depression and unemployment.

_____ . *Microeconomics*. Vol. 1 in *Economic Analysis*. 4th ed. New York: Harper & Row, 1966.

In chapter 4, Boulding provides a fine review of the meaning of equilibrium (partial and general) and disequilibrium. The use of mathematics is kept to a minimum—a few basic graphs—so that the material can be understood by those with a modest background in economic theory.

Bradley, Michael E. *Microeconomics*. 2d ed. Glenview, Ill.: Scott, Foresman, 1985.

This very brief elementary discussion of oligopoly includes duopoly and strategic decision making. Chapter 17 deals with the role of government in the market economy to correct for market failures that are caused by externalities and public goods. An introductory economics text that provides some of the basic analytical tools to deal with public goods issues.

_____ . "Mill on Proprietorship, Productivity, and Population: A Theoretical Reappraisal." *History of Political Economy* 15 (Fall, 1983): 423-449.

A restatement and critique of John Stuart Mill's arguments on land reform and peasant proprietorship. Essentially a theoretical article, but the general arguments are fairly accessible.

Branson, William H. *Macroeconomic Theory and Policy*. 2d ed. New York: Harper & Row, 1989.

Chapter 12 gives a very complete version of the life-cycle model, but comprehending it requires a solid analytical background.

Brazelton, W. Robert. "Alvin Harvey Hansen: Economic Growth and a More Perfect Society." *The American Journal of Economics and Sociology* 48 (October, 1989): 427-440.

Analyzes the growth concepts of the 1930's and their policy implications. Sets up the historical background to the development of growth analysis.

_____ . *Leon H. Keyserling and Mary Dublin Keyserling: Growth and Equity, Over Fifty Years of Economic Policy and Analysis*. Independence, Mo.: Truman Memorial Library, 1989.

A comprehensive analysis of the policy critiques from 1945 to 1984 of Keyserling, the chief economic adviser to President Truman. For those with extensive background and/or interest.

Brealey, Richard A. *An Introduction to Risk and Return from Common Stocks*. Cambridge, Mass.: MIT Press, 1969.
A short, well-written book that explains the linkage between risk and stock prices. There are also excellent discussions of portfolio diversification, the relationship between risk and expected rate of return, and the use of the standard deviation as a measure of risk. An excellent introduction to the concepts of risk for the investor.

Bressler, Barry. *A Unified Introduction to Mathematical Economics*. New York: Harper & Row, 1975.
This textbook provides a particularly thorough and approachable introduction to mathematical concepts of optima and to the underlying mathematical concepts and many applications.

Brinkman, Richard L. *Cultural Economics*. Portland, Oreg.: Hapi Press, 1981.
Cultural economics represents a theory and conception of the economic process in the framework of culture evolution. A primary emphasis of this study, using a holistic and interdisciplinary methodology, concerns the conceptual distinction between economic growth and economic development.

Bristol, James D. *An Introduction to Linear Programming*. Boston: D. C. Heath, 1963.
Designed for high school and beginning college students, this book relies on graphs and illustrations rather than algebra as an approach to explaining the assignment model.

Bronfenbrenner, Martin. *Income Distribution Theory*. New York: Aldine Atherton, 1971.
A standard presentation of the neoclassical theory of distribution in a clear and concise fashion.

Bronfenbrenner, Martin, and Franklyn D. Holzman. "Survey of Inflation Theory." *American Economic Review* 53 (September, 1963): 593-661.
Though written for professionals, the basic ideas are clearly expressed and an excellent bibliography of the earlier literature is surveyed.

Brown, Murray, Kazuo Sato, and Paul Zarembka. *Essays in Modern Capital Theory*. Amsterdam: North-Holland, 1976.
A collection of articles by eminent capital theorists illustrates new developments in capital theory as well as the continuing controversies

that divide the economics profession. Suitable for advanced undergraduate economics students and specialists.

Brown, Stephen J., and David S. Sibley. *The Theory of Public Utility
Pricing.* Cambridge, England: Cambridge University Press, 1986.
   The presentation is at a fairly technical level, but the first three chapters
   provide a good introduction that should be understandable by a careful
   reader.

Browning, Edgar K., and Jacqueline M. Browning. *Microeconomic Theory and Applications.* 3d ed. Glenview, Ill.: Scott, Foresman, 1989.
   A clear and technically undemanding intermediate microeconomic
   theory text. Chapters 5, 6, and 18 provide a good introduction to the
   elements of welfare economics.

Brozen, Yale, ed. *The Competitive Economy.* Morristown, N.J.: General
Learning Press, 1975.
   Brozen has edited a fine book of selected readings on imperfect
   competition, regulation, antitrust, and some applications of antitrust
   law with contributions from Kenneth J. Arrow, Arthur Laffer, Joseph
   Schumpeter, George J. Stigler, J. Fred Weston, and others. Excellent
   for nonspecialists and college students.

Brus, Wlodzimierz, and Kazimierz Laski. *From Marx to the Market:
Socialism in Search of an Economic System.* Oxford, England: Clarendon
Press, 1989.
   A sustained examination of the possibility of market socialism.

Buchanan, James. "The Coase Theorem and the Theory of the State." In
The Theory of Public Choice II, edited by James Buchanan and Robert
Tollison. Ann Arbor: University of Michigan Press, 1984.
   An extension of Coase's theorem to the governmental realm. Uses
   simple numerical examples and so should be understandable to the
   general reader.

_____ . *Cost and Choice.* Chicago: Markham, 1969.
   The definitive work on opportunity cost.

Buchanan, James M., and Robert D. Tollison, eds. *Theory of Public
Choice: Political Applications of Economics.* Ann Arbor: University of
Michigan Press, 1972.
   This collection contains many of Buchanan's more important contri-
   butions to public choice theory, including "Toward Analysis of Closed

Behavioral Systems" and "Fiscal Policy and Fiscal Preference." Other influential papers are Tollison's "The Political Economy of the Military Draft," Richard E. Wagner's "Optimality in Local Debt Limitation," and Gordon Tullock's "Economic Imperialism."

Buchanan, James M., and Gordon Tullock. *The Calculus of Consent*. Ann Arbor: University of Michigan Press, 1962.
   Uses economic methods to analyze political decision making. A mostly nontechnical discussion of how governments use and alter property rights in modern societies, and of the ways private citizens do or do not control the actions of governments.

Bulmer-Thomas, Victor. *Input-Output Analysis in Developing Countries: Sources, Methods, and Applications*. New York: John Wiley & Sons, 1982.
   As suggested by its title, this book focuses on input-output applications in developing countries. Its primary value, however, lies in its clear and thorough discussion of difficult empirical issues that arise in preparing transactions tables and in applying input-output analysis.

Bureau of Economic Analysis. *Regional Multipliers: A User Handbook for the Regional Input-Output Modeling System*. Washington, D.C.: U.S. Department of Commerce, 1986.
   A practical guide for the economist who is trying to apply the multiplier theory to models of regional economies.

Burmeister, Edwin. *Capital Theory and Dynamics*. Cambridge, England: Cambridge University Press, 1980.
   A systematic treatment of capital theories and debates. Highly comprehensive, but requires a substantial knowledge of mathematics. Recommended for advanced undergraduates and graduate students.

Burmeister, Edwin, and A. Rodney Dobell. *Mathematical Theories of Economic Growth*. New York: Macmillan, 1970.
   A textbook that covers in detail descriptive neoclassical growth models, as well as optimal growth literature. Uses high-level mathematics and for this reason is appropriate for advanced undergraduates and specialists.

Buse, Rueben C., and Daniel W. Bromley. *Applied Economics*. Ames: Iowa State University Press, 1975.

Chapters 6 and 8 provide a somewhat rigorous review of the economics behind firm decision making. The novice could use this text for researching details in extensive study.

Caatephores, George. *An Introduction to Marxist Economics*. New York: New York University Press, 1989.

This comprehensive review of the key factors of economic analysis that are contained in Marxism begins with the theory of historical materialism, the labor theory of value, and the question of money and growth. Also focuses on the way in which, according to Marxist theory, capitalism was responsible for the distortion in these areas.

Cagan, Phillip. "The Monetary Dynamics of Hyperinflation." In *Studies in the Quantity Theory of Money*, edited by Milton Friedman. Chicago: University of Chicago Press, 1956.

A very famous research paper involving the study of seven hyperinflations. Although its intended audience is professional economists, much of the paper can be understood by noneconomists.

_____. *Persistent Inflation*. New York: Columbia University Press, 1979.

A leading monetarist examines inflation theory and history. Chapter 2 compares monetary and cost-push inflation theories.

Caravan, Bernard. *Economics for Beginners*. New York: Pantheon Books, 1983.

Although not strictly on economic systems, the book covers seven leading economists (including Karl Marx and John Maynard Keynes) and their views on the labor theory of value, capital, and profit. The comic-book style allows for easy reading and comparison of theories and development.

Carlson, Sune. *A Study on the Pure Theory of Production*. London: P. S. King, 1939.

This seminal work is an early survey of the main principles of production theory that are typically found in modern textbook presentations.

Carson, Richard L. *Comparative Economic Systems*. New York: Macmillan, 1973.

Part 3 deals with the economics of command economies. Most of Carson's predictions of the future of command economies are understandably dated; however, the text deals extensively with the underlying logic of command economies and the institutional and practical problems in formulating and executing plans. Technical material is largely relegated to chapter appendices.

Carson, Robert B. *Economic Issues Today: Alternative Approaches.* 5th ed. New York: St. Martin's Press, 1991.
    Examines a number of policy issues, presenting both liberal and conservative views. Chapters 9 and 10 are related to employment theory. Chapter 9 analyzes the possibility of another "Great Depression," while chapter 10 examines the best method of stimulating economic (and employment) growth. Chapter 12 examines the issue of unemployment, with specific attention given to official measures of unemployment.

_____. *What Economists Know: An Economic Policy Primer for the 1990's and Beyond.* New York: St. Martin's Press, 1990.
    Surveys the state of the discipline and focuses on what has been learned over the last half century. Argues that economic reasoning and policy-making is evolutionary and requires adaptations. Explores the possibilities and limits of the discipline, especially in the macroeconomic context. Clearly written; intended for nonspecialists and undergraduate students.

Case, Karl E., and Ray C. Fair. *Principles of Economics.* Englewood Cliffs, N.J.: Prentice-Hall, 1989.
    Most introductory texts in economics have some brief discussion of the role of models in economics. Chapter 1 presents one of the best.

Castles, Francis G. *The Social Democratic Image of Society.* London: Routledge & Kegan Paul, 1978.
    An excellent study of the particular nature of Swedish social democracy and the dominant role of socialist ideology in Sweden. Suitable for a general audience.

Chamberlain, John. *The Roots of Capitalism.* Princeton, N.J.: D. Van Nostrand, 1959.
    Analyzes capitalism in general and the beginnings of the capitalist mode of thought, and focuses particularly on the American variation on the capitalist theme. Somewhat ideological in the views of alternatives to capitalism, but insightful in the discussion of the human basis of capitalist organization.

Chamberlin, Edward H. *The Theory of Monopolistic Competition.* 8th ed. Cambridge, Mass.: Harvard University Press, 1962.

Chapter 3 contains a brief historical summary of Antoine Augustin Cournot, Joseph Bertrand, Francis Ysidro Edgeworth, A. C. Pigou, and Alfred Marshall on duopoly, as well as Chamberlin's own analysis of duopoly. There is some technical economics, and Chamberlin's style is sometimes difficult.

Chandler, Lester V. *America's Greatest Depression, 1929-1941.* New York: Harper & Row, 1970.
An excellent overview of the conditions leading to the Depression and of governmental policy responses. Descriptive and factual with emphasis on the events and institutional structure of the period.

Chiang, Alpha. *Fundamental Methods of Mathematical Economics.* 3d ed. New York: McGraw-Hill, 1984.
A standard textbook of mathematical economics in most graduate and undergraduate programs in economics in the United States. Defines the range of mathematical modeling tools which modern economists are expected to know. A large, difficult, but rewarding book.

Chow, Gregory C. *Analysis and Control of Dynamic Economic Systems.* New York: John Wiley & Sons, 1975.
Chow provides a brief introduction to the spectrum, gain, and coherence and presents a large number of applications of spectral analysis to macroeconomics, as well as extensive references to other economists' work on the subject.

Clark, John Bates. *The Distribution of Wealth.* New York: Macmillan, 1899.
The most influential presentation of the view that marginal productivity theory shows that workers are not exploited in a capitalist economy. Argues that each factor of production receives its marginal value product and that workers cannot be exploited if they receive all that they produce.

Clark, John M. "Business Acceleration and the Law of Demand: A Technical Factor in Economic Cycles." *Journal of Political Economy* 25 (March, 1917): 217-235.
The original article explaining the acceleration principle.

_____ . *Strategic Factors in Business Cycles.* New York: National Bureau of Economic Research, 1935.
Much of part 2, on strategic factors in business cycles, is devoted to the acceleration principle, especially pages 33-44.

Cliff, Tony. *State Capitalism in Russia*. London: Pluto Press, 1974.
This 309-page book provides an enormously powerful and in many ways original Marxist analysis of the Stalinist Soviet Union. As its title suggests, the author firmly believes that Soviet society is state capitalism. What is state capitalism and how it came about are the major themes of the book.

Clower, Robert, et al. *Growth Without Development*. Evanston, Ill.: Northwestern University Press, 1966.
Using the Liberian example as a case in point, the argument presented is that the economic growth in primary commodities produced by foreign concessions was not accompanied by structural or institutional change.

Clower, Robert W., Philip E. Graves, and Robert L. Sexton. *Intermediate Microeconomics*. New York: Harcourt Brace Jovanovich, 1988.
Contains a discussion on cost-plus pricing in chapter 12.

Coase, Ronald H. "The Nature of the Firm." *Economica* 4, nos. 13-16 (1937): 386-405. Reprint. *Readings in Price Theory*, edited by Richard E. Neel. Cincinnati: South-Western, 1973.
A theoretical approach to a general definition of a business firm. Coase focuses on the firm as a way to reduce transactions costs by reducing the number of contracts required to coordinate the use of resources within the firm.

_____. "The Problem of Social Cost." *The Journal of Law and Economics* 3 (October, 1960): 1-44.
Coase originally introduced his ideas on solving externalities in this article. The examples are simple with a few easy-to-understand tables and can be understood by anyone at the high school level or above. Other economists took the ideas in this article in order to formulate Coase's theorem.

Coleman, Jules. *Markets, Morals, and the Law*. Cambridge, England: Cambridge University Press, 1988.
A collection of papers by a professional philosopher who is one of the most acute expositors and critics of law and economics. Coleman defends a moral analysis of torts. Although some of the articles are quite technical, Coleman is an exceedingly clear writer with good pedagogic instincts.

Commons, John R. *The Economics of Collective Action*. New York: Macmillan, 1950.

While Commons' *Institutional Economics* was intended for specialists, this volume sought to explain his view of institutionalism to a broader audience. Contains a biographical sketch by Selig Perlman (a student of Commons), an introduction and supplemental essay—on Commons' point of view—by Kenneth Parsons (also a student of Commons), and a bibliography of Commons' writings.

Cook, Timothy Q., and Timothy D. Rowe, eds. *Instruments of the Money Market*. 6th ed. Richmond, Va.: Federal Reserve Bank of Richmond, 1986.

A detailed description of money market instruments and their interest yields. Includes an examination of such instruments as certificates of deposit, Eurodollars, Treasury bills, commercial paper, and options on short-term interest rate futures. Includes a subject index.

Cooter, Robert, and Thomas Ulen. *Law and Economics*. Glenview, Ill.: Scott, Foresman, 1988.

This textbook, an important collaborative effort by a leading academic lawyer and a professional economist, provides a very thorough overview of a number of areas of the law that have been examined through economic means. Intended for advanced undergraduate students but presupposes no previous work in either law or economics.

Corden, W. M. *The Theory of Protection*. Oxford, England: Clarendon Press, 1971.

This classic work assesses the theoretical impact of tariffs and quotas on countries and industries. Suitable for those readers with a background and interest in economic theory as applied to international trade.

Cornwall, Richard R. *Introduction to the Use of General Equilibrium Analysis*. Amsterdam: North-Holland, 1984.

A methodical, patient introduction to general equilibrium theory. Very accessible to college economics students, this book intermingles historical developments in the field, modern notation, and difficult theory. Particularly strong in the area of computing general equilibrium solutions.

Cournot, Antoine Augustin. *Mathematical Principles of the Theory of Wealth*. 1838. Reprint. New York: Augustus M. Kelley, 1971.

Chapter 7 contains Cournot's duopoly model. Cournot's approach is mathematical, but reading the original source is valuable for those with some calculus background.

Daellenbach, Hans G., and Earl J. Bell. *User's Guide to Linear Programming*. Englewood Cliffs, N.J.: Prentice-Hall, 1970.

This book approaches the assignment problem from the perspective of a decision maker and focuses on recognizing problems and formulating models rather than on solving the models.

Dantzig, George B. *Linear Programming and Extensions*. Princeton, N.J.: Princeton University Press, 1963.

The classical reference to linear programming, including a section on the assignment problem. It is mathematically sophisticated and not recommended for the nontechnical reader.

Daugherty, Carroll R., and Marion R. Daugherty. *Principles of Political Economy*. Boston: Houghton Mifflin, 1950.

This text, which is outdated in many ways but still excellent on many subjects, contains a full treatment of the issue of production possibilities under other names.

Davis, David Howard. *Energy Politics*. New York: St. Martin's Press, 1982.

An excellent readable account of the history of energy policy-making in each fuel area, and the degree of regulation experienced by each area in the American political process.

Deaton, Angus, and John Muellbauer. *Economics and Consumer Behavior*. Cambridge, England: Cambridge University Press, 1980.

A presentation of several studies that utilized Engel's law. Although it is designed for the economist, this text has a substantial bibliography that allows the interested reader to select future reading from the many studies that have individual merit. Presents data from many different time periods and view points.

Debreu, Gerard. "Existence of Competitive Equilibrium." In *Handbook of Mathematical Economics*, edited by Kenneth J. Arrow and Michael D. Intriligator. Vol. 2. Amsterdam: North-Holland, 1982.

A terse survey of the advances in general equilibrium theory, this chapter focuses on the consistency of optimizing behavior among the economic agents, investigates the excess demand approach to equilibrium, and presents the model of a continuum of agents which most accurately reflects a competitive economy.

_____ . *Mathematical Economics.* Cambridge, England: Cambridge University Press, 1983.
A collection of twenty of Debreu's most important papers, this book reproduces the seminal Arrow and Debreu paper of 1954.

_____ . *Theory of Value.* New Haven, Conn.: Yale University Press, 1959.
A rigorous attempt to state the theory of utility and relate it to the concept of general equilibrium. This work should be attempted only after some of the other works listed, as it is likely to prove difficult for students. The main ideas, however, can be grasped even if the technical details prove unmanageable. The student will acquire from the book a sense of the exacting nature of mathematical rigor.

DeGregori, Thomas R. "Resources Are Not, They Become: An Institutional Theory." *Journal of Economic Issues* 21 (September, 1987): 1241-1263.
Presents empirical evidence that the real price of resources has fallen and that reserves have generally increased since the limits-to-growth theorists predicted increasing scarcity and the rising prices of resources.

_____ . *A Theory of Technology: Continuity and Change in Human Development.* Ames: Iowa State University Press, 1985.
Claims that natural resources are a function of technology. A comprehensive theory of the nature of technology is offered as a framework for defining resources and how they are created.

Denison, Edward F. *Why Growth Rates Differ: Postwar Experience in Nine Western Countries.* Washington, D.C.: Brookings Institution, 1967.
One in a series of studies by Denison on the causes of economic growth in the United States and elsewhere. In these studies, Denison attempts to differentiate the extent to which economic growth is attributable to growth of the factors of production.

Dernburg, Thomas F. *Global Macroeconomics.* New York: Harper & Row, 1989.
Chapter 13 offers an enjoyable account of the international monetary system to 1973. Chapters 1 through 3 provide a cryptic and sometimes

hard-to-follow introduction to the basic issues of the international monetary system.

Dernburg, Thomas F., and Duncan M. McDougall. *Macroeconomics: The Measurement, Analysis, and Control of Aggregate Economic Activity.* New York: McGraw-Hill, 1976.
If one has a good grasp on the concepts, this book will serve as a good second source. It presents all of the major macroeconomic concepts, if in a manner that is somewhat hard to read.

Dewey, Donald. *Modern Capital Theory.* New York: Columbia University Press, 1965.
One of the few books on capital theory that does not require much mathematics. Highlights the fundamental notions of capital theory by avoiding the technical details. Suitable for specialists and nonspecialists alike.

Diamond, Peter, and Michael Rothschild. *Uncertainty in Economics: Readings and Exercises.* Rev. ed. New York: Academic Press, 1989.
This set of readings was compiled from several academic economic journals and contains many of the classic articles written on uncertainty in economics. Sections include individual static choice, static general equilibrium, and dynamic models. Exercises are also included. The articles vary greatly in terms of technical sophistication. Generally not for the beginner.

Diewert, W. E. "Duality Approaches to Microeconomic Theory." In *Handbook of Mathematical Economics*, edited by K. J. Arrow and M. D. Intriligator. Vol. 2. New York: Elsevier, 1982.
Slightly more pedagogical than Diewert's 1974 piece, this article provides an excellent introduction to the general theory of duality. Includes an exhaustive reference list.

Dillard, Dudley. *The Economics of John Maynard Keynes: The Theory of a Monetary Economy.* Englewood Cliffs, N.J.: Prentice-Hall, 1948.
One of the first, and clearest, expositions of Keynes's approach. Chapter 3 specifically deals with Keynes's general theory of employment.

Dolan, Edwin G., and David E. Lindsey. *Economics.* Chicago: Dryden Press, 1988.

This textbook argues that prices reflect relative scarcity, reviews the tasks of markets, and describes Smith's argument that the wealth of nations was the result not of accumulating gold or silver, as the mercantilists believed, but of working and trading in free markets.

_____ . *Microeconomics*. Chicago: Dryden Press, 1988.
This text, like many other economic texts, contains useful passages on subsidies. Chapters 3 and 5 provide good examples of subsidies, as well as their effects on demand and supply. Recommended for college students.

Doll, John P., and Frank Orazem. *Production Economics: Theory with Applications*. 2d ed. New York: John Wiley & Sons, 1984.
Primarily a college text for students of agricultural economics. A brief section in Chapter 2 on the costs of production, however, can be helpful to the beginner. The mathematics can be set aside to a certain extent, while the examples provide a sound understanding of the decision process. Many less complicated examples also help the reader to grasp cost-of-production concepts.

Domar, Evsey. "Capital Expansion, Rate of Growth, and Employment." *Econometrics* 14 (April, 1946): 137-147.
A basic beginning of growth analysis in a professional journal that is usually known for its mathematical analyses.

_____ . "Expansion and Employment." *American Economic Review* 27 (March, 1947): 34-55.
The more basic elements of Domar's analysis without extensive mathematical concepts.

Dorfman, Robert. *Prices and Markets*. 2d ed. Englewood Cliffs, N.J.: Prentice-Hall, 1972.
An analysis of how an economy that is based on private decision-making functions and of its social implications.

_____ . *Prices and Markets*. 3d ed. Englewood Cliffs, N.J.: Prentice-Hall, 1978.
One of Prentice-Hall's Foundations of Modern Economics series, written to be a basic core for a college course in economics. Dorfman develops the determinants of supply and demand, as well as market price determination under competition, monopoly, and oligopoly. The efficiency aspects of the free market pricing system are examined.

Dorfman, Robert, Paul A. Samuelson, and Robert M. Solow. *Linear Programming and Economic Analysis*. New York: McGraw-Hill, 1958.
The classic reference on linear programming.

Dornbusch, Rudiger, and Stanley Fischer. *Macroeconomics*. 5th ed. New York: McGraw-Hill, 1990.
An intermediate text that goes beyond a rudimentary treatment and outlines the source of discrepancies that led to theoretical developments in the consumption function. The drawbacks of this book are that it is densely written and formally presented, which may make it a difficult study. Includes numerous references to lead the student to further investigation. Any intermediate macroeconomics text with references may serve as a substitute.

Dosi, Giovanni, Christopher Freeman, Richard Nelson, Gerald Silverberg, and Luc Soete. *Technical Change and Economic Theory*. New York: Pinter, 1988.
An exhaustive and oppressively long treatment of many of the institutional aspects of innovation. This volume might be seen as less than mainstream in its approach, but it does offer discussions that are not found elsewhere, including a chapter on innovation and less developed countries.

Dougan, W. R. "Giffen Goods and the Law of Demand." *Journal of Political Economy* 90 (August, 1982): 809-815.
An explanation of why a Giffen good might not be observed even if it did exist.

Dougherty, Christopher. *Interest and Profit*. New York: Columbia University Press, 1980.
An advanced but very readable text that examines the neoclassical approach to capital; the relationship of time preference, profit, and interest to investment from an indifference curve and consumption possibilities framework; extensions and a critique of the Fisher model; the role of taxation in investment and saving; public investment; and the equilibrium of savings and investment. A good bibliography and an index are provided.

Douglas, Paul H. "Are There Laws of Production?" *American Economic Review* 38 (1948): 1-41.
An excellent discourse on classical production and distribution theory, the development and generalization of the Cobb-Douglas production

function, and the empirical results prior to 1948. Douglas was one of the codiscoverers of the production specification bearing his name and that of Cobb. The author served as a senator from Illinois.

Dowling, Edward T. *Introduction to Mathematical Economics*. 2d ed. New York: McGraw-Hill, 1991.

In this superb text/workbook, Dowling proves to be extremely strong in the area of the instruction of techniques. Covers calculus, linear algebra, difference and differential equations, and the calculus of variations. An excellent point of departure for beginners.

_____. *Mathematics for Economists*. New York: McGraw-Hill, 1980.

A modern text giving a superb intuitive and formal presentation of linear programming and the associated duality. Very accessible.

Downing, Paul B. *Environmental Economics and Policy*. Boston: Little, Brown, 1984.

A fine textbook addressed to those who have taken an introductory course in microeconomics.

Downs, Anthony. *An Economic Theory of Democracy*. New York: Harper, 1957.

The ideas are profound, but the exposition is simple. A pioneering effort to apply economic logic to the political process.

Dubins, Lester E., and E. H. Spanier "How to Cut a Cake Fairly." *American Mathematical Monthly* 68 (1961): 1-17.

A seminal article in the fair division literature, presented at a fairly high technical level.

Duesenberry, James S. *Income, Saving, and the Theory of Consumer Behavior*. Cambridge, Mass.: Harvard University Press, 1949.

One of the classic works on the savings function, this study is synonymous with the term "relative income hypothesis." Although some sections of the book are accessible only to professional economists, a few of the early sections are very readable and a must for anyone interested in the origins of this particular area of economics.

Dwyer, Gerald P., and Cotton M. Lindsay. "Robert Giffen and the Irish Potato." *American Economic Review* 74 (March, 1984): 188-192.

This short article presents a definitive argument as to why the Irish potato story could not have happened in the manner that it has been explained. Simple demand-supply analysis is used to illustrate the main point, but the main line of reasoning is readily accessible to the general reader. An extended list of references pertaining to the Giffen paradox and the potato is offered.

Eagley, Robert V. *The Structure of Classical Economic Theory.* New York: Oxford University Press, 1974.
A relatively short (140-page) book which provides a detailed description of the underlying analytical structure of classical economics. Concludes that classical theory's central concept is capital.

Eaton, B. Curtis, and Diane F. Eaton. *Microeconomics.* New York: W. H. Freeman, 1988.
The first three sections of chapter 10 give a clear presentation of perfect competition, the Walrasian auctioneer, and information contents. Read chapter 6 to understand attitudes toward risk. Analytically rigorous (without relying on calculus), but widely accessible. Suitable for college students and general audiences who appreciate graphic techniques.

Eatwell, John, Murray Milgate, and Peter Newman, eds. *The New Palgrave: A Dictionary of Economics.* 4 vols. London: Macmillan, 1987.
The entry under currencies is a good overview of the definition, functions, and history of currency in the world context.

Ebenstein, William, and Edwin Fogelman. *Today's Isms: Communism, Fascism, Capitalism, Socialism.* Englewood Cliffs, N.J.: Prentice-Hall, 1985.
Gives a slightly different classification for systems and expands on the socialism of Owen and the Fabian socialists. It is, however, dated regarding specific countries and misses some of the better socialist theorists.

Eggert, Jim. *What Is Economics?* Los Altos, Calif.: Kaufman, 1987.
Treats both microeconomic and macroeconomic principles and ideas in a manner which the general reader will appreciate and understand. The illustrations are not too difficult and tend to emphasize concerns that are universal and timeless. A good work.

Ehrenberg, A. S. C., and F. G. Pyatt, eds. *Consumer Behavior: Selected Readings*. Baltimore: Penguin Books, 1971.
Part 4 of this book—"Economic Factors"—contains three articles, by Robert Ferber, Richard Stone et al., and Arthur S. Goldberger and Maw Lin Lee, dealing with aspects of income elasticity.

Eisner, Robert. *The Total Incomes System of Accounts*. Chicago: University of Chicago Press, 1989.
A thorough study of the national income and product accounts. Includes the statistical methodology and real-world relevance of the net national product and capital consumption allowances. Also contains detailed tables of data for selected years.

Elliott, John. *Comparative Economic Systems*. Belmont: Calif.: Wadsworth, 1985.
This book covers in a comprehensive way important contributors to theory of economic systems, as well as the theoretical systems themselves. Geared to serious students of economics.

Elster, Jon. *Making Sense of Marx*. Cambridge, England: Cambridge University Press, 1985.
A detailed discussion of the labor theory of value. Most of the standard criticisms are given, as well as some new ones. Elster also raises difficulties for the marginalist case against exploitation, by asking why workers should receive only the value that is added by the last unit of labor.

Engels, Friedrich. *Anti-Duhring: Herr Eugen Duhring's Revolution in Science*. New York: International Publishers, 1976.
Written by the closest friend of Karl Marx, this 365-page work is one of the best books on the major issues of Marxism. In extremely clear language, it provides a systematic statement about Marxist philosophy as a method of analysis, political economy of capitalism, and communism (scientific socialism).

Etzioni, Amitai. *The Moral Dimension*. New York: Free Press, 1988.
A much-discussed espousal and presentation of the normative economic viewpoint by a sociologist. Although the criticisms of positive economics are not always on target, this large book is rich in constructive contributions to the normative-economic alternative view, especially (as the title would suggest) when the role of morality in real human behavior is concerned.

Evans, Paul. "Do Budget Deficits Raise Nominal Interest Rates? Evidence from Six Countries." *Journal of Monetary Economics* 20 (September, 1987): 281-300.

A moderately technical article which argues that the evidence does not support the hypothesis that government deficits raise interest rates and cause crowding out.

Evensky, Jerry. *Economic Ideas and Issues: A Systematic Approach to Critical Thinking.* Englewood Cliffs, N.J.: Prentice-Hall, 1987.

Presents economic ideas and issues in a bit more advanced level and style, using graphical illustrations. Yet, the explanation of microeconomic theories is quite clear and suitable for both high school seniors and undergraduate students. Also presents background theories that underlie economic analysis. Some items in the appendix will interest the general reader.

Feiwel, George R., ed. *Arrow and the Ascent of Modern Economic Theory.* London: Macmillan, 1987.

An anthology that presents developments in modern economic theory, including advances in production theory at the frontiers of economics and the potential and limits of the market.

_____, ed. *Arrow and the Foundations of the Theory of Economic Policy.* London: Macmillan, 1987.

An anthology that centers on modern welfare economic theory, including problems of efficiency, distributive justice, and democracy.

_____. *Cost: The Various Meanings of the Concept.* Edmonton: University of Alberta, 1964.

Review of some of the basic cost concepts as viewed by the accountant and the economist.

_____, ed. *The Economics of Imperfect Competition and Employment.* London: Macmillan, 1989.

An anthology that includes a number of papers applying the game-theoretic method to such problems as unemployment, imperfect competition, and oligopoly.

_____. *The Intellectual Capital of Michal Kalecki.* Knoxville: University of Tennessee Press, 1975.

Chapter 3 presents an account of Kalecki's development of cost-plus pricing as a foundation for the theory of output and distribution as a whole.

_____ , ed. *Issues in Contemporary Macroeconomics and Distribution*. London: Macmillan, 1985.

This compilation surveys major topics in macroeconomic theory and policy from different vantage points. Discusses the major issues in the theory of output and employment, including the monetarist counter-revolutions (pages 24-69). This compilation also surveys major topics in microeconomics, including alternative theories of the firm and welfare economics.

_____ , ed. *Joan Robinson and Modern Economic Theory*. London: Macmillan, 1989.

Among other things, the essays in this anthology discuss the developments in and critiques of Marshallian economics and the formidable question of incorporating time into modern economic analysis.

Feldman, Allan, and A. Kirman. "Fairness and Envy." *American Economic Review* 64, no. 4 (1974): 995-1005.

Feldman and Kirman show that fairness, once established in an economy, can be lost through standard economic trade. They also point out that equity is not subject to degree; an allocation either is or is not equitable.

Feldstein, Martin, and Alan Auerbach. "Inventory Behavior in Durable Goods Manufacturing: The Target Adjustment Model." *Brookings Papers on Economic Activity* 6 (1976): 351-408.

Feldstein and Auerbach explain the stock adjustment and flexible accelerator models of inventory accumulation. They confront the models with post-World War II U.S. data. Accessible to the lay reader.

Ferguson, C. E. *Microeconomic Theory*. Rev. ed. Homewood, Ill.: Richard D. Irwin, 1969.

This classic microeconomics text explains, in a particularly clear way, the differences in approaches to applying utility theory.

_____ . *The Neoclassical Theory of Production and Distribution*. New York: Cambridge University Press, 1969.

An encyclopedic treatment of neoclassical production theory, this book covers some topics typically circumvented by other works on production. These subjects include multiproduct firms, vintage capital models, a taxonomy of technological change, and the learning-by-doing approach.

Ferguson, C. E., and John Gould. *Microeconomic Theory*. Homewood, Ill.: Richard D. Irwin, 1975.
An advanced text used in college economics programs. Presents elasticities in some detail. An outstanding feature of the book is its collection of questions and problems concerning economic concepts, including price, cross-price, and income elasticity of demand, as well as price elasticity of supply and the elasticity of substitution. Also gives elasticity estimates for major consumer goods.

Ferguson, C. E., and S. C. Maurice. *Economic Analysis*. Homewood, Ill.: Richard D. Irwin, 1970.
Designed as an intermediate microeconomic theory text. Chapter 11 summarizes general equilibrium analysis and its relationship to welfare economics. The use of mathematics is minimized—simple equations only—but some knowledge of microeconomic theory is required.

Fetter, Frank A. *Capital, Interest, and Rent*. Edited by Murray N. Rothbard. Kansas City: Sheed Andrews and McMeed, 1977.
Fetter's great contributions to interest rate theory were to emphasize that the productivity of capital was inherently subjective and to develop the implications of this insight for rent and the prices of durable capital goods.

——————. *Economic Principles*. New York: Century, 1915.
A pioneering account of the view of rent, which has replaced David Ricardo's theory in mainstream economics. Land is regarded as a capital asset and its price is not explained according to a theory that applies uniquely to it. As a result, the law of diminishing returns does not play a direct part in the explanation of rent.

Fischer, Stanley, and Franco Modigliani*gliani, Franco, and Stanley Fischer*. *"Towards an Understanding of the Real Effects and Costs of Inflation." Weltwirtschaftliches Archiv* 114 (1978): 810-833.
An extensive listing and discussion of the real effects of inflation. Although it is a journal article, it is accessible to a general audience.

Fisher, Franklin M. "Games Economists Play: A Noncooperative View." *RAND Journal of Economics* 20 (Spring, 1989): 113-124.
Provides a brief summary of oligopoly theory, both before and after the advent of the game-theoretic approach, and argues that generally game theory is the wrong way of approaching the problem.

Fisher, Irving. *The Theory of Interest*. New York: Macmillan, 1930.
Further develops the ideas that were first published in *Appreciation and Interest* (1896) and *The Rate of Interest* (1907). A commanding synthesis of theory and empirical analysis, with many original insights and clarifications. Much of contemporary monetary economics and finance is found in this classic, including continuous and discrete compounding, nominal versus real interest rates, high versus rising prices, and distributed lag effects.

Fitzgibbons, Athol. *Keynes's Vision: A New Political Economy*. New York: Oxford University Press, 1988.
Focuses on the thinking of John Maynard Keynes in economic and political matters, as well as his approach to economic policy. Written for noneconomists who are interested in Keynes's philosophical writings.

Foley, Duncan K. *Understanding Capital*. Cambridge, Mass.: Harvard University Press, 1986.
Written as a general introduction to Karl Marx's economic theory. The section on method is good, and chapter 4 provides an account of mechanization as an inherent feature of capitalist production. The references provide a nearly comprehensive list of pertinent literature on various subjects.

Fossati, Eraldo. *The Theory of General Static Equilibrium*. Edited by G. L. S. Shackle. New York: Augustus M. Kelley, 1965.
An introduction to general equilibrium theory that develops the mathematics in a way that does not intimidate those who are not mathematically inclined.

Frank, Robert H. *Choosing the Right Pond: Human Behavior and the Quest for Status*. New York: Oxford University Press, 1985.
The definitive modern source on relative standing issues, this highly readable and entertaining book explores the wide range of consequences associated with concern for relative standing and the proper policy responses to these concerns.

_____. *Microeconomics and Behavior*. New York: McGraw-Hill, 1990.
Chapters 7, 8, 18, 19, and 20 in this intermediate-level textbook give a good overview of the Pareto optimum and its applications in modern economics, especially with respect to public policy (chapters 18, 19,

and 20), and also of some of the evidence that people do not always choose the optimal decision (chapters 7 and 8).

Freedman, Robert, ed. *Marx on Economics*. New York: Harcourt, Brace & World, 1961.

As noted on the cover of this 290-page book, it is "[t]he first systematic compilation of Karl Marx's economic theories and critique of capitalism, drawn from all his writings and presented in a logical order with brief summaries of the argument."

Freeman, Richard B. *The Overeducated American*. New York: Academic Press, 1976.

Written to inform the general public, this book illustrates how the market for college graduates turned from a shortage into an excess supply in the early 1970's. Its 218 pages contain details on occupational, ethnic, and gender differences.

Friedman, David D. *Price Theory*. Cincinnati: South-Western, 1986.

A very good but idiosyncratic intermediate-level microeconomics text. Freidman, who is the son of famed economist Milton Freidman, not only writes lucidly but also dares to apply economic theory to unconventional topics such as war, marriage, and theft. His discussion of Arrow's theorem is especially good. Designed for college students, but many sections may be understood by the general reader.

Friedman, James W. "Duopoly." In *The New Palgrave: A Dictionary of Economics*, edited by John Eatwell, Murray Milgate, and Peter Newman. Vol. 1. London: Macmillan, 1987.

Brief, quite technical introduction to duopoly theory that makes extensive use of game theory. Contains a short, useful bibliography of original sources.

_____ . *Game Theory with Applications to Economics*. New York: Oxford University Press, 1986.

Unfortunately, all references which focus on game theory require the reader to understand some basic linear algebra and calculus. This book is one of the least technical references on game theory. Friedman presents game theory, starting with simple models and proceeding to the more complex, but more realistic, models.

_____ . *Oligopoly and the Theory of Games*. Amsterdam: North-Holland, 1977.

Friedman first presents traditional models of oligopolistic behavior (such as the kinked demand curve model, the collusion model, and the leader-follower model). Then he presents game theory, starting with simple models and proceeding to the more complex models. This book is less technical than Friedman's *Game Theory with Applications to Economics*.

Friedman, Milton. *Essays in Positive Economics*. Chicago: University of Chicago Press, 1963.
An example of the influence of logical positivism on a key twentieth century economist. Friedman views ethical statements as nonscientific and reconciles this view with his own very pronounced advocacy of various policy measures by claiming that most people agree on ends; disputes largely consist of conflicting views on how these ends are to be attained. Questions of this sort, unlike values themselves, are amenable to scientific treatment. Useful for the Chicago approach to market structure. Without rejecting the model of perfect competition, Friedman rejects the usual justifications for government antimonopoly measures. The American economy measures up quite well to the perfect competition model. Government intervention will worsen matters because the governmental authorities lack the ability to "fine-tune" the economy.

_____. *The Essence of Friedman*. Edited by Kurt Leude. Stanford, Calif.: Hoover Institution Press, 1987.
This collection of Friedman's writings contains major essays dealing with monetarism. Although "The Quantity Theory: A Restatement" requires some mathematical background, "The Supply of Money and Changes in Prices and Output" will be of interest to the general reader. Friedman clearly explains, in his logical style, the tenets of monetarism.

_____. "The Marshallian Demand Curve." *The Journal of Political Economy* 57 (December, 1949): 463-495.
Friedman's purpose is twofold: first, to argue that real income, rather than nominal income, should be held constant along a demand curve, for both theoretical and empirical reasons; and second, to argue that Alfred Marshall's work is consistent with a real income constant demand curve, although Marshall was vague on this point. Friedman provides an interesting description of the history and evolution of this aspect of demand theory. The article is accessible to readers with some

background in economics. There is some mathematical exposition, but this can be skimmed.

_____ . *Price Theory.* Chicago: Aldine, 1976.
Chapter 5, entitled "The Relationships Between Supply Curves and Cost Curves," is a classic reference on industry supply curves and their derivation from individual firm cost curves.

_____ . "The Quantity Theory of Money: A Restatement." In *Studies in the Quantity Theory of Money*, edited by Milton Friedman. Chicago: University of Chicago Press, 1956.
This difficult article by a Nobel laureate in economics could be regarded as the definitive beginning of modern-day monetarism and the monetarist view that eventually deficit spending will crowd out an equal amount of private spending.

_____ . "The Role of Monetary Policy." *American Economic Review* 58 (March, 1968): 1-17.
The premier monetarist's presidential address to the American Economic Association presents his basic theory relating money, unemployment, and inflation with exceptional clarity and brevity.

_____ . *Studies in the Quantity Theory of Money.* Chicago: University of Chicago Press, 1956.
A seminal work which lays out the modern quantity theory of money. The first chapter contains Friedman's famous restatement of the quantity theory, and the remaining chapters contain articles by other leading monetarists on empirical and theoretical issues supporting the quantity theory.

_____ . *A Theory of the Consumption Function.* Princeton, N.J.: Princeton University Press, 1957.
Shows the connection between Ernst Engel's work and post-Keynesian notions of the consumption function. This volume ties in the work of post-Keynesian economists in family consumption with Friedman's work on the concept of lifetime income and helps explain some of the anomalies that arise in Engel's law from ignoring lifetime income concepts. Contains a masterful presentation of the permanent income hypothesis. Friedman solidly grounds his explanation of consumption on economic theory, carefully considers the role of bias in econometric analysis, and reviews practically the data then available.

Friedman, Milton, and Rose D. Friedman. *Capitalism and Freedom.* Chicago: University of Chicago Press, 1975.

This volume summarizes a number of topics covered by Friedman in a series of lectures delivered under the auspices of the Volker Foundation in 1956. They tend to emphasize the importance of free economic enterprise for fostering a free political system.

_____. *Free to Choose: A Personal Statement.* New York: Harcourt Brace Jovanovich, 1980.

This series of essays addresses what the Friedmans considered to be the most essential issues facing U.S. and world society in the last quarter of the twentieth century. They include typical Chicago School concerns: "The Tyranny of Controls," "The Cure for Inflation," and others.

Frisch, Ragnar. *Theory of Production.* Chicago: Rand McNally, 1965.

A leading economist examines the fundamentals of production theory.

Fromm, Gary, and Lawrence R. Klein. "A Comparison of Eleven Econometric Models of the United States." *American Economic Review* 63 (May, 1973): 385.

Economists have used econometrics to try to estimate the size of the multiplier in the real world. These estimates are then used in econometric models to allow economists to predict, for example, the effects of an increase of government spending on the economy. This article looks at the size of the multiplier used in several econometric models of the U.S. economy.

Frowen, Stephen, ed. *Unknowledge and Choice in Economics.* New York: St. Martin's Press, 1990.

This 245-page book covers a wide array of topics on theories of expectations and decision making under uncertainty. Specific topics include the role of time in expectations and applications to financial markets and investment decisions by various well-known economists. Suitable for college students.

Froyen, Richard T. *Macroeconomics: Theories and Policies.* New York: Macmillan, 1990.

An intermediate book which contains a lengthy discussion of American business cycles, the dual problems of unemployment and inflation, and policy responses to the cycle. Suitable for upper-level undergraduates.

Fuchs, Victor R. *How We Live.* Cambridge, Mass.: Harvard University Press, 1983.
A fascinating, widely acclaimed book on the family, on the various choices made between birth and old age. Puts human capital investment activities in a broader context. Suitable for advanced high school and undergraduate students. 293 pages.

Furnham, Adrian, and Alan Lewis. *The Economic Mind.* New York: St. Martin's Press, 1986.
An extensive, well-written, and critical review of psychological research applied to economic phenomena. Topics covered include economic socialization, poverty, unemployment and work, savings and gambling, consumer choice, and taxation. Although the focus is on the contributions of psychologists, the discussion is accessible to a broad academic audience.

Furubotn, Eirik G., and Svetozar Pejovich, eds. *The Economics of Property Rights.* Cambridge, Mass.: Ballinger, 1974.
One of the best books on the wide range of issues revolving around the issue of property rights. Some of the articles are somewhat technical, but most do not require any specialized knowledge of economic theory.

Fuss, M., and D. L. McFadden, eds. *Production Economics: A Dual Approach to Theory and Applications.* New York: Elsevier, 1978.
The premier reference linking the formal duality theory and its use in econometric studies.

Galbraith, John Kenneth. *The Affluent Society.* 3d ed. Boston: Houghton Mifflin, 1976.
A brilliant work that can be read with great profit by everyone. Dismissing the views of other economists, Galbraith proposes much greater government spending to end poverty and argues that the United States is rich enough to afford it. With Michael Harrington's *The Other America*, this book helped to make the public aware of the problem of poverty. Considered to be the classic critique of modern, industrialized societies' narrow definitions of growth. This book catalyzed a long series of critiques of growth as the central focus of economic performance. Galbraith argues that society contains a strong bias against providing adequate resources to the public sector, a view opposite to that of James Buchanan. Galbraith provides a critical perspective on advertising relative to the economics of modern consumer society. He deplores the myopia of economists in ignoring the roles that are played

by advertising and salesmanship in the modern economy. This book is only one of the many places in which he supports the notion that inflation has an important cost-push dimension.

_____ . *Economics and the Public Purpose.* Boston: Houghton Mifflin, 1973.

Galbraith is among the best-known and most widely read institutionalists. This volume, which builds on a number of his earlier works, criticizes neoclassical economics and its interpretation of the post-World War II American economy. It also presents both an alternative model of the economy (and economic problems) and suggestions for economic reform.

_____ . *Economics in Perspective.* Boston: Houghton Mifflin, 1989.

Drawing on one of the most distinguished careers in economics, Galbraith relates how changing economic and social factors influenced economic theory and policy. Particularly good for twentieth century developments, in which Galbraith was a major player.

_____ . *The Great Crash, 1929.* Boston: Houghton Mifflin, 1961.

A very readable and nontechnical discussion of the events surrounding the stock market crash in the fall of 1929.

_____ . *Money: Whence It Came, Where It Went.* Boston: Houghton Mifflin, 1975.

Galbraith, in his best style, gives an excellent history of the development of money, including currency. Primarily an account of the development of money in the United States, the first six chapters are especially rich in their discussion of currency.

_____ . *A Theory of Price Control.* Cambridge, Mass.: Harvard University Press, 1952.

The U.S. price czar during World War II explains how prices are actually set in the American economy. He then argues for wage and price controls as a necessary part of the fight against inflation. This work requires some knowledge of economics but should be understandable by both the educated layperson and college students.

Galbraith, John Kenneth, and Nicole Salinger. *Almost Everyone's Guide to Economics.* New York: Bantam Books, 1978.

This readable, 161-page paperback discusses such topics as what is economics, economic systems, what happened to the market, and monetary and fiscal policy. Galbraith says that liberal economists and politicians pretend that competitive markets work while corporations do not use their power to compete.

Gilder, George. *Wealth and Poverty*. New York: Basic Books, 1981.
This book supposedly influenced Ronald Reagan to run for president on a supply-side economic program. The program, calling for successive annual cuts in income tax rates, supposedly would have raised tax revenues, thus balancing the budget by 1984. Because saving was required as a precondition for investment, Gilder called for an increase in the inequality of income distribution.

Ginzburg, Andrea. "Ricardian Socialists." In *The New Palgrave: A Dictionary of Economics*, edited by John Eatwell, Murray Milgate, and Peter Newman. Vol. 4. New York: Stockton Press, 1987.
An excellent summary of "Ricardian" socialism and the major figures in the movement. There is no technical material, but some of the arguments assume some economic background.

Gittinger, J. Price, Joanne Leslie, and Caroline Hoisington. *Food Policy: Integrating Supply, Distribution, and Consumption*. Baltimore: The Johns Hopkins University Press, 1987.
Contains articles on the various components of a broadly based food policy approach to the supply, distribution, and consumption of food.

Glahe, Fred R., and Dwight R. Lee. *Microeconomics Theory and Applications*. New York: Harcourt Brace Jovanovich, 1989.
A popular textbook at the intermediate level in college economics courses. Like other texts that are used in intermediate microeconomics courses, major portions are devoted to indifference analysis and isoquant-isocost analysis. Those topics are founded on substitution, which is well treated here. This book shines in the application of marginal rate of substitution tools to specific cases, such as leisure-income substitution and food subsidies.

Godwin, William. *An Enquiry Concerning Political Justice and Its Influence on General Virtue and Happiness*. 1793. Reprint. 2 vols. New York: Alfred A. Knopf, 1926.
One of the most influential books of its time, it evoked in Thomas Robert Malthus an extremely pessimistic reaction against the overoptimistic views of Godwin about the future of humankind. Godwin thought that the future of the human race would hold a reign of reason,

happiness, justice, and equality for all. In his essay on population, Malthus replaced this view with one which showed that the future of humankind was doomed by overpopulation, wars, epidemics, and famines.

Goodall, Brian. *The Economics of Urban Areas.* New York: Pergamon Press, 1974.

This book provides a good overview of the economic forces at work in the urban area. It offers a particularly good, nontechnical explanation of the most important urban models.

Gorbachev, Mikhail. *Perestroika.* New York: Harper & Row, 1987.

In this book, Soviet president Gorbachev discusses the need for restructuring the Soviet system in the 1980's. The readable text provides insight into the thinking of the original architect of modern change in the Soviet Union.

Gordon, Lawrence A., et al. *The Pricing Decision.* New York: National Association of Accountants, 1981.

A survey of how manufacturing firms in the United States and Canada actually make pricing decisions.

Gordon, Robert J. *Macroeconomics.* 5th ed. Glenview, Ill.: Scott, Foresman, 1990.

Contains an excellent discussion of the acceleration principle on pages 582-589. Both the simple accelerator and the flexible accelerator are covered. Pages 339 to 350 give a straightforward presentation of some of the issues involved and some of the evidence from both the United States and two hyperinflation cases: Germany in the early 1920's and Bolivia in 1985.

_____ , ed. *Milton Friedman's Monetary Framework.* Chicago: University of Chicago Press, 1974.

Friedman's own summary of his analysis contains real balance effects, as pointed out in the critical essay of Don Patinkin (especially pages 119-120). Friedman refuses, however, to acknowledge that this is what he is doing.

Gordon, Wendell. *Institutional Economics: The Changing System.* Austin: University of Texas Press, 1980.

Gordon builds on the work of Thorstein Veblen, Clarence Ayres, and the pragmatic philosophers to develop an institutionalist view of economic activity. This perspective is then compared with conventional,

Marxist, and other economic approaches. The book closes by considering both institutionalist research methods and a number of empirical applications.

Gramlich, Edward M. *A Guide to Benefit-Cost Analysis*. 2d ed. Englewood Cliffs, N.J.: Prentice-Hall, 1990.
Probably the best single introduction to cost-benefit analysis, this textbook contains exercises at the end of each chapter and the answers to all of these exercises in the back. It is thorough and simply written, but to fully appreciate it, the reader should have some background in microeconomics.

Grampp, William D. *The Classical View*. Vol. 2 in *Economic Liberalism*. New York: Random House, 1965.
A clear, accurate, and critical synthesis of the subject, excellent for nonspecialists. Although there are no illustrative materials, there are informative footnotes in place of a bibliography and a helpful index. Essential for introductory reading.

Greene, William H. *Econometric Analysis*. New York: Macmillan, 1990.
A comprehensive text on the general subject of econometrics. The chapters on models with discrete and limited dependent variables (pages 661-754) provide a comprehensive and straightforward overview of the subject.

Greenway, David, ed. *Current Issues in Macroeconomics*. Current Issues in Economic Series 2. New York: St. Martin's Press, 1989.
A collection of ten papers. Examines changes in macroeconomic thinking. The papers focus on recent discussion relating to New Classical macroeconomics, the role of expectations, political business cycles, macroeconomic interdependence and policy coordination, and other topics. Well written; primarily intended for undergraduates, but mature nonspecialists can also benefit. Bibliography; author and subject indexes.

Gregory, Paul R., and Roy J. Ruffin. *Basic Macroeconomics*. Glenview, Ill.: Scott, Foresman, 1989.
A standard textbook that is used in principles of macroeconomic classes. Chapter 7 presents the standard treatment of the multiplier principle. Chapter 9 discusses the relation between the multiplier and the crowding-out effect.

Gregory, Paul R., and Robert C. Stuart. *Comparative Economic Systems.* 3d ed. Boston: Houghton Mifflin, 1989.

Although it is designed for students with a background in basic economics, the text is very readable. Chapters 5 and 7 are most relevant to the command economy. This textbook is one of the better ones in terms of covering both theory and operating systems (countries). Includes graphs and formulas that will be of interest to those with some economics background.

Gruchy, Allan G. *The Reconstruction of Economics: An Analysis of the Fundamentals of Institutional Economics.* Westport, Conn.: Greenwood Press, 1987.

This volume provides an excellent overview of institutionalist preconceptions, analyses (including a fresh look at the dual economy), and policy proposals. The author devoted much of his life to chronicling the development of institutional thought, and this work distills his findings into one concise and accessible book.

Gwartney, James D., and Richard L. Stroup. *Economics: Private and Public Choice.* 4th ed. New York: Harcourt Brace Jovanovich, 1987.

This elementary economics textbook is one of the few that develop the causes and consequences of aggregate demand and supply free from a Keynesian slant. Chapter 30 provides an excellent treatment of government decision making, offering not only a description of public choice theory but also reasons that the public sector at times has difficulty achieving its objectives. Suitable for advanced high school and college students.

Hacche, Graham. *The Theory of Economic Growth: An Introduction.* New York: St. Martin's Press, 1979.

An introductory book on growth theories that relies on a limited use of mathematics to describe various growth models. Also focuses on the discussion of technical change. Appropriate for undergraduate economic students.

Hadjimatheou, George. *Consumer Economics After Keynes.* Brighton, England: Wheatsheaf Books, 1987.

A fine survey of consumption economics.

Hahn, Frank H. *Equilibrium and Macroeconomics.* Oxford, England: Basil Blackwell, 1984.

By one of the leading supporters of the neoclassical synthesis. Hahn argues that Piero Sraffa's system is compatible with the standard view. Contains no true propositions that the neoclassical synthesis does not already incorporate. Hahn illustrates one type of neoclassical response to Sraffa's criticism: Some of his suggestions, such as reswitching, are incorporated into the mainstream. Hahn is mostly critical of New Classical economics for its strict interpretation of Say's Law.

_____ . "On the Notion of Equilibrium in Economics." In *Macroeconomics and Equilibrium*. Cambridge, Mass.: MIT Press, 1982.
A classic defense of neoclassical general equilibrium which contains a rebuttal to attacks made by Kornai and Kaldor.

Hailstones, Thomas. *Basic Economics*. 7th ed. Cincinnati: South-Western, 1988.
An economics textbook written for the beginning student or for those who require only a basic understanding of economic problems. The first half of the book is devoted to microeconomic topics, and the section on prices is especially well written. A good introductory text.

Halcrow, Harold G. *Economics of Agriculture*. New York: McGraw-Hill, 1980.
Chapters 4 through 7 provide a brief description of costs of production, revenues, demand and supply, and production functions. This text is written for students of economics, but the nonspecialist should have little trouble following the ideas.

Hall, Robert E. "Stochastic Implications of the Life Cycle Permanent Income Hypothesis: Theory and Evidence." *Journal of Political Economy* 86 (December, 1978): 971-987.
Hall and Thomas S. Sargent can be considered co-discoverers of the rational expectations-permanent income hypothesis. With rational expectations, changes in consumption spending do not slowly and mechanistically follow changes in income, but can occur quickly after a macroeconomic "shock."

Hall, Robert E., and John B. Taylor. *Macroeconomics: Theory, Performance, and Policy*. New York: W. W. Norton, 1988.
A very good intermediate macroeconomics text. If one is interested in the theoretical aspects of macroeconomic concepts, this is a fine place to start.

Hammersley, J. M., and D. C. Handscomb. *Monte Carlo Methods.* New York: Barnes & Noble Books, 1964.

Although first published in 1964, this book remains a definitive reference for Monte Carlo methods, providing an excellent presentation of their principles and applications. Chapter 1 discusses the nature of Monte Carlo methods for the general audience.

Hamouda, O. F., ed. *Controversies in Political Economy: Selected Essays of G. C. Harcourt.* New York: New York University Press, 1986.

A collection of essays written by Harcourt, a famous economist who is quite good at summarizing and explaining difficult theories for general audiences. In part 3, three essays on the "capital debate" or "Cambridge controversy" examine the problems that are faced by neoclassical theory in dealing with the determination of profit. While Harcourt has probably written the simplest and clearest exposition of this topic that is available, nonspecialists will find these essays difficult.

Hansen, Alvin. *Fiscal Policy and Business Cycles.* New York: W. W. Norton, 1941.

A persistent theme of Hansen's work, originating in his famous Harvard seminar in the late 1930's, was that unemployment was caused by a failure of private investment to match the level of saving at full employment income. With the effectiveness of monetary policy reduced by inelasticity, and with high liquidity preference in a sluggish economy, aggregate demand would have to be supplemented by fiscal expenditures to reach the required level. Drawing on his 1937 presidential address to the American Economic Association, Hansen placed the Keynesian model in a historical perspective and originated the secular stagnation thesis. After World War II, Paul Samuelson devised an alternative secular exhilaration thesis and his so-called neoclassical synthesis, which Hansen subsequently accepted.

_____. *A Guide to Keynes.* New York: McGraw-Hill, 1953.

In Hansen's words, this is a "tutorial guide of the *General Theory*." Written in a much more accessible manner, it is a classic restatement, along with Hansen's own opinions of *The General Theory of Employment, Interest, and Money* (1936). This is essential reading for those interested in a study of John Maynard Keynes and the consumption function. Includes an enumeration and brief overview of the determinants of consumption as originally propounded by Keynes.

Harcourt, G. C. *Some Cambridge Controversies in the Theory of Capital.* Cambridge, England: Cambridge University Press, 1972.

A very detailed account of Piero Sraffa's system, by a strong supporter. The details of the debate over reswitching between the neo-Ricardians, on the one hand, and Paul A. Samuelson and Robert M. Solow, on the other, are explained in abundant detail.

Harcourt, Geoffrey C., and N. F. Laing, eds. *Capital and Growth.* Harmondsworth, Middlesex, England: Penguin Books, 1971.

A collection of articles that brings together the most important contributions in capital theory. Some articles are quite technical, but some can be read by undergraduates.

Harris, Seymour. *John Maynard Keynes: Economist and Policy Maker.* New York: Charles Scribner's Sons, 1955.

One economist's study of another, this work concentrates on Keynes's practical objectives more than upon his personality or philosophy. It is written for the nonspecialist and avoids the equations familiar to professionals. Notes are skimpy and, like the brief bibliography, somewhat dated. Still, a useful introductory study.

Harrod, Roy F. "An Essay in Dynamic Theory." *American Journal* 49 (March, 1939): 14-33.

A basic analysis of Harrod's growth analysis with some, but not extensive, mathematical constructs.

_____. *The Life of John Maynard Keynes.* London: Macmillan, 1952.

A colleague of Keynes, Harrod produced the first official biography of the man drawing heavily on then private and unpublished materials. There have since been other biographies, some more critical than this one, but Harrod remains essential reading. Contains interesting photographs of Keynes, his family, and friends. There is no bibliography, as the study builds on private papers and correspondence, but the index is helpful.

_____. *Towards a Dynamic Economics.* London: Macmillan, 1948.

A series of essays on the topic of economic growth and its implications to various sectors of the economy. The analysis is intensive. Among other things, Harrod suggests that capitalists give up the idea of charging nominal interest rates to pacify the socialists.

Haveman, Robert. *Starting Even*. New York: Simon & Schuster, 1988. Haveman argues that poverty can be reduced without any negative economic consequences if current antipoverty policies are radically redesigned. Haveman's analysis of past successes and failures in reducing poverty, and his policy proposals, are generally very good.

Havrilesky, Thomas M., ed. *Modern Concepts in Macroeconomics*. Arlington Heights, Ill.: Harlan Davidson, 1985. A collection of essays written by leading economists examining issues in macroeconomics. Two essays are of special interest: "A Survey of Large-Scale Macroeconomic Models: Their Workings and Shortcomings" is a nontechnical introduction to the large-scale macroeconomic models being used by forecasting firms, the government, and industry. Also reprinted is the Congressional Budget Office's "Outlook for Fiscal Policy," which shows how a macroeconomic model influences policy decisions.

Hayashi, Fumio. "The Permanent Income Hypothesis: Estimation and Testing by Instrumental Variables." *Journal of Political Economy* 90 (October, 1982): 895-916. Hayashi shows that most of the overreaction of consumption expenditure to changes in income is in spending on consumer durable goods such as automobiles and household appliances and furniture.

_____. "Why Is Japan's Savings Rate So Apparently High?" In *NBER Macroeconomics Annual*, edited by Stanley Fischer. Cambridge, Mass.: MIT Press, 1986. Hayashi examines if Japan's high rate of savings can be explained by economic theory or if it can be attributable to Japanese people being "different."

Hayek, Friedrich A. von, ed. *Collectivist Economic Planning*. London: Routledge, 1935. Contains a number of important essays giving the Austrian view of the calculation controversy. Hayek contributes a detailed analysis of the market-socialist scheme of Oskar R. Lange, a leading socialist reply to the calculation argument. Because Hayek stressed the practical difficulties of socialism, it is sometimes claimed that he retreated from Ludwig von Mises' argument that socialist calculation is impossible. This, however, is much disputed. The collection reprints the basic papers on general equilibrium by Enrico Barone and Vilfredo Pareto.

_____. *Individualism and Economic Order*. Chicago: University of Chicago Press, 1948.

This book features Hayek's tremendously important essay on the knowledge problem.

_____. *Prices and Production*. London: Routledge & Kegan Paul, 1931.

Perhaps the most influential Austrian account of the natural and market rates. Hayek uses Wicksellian concepts to explain the structure of production, diagrammed in the famous Hayekian triangles. The key to the business cycle is a fall in the market rate of interest below the natural rate, encouraging overinvestment in capital goods. The depression is the process of readjustment to the correct natural rate.

_____. *Profits, Interest, and Investment*. London: Routledge & Kegan Paul, 1939.

Contains the basic statement of the Ricardo-Hayek effect, which is set forward in the context of the Austrian theory of business cycles. Hayek places great stress on the structure of production, and his "Hayekian triangles" are presented.

_____. "The Ricardo Effect." *Economica* 9 (May, 1942): 127-152.

Hayek defends his view from the criticisms of Kaldor (see below) and others. He elaborately discusses the way individual firms make investment decisions, particularly stressing differences in interest rates between higher- and lower-order goods. The effects of capital turnover receives much emphasis.

_____. *Studies in Politics, Philosophy, and Economics*. Chicago: University of Chicago Press, 1974.

Defends the Ricardo-Hayek effect. The doctrine has been misunderstood by its critics and really is little but elementary common sense. Probably the best introduction to the subject for the general reader. The setting of the effect within Austrian business cycle theory does not receive detailed treatment.

Hazlitt, Henry. *The Failure of the New Economics: An Analysis of the Keynesian Fallacies*. New York: D. Van Nostrand, 1959.

A very unusual book. Hazlitt presents a chapter-by-chapter, almost page-by-page, critique of John Maynard Keynes's work and, implicitly, a spirited defense of Say's Law. May be profitably read by anyone.

Heilbroner, Robert. *Behind the Veil of Economics*. New York: W. W. Norton, 1988.

Heilbroner, as always in his many books, attempts to rehabilitate Marxian economics; as always, he fails, but in a thought-provoking and readable manner. Especially relevant are two essays, "The World of Work" and "The Problem of Value," both of which include a discussion of the labor theory of value.

_____. *The Making of Economic Society*. Englewood Cliffs, N.J.: Prentice-Hall, 1962.

A rather abstract but nontechnical analysis of the deep structure of economic systems, including the often tacit agreements regarding property and individual property rights.

Heilbroner, Robert, and James K. Galbraith. *The Economic Problem*. Englewood Cliffs, N.J.: Prentice-Hall, 1987.

The two chapters on supply and demand and market dynamics are especially relevant. Heilbroner's style of writing is interesting and concise, with many real-life illustrations. Includes graphs and a glossary. An excellent book for the lay reader.

Heilbroner, Robert, and Lester Thurow. *Economics Explained*. New York: Simon & Schuster, 1987.

The best introduction to a wide variety of economic topics, explained in simple terms for a general audience. Chapters 5 through 9 are related to employment theory; chapter 7 contains a clear and concise explanation of the multiplier process.

Heilbrun, James. *Urban Economics and Public Policy*. 3d ed. New York: St. Martin's Press, 1987.

Provides a comprehensive overview of urban economics, but the emphasis is on application of the theories to public policy.

Hendershott, Patric H., ed. *The Level and Composition of Household Saving*. Cambridge, Mass.: Ballinger, 1985.

A collection of articles which analyzes trends regarding household saving by various demographic groups. Some of these articles would be appropriate for the nonspecialist.

Henderson, James M., and Richard E. Quandt. *Microeconomic Theory*. 3d. ed. New York: McGraw-Hill, 1980.

Henderson and Quandt show how a system of equations can be used to model an individual consumer's demands for goods and services and the supply of labor, as well as an individual firm's supplies of goods and services and its demands for the inputs (including labor) that it needs to produce these products. They also show how the consumers' and firms' equations can be combined into a system of equations which describes the behavior of the overall economy.

Hey, John D. *Uncertainty in Microeconomics.* New York: New York University Press, 1979.

Centering on the traditional areas of microeconomics (consumer, firm, and market models), the author gives a most thorough survey of the literature on uncertainty in economics. While less of an instructional volume than that of C. J. McKenna regarding the use of technique, this book provides an overview of the direction of completed and ongoing research. Very readable, particularly for the nonspecialist.

Hey, John D., and Peter J. Lambert. *Surveys in the Economics of Uncertainty.* New York: Basil Blackwell, 1987.

A collection of surveys focusing on individual choice, principal-agent problems, labor contracts, and tax evasion.

Heyne, Paul. *The Economic Way of Thinking.* 5th ed. New York: Macmillan, 1987.

A brief text of microeconomics and macroeconomics. Quite sufficient without being compendious. The emphasis is on economic thinking rather than analysis or policy. Contains a good discussion on the "myth of material wealth."

_____ . *Microeconomics.* New York: Macmillan, 1991.

Chapter 2 is especially relevant because it develops the concept of demand by considering substitutes. This is one of the more basic undergraduate economics texts. Noteworthy is the clarity of language and the large number of questions for discussion: There are at least thirty at the end of each chapter.

Hicks, John R. *Capital and Growth.* New York: Oxford University Press, 1965.

Presents the initial elucidation of the fix-flex price distinction.

_____ . *A Revision of Demand Theory.* Oxford, England: Clarendon Press, 1956.

A revision of Hicks's earlier work, providing a thorough geometrical analysis of the income and substitution effects for normal, inferior, and Giffen goods.

_____. *Value and Capital*. 1939. 2d ed. Oxford, England: Clarendon Press, 1946.

This seminal work by the Nobel laureate developed the first comprehensive framework for systematically analyzing the theory of consumer choice. Hicks was the person who coined the term "inferior good." Advanced economics and a good grasp of indifference curve analysis are required in order to follow the more technical aspects of deriving demand curves. Hicks describes how a system of equations can be used to construct models of an individual consumer's demands for goods and services, the supply of labor, and an individual firm's supplies of goods and services and that firm's demands for inputs. Hicks also examines how these equations and models can be combined into a larger system of equations which can describe the behavior of an overall economy.

Hildenbrand, Werner, and Alan Kirman. *Equilibrium Analysis*. Rev. ed. Amsterdam: North-Holland, 1988.

An updating of an earlier text which heuristically compares and contrasts the two themes of price decentralization (from Léon Walras) and the core (from Francis Ysidro Edgeworth)—the two main approaches to general equilibrium analysis. An excellent formal primer, though it assumes some familiarity with calculus.

Hill, Christopher T., and James M. Utterback, eds. *Technological Innovation for a Dynamic Economy*. New York: Pergamon Press, 1979.

Analyzes and reviews the principal characteristics of the innovation process, its consequences, and the ways governments deal with it.

Hillier, Frederick S., and Gerald J. Lieberman. *Introduction to Operations Research*. San Francisco: Holden-Day, 1967.

A high-level book that provides a rigorous treatment of the assignment problem, as well as other operations research topics. Chapter 6 deals with the assignment problem. Recommended to those with appropriate mathematical proficiency.

Hirsch, Fred. *Social Limits to Growth*. Cambridge, Mass.: Harvard University Press, 1976.

An influential book in which Hirsch explores the consequences associated with the existence of "positional goods," those goods whose value or enjoyment depends on whether others are consuming the goods. Accessible to a general audience, the book shows that concern about relative standing should not be dismissed as irrational, since relative standing is often instrumental in achieving other absolute goals.

Hirshleifer, Jack. *Price Theory and Applications.* 2d ed. Englewood Cliffs, N.J.: Prentice-Hall, 1970.

Chapters 3 through 6 provide a comprehensive treatment of the theory of demand, including income effects and the new approach to demand theory. Chapter 7 provides an excellent explanation of exchange equilibrium and related topics. Hirshleifer does a fine job of integrating traditional theory with new developments and examples of empirical studies. For those who can handle fairly sophisticated graphical analysis, including Edgeworth box diagrams. Hirshleifer uses interesting examples, one of which involves exchange between the North and South at the time of the Civil War.

_____. *Time, Uncertainty, and Information.* New York: Basil Blackwell, 1989.

This 306-page book provides an essential guide for college students who are interested in the economics of uncertainty and expectations. Topics include information theory, uncertainty and expectations in economics, and investments and decision making under risk. Also suitable for noneconomists.

Hoffman, Elizabeth, and Matthew L. Spitzer. "Experimental Law and Economics: An Introduction." *Columbia Law Review* 85, no. 5 (1985): 991-1036.

A thorough introduction to the technique and literature of experimental economics up to 1985. This article is written for lawyers but accessible to nonspecialists. Includes in-depth analyses of several classic experimental research projects.

Hollander, Samuel. *The Economics of Adam Smith.* Toronto: University of Toronto Press, 1973.

Examines Smith's views with an emphasis on a competitive economy's general equilibrium tendencies.

_____. *The Economics of David Ricardo.* Toronto: University of Toronto Press, 1979.

A massive study of Ricardian economics, written from a very strong point of view. There is relatively little technical theoretical material. Arguments are developed in great detail from Ricardo's writings.

Holtzman, Franklyn D., ed. *Readings on the Soviet Economy*. Chicago: Rand McNally, 1962.

Long out of print, this is a very valuable collection of early Western articles and papers on the Soviet economy. Provides valuable information on the "classic" Soviet command economy. Economic background required varies, but most items are designed for the general reader.

Hoover, Kevin D. *The New Classical Macroeconomics: A Skeptical Inquiry*. New York: Basil Blackwell, 1988.

Examines and elaborates on the application of New Classical thought doctrine to particular macroeconomic issues. Discusses the Phillips curve approach to stagflation and examines several prominent New Classical models in that context. Explores the limits of macroeconomic policies. Index.

Houthakker, H. S., and Lester D. Taylor. *Consumer Demand in the United States, 1929-1970: Analyses and Projections*. 2d ed. Cambridge, Mass.: Harvard University Press, 1970.

A fairly technical treatise that is interesting from the standpoint of income elasticity because it contains empirical estimates, using historical data, of a wide variety of commodities. Contains tables and discussion that show the income elasticity of demand for various classifications of goods. Provides insight into the value of using Engel's law methodology in determining income elasticities and cross elasticities in the United States. The work in forecasting such figures is especially valuable.

Howard, Michael. *Profits in Economic Theory*. New York: St. Martin's Press, 1983.

Howard presents a basic review of the economic concepts underlying profit maximization. Of interest to the more advanced reader are sections that provide sound mathematical models of profit maximization.

Howson, Colin, and Peter Urbach. *Scientific Reasoning: The Bayesian Approach*. La Salle, Ill.: Open Court, 1989.

Provides a good introduction to Bayesian inference from a philosophical and historical perspective. Demonstrates how Bayesian methods overcome logical inconsistencies problems. A knowledge of advanced mathematics is not assumed.

Hultgren, Thor. *Cost, Prices, and Profits: Their Cyclical Relations.* New York: Columbia University Press, 1965.

Written and edited by a well-respected expert, this book provides an extensive review of business cycles and their relationship to the net revenues that are generated by firms over time. The book reads well and is a good resource for the beginner.

Hutt, W. H. *Economists and the Public.* London: Jonathan Cape, 1936.

Hutt, a disciple of Edwin Cannan, supports nineteenth century utilitarianism. Because in his view the free market best promotes the growth of wealth, it is the function of the economist to make the general public aware of the benefits of the market.

Ingrao, Bruna, and Giorgio Israel. *The Invisible Hand.* Cambridge, Mass.: MIT Press, 1990.

Provides a critical history of the development of general equilibrium theory. Especially strong on the influence of the natural sciences and philosophy upon general equilibrium theories.

Intriligator, Michael D. *Econometric Models: Techniques and Applications.* Englewood Cliffs, N.J.: Prentice-Hall, 1978.

Demonstrates how simultaneous equation models of economic behavior are constructed and how the parameters of these models can be estimated, using real-world data. Also describes how the estimated versions of these models can be used to forecast economic behavior and to examine the impacts of various economic policies.

_____. *Mathematical Optimization and Economic Theory.* Englewood Cliffs, N.J.: Prentice-Hall, 1971.

Examines the function of a system of equations as it relates to models of individual consumer demands, the supply of labor, and the behavior of individual firms in production and the demand for inputs. These equations can be combined into a system of equations which describes the behavior of the overall economy. Intriligator shows how such a system of equations can be used to analyze the impact of various "controls" on the behavior of economic variables. These controls range from the monetary and fiscal policies used to control the macroeconomy to the prices used by an individual firm to control its market share.

Isaac, R. Mark. "Laboratory Experimental Economics as a Tool in Public Policy Analysis." *Social Science Journal* 20, no. 3, (1983): 45-58.
A readable introduction to how laboratory experiments can be used to inform policy analysis and regulation. Includes analyses of several experimental projects that did have an effect on public policy.

Isard, Walter. *Methods of Regional Analysis.* Cambridge, Mass.: MIT Press, 1960.
Isard, one of the prominent regional economists, provides in this work a comprehensive guide to the science and methods of doing regional economics.

Jacobs, Jane. *The Economy of Cities.* New York: Random House, 1969.
An excellent accounting of the development process. Although theoretical, it is quite readable. The basic principles that Jacobs outlines can be as easily applied to regional development as to cities.

James, Estelle, and Susan Rose-Ackerman. *The Nonprofit Enterprise in Market Economies.* Fundamentals of Pure and Applied Economics, Vol. 9. Chur, Switzerland: Harwood Academic Publishers, 1986.
A good, if somewhat technical, survey. This book focuses more on the behavior of individual nonprofit organizations than on their role in the overall economy.

Jenkins, Gwilym M., and Donald G. Watts. *Spectral Analysis and Its Applications.* Oakland, Calif.: Holden-Day, 1968.
This work is complete but technical. Contains examples from several different fields, not just economics. Introduces the concept of the spectrum, explains the techniques that are used to estimate it, and presents several examples. Also examines the concepts of the gain and coherence, with examples.

Jevons, William Stanley. *Theory of Political Economy.* 1871. Reprint. New York: Kelley and Millman, 1957.
Contains an early development of the concept of marginal utility (benefit). Antiquated language makes the book difficult to understand in places.

Johnson, D. Gale, ed. *The Politics of Food: Producing and Distributing the World's Food Supply.* Chicago: Chicago Council on Foreign Relations, 1980.

A very useful analysis of the world food supply and the problems of distribution by a number of well-known economists, writing from a variety of points of view.

Jones, Hywel G. *An Introduction to Modern Theories of Economic Growth.* New York: McGraw-Hill, 1976.
Probably one of the few books on growth models that does not require calculus. An excellent exposition of the fundamental properties of various growth models supplemented by the historical background of the underlying theories. Appropriate for undergraduates and a general audience.

Judge, George G., W. Griffiths, R. Hill, H. Lutkepohl, and T. Lee. *The Theory and Practice of Econometrics.* 2d. ed. New York: John Wiley & Sons, 1985.
Spectral analysis is presented in chapters 7, 8, and 16. In chapter 7, the authors introduce the spectrum, the methods that can be used to estimate it, and a bibliography. In chapter 8, a second method for estimating the spectrum is presented. In chapter 16, the technique that is used to estimate the joint spectrum of several time series is presented, as well as bibliography.

Junakar, P. N. *Investment: Theories and Evidence.* London: Macmillan, 1972.
This short book contains mostly theories and little evidence. Chapter 3 explains both the simple accelerator and the flexible accelerator.

Juster, F. Thomas, and Kenneth C. Land. *Social Accounting Systems.* New York: Academic Press, 1981.
A book of essays on social accounting, some of which are concerned with national income and product accounts.

Kahn, Alfred E. *The Economics of Regulation: Principles and Institutions.* Cambridge, Mass: MIT Press, 1988.
Two sections of different chapters are devoted to the Averch-Johnson effect. The first deals with incentives and distortions, while the second section examines possible positive aspects of the effect.

Kaldor, Nicholas. "Alternative Theories of Distribution." In *Essays on Value and Distribution.* 2d ed. London: Duckworth, 1980.
Kaldor develops a theory of distribution based on the economic theories of John Maynard Keynes. This article laid the foundation of the post-Keynesian theory of distribution.

_____. *Causes of the Slow Rate of Economic Growth in the United Kingdom*. Cambridge, England: Cambridge University Press, 1966.
An important study of increasing returns, by a close associate of John Maynard Keynes. Kaldor distinguishes between increasing returns because of scale and other types of increasing returns. The former involve the law of diminishing returns, because they exist when the optimal proportion of factors of production has not yet been reached. The latter, which Kaldor thinks are of greater importance, relate to technological changes and are not directly affected by diminishing returns.

_____. *Economics Without Equilibrium*. Armonk, N.Y.: M. E. Sharpe, 1983.
Kaldor was a leading critic of general equilibrium theory, and this short book was his final contribution to the debate. Kaldor also offers some alternative concepts and tools to replace general equilibrium.

_____. "Professor Hayek and the Concertina Effect." *Economica* 9 (November, 1942): 359-382.
Mercilessly satirizes Friedrich A. von Hayek's account of the Ricardo effect. Kaldor stresses the counterintuitive nature of Hayek's view: Spending on consumption will decrease employment. Kaldor contends that a cycle of expansion and decline will result, according to the Hayek effect. This, Kaldor thinks, is also contrary to reasonable belief.

Kalecki, Michal. *Selected Essays on the Dynamics of the Capitalist Economy*. Cambridge, England: Cambridge University Press, 1971.
Contains the essentials of Kalecki's theory of effective demand and income distribution and his novel theory of the firm. Chapters 5 through 10 and 14 present Kalecki's insights into the question of the distribution of income, which extend Karl Marx's analysis of the class struggle to include the element of monopoly. Part 2 deals with the theoretical development of cost-plus pricing in connection with the development of the theory of effective demand and income distribution.

_____. *Studies in the Theory of the Business Cycle, 1933-1939*. With an introduction by Joan Robinson. New York: A. M. Keley, 1966.
Contains material first appearing in Polish and buttressing Robinson's claim that Kalecki was a forerunner of Keynes.

_____ . *Theory of Economic Dynamics.* London: Allen & Unwin, 1954.
Contains an exposition of Kalecki's profit equation, as well as his theory of business cycles. Although much of the analysis concerns profit at the macroeconomic level, Kalecki also explains the markup theory of the determination of micro level profits. Nonspecialists will find this book moderately difficult.

Kaplinsky, Raphael. *Automation: The Technology and Society.* Harlow, England: Longman, 1984.
Using many good examples and graphs, this book relates how the new automation affects both production and management and makes possible the "unmanned factory of the future." Kaplinsky stresses the potential adverse social impact of automation and the prospects for mitigating its negative consequences.

Katona, George. *The Powerful Consumer.* New York: McGraw-Hill, 1960.
Although not couched in the terminology of the rational expectations-permanent income hypothesis, Katona's public opinion surveys demonstrate that consumer confidence can dramatically change after "macroeconomic news."

Katz, Michael L., and Harvey S. Rosen. *Microeconomics.* Homewood, Ill.: Richard D. Irwin, 1991.
A brilliantly written and understandable textbook of microeconomic theory at the intermediate level which provides a wealth of applications. The mathematics is mainly in the form of diagrams, which are accessible to the general reader. Deals with perfect and imperfect competition.

Kearl, J. R., C. I. Pope, G. T. Whiting, and L. T. Wimmer. "A Confusion of Economists?" *American Economic Review* 69 (May, 1979): 28-37.
This article, in a leading economics journal, reports the results of a survey of economists. These findings have often been used to demonstrate that there is much agreement among economists on many government policy issues. Suitable for advanced high school students and undergraduates.

Kelso, Louis, and Mortimer Adler. *The Capitalist Manifesto.* New York: Random House, 1958.

This small book launched the movement for employee stock owner-ship plans (ESOPs) in the United States. It outlines the author's conception of a modern Jeffersonian democracy and the role of employee-ownership in it.

Kemmerer, Edwin L. *The ABC of Inflation*. New York: McGraw-Hill, 1942.
A good statement of the pre-Keynesian monetary view of inflation.

Kemp, Murray C., ed. *Production Sets*. New York: Academic Press, 1982.
This collection of essays offers a modern look at production theory using a set-theoretic approach, methods which have dominated general equilibrium analysis.

Kendrick, John W. *Economic Accounts and Their Use*. New York: McGraw-Hill, 1972.
Describes, in considerable detail, the system of national income and production accounting that was in use in the United States during the early 1970's. Not quite up to date, as there have been some changes in the accounting system since the early 1970's, but still a good introduction to NIPAs.

_____ . *International Causes of Productivity and Causes of the Slowdown*. Cambridge, Mass.: Ballinger, 1984.
One of a number of attempts to explain the slowdown in productivity growth that characterized the United States and other countries during the 1970's.

Kennedy, Peter. *A Guide to Econometrics*. Cambridge, Mass.: MIT Press, 1984.
Essential for all econometrics students. It provides excellent intuitive explanations of the theory of econometrics using a minimum of mathematics. Appendices following each chapter quickly present the material in mathematical notation. Kennedy's book should be used as a companion text, as it does not provide examples of applications.

Keynes, John Maynard. "The General Theory of Employment." *The Quarterly Journal of Economics* 17 (February, 1937): 44-49.
In this short article, Keynes summarized his theory of employment, which had been presented in his book in 1936. Nonspecialists may find this exposition a bit easier to understand.

_____ . *The General Theory of Employment, Interest, and Money.* 1936. Reprint. London: Harcourt Brace Jovanovich, 1964.

The most influential macroeconomics book of the twentieth century. The most important chapters are those on the classical labor market, the consumption function, and the demand for money. Follows a Marshallian general equilibrium approach. Continues the emphasis of *A Treatise on Money* on cases in which the market rate of interest is too high to permit a level of investment that sustains fully employment. The natural rate of interest is deemphasized as a component of the market rate, which is ascribed almost entirely to monetary factors.

_____ . "The Process of Capital Formation." In *The Collected Writings.* Vol. 15. 2d ed. London: Macmillan, 1987.

In this brief article, Keynes explains why saving and investment must be identical, why investment must determine saving, and how investment is financed.

_____ . *A Treatise on Money.* 2 vols. London: Macmillan, 1930.

A work of fundamental importance, not superseded by the later *The General Theory of Employment, Interest, and Money.* Using the same Wicksellian concepts as Hayek, Keynes arrived at a diametrically opposed view of business cycles. Cases in which the natural rate of interest is below the monetary rate are of crucial significance. The bottlenecks that result from this divergence are not subject to automatic correction by the market. The Austrian model, in which the natural rate is below the market rate, is held to be irrelevant to the real world.

Kiker, B. F., ed. *Investment in Human Capital.* Columbia: University of South Carolina Press, 1971.

This 608-page book brings together thirty-one of the most important contributions to the theory of human capital up to 1970. A few of the articles are quite technical, but it is an excellent collection covering the full breadth of human capital investment activities and providing many rich insights.

Kim, Kyun. *Equilibrium Business Cycle Theory in Historical Perspective.* Cambridge, England: Cambridge University Press, 1987.

Kim traces the historical development of econometric macroeconomic models, relating these models to their ability to explain business cycle phenomena such as inflation and unemployment. Discusses more recent approaches to macroeconomic econometrics. Some readers may find this book to be too technical.

Kirzner, Israel M. *Competition and Entrepreneurship*. Chicago: University of Chicago Press, 1973.
Presents the Austrian theory of competition.

_____. *The Economic Point of View*. Princeton, N.J.: Van Nostrand, 1960.
A sympathetic critique and extension of Lionel Robbins' synthesis of the Austrian and English foundations of economics.

Kivenson, Gilbert. *The Art and Science of Inventing*. 2d ed. New York: Van Nostrand Reinhold, 1982.
A basic work by a teacher of inventing techniques covering the range from fundamental scientific principles to the economic aspects of the process. The numerous diagrams are understandable to those without scientific or engineering background.

Klein, Lawrence R. *The Keynesian Revolution*. New York: Macmillan, 1961.
A most useful study for those who have prior knowledge of basic economics. Klein is critical and judicious but still pro-Keynesian. The discussion lacks some historical perspective on Keynes's ideas and influences—it was originally published in 1947—but the technical discussions are valuable. The index is helpful, but there are few notes and there is no bibliography.

_____. "The Neoclassical Tradition of Keynesian Economics and the Generalized Model." In *Samuelson and Neoclassical Economics*, edited by George R. Feiwel. Boston: Kluwer-Nijhoff, 1982.
A generalized model of both the supply and demand sides of the economy and discussion of policy implications.

_____. "Whither Econometrics?" In *Economic Theory and Econometrics*, edited by J. Marquez. Philadelphia: University of Pennsylvania Press, 1985.
This chapter provides an excellent but brief history of the development and growth of econometrics as an offshoot of correlation and regression. Though the target audience is a highly specialized one, the text is not very technical.

Knight, Frank H. *The Ethics of Competition*. London: George Allen & Unwin, 1935.

This historically important collection of articles includes the well-known "Cost of Production and Price over Long and Short Periods," as well as Knight's "Fallacies in the Interpretation of Social Cost."

_____. *Risk, Uncertainty, and Profit.* Boston: Houghton Mifflin, 1921.

In the first work to draw a meaningful distinction between risk and uncertainty, Knight puts forth his theory that profit is the result of a lack of perfect foresight. Anticipates the secular decline in interest rates.

Kohler, Heinz. *Intermediate Microeconomics.* 3d ed. Glenview, Ill.: Scott, Foresman, 1990.

This intermediate-level text presents a good study of indifference curve analysis and the sorting out of the income and substitution effects brought about by a change in the relative prices of goods. A clear discussion of the Giffen good case and the conditions required to produce an upward-sloping demand curve.

Koopmans, Tjalling C. "Stationary Ordinal Utility and Impatience." *Econometrica* 28 (April, 1960): 287-309.

Represents lifetime utility as a discounted sum of each year's utility. Insofar as each year's utility function features diminishing marginal utility, however, impatience would be implicit in the differing values of goods as time passes if incomes were increasing over time. Thus, the discounting of future years' utilities in Koopmans' model represents an underestimation of the future.

_____. *Three Essays on the State of Economic Science.* New York: McGraw-Hill, 1957.

This source brings the reader to the frontiers of modern mathematical economics with surprisingly little difficulty. Suitable for college students.

Kornai, Janos. *Anti-Equilibrium.* New York: North-Holland, 1971.

A strong critique of neoclassical general equilibrium. Kornai attacks the validity of the underlying assumptions of neoclassical general equilibrium theory for being inappropriate for modeling economic behavior in an advanced capitalist economy and for not following standard scientific procedures in theory construction.

_____ . *Contradictions and Dilemmas: Studies on the Socialist Economy and Society.* Cambridge, Mass.: MIT Press, 1986.
A collection of many of Kornai's previously published articles. This is an advanced work on the problems facing planned economies as they introduce more market mechanisms and grapple with the implications of the profit motive.

_____ . *The Socialist System: The Political Economy of Socialism.* Princeton, N.J.: Princeton University Press, 1992.
The author, who divides his time between Budapest and Harvard, is the foremost contemporary Hungarian economist, famous for his earlier work on anti-equilibrium. He presents a comprehensive critique of socialism.

Kregel, Jan A. "Conceptions of Equilibrium: The Logic of Choice and the Logic of Production." In *Subjectivity, Intelligibility, and Economic Understanding*, edited by Israel Kirzner. New York: New York University Press, 1986.
This chapter is an excellent demonstration of the differences between structural and behavioral traditions of general equilibrium, coming down strongly on the side of the structural variety.

_____ . "The Multiplier and Liquidity Preference: Two Sides of the Theory of Effective Demand." In *The Foundations of Keynesian Analysis: Proceedings of a Conference Held at the University of Paris I-Pantheon-Sorbonne*, edited by Alain Barrere. New York: St. Martin's Press, 1988.
This difficult article explains the relation between John Maynard Keynes's theory of the multiplier and his liquidity preference theory. Kregel argues that each theory is an important component of Keynes's argument that aggregate effective demand determines income and employment. Not for nonspecialists.

_____ . *Rate of Profit, Distribution, and Growth: Two Views.* London: Macmillan, 1971.
Kregel examines the neoclassical theory of profit, the "Cambridge controversy," the Cambridge (or post-Keynesian) approach to profit, and the relation between profit and economic growth. Probably the best single source on profit theory, covering a wide range of viewpoints and topics.

Kreps, David M. *A Course in Microeconomic Theory*. Princeton, N.J.: Princeton University Press, 1990.

An innovative textbook which specifically addresses general equilibrium analysis, capturing developments at the frontiers of economic theory.

_____ . *Game Theory and Economic Modelling*. New York: Oxford University Press, 1990.

This textbook examines why game theory has become such an important tool for economic analysis. Provides a conceptual background and explores the strengths and weaknesses and the future of game theory as a tool for economists.

Krugman, Paul. *Peddling Prosperity in the Age of Diminished Expectations*. New York: W. W. Norton, 1994.

Kurgman claims that no major United States economist became a supporter of supply-side economics. To reach this conclusion, he emphasizes Robert Mundell's eccentricities and overlooks Walter Heller, who finally admitted in the mid-1980's that he had been the first practicing supply-side economist, even though he did not have the insight to recognize the need for a new term to sell "commercial Keynesianism," the term used by Robert Lekachman in *Age of Keynes* to describe Keynesians who are eager to cut tax rates. Krugman is especially critical of the media pundits. As a so-called "New Keynesian," he presents insightful critiques of monetarism, rational expectations, and the New Classical schools.

Kuenne, Robert E. *The Theory of General Equilibrium*. Princeton, N.J.: Princeton University Press, 1963.

A lengthy book on classical general equilibrium theory which contains a good discussion of Walras' Law. Unfortunately, the book also contains numerous errors.

Kuhn, T. S. *The Structure of Scientific Revolutions*. Chicago: University of Chicago Press, 1962.

This slim book revolutionized the thinking of historians and philosophers of science in the 1960's and 1970's, raising doubts about the role of evidence and especially of disconfirmation in the sciences generally. Many economists critical of positive economics have borrowed ideas from it.

Kuperberg, Mark, and Charles Beitz, eds. *Law, Economics, and Philosophy: A Critical Introduction with Applications to the Law of Torts.* Totowa, N.J.: Rowman & Allanheld, 1983.

This anthology of professional papers contains the work of some of the most prominent scholars working in this area, as well as the thoughts of some of its most important critics. The papers are all aimed at a professional scholarly audience, but most should be accessible to nonexperts. The collection includes one particularly important paper, Ronald H. Coase's "The Problem of Social Cost."

Kuttner, Robert. *The End of Laissez Faire, National Purpose, the Global Economy After the Cold War.* New York: Knopf, 1991.

Kuttner calls for a "new economic strategy—located between a free market and a command economy—for the 1990's" and sees the world as heading toward a global Keynesianism. This is a work of historical scholarship from the Great Depression of 1929 to the Great Liberation of 1989. Kuttner believes that a planning coalition, including segments of business, is forming.

Kuznets, Simon. *Modern Economic Growth.* New Haven, Conn.: Yale University Press, 1966.

This is perhaps the best work by Kuznets for an understanding of his conception of modern economic growth. Another source from among his prolific contributions to the literature is his Nobel address that appears in the *American Economic Review* 63 (June, 1973): 247-258. Kuznets frequently draws attention to "social invention" and the conception of social technology. A good reference in this context by the same author is *Economic Development, the Family, and Income Distribution* (Cambridge: England: Cambridge University Press, 1989).

_____. "Modern Economic Growth: Findings and Reflections." *American Economic Review* 63, no. 3 (1973): 247-258.

This article summarizes the findings of Nobel Prize-winning economist Kuznets on the historical record of economic growth. Kuznets identifies six characteristic features that are manifested in the growth process of almost every developed nation.

Kyburg, Henry E., Jr., and Howard E. Smokler, eds. *Studies in Subjective Probability.* Huntington, N.Y.: R. E. Krieger, 1980.

One of the best collections of important works in subjective probability which forms the basis for Bayesian inference. Some of the articles are mathematically technical, while others are literary.

Landau, Ralph, and Dale W. Jorgenson, eds. *Technology and Economic Policy*. Cambridge, Mass.: Ballinger, 1986.

Develops an understanding of the interrelationship between issues in economics (especially business taxation) and technological innovation.

Landau, Ralph, and Nathan Rosenberg, eds. *The Positive Sum Strategy: Harnessing Technology for Economic Growth*. Washington, D.C.: National Academy Press, 1986.

Specific themes include how the innovative process innovation actually works in the United States and Japan in different industries; role of educational, financial, and other key infrastructures; effect of government policies; and how economics and technology might work more constructively together. Outstanding contributors are engineers who are knowledgeable about technologies and economists who are knowledgeable about the functioning of markets.

Landis, William M., and Richard A. Posner. *The Economic Structure of Tort Law*. Cambridge, Mass.: Harvard University Press, 1987.

Posner is one of the early and most influential proponents of law and economics; he has collaborated with Landis on a number of previous occasions. This book constitutes an extensive examination of tort law and a spirited defense of the positive theory of law and economics.

Leamer, Edward E. *Specification Searches: Ad Hoc Inference with Nonexperimental Data*. New York: John Wiley & Sons, 1978.

An influential work that takes a critical view of classical inference in econometrics. An especially important book for statistical researchers working with observational data. Requires a background of calculus and linear algebra.

Lekachman, Robert, ed. *Keynes and the Classics*. Boston: D. C. Heath, 1964.

A brief, popular work, clearly collected and written for nonspecialists by well-known economists, some of whom are frank critics of Keynesian philosophy and policies. Notes are lacking, and the bibliography and index are not particularly helpful. Still, these essays are informative.

_____ , ed. *Keynes' General Theory: Reports of Three Decades.*
New York: St. Martin's Press, 1964.

Distinguished economists, in this collection of well-written assessments, discuss some of Keynes's lasting influences and some of the problems posed in and by his theories when transformed into public policies. Most essays have good notes and supplemental references. The index is modest. A useful preliminary updating of Keynes's impact.

Leone, Bruno. *Socialism: Opposing Viewpoints.* 2d rev. ed. St. Paul, Minn.: Greenhaven Press, 1986.

Under the broad term "socialism," Leone covers the thoughts of many authors on different forms of socialism and communism. He covers theoretical arguments as well as specific topics, such as "Socialism Is the Community of Christians." The book will not synthesize, but introduces different viewpoints.

Leontief, Wassily. *Input-Output Economics.* New York: Oxford University Press, 1986.

Nobel laureate Leontief presents the system of equations that he believes can be used to describe the behavior of the economy. He then uses his system to analyze wages, prices, profits, taxes, foreign trade, air pollution, population growth, arms control, and the distribution of work and income.

Leontief, Wassily, and Faye Duchin. *The Future Impact of Automation on Workers.* New York: Oxford University Press, 1986.

Covers automation in manufacturing, office work, education, and health care and uses an input-output model to draw conclusions for overall employment and individual occupations in the year 2000. The summary assessment is that the displacement of labor that will be attributable to computer-based automation is not likely, by itself, to proceed so quickly as to be unmanageably disruptive to the U.S. economy. Education and retraining to smooth accommodation are recommended.

Lerner, Abba. *Economics of Control: The Principles of Welfare Economics.* New York: Macmillan, 1944.

Written during World War II, this volume contains Lerner's idea of what principles should govern a socialist country and expands on Oskar Lange's work. His chapter on functional finance appeared earlier in *Social Research* and caused John Maynard Keynes to regard Lerner as an impractical dreamer. Later, the two met, and Keynes agreed that

Lerner's functional finance was a logical extension of Keynesian economics. David Colander's account of this meeting appeared in the *Journal of Economic Literature* in December of 1984.

Levi, Maurice. *Thinking Economically.* New York: Basic Books, 1985.
A series of refreshingly informal applications of economic principles. Chapter 9, "Thinking Opportunistically," is an application of the opportunity cost principle to explain rents and wages.

Lewis, Frank L. *Optimal Estimation: With an Introduction to Stochastic Control Theory.* New York: Wiley-Interscience, 1986.
Lewis introduces continuous-time stochastic models and then presents an estimation technique which can be used to estimate the structure of a system of continuous-time stochastic equations and forecast the future behavior of that system. Kalman filtering is the most important of such techniques. Also shows how an economist can model the impact of attempts to control a system of equations and thus the economy, such as with monetary and/or fiscal policy.

Lewis, W. Arthur. *Theory of Economic Growth.* London: Allen & Unwin, 1955.
Lewis presents the classic statement of the nature of economic growth in less developed countries. This work has had an enormous influence on the emergence of a separate discipline—development economics—that devised plans for Third World countries to stimulate their economic growth.

Lieber, Nancy, ed. *Eurosocialism and America.* Philadelphia: Temple University Press, 1982.
This book presents a collection of articles presented at a conference sponsored by the Institute for Democratic Socialism. Includes an article by Michael Harrington (the leading figure of the social democratic movement in the United States) on the distinguishing features of democratic socialism and other reviews by the prominent leaders of European social democracy, such as François Mitterrand, Willy Brandt, and Olaf Palme. A useful collection for those who want to acquire a broad perspective on social democracy.

Lindley, D. V. *Introduction to Probability and Statistics from a Bayesian Viewpoint.* Cambridge, England: Cambridge University Press, 1965.
A comprehensive introduction to probability and statistics. Requires some knowledge of calculus.

Lintner, John. "The Distribution of Incomes of Corporations Among Dividends, Retained Earnings, and Taxes." *American Economic Review* 46 (May, 1956): 97-113.

This is a classic study, presenting the results of a survey of corporate managers concerning their views on dividend policy. Contains one of the earliest analyses of how corporations actually set dividend policy. Suitable for college students.

Lipset, Seymour M. *The Sociology of Marxism.* Berkeley: University of California Press, 1963.

A brief essay in response to *Marxism: An Historical and Critical Study* (New York: Praeger, 1961), by George Lichtheim. As the title of Lipset's essay suggests, the treatment of Marxism as a theory of social, as well as economic, organization receives primary attention.

Lipsey, R. G., and Kelvin Lancaster. "The General Theory of Second Best." *Review of Economic Studies* 24, no. 1 (1956): 11-32.

The standard reference for the theory of second best. Some of the presentation is rather technical, but the general discussion is understandable to the interested lay reader.

Lipsey, Richard, et al. *Microeconomics.* 9th ed. New York: Harper & Row, 1990.

A popular textbook for the first year college economics course. It contains a fairly full account of the price elasticities of demand and supply and income elasticity of demand. The chapter on elasticity and market adjustment contains estimates of elasticities, for example, the estimated elasticity of sugar, gasoline, cigarettes, beer, automobiles, and whole milk. Contains little mathematics.

Lipsey, Richard G., Peter O. Steiner, Douglas Purvis, and Paul N. Courant. *Economics.* 9th ed. New York: Harper & Row, 1990.

A textbook widely used at the introductory level. Chapters 4 through 6 define markets, demand and supply, and the elasticity of demand. A wide variety of phenomena, such as rent controls, price supports, and farm policy in the United States, are explained well. Chapters 12 through 15 consider the problems of pricing in competitive and noncompetitive market structures.

Lloyd, Peter E., and Peter Dicken. *Location in Space: A Theoretical Approach to Economic Geography.* New York: Harper & Row, 1972.

Despite its title, a very practical and applied introduction to the study of regional economics. This text is particularly strong in its coverage of spatial location. The illustrations that it uses in the treatment of this topic are considerable and an excellent aid to understanding. Contains an excellent bibliography.

Lorie, James H., Peter Dodd, and Mary T. Hamilton. *The Stock Market: Theories and Evidence.* 2d ed. Homewood, Ill.: Richard D. Irwin, 1985.
An excellent introduction to many of the principles relevant to the valuation of common stocks. Contains a good discussion of the efficient markets hypothesis. Suitable for undergraduates.

Lucas, Robert E., and Thomas J. Sargent, eds. *Rational Expectations and Econometric Practice.* Minneapolis: University of Minnesota Press, 1981.
This collection of journal articles contains some of the seminal uses of the rational expectations approach to both empirical and theoretical work in economics. Also contains the original papers by John F. Muth. Suitable for advanced undergraduates and graduate students.

Luce, R. Duncan, and Howard Raiffa. *Games and Decisions.* New York: John Wiley & Sons, 1957.
A standard and very influential early introduction to game theory.

MacAvoy, Paul W. *Energy Policy: An Economic Analysis.* New York: W. W. Norton, 1983.
A standard college text for energy economics courses, MacAvoy's work offers a clear and concise analysis of the economics of the oil, gas, coal, and electrical power industries in the United States, and of the frequently counterproductive policies which were passed to regulate them following the oil crisis of 1973.

McCloskey, Donald. *The Rhetoric of Economics.* Madison: University of Wisconsin Press, 1985.
This widely discussed book is a criticism of positive economics by a former positive economist. Economic theory, statistics, and the use of evidence are considered as exercises in persuasion, and are evaluated as such.

McConnell, Campbell R., and Stanley Brue. *Economics.* 11th ed. New York: McGraw-Hill, 1990.
This popular textbook presents the kinked demand curve model, the collusion model, the leader-follower model, and the game theory

model. Contains a very complete treatment of the collusion model and the leader-follower model. The authors devote a chapter to the topic of income inequality and redistribution policies. Chapter 37, "Income Distribution: Inequality and Poverty," includes a nontechnical balanced presentation of a wide range of income inequality issues. Chapter 22, "Rural Economics: The Farm Problem," covers some basic principles of agricultural economics.

McCulloch, J. Huston. "The Austrian Theory of the Marginal Use and of Ordinal Marginal Utility." *Zeitschrift für Nationalökonmie* 37, no. 3-4 (1977): 249-280.

A technical, but still readable, modern development of the Austrian theory of marginal utility.

_____. *Money and Inflation: A Monetarist View.* 2d ed. New York: Academic Press, 1982.

This 100-page paperback is designed to give college students an introduction to the analysis of inflation.

McEachern, William A. *Economics: A Contemporary Introduction.* Cincinnati: South-Western, 1991.

A college-level introductory text that explains substitution effects and the marginal rates of substitution, in both consumption and production, clearly and well in separate appendices. Supports the words with excellent graphical aids, printed in color. Especially good is the appendix to chapter 20. For readers who are interested in a clear explanation of the marginal rate of technical substitution.

McFadden, Daniel. "Cost, Revenue, and Profit Functions." In *Production Economics: A Dual Approach to Theory and Applications*, edited by Melvyn A. Fuss and Daniel McFadden. Amsterdam: North-Holland, 1978.

A formal piece on the technical relationships between cost and profit functions.

MacFadyen, Alan J., and Heather W. MacFadyen, eds. *Economic Psychology: Intersections in Theory and Applications.* New York: Elsevier Science, 1986.

A collection of largely conceptual and theoretical readings. Although some papers are relatively technical, it presents perhaps the broadest and most balanced view of the field including contributions from a broad range of psychologists and from economists.

Machlup, Fritz. "Monopoly and Competition: A Clarification of Market Positions." *American Economic Review* 26 (September, 1937): 445-451. Reprinted in *Readings in Microeconomics*, edited by David R. Kamerschen. Cleveland: World Publishing, 1967.

A clear explanation of various market structures by one of America's best-known economists.

Mack, Ruth P. "Economics of Consumption." In *A Survey of Contemporary Economics*. Vol. 2, edited by B. F. Haley. Homewood, Ill.: Richard D. Irwin, 1952.

Despite its age, this article contains an excellent discussion of the concept of income elasticity, some limitations of the concept, and caveats regarding its use.

MacKay, Alfred F. *Arrow's Theorem: The Paradox of Social Choice*. New Haven, Conn.: Yale University Press, 1980.

An excellent summary and critique of Arrow's theorem. MacKay, a professor of philosophy, succeeds in reducing Arrow's rather intimidating mathematical proofs to a manageable verbal treatment. Furthermore, MacKay—who is troubled by Arrow's conclusion—offers a possible escape from the paradox by suggesting that Arrow's theorem may be viewed as a peculiar sort of infinite regress. Useful to specialists, college students, and the general reader.

McKenna, C. J. *The Economics of Uncertainty*. New York: Oxford University Press, 1986.

An excellent exposition of the effects of uncertainty when applied to utility theory, the theory of the firm, futures markets, saving behavior, insurance, signaling, and search. Although familiarity with calculus is helpful, this is a superb introductory work for one interested in acquiring the techniques of analysis employed in the study of uncertainty.

McNulty, Paul J. "Economic Theory and the Meaning of Competition." *Quarterly Journal of Economics* 74 (November, 1960): 639-656. Reprinted in *Readings in Price Theory*, edited by Richard E. Neel. Cincinnati: South-Western, 1973.

Contains a somewhat difficult but understandable critical discussion of the inadequacy of the meaning of perfect competition in traditional economic theory. This traditional theory does not explain how and why competitive economies further economic growth. To understand the dynamic character of free markets, the meaning of competition in Adam Smith is more relevant.

Maddala, G. S., and Ellen Miller. *Microeconomics.* New York: McGraw-Hill, 1989.

Part 5 in this intermediate-level college economics text provides a good overview of the concepts of Pareto optimum, intertemporal optimum, and risk and uncertainty, with their applications in economics.

Maier, Charles S. "The Politics of Inflation in the Twentieth Century." In *The Political Economy of Inflation*, edited by Fred Hirsch and John H. Goldthorpe. London: Martin Robertson, 1978.

Contains a good discussion of hyperinflation and the politics that surrounded it in several countries.

Maital, Shlomo, ed. *Applied Behavioral Economics.* 2 vols. New York: New York University Press, 1988.

A very large collection of both theoretical and empirical research papers drawn from the 1986 International Conference on Economics and Psychology. Covers a broad range of topics including tax evasion, entrepreneurship, social security, the family, labor relations, and managerial behavior. The sheer size of this collection and the relatively technical nature of some papers make it of more interest to the specialist.

———. *Economic Games People Play.* New York: Basic Books, 1984.

A short but clear introduction to John von Neumann's theory. Suitable for a general audience.

———. *Minds, Markets, and Money: Psychological Foundations of Economic Behavior.* New York: Basic Books, 1982.

A concise, and perhaps the best, introduction to the field. While a little polemical in tone in some places, it is very readable and covers a broad range of topics, including economic socialization, human productivity, the psychology of borrowing, investment, inflation, gambling, and tax evasion. Suitable for a general audience.

Malinvaud, Edmond C. *The Theory of Unemployment Reconsidered.* Oxford, England: Basil Blackwell, 1977.

A representative study of the "French school" that is not too abstract or difficult for the general reader to understand.

Malkiel, Burton G. *A Random Walk Down Wall Street.* 4th ed. New York: W. W. Norton, 1985.

A very readable discussion of research on the stock market in the 1980's, including efficient markets, that is relevant to stock valuation. Suitable for undergraduates.

Malthus, Thomas Robert. *An Essay on the Principle of Population.* London: J. Johnson, 1798.

First published anonymously, this essay was a reaction against the overly optimistic and liberal views of William Godwin, the Marquis de Condorcet, and other intellectuals who believed that the condition of the human race could be improved through social and economic policies. Malthus argued that poverty and hunger were not the result of human institutions but rather that of natural forces, such as unmatched growth rates of population and means of subsistence.

_____ . *An Inquiry into the Nature and Progress of Rent.* 1815. Reprint. Baltimore: The Johns Hopkins University Press, 1903.

In this work, Malthus related an increase in rent to an increase in food prices, which in turn results from the difficulty of growing food for an ever-increasing population. Thus, the basis of his theory of rent is the application of the same principle that also underlies his theory of population.

_____ . *Principles of Political Economy.* 1820. Reprint of 2d ed. New York: Augustus M. Kelley, 1951.

In this book, Malthus expanded his theory of general gluts and showed that the cause of depressions and business slumps is the problem of inadequate effective demand. It was this contribution which brought him the admiration of John Maynard Keynes, who considered him his forerunner. As facts and history have contradicted the prognosis of his theory of population, Malthus' place in the history of economic thought rests mainly with his theory of general gluts.

Mandel, Ernest. *Long Waves of Capitalist Development.* Cambridge, U.K.: Cambridge University Press, 1980.

This small volume is based on Mandel's Marshall lectures at Cambridge University in 1978. Mandel divides the postwar period into two parts: the "golden years" before 1972, which surprised both Marxists and non-Marxists, and the subsequent stagnation. Mandel is sympathetic to long waves, or Kondratieff cycles, as an explanation for the stagnation after 1972. Other believers in Kondratieff, such as David Gordon, are mentioned.

Mann, Charles K., and Barbara Huddleston, eds. *Food Policy: Framework for Analysis and Action*. Bloomington: Indiana University Press, 1986.

Provides an excellent overview of all the issues of food policy analysis: production, consumption, nutrition, and political systems. The most noted writers on the subject have written articles and several country case studies are included.

Mansfield, Edwin, and Nariman Behravesh. *Economics U$A*. New York: W. W. Norton, 1986.

The companion volume to the Public Broadcasting Service (PBS) series of the same name, the book is a readable guide to the basic ideas of economics. The telecourse was designed to use economic events in the United States, present and past, to explain the principles of economics. The aim of the book is to show how the knowledge of those basic ideas can help foster an understanding of the complexities of the U.S. economy.

Mansfield, Edwin, John Rapoport, Anthony Romeo, Edmond Villani, Samuel Wagner, and Frank Jusic. *The Production and Application of New Industrial Technology*. New York: W. W. Norton, 1977.

A bit dated, but very thorough development of many of the topics related to innovation. Contains some statistical and graphical analysis, but is not too mathematical. Particularly appropriate for an academic investigation.

Marshall, Alfred. *Money, Credit, and Commerce*. London: Macmillan, 1929.

In a book written late in Marshall's life, he makes extensive use of offer curves in an appendix. They are a device that he had developed several decades earlier. Very attentive reading is required in order to follow the appendices.

——————. *Principles of Economics*. 9th variorum ed. London: Macmillan, 1961.

Marshall devised the core of what is called neoclassical economics. He wrote this book for an audience of enlightened businesspeople. All mathematics and graphs are in footnotes and appendices, and not in the text. His style is clear and facile, though sometimes tedious. He also tends to simplify his analysis to the point of sweeping much aside. Nevertheless, Marshall is the most accessible of the great economists.

Volume 1 of the ninth edition is the text of the eighth edition (Marshall's last revision, published in 1920) and is sufficient for nearly all readers.

Marx, Karl. *Capital: A Critique of Political Economy.* Edited by Friedrich Engels. 3 vols. New York: International Publishers, 1967.

This is the seminal work of the Marxist critique of capitalism. Marx's classic work on his theory of the functioning of capitalist economies. Contains his labor theory of value, which explains the source of profit as the ability of labor to produce surplus value. While this is a difficult book, it is rewarding.

_____. *The Grundrisse.* Edited and translated by David McLellan. New York: Harper & Row, 1971.

This book establishes the Marxist view of the linkage among distribution, exchange, and consumption. Contains Marx's analyses on exploitation, the role of money, and alienation.

_____. *Wage-Labour and Capital.* Peking: Foreign Languages Press, 1978.

This fifty-three page collection of articles is one of Marx's first attempts to define his understanding of the essence of capitalist society. Here he plainly declares that the core of capitalism is wage labor: labor of workers exploited by the capitalist class for the sake of surplus value (profit).

Marx, Karl, and Friedrich Engels. *The German Ideology.* Edited by C. J. Arthur. New York: International Publishers, 1970.

This passionate masterpiece of young Marx and Engels (not intended for publication) was published because it contained "the new world outlook." The development of the division of labor and private property and their subsequent abolition in communist society are the main themes of the manuscript.

Meadows, Donella H., et al. *The Limits to Growth: A Report for the Club of Rome's Project on the Predicament of Mankind.* New York: Universe Books, 1974.

This study caused a stir when first published. Many economists have refuted the thesis of this book, which has decreased its interest for some. The position that the world is on the verge of resource exhaustion, however, remains a serious concern.

Meimaroglon, M. C. "Break-Even Analysis with Stepwise Varying Marginal Costs and Revenues." *Budgeting* 13 (November, 1964): 1-7.

A good article that shows how break-even analysis can be used in conditions in which both price and cost per unit are changing.

Meiselman, David, and Arthur Laffer, eds. *The Phenomenon of Worldwide Inflation*. Washington, D.C.: American Enterprise Institute, 1975.
Thoughtful and readable conference papers. Those by Meiselman, James Duesenberry, and Edwin Phelps are particularly relevant to demand-pull inflation.

Menger, Carl. *Principles of Economics*. Translated by J. Dingwall and B.F. Hoselitz. 1871. Reprint. New York: New York University Press, 1981.
In addition to presenting the Austrian contribution to the marginalist revolution, there is the first, brilliant statement of the Austrian theory of money in chapter 8.

Metzger, Robert W. *Elementary Mathematical Programming*. New York: John Wiley & Sons, 1958.
An elementary description of several methods of mathematical programming. This book was designed for people in business and industry with a minimal mathematical background.

Milgate, Murray. "Equilibrium: Development of the Concept." In *The New Palgrave: A Dictionary of Economics*, edited by John Eatwell, Murray Milgate, and Peter Newman. New York: Stockton Press, 1987.
A brief but thorough summary of the development of the concept of equilibrium and its contribution to economic theory. For those with little formal training in economics, extended descriptions of long-run, general, and partial equilibrium and related topics would be difficult to wade through. This reading provides a solid introduction without excessive detail. Most suitable for college students.

Mill, John Stuart. *Principles of Political Economy*. Reprint. Toronto: Toronto University Press, 1965.
Mill was one of the major figures in the evolution of classical and neoclassical economic thought. He was also an ardent proponent of land reforms that would product a class of small farms with peasant proprietors. Chapters 6 through 10 in book 2 contain the best statement of the classical land reform argument.

Miller, Roger L. *Economics Today*. New York: Harper & Row, 1979.
A comprehensive, readable, and understandable presentation of the subject of economics. Single-page biographical sketches of leading economists give their views and contributions to the field. The princi-

ples of economics as a social science are related by examples, activities, problems, and events in the real world.

Miller, Roger LeRoy, and Russell Shannon. *The Economics of Macro Issues*. 5th ed. St. Paul, Minn.: West, 1986.

This interesting collection of short articles on macroeconomic topics includes a discussion of political business cycles and industrial policy, both of which are issues that some charge illustrate the shortsightedness of government. Suitable for a general audience.

Miller, Ronald E., and Peter D. Blair. *Input-Output Analysis: Foundations and Extensions*. Englewood Cliffs, N.J.: Prentice-Hall, 1985.

This publication is widely used as a textbook and reference work on input-output analysis. The basic model and some of its extensions are presented in detail. The authors assume a knowledge of matrix algebra, making the book appropriate for the advanced undergraduate level and above.

Mills, Edwin S., and Bruce W. Hamilton. *Urban Economics*. 4th ed. Glenview. Ill.: Scott, Foresman, 1989.

Absolutely the best book on urban economics for the general reader. The book provides a comprehensive overview of the field. It is one of the few books in the field that is not too technical for most readers.

Minford, Patrick, and David Peel. *Rational Expectations and the New Macroeconomics*. Oxford, England: Basil Blackwell, 1983.

This reference book will be useful to graduate students and researchers who want to work their way through the Keynesian/New Classical debates. It explains the mathematics of the New Classical proposition that discretionary policy is ineffective, but concludes that built-in stabilizers remain effective because of their informational advantage.

Mirowski, Philip. *More Heat than Light*. Cambridge, England: Cambridge University Press, 1989.

Mirowski draws out the influence of physics on the development of economic theories, particularly neoclassical economics, and critically analyzes the inherent limitations of this activity. Brilliant and stimulating, but difficult for those not familiar with physics or the history of economics.

Mises, Ludwig von. "Economic Calculation in the Socialist Common-wealth." In *Collectivist Economic Planning*, edited by Friedrich A. von Hayek. London: Routledge, 1935.
The most famous article in the entire controversy over central planning. Writing in 1920, when War Communism in Soviet Russia had brought the country's economy to near-total collapse, Mises argued that a socialist economy could not achieve economic efficiency. To do so, calculation in a common measure is needed; otherwise, competing projects cannot be rationally assessed. Only money can fulfill this role, and in socialism, no money exists.

_____. *Human Action*. Chicago: Henry Regnery, 1966.
The leading proponent of Austrian economics and Friedrich A. von Hayek's mentor, Mises contends that the Hayek effect should be rejected: Increases in spending on machinery need not increase pro-ductivity. The effect is not properly part of Austrian business cycle theory and leads to the policy prescription of "forced saving," which Mises rejects. Mises contends that the law of diminishing returns can be derived from the self-evident axiom that human beings act. The law requires no empirical confirmation. Mises rejects the use of general equilibrium analysis as based on a model that does not apply to the real world. Solving the equations avails the central planner nothing. Market socialism also is indicted. The requirements for a workable market include free trading in shares, and no system with this feature qualifies as socialist.

_____. *Socialism*. Indianapolis: Liberty Fund, 1981.
A reprint of a work whose German original appeared in 1922, this is Mises' most comprehensive assessment of socialism. He replies to critics of his calculation argument. He expresses surprise at efforts to introduce money into socialist systems, which violates the concept of socialism as it has been ordinarily understood. Although market social-ism is not directly analyzed, the closely related system of workers' cooperatives is treated in detail in the section entitled "Syndicalism."

_____. *The Theory of Money and Credit*. Translated by H. E. Batson. London: Jonathan Cape, 1934.
This work first appeared in German in 1912 and is the fundamental Austrian work on monetary theory. It employs Wicksellian insights extensively and introduces the concept of forced savings. The notion of the natural rate of interest is basic to the book's fundamental aim: the integration of monetary theory with price theory.

Mishan, E. J. *Cost Benefit Analysis*. Rev. ed. New York: Praeger, 1976.
    Mishan is a welfare economist, and, while introducing the techniques
    of cost-benefit analysis, he also explains the difference between the
    task of analyzing a project for a profit making firm and analyzing one
    for the government whose objective is not profit but social welfare.

Modigliani, Franco. *The Debate over Stabilization Policy*. New York:
Cambridge University Press, 1986.
    Consists of four lectures given by Nobel laureate Modigliani at Luigi
    Bocconi University. Shows how a particular macroeconomic model,
    the IS-LM model, can be used to formulate economic policy and to
    analyze the economy. The reader should have some familiarity with
    the IS-LM model.

_____ . "Life Cycle, Individual Thrift, and the Wealth of Nations." *American Economic Review* 76 (June, 1986): 297-313.
    This article is Modigliani's Nobel lecture in which he develops many
    of the implications of the life-cycle permanent income hypothesis.

Morgan, Theodore. "The Theory of Error in Centrally Directed Systems."
Quarterly Journal of Economics 78 (August, 1964): 395-419.
    This is an excellent and very readable, although quite old, article.
    Morgan provides valuable insights into command economies by com-
    paring aspects of Soviet central planning and decision making in a large
    corporation.

Morley, Samuel. *Inflation and Unemployment*. Chicago: Dryden Press,
1983.
    A balanced presentation of both the classical and Keynesian views of
    the Phillips curve. Appropriate for both undergraduates and the general
    reader.

Mueller, Dennis C. *Public Choice II: A Revised Edition of Public Choice*.
Cambridge, England: Cambridge University Press, 1989.
    A revision and expansion of Mueller's 1979 work to include coverage
    of the large body of public choice scholarship that had been published
    in the interval. Reflecting the rapid growth of the field, this volume is
    more than 40 percent longer than its predecessor. Mueller did make an
    effort to make this version more "student friendly," but the work
    remains tough going for nonspecialists. Insofar as Mueller's personal
    value judgments intrude, his bias is in the direction of rebutting the
    "pessimistic interpretation of the implications of the social-public

choice literature . . . regarding the potential of democratic institutions."

Murad, Anatol. *What Keynes Means: A Critical Clarification of the Economic Theories of John Maynard Keynes*. New York: Bookman Associates, 1962.

A brief and well-written analysis of the major parts of John Maynard Keynes's theories, including the consumption function and the marginal propensity to consume, and the importance of each part of the theory to the entire scheme.

Mushkin, Selma J., ed. *Public Prices for Public Products*. Washington, D.C.: Urban Institute, 1972.

Perhaps the most complete set of readings on the topic in existence. A few of the articles may be difficult for the nonspecialist, but most are easy to follow.

Myrdal, Gunnar. "What Is Development?" *Journal of Economic Issues* 8 (December, 1974): 729-736.

The Nobel laureate Myrdal is recognized for his emphasis on noneconomic variables as well as the dynamics of circular and cumulative causation and their relevance to economic analysis. Myrdal's definition of development as "the movement upward of the entire social system" represents the opposite polarity from that of the neoclassical conception. Though he is internationally recognized as one of the leading social scientists of the twentieth century, his concepts and theories have not penetrated the basic U.S. textbooks and curriculum (mainstream economics). Major works by Myrdal are the *Asian Drama* (1968) and *Rich Lands and Poor* (1957).

Nagle, Thomas T. *The Strategy and Tactics of Pricing*. Englewood Cliffs, N.J.: Prentice-Hall, 1987.

An extensive treatment of pricing by private firms, in both theory and practice, which is easily accessible for the average reader.

Naylor, Thomas H. *Computer Simulation Experiments with Models of Economic Systems*. New York: John Wiley & Sons, 1971.

The concepts are illustrated by examples of simulations in economics. This book is different from other books, because it provides detailed discussions and examples of simulations of the models developed by firms and industries.

Nell, Edward. *Prosperity and Public Spending: Transformational Growth and the Role of Government*. Winchester, Mass.: Unwin Hyman, 1988.
A critical evaluation of supply-side economics. Argues that the role of government, including government deficits, is essential to the maintenance of economic prosperity. Argues that deficits are not necessarily inflationary, nor the source of "crowding out," nor does public debt create burden on future generations. Discusses the questions of public expenditure policy in a demand-constrained environment. Strong Keynesian orientation. Primarily suited to the more specialized readers. Index included.

Nelson, Richard, and Sidney Winter. *An Evolutionary Theory of Economic Change*. Cambridge, Mass.: Harvard University Press, 1982.
A lucidly written, but somewhat advanced, treatment of the inadequacies of high neoclassical theory, with particular regard to perfect knowledge and conflicting interests in large-scale organizations. Contains a rich treatment of Joseph Schumpeter's theories. Nelson and Winter's own model of a stochastically based evolutionary system constitutes half the book. A major contribution to economic analysis.

Nerlove, Marc. *Estimation and Identification of Cobb-Douglas Production Functions*. Chicago: Rand McNally, 1965.
The main thrust of this work is to apply modern production theory empirically. Focusing on the Cobb-Douglas production function, Nerlove demonstrates how this production formula has been, and can be, statistically estimated.

Ng, Yew-Kwang. "Harcourt's Survey of Capital Theory." *Economic Record* 50 (March, 1974): 119-129.
Ng argues that Piero Sraffa's model does not provide a complete account of price. Methods of production are given at the outset, and why particular technique is used receives no explanation. Sraffa ignores the role of consumer preferences in determining some of the key variables in his system.

_____. "Towards a Theory of Third Best." *Public Finance* 21, no. 1 (1967): 1-15.
An extension of the theory of the second best, aimed at developing decision rules for general, rather than specific, cases that can be helpful in incorporating the constraints that prevent first-best solutions in ways that generally will produce socially desired results.

Nicholson, Walter A. *Microeconomic Theory*. 4th ed. Chicago: Dryden Press, 1989.

One does not find offer curves discussed as a tool of general equilibrium theory in many intermediate microeconomic textbooks, but this is a relatively advanced intermediate book that contains a good discussion of the subject.

Nordhaus, William D. "What's Wrong with a Declining National Savings Rate?" *Challenge* 32 (July/August, 1989): 22-26.

One article from a series in *Challenge* which examines the low saving rate of the United States during the 1980's. Nordhaus argues that consumption must be lowered to promote economic growth and higher future living standards through more investment.

Nozick, Robert. *Anarchy, State, and Utopia*. Oxford, England: Basil Blackwell, 1974.

Nozick is a philosopher who provides a nonutilitarian alternative based on "fair exchange" of "just entitlements." His conclusions represent the nonegalitarian extreme.

O'Donnell, R. M. *Keynes: Philosophy, Economics, and Politics*. London: Macmillan, 1989.

A thorough, well-written, lucid examination of Keynes's work. Technical discussions are minimal. The Australian author carefully handles his sources, and there are many fine quotations culled from Keynes's writings on a variety of relevant topics. Chapter notes are extensive and informative and the annotated bibliography helpful, as is the double-columned index.

O'Driscoll, Gerald P., Jr., ed. *Adam Smith and Modern Political Economy: Bicentennial Essays on "The Wealth of Nations."* Ames: Iowa State University Press, 1979.

Incorporates ten of eleven bicentennial papers delivered at the University of California at Santa Barbara in early 1976. Joseph Cropsey's essay on the invisible hand is especially well done, including the distinction between doing what one desires and self-legislation.

Okun, Arthur. *Economics for Policy Making*. Edited by J. Pechman. Washington, D.C.: Brookings Institution, 1983.

A collection of essays by a chief adviser to Presidents John F. Kennedy and Lyndon B. Johnson who was a very influential spokesman and contributor to the Keynesian view of the Phillips curve. Appropriate for almost any reader, from the general audience to graduate students.

_____. *Equality and Efficiency: The Big Tradeoff.* Washington, D.C.: Brookings Institution, 1975.

Considered to be a classic statement on the issues raised by attempts to increase the equality of wages. Offers an engaging and accessible framework for thinking about distributional issues and incorporating them into a social welfare framework. The classic statement of looking at the costs and benefits of income redistribution policies. Very readable.

Olson, Mancur L. *The Logic of Collective Action.* Cambridge, Mass.: Harvard University Press, 1965.

Olson attempts to generalize and apply the theory of public goods.

Panico, Carlo. *Interest and Profit in the Theories of Value and Distribution.* New York: St. Martin's Press, 1988.

Examines various theoretical approaches to profit, including the neoclassical approach and Karl Marx's approach, at a fairly advanced level.

Pasinetti, Luigi, and Roberto Scazzieri. "Capital Theory: Paradoxes." In *The New Palgrave: A Dictionary of Economics*, edited by John Eatwell, Murray Milgate, and Peter Newman. London: Macmillan, 1987.

A concise and clear summary of the capital controversy by one of its leading participants. Pasinetti. Suitable for undergraduate economics students as well as professional economists.

Pasour, E. C., Jr. "Economic Efficiency: Touchstone or Mirage?" *The Intercollegiate Review* 17 (Fall/Winter, 1981): 33-44.

Coming from an Austrian school point of view, this paper argues that the theoretical standard of economic efficiency is practically unattainable and that common sense must be used in the real world. A good antidote to applying theory too strictly. Accessible to college and advanced high school students.

Patinkin, Don. *Money, Interest, and Prices.* White Plains, N.Y.: Row, Peterson, 1956. 2d ed. New York: Harper & Row, 1965.

These are the definitive works on the real balance effect. It is put into a context of a fully developed micro-macro theoretical model. Emphasis shifts from the disequilibrium approach (first edition) to the wealth-based approach (second edition).

_____. "Price Flexibility and Full Employment." *American Economic Review* 38 (September, 1948): 543-564.

Reviews the debate concerning whether price reductions can restore full employment when aggregate demand has declined. This was the context out of which the real balance effect emerged.

Peach, James. "Distribution and Economic Progress." In *Evolutionary Economics*, edited by Marc Tool. 2 vols. Armonk, N.Y.: M. E. Sharpe, 1988.

The merits of this work, which is part of a collection of essays on institutional economics, are its highlighting of the role that power plays in determining the distribution of a society's output.

Peterson, Wallace C. *Income, Employment, and Economic Growth*. 5th ed. New York: W. W. Norton, 1948.

A basic college undergraduate text in macroeconomics with a thorough, simplified version of the Harrod-Domar model, minimizing its mathematical constructs.

Phelps, Edmund. *Inflation Policy and Unemployment Theory: The Cost Benefit Approach to Monetary Planning*. New York: W. W. Norton, 1972.

This classic book combines a discussion of a theory behind the Phillips curve, the costs of inflation and unemployment, and the implications of the curve for policy-making. Accessible to the general reader and to undergraduates. Although a bit dated, it would also be interesting reading for graduate students.

Phlips, Louis. *Applied Consumption Analysis*. Rev. ed. Amsterdam: North-Holland, 1983.

An excellent survey of both demand theory and the econometric estimation of demand relationships. Phlips is successful in showing the connection between pure theory and empirical modeling. Several topics are covered including cost-of-living indexes, dynamic demand functions, and dynamic demand systems.

_____. *The Economics of Imperfect Information*. New York: Cambridge University Press, 1988.

Chapter 4 is devoted to auctions. Most readers will benefit from reading the first five pages of chapter 4; the rest of that chapter is technical and suitable for those with a solid background in economics and statistics.

Pigou, Arthur. *The Economics of Welfare*. London: Macmillan, 1920.

Very influential, a classic in the special field of welfare economics. Pigou distinguishes "social cost" from "private cost" and "social benefit" from "private benefit." He proposes that governments tax producers in order to eliminate an excess of social cost over private cost and subsidize consumers in order to eliminate an excess of social benefit over private benefit. Recommended for specialists and college students.

_____ , ed. *Memorials of Alfred Marshall*. London: Macmillan, 1925.

Pigou was Alfred Marshall's student, his successor to the chair in political economy at Cambridge and himself a major figure in the development of neoclassical economics. This volume, compiled after Marshall's death, contains obituaries of Marshall (including John Maynard Keynes's magnificent biographical obituary), selections from Marshall's writings, and correspondence.

Polanyi, Karl. *The Great Transformation*. New York: Farrar and Rinehart, 1944.

A brilliantly conceived, splendidly written, and provocative work of great value to specialists and nonspecialists alike. No one else has fastened so insightfully on the problems of acquainting the eighteenth century world with the idea of a market economy. Invaluable. Few footnotes; the bibliography and index are modest but helpful.

Polinsky, A. Mitchell. *An Introduction to Law and Economics*. Boston: Little, Brown, 1983.

A strikingly successful short introduction to the field. Polinsky is trained in both economics and the law, and he is an excellent pedagogue. Contains numerous quantitative examples, but presupposes no mathematical training beyond simple arithmetic. One particularly attractive feature of the book is its inclusion of the effects of insurance on the economic analysis of torts.

Pollak, Robert A. *The Theory of the Cost of Living Index*. New York: Oxford University Press, 1989.

A collection of four essays on the theory of cost of living. Written at a fairly high level.

Pool, John Charles, and Ross M. LaRoe. *The Instant Economist*. Reading, Mass.: Addison-Wesley, 1985.

A small paperback for noneconomists, written in plain, nontechnical language. Chapter 1 deals with macroeconomics from a business perspective. Fiscal and monetary policy are explained without graphs.

Popper, Karl R. *The Logic of Scientific Discovery*. London: Hutchinson University Library, 1959.

An extremely influential work on scientific method. Many economists regard it as the key work in this area. Although not a logical positivist, Popper maintains that normative statements are imperatives that cannot be deduced from facts and cannot be proved by other means.

Porter, Michael. *The Competitive Advantage of Nations*. New York: Free Press, 1990.

Based on his assessment of the competitive advantages of the United States, Porter advocates increased investment spending, research and development, and higher quality education. He dismisses the recovery of economic growth in the United States during the 1980's as "one-shot restructuring" the impact of which "may be short-lived."

Preston, A. J., and A. R. Pagan. *The Theory of Economic Policy: Statics and Dynamics*. Cambridge, England: Cambridge University Press, 1982.

For those who wish to review the most recent developments in the theory of economic policy, this book provides a complete theoretical treatment of both the static and dynamic aspects. It is intended for the mathematical sophisticate with a knowledge of matrix algebra.

Przeworski, Adam. *Capitalism and Social Democracy*. Cambridge, England: Cambridge University Press, 1985.

This book brings together some of the previously published articles and two new ones by Przeworski. These articles examine, from a neo-Marxist perspective, the dilemma of social democracy that moves more to the Right the more it tries to win electoral majority. Suitable for specialists and advanced students of history and political science.

Quirk, James P. *Intermediate Microeconomics*. 3d ed. Chicago: Science Research Associates, 1986.

This undergraduate price and value theory text provides an accessible treatment of all the standard microeconomic exercises in partial equilibrium. Especially good in the area of single market price determination.

Raiffa, Howard. *Decision Analysis*. Reading, Mass.: Addison-Wesley, 1968.

A classical introductory book on probability and decision making. Highly recommended for college students.

Raiklin, Ernest. "After Gorbachev? A Mechanism for the Transformation of Totalitarian State Capitalism into Authoritarian Mixed Capitalism." *The Journal of Social, Political and Economic Studies* 14 (1989): 1-105. This 105-page piece outlines the contemporary hazards facing the Soviet socioeconomic and political system and remedies for overcoming them. It points out the most probable road Soviet society might take. Accompanied by an updated bibliography on the subject.

_____. "The Soviet Union in Transition (The Question Is Open to Discussion)." *International Journal of Social Economics* 15, no. 7 (1988). This article discusses the nature of Soviet society, the Soviet problems, and the menu of solutions available to the Soviet leadership.

Ramsey, Frank P. "A Mathematical Theory of Saving." *Economic Journal* 38 (December, 1928): 543-559. Reflecting his distaste for impatience because of the underestimation of the future, Ramsey represents lifetime utility as the undiscounted sum of each year's utility. If there is impatience in this model, then it would only be because incomes are increasing over time.

Ranadive, K. R. *Income Distribution: The Unsolved Puzzle.* Oxford, England: Oxford University Press, 1978. A very good introduction to the various theories of distribution. Advanced, but not overly so.

Randall, Alan. "Market Solutions to Externality Problems: Theory and Practice." *American Journal of Agricultural Economics* 54 (May, 1972): 175-183. Randall examines the applicability of Coase's theorem when legal liability rules change. The article is a bit more difficult than the others listed here but the ideas should be grasped at the undergraduate level or above.

Rasmusen, Eric. *Game Theory and Information.* New York: Basil Blackwell, 1989. A technical text suitable for upper-level undergraduate students or graduate audiences. Chapter 11 deals with both private-value and common-value auctions. General readers should examine the first two sections of chapter 11.

Rawls, John. *A Theory of Justice*. Cambridge, Mass.: Harvard University Press, 1971.
Rawls is a philosopher seeking the ethical foundations underlying social welfare functions.

Reisman, David. *Thorstein Veblen: A Critical Interpretation*. New York: Charles Scribner's Sons, 1960.
A brief, well-written, critical analysis of Veblen and his career that respectfully defuses Veblen's caricature of the leisure class. A fine corrective to the prejudices of Veblen devotees. Contains few notes, a good select bibliography, and a useful index. An essential source.

Rhoads, Steven E. *The Economist's View of the World*. Cambridge, England: Cambridge University Press, 1985.
Designed for the noneconomist who wants to understand basic microeconomic concepts and how they influence (or could influence) governmental policy. Several chapter deal with the concept of externalities and their use in justifying government intervention.

Ricardo, David. *The Principles of Political Economy and Taxation*. 1821. 3d. ed. New York: E. P. Dutton, 1911.
There is no substitute for reading original sources, but reading Ricardo is not fun. Although there is no overtly technical material, there are intricate analytical arguments. Ricardo's writing style is also a source of difficulty. The rewards are worth the effort.

Richardson, H. W. *The New Urban Economics and Alternatives*. London: Dion, 1977.
This book limits itself to a discussion of the Muth/Mills-type urban model called the new urban economics. It is a bit technical for the general reader, but the text is substantial enough to allow the reader to skip the equations.

_____ . *Regional Economics*. New York: Praeger, 1969.
One of the standard graduate treatments of regional economics. Recommended for the serious and more advanced students.

Richardson, Jacques G., ed. *Windows on Creativity and Invention*. Mt. Airy, Md.: Lomond, 1988.
A very imaginative, UNESCO-generated collection of contributions by international practitioners in the artistic and scientific fields, providing mostly offbeat insights into the creative process, with references

to its intellectual and economic environments. Scantily illustrated but adequately annotated.

RIUS. *Marx for Beginners*. New York: Pantheon Books, 1974.
Presents the theory of Karl Marx in a fun, comic-book style. It gives thorough coverage of Marx's theory (history and origins, capital, labor, and the class struggle), presenting complex ideas in a digestible way.

Robbins, Lionel. *An Essay on the Nature and Significance of Economic Science*. London: Macmillan, 1935.
A classic statement on the methodology and subject matter of economics, this book stresses the role of logic and the central position of scarcity in economic theory. This book has had a very great influence on the development of economic theory. Although not completely Austrian in approach, it was quite sympathetic to this school and helped win for the Austrian approach a sympathetic hearing in Great Britain. Robbins' method is deductive, and he is very favorable to the ability of the market to meet the criteria of economic efficiency without the need for extensive government intervention.

Roberts, Paul Craig. *The Supply Side Revolution*. Cambridge, Mass.: Harvard University Press, 1984.
A leading supply-side economist's inside account of policy-making in Washington, D.C.

Robinson, Joan. *Accumulation of Capital*. 1956. Reprint. London: Macmillan, 1966.
The generalization of John Maynard Keynes's short-run theory of employment into the long run by one of Keynes's leading younger colleagues.

_____ . *Economic Heresies*. New York: Basic Books, 1971.
A critical look at the fundamental concepts and issues in the theories of price, distribution, and accumulation.

_____ . *The Theory of Imperfect Competition*. London: Macmillan, 1934.
Chapter 15, "Price Discrimination," describes price discrimination by a monopolist using graphical illustration. Chapter 16, "The Moral of Price Discrimination," examines whether price discrimination is harmful or beneficial to consumers or society as a whole. Suitable for college students.

Romano, Richard, and Melvin Leiman, eds. *Views on Capitalism*. Beverly Hills, Calif.: Glencoe Press, 1970.
A highly readable collection of essays on capitalism from conservative, liberal, and radical perspectives. Includes a broad range of authors, from Adam Smith to Karl Marx to Milton Friedman and Senator Daniel P. Moynihan.

Rosen, Sam. *National Income and Other Social Accounts*. New York: Holt, Rinehart and Winston, 1972.
Contains an excellent exposition of national income and product accounting. There have been some changes in the system of accounts since 1972, but this book remains helpful for gaining an understanding of national income accounting.

Rosenberg, Nathan, ed. *The Economics of Technological Change*. Baltimore: Penguin Books, 1971.
Contains several seminal papers exploring the causes and consequences of technological change. See especially those by Schumpeter, Schmookler, Nelson, Arrow, Mansfield, Abramovitz, Solow, and Denison.

_____. "Innovative Responses to Materials Shortages." *American Economic Review* 63 (May, 1973): 31-36.
Explores the way in which humans respond with creative technological change to short-term resource scarcities.

_____. *Inside the Black Box: Technology and Economics*. New York: Cambridge University Press, 1982.
Contains an excellent discussion of the relation between market structure and innovation. Also contains a historical and international perspective on the subject. Nontechnical and provides good references.

Rostow, Walt W. *The Stages of Economic Growth: A Non-Communist Manifesto*. Cambridge, England: Cambridge University Press, 1961.
This extremely influential book has guided much work in economic planning because it presents the theoretical stages through which a growing economy should develop and thus sets a framework for what steps planners should take in order to stimulate economic growth.

_____. *Theories of Economic Growth from David Hume to the Present*. New York: Oxford University Press, 1990.
A panoramic survey of ideas on the nature and causes of economic development.

Rothbard, Murray N. *Man, Economy, and State.* 2 vols. Princeton, N.J.: Van Nostrand, 1962.

  Gives a careful statement of the deductive proof of diminishing returns, by a leading American member of the Austrian school. Rothbard, like his mentor, Ludwig von Mises, is a deductivist. He contends that the premise of imperfect substitutability is capable of deductive proof.

Rowley, J. C. R., and P. K. Trivedi. *Econometrics of Investment.* New York: John Wiley & Sons, 1975.

  Integrates inventory investment in the broader theory of investment by the firm. Requires considerable mathematical and statistical sophistication.

Rowthorn, Bob. *Capitalism, Conflict, and Inflation.* London: Lawrence & Wishart, 1980.

  Rowthorn criticizes Piero Sraffa from a Marxist point of view. Sraffa's analysis of production is too abstract. It ignores the social dimension of production and leaves classes out of the account. By its emphasis on exchange values, it fails to account for the creation of surplus value. Only the use of labor values is adequate to this task.

Ruffin, Roy, and Paul R. Gregory. *Principles of Macroeconomics.* Glenview, Ill.: Scott, Foresman, 1986.

  An introductory book of macroeconomics. Provides an extensive discussion of the basics of the real and nominal gross national products as part of the national income and product accounts system. Also successfully relates this information to governmental policy and the framework of the whole economy.

Salvatore, Dominick. *Microeconomics.* New York: HarperCollins, 1991.

  An outstanding text that gives a particularly insightful presentation of supply theory, as based on the profit-maximizing (cost-minimizing) behavior of firms. A graphical derivation of market supply from firm cost curves lends greatly to the understanding of the nature of supply. The short-run and long-run distinction is carefully analyzed. A most thorough and highly recommended reference, quite accessible to those with very little background.

Samuelson, Paul A. "Complementarity: An Essay on the Fortieth Anniversary of the Hicks-Allen Revolution in Demand Theory." *Journal of Economic Literature* 12 (1974): 1255-1289.

Although this is somewhat technical in its discussion of complementarity as it relates to economic theory, it can be understood and enjoyed by the lay reader.

_____. "Diagrammatic Exposition of a Theory of Public Expenditure." *Review of Economics and Statistics* 37 (November, 1955): 350-356. Reprinted in *Microeconomics: Selected Readings*, edited by Edward Mansfield. New York: W. W. Norton, 1985.
One of Samuelson's two seminal articles on public goods. This article contains a considerable amount of technical economics, mostly graphical analysis, but is generally accessible to those with a basic grasp of intermediate microeconomic theory.

_____. *Economics*. New York: McGraw-Hill, 1948.
The first important principles of economics text to emphasize macroeconomic issues, and perhaps the first to use the simple production possibilities curve to illustrate the problems of scarcity and choice that confront every society.

_____. "An Exact Consumption-Loan Model of Interest." *Journal of Political Economy* 66 (December, 1958): 467-482.
Samuelson presents an alternative proof of von Neumann's theorem that the real rate of interest is equal to the biological growth rate, except that, instead of relying on production technologies, Samuelson completely abstracts from production and relies only on retirement provision.

_____. *Foundations of Economic Analysis*. Cambridge, Mass.: Harvard University Press, 1947.
Samuelson describes how a system of equations can be used to model an individual consumer's demands for goods and services, the supply of labor, and how such systems of equations also can be used to model an individual firm's supplies of goods and services and its demands for the inputs (including labor) that it needs to produce the goods and services that it supplies. He then shows how the consumers' and firms' equations can be combined into a system of equations that describes the behavior of the overall economy.

_____. "Interactions Between the Multiplier Analysis and the Principle of Acceleration." $I!Accelerator*Review of Economics and Statistics* 20 (May, 1939): 28-33.

The original article describing interaction between the multiplier and the accelerator.

_____ . "A Summing Up." *The Quarterly Journal of Economics* 80 (November, 1966): 568-583.

A concise summary of the debates on the reswitching of techniques given by one of the protagonists of the capital debates, Nobel laureate Samuelson. Suitable for undergraduates and specialists.

Samuelson, Paul A., and William D. Nordhaus. *Economics.* 13th ed. New York: McGraw-Hill, 1989.

Considered to be a classic. The five most popular models of oligopoly are presented, with emphasis on the collusion model, the limit-pricing model, and the kinked demand curve model.

Sargent, Thomas. *Rational Expectations and Inflation.* New York: Harper & Row, 1986.

A leading practitioner of the new classical approach to economics explains why the rational expectations view supports the anti-inflation efforts of U.S. President Ronald Reagan and British Prime Minister Margaret Thatcher. While there is some formal modeling, the book's verbal approach makes it both lively reading and accessible to a general audience.

Sato, Kazuo. *Production Functions and Aggregation.* Amsterdam: North-Holland, 1975.

Although the microeconomic theory of production is well understood, the study of macroeconomic or aggregate production functions is less established. This monograph is an examination of the nature, properties, and statistical estimation of aggregate production functions.

Say, Jean-Baptiste. *A Treatise on Political Economy.* Translated by C. R. Prinsep. 4th ed. Reprint. New York: Augustus M. Kelley, 1971.

Originally published in 1821, this is one of the most famous books in the history of economics. Say both extends and improves upon the earlier *An Inquiry into the Nature and Causes of the Wealth of Nations* by Adam Smith. Regarding Gresham's law, Say argues that the only appropriate role for government is to mint coins; government should never impose legal exchange rates between types of money.

Scherer, F. M. *Industrial Market Structure and Economic Performance.* Chicago: Rand McNally, 1980.

An excellent reference for understanding all the issues that are behind entry barriers. Some of the chapters may be a little intense for the beginner. The introductions and examples that are given, however, can be helpful to nonspecialists.

Schmukler, Nathan, and Edward Marcus, eds. *Inflation Through the Ages: Economic, Social, Psychological, and Historical Aspects.* New York: Columbia University Press, 1983.

This volume contains fifty-four papers extending over nearly nine hundred pages and providing a treasure trove of material. Contains Tobin's 1983 paper referred to above. Cost-push issues come out particularly in part 3, "Policy Issues." The quality of the articles is quite uneven.

Schreiber, Arthur F., and Richard B. Clemmer. *Economics of Urban Problems.* 3d ed. Boston: Houghton Mifflin, 1982.

This book focuses on applying urban economic theory to common urban problems. The problems of urban poverty, housing, transportation, pollution, and crime are emphasized.

Schultz, Henry. *The Theory and Measurement of Demand.* Chicago: University of Chicago Press, 1938.

The classic volume on statistical demand estimation, this book has a brief theoretical section, followed by numerous empirical studies.

Schultze, Charles L. *National Income Analysis.* Englewood Cliffs, N.J.: Prentice-Hall, 1971.

Though this book is dated, it provides the nontechnical reader with good definitions and explanations of national accounts.

Schumacher, E. F. *Small Is Beautiful: Economics as If People Mattered.* New York: Harper & Row, 1975.

This thought-provoking, 305-page paperback on meta-economics identifies a bigger-is-better bias of conventional economics, which allegedly ignores the needs of people, the environment, and the future. Schumacher argues that the market is the institutionalization of greed, and that the lack of a concept of "enough" destroys the human spirit.

Schumpeter, Joseph A. *Capitalism, Socialism, and Democracy.* 2d ed. New York: Harper & Brothers, 1947.

An unusual assessment of central planning by a leading Walrasian. Although hostile to socialism, Schumpeter maintains that the calculation argument fails. By valuing consumption goods, consumers automatically impute values to the factors of production that constitute them. There is no calculation problem, and work by Enrico Barone and Vilfredo Pareto showed this before Mises.

Schwartzman, David. *Economic Policy: An Agenda for the Nineties.* New York: Praeger, 1989.
Argues against the view that government deficit is the key economic problem, but that it should be reduced—mainly by increasing taxes. Contends that high interest rates of the early 1980's were the result of tight monetary policies. Critically examines the economic priorities faced by President George Bush. Advocates greater federal assistance for state and local government services. Selected bibliography. Index included.

Seidman, Laurence S. *Macroeconomics.* San Diego: Harcourt Brace Jovanovich, 1987.
An excellent intermediate college-level text containing one of the most up-to-date and evenhanded treatments of the savings function. Unlike many texts that ignore the relative income hypothesis, Seidman's text carefully and accurately integrates the latest work on the relative income approach into the discussion of the savings function.

_____. *Saving for America's Economic Future: Parables and Policies.* Armonk, N.Y.: M. E. Sharpe, 1990.
A fascinating and insightful set of policy recommendations directed toward assuring that the United States can maintain a high standard of living relative to that of other countries. Seidman's discussion touches on controversial topics such as consumption taxes, how to balance the federal budget, education vouchers, social security, and many others. Entertaining and accessible to a general audience.

Sen, Amartya, ed. *Growth Economics.* Harmondsworth, Middlesex, England: Penguin Books, 1971.
A collection of the classic articles written by the pioneers in growth theory. Although most of the articles are highly mathematical, there are some that do not involve too much mathematics and hence can be read by undergraduates. Appropriate for advanced undergraduates and specialists.

_____. *Poverty and Famines: An Essay on Entitlement and Deprivation.* Oxford, England: Clarendon Press, 1981.

Sen distinguishes between starvation caused by general lack of food and starvation caused by lack of entitlement to food. Because of the entitlement issue, Sen sees little value in trying to relate population to total food supply.

Shackle, G. L. S. *Epistemics and Economics: A Critique of Economic Doctrine.* Cambridge, England: Cambridge University Press, 1972.

This 482-page book is a classic in expectations theory within the economics discipline. Provides a philosophical view and the foundation for the theory of expectations with emphasis on the time dimension in decision making. Suitable for college students.

Shaikh, Anwar. "Capital as a Social Relation." In *The New Palgrave: A Dictionary of Economics*, edited by John Eatwell, Murray Milgate, and Peter Newman. London: Macmillan, 1987.

A clear summary of the interpretation of capital from a Marxian perspective. Suitable for a general audience.

_____. "Marx's Theory of Value and the 'Transformation Problem'." In *The Subtle Anatomy of Capitalism*, edited by Jesse Schwartz. Santa Monica, Calif.: Goodyear, 1977.

Begins with the centrality of production and its importance as a point of departure for the labor theory of value. The connection among values, direct prices, and prices of production, as well as the necessity of money, is analyzed with illuminating precision. A solution to the so-called transformation problem is presented.

Shand, Alexander H. *The Capitalist Alternative: An Introduction to Neo-Austrian Economics.* New York: New York University Press, 1984.

A wide-ranging survey of contemporary Austrian school economics.

Shapiro, Milton. *Foundations of the Market-Price System.* New York: St. Martin's Press, 1983.

A reprint of the author's Ph.D. dissertation. Introduces readers to the determination of market prices using supply and demand tools, and contains a bibliography that may be of some help to intermediate students. Difficult to read and definitely not for the novice.

Shapiro, Nina. "The Revolutionary Character of Post-Keynesian Economics." *Journal of Economic Issues* 11 (September, 1977): 3.

A clear statement of the connection between profits and investment, and the self-sustaining nature of the capitalist growth process, as contained in the theories of John Maynard Keynes and Michal Kalecki.

Sharp, Ansel, Charles A. Register, and Richard H. Leftwich. *The Economics of Social Issues*. Homewood, Ill.: BPI/Irwin, 1990.

This book introduces economic concepts by way of analyzing various social problems of the day. For example, price elasticity of supply is used in analyzing the (elastic) supply of physicians, when immigration of trained doctors is permitted. It is easy to read. To gain an insight into the uses of elasticity, rather than elasticity for its own sake, this book serves well.

Sheffrin, Steven. *Rational Expectations*. Cambridge, England: Cambridge University Press, 1983.

An excellent primer for understanding the rational expectations approach. Accessible to the general reader but could also be used as an introduction for undergraduates and graduate students.

Shephard, Ronald W. *Theory of Cost and Production Functions*. Princeton, N.J.: Princeton University Press, 1970.

The classic treatment of the duality relationships between production functions and cost functions. This book is necessarily rather technical, and it presumes some mathematical sophistication.

Shubik, Martin. *Game Theory in the Social Sciences*. 2 vols. Cambridge, Mass.: MIT Press, 1982.

An incisive survey of developments in the conceptual apparatus and applications of game theory which assesses its usefulness and record of performance in the social sciences.

Silberberg, Eugene. *The Structure of Economics*. 2d ed. New York: McGraw-Hill, 1990.

A technical survey of recent advanced theoretical developments in demand theory. Silberberg provides a brief exposition of demand estimation and several examples of functional form specification in chapter 11. He applies mathematical models to the theory of the firm, the theory of the consumer, general equilibrium analysis, and intertemporal optimization. This mathematical economics text places duality in its proper context by setting out the constrained optimization so frequently encountered in economics, then deriving Roy's Identity and Shephard's Lemma as special instances of duality. The first chapter of this textbook presents an overview of marginalist economics suitable for the general reader.

Silk, Leonard, ed. *Capitalism: The Moving Target.* New York: Praeger, 1974.

A collection of essays on the pros and cons of the modern, particularly the American, version of capitalist society, including the political and social institutions associated with a capitalist economy. Squarely faces some of the most troubling issues of modern capitalist societies, but offers few concrete solutions.

Simon, Julian L. *The Ultimate Resource.* Princeton, N.J.: Princeton University Press, 1981.

Simon is a controversial author and articulate spokesperson for the thesis that resources are not finite. The ultimate resource of the title is human intelligence.

Slawson, W. David. *The New Inflation: The Collapse of Free Markets.* Princeton, N.J.: Princeton University Press, 1981.

A particularly forceful and dogmatic statement of the cost-push view. Not surprisingly, Slawson ends with a plea for comprehensive government control of wages, prices, and many other variables. Not many present-day economists would support this.

Smith, Adam. *The Essential Adam Smith.* Edited by Robert L. Heilbroner and Laurence Malone. New York: W. W. Norton, 1988.

Contains selections from *An Inquiry into the Nature and Causes of the Wealth of Nations*, as well as Smith's other important book, *The Theory of Moral Sentiments.* Although the introductory essays before each section are excellent, the real treat here is Smith—there is no substitute for the real thing.

_____ . *An Inquiry into the Nature and Causes of the Wealth of Nations.* 1776. Reprint. New York: Modern Library, 1937.

This reasonably priced edition uses the introduction notes, marginal summary, and enlarged index of Edwin Cannan and is considered by many to be the definitive edition of this work. Rich, varied, fascinating, and diverse, the book is approximately one thousand pages of intelligent discourse about economy and society. It is the founding work of modern economics. Smith's was one of the first statements on the long-run tendency of profits to become zero, with nonzero profits leading to changes in production. Book 5 is Smith's analysis of the role of government in the economy. Chapter 1, "Expenses of the Sovereign or Commonwealth," deals with government expenditures. In the first systematic analysis of market economics, Smith laid the foundation for much of modern economics, including the relationship between time and supply elasticity. In addition to its historical importance, the book contains analyses of markets and government policies that remain relevant. Suitable for the general reader, and required reading for anyone who is truly interested in economics.

Smith, Vernon L. "Experimental Methods in Economics." In *The New Palgrave: A Dictionary of Economics*, edited by John Eatwell, Murray Milgate, and Peter Newman. London: Macmillan, 1987.
   The best introduction to experimental economics available in print in 1990. The presentation may be somewhat advanced for some readers.

_____ . "Microeconomic Systems as an Experimental Science." *American Economic Review* 72, no. 5 (1982): 923-955.
   The best introduction to the approach to experimental economics is outlined in this article, but the presentation may be somewhat advanced for some readers.

Smith, Vincent Kerry. *Monte Carlo Methods: Their Role for Econometrics*. Lexington, Mass.: Lexington Books, 1973.
   A good survey of the role of Monte Carlo simulations in the evaluation of estimation techniques in econometrics. Provides an extensive list of references of applications of Monte Carlo methods in the comparison of econometric estimators. Suitable for college students.

Solberg, Eric J. *Intermediate Microeconomics*. Plano, Tex.: Business Publications, 1982.
   A good modern undergraduate text in microeconomics in which Solberg clearly presents axiomatic consumer theory as distinct from the nineteenth century marginalist perspective, which still dominates many texts.

Solow, Robert M. *Capital Theory and the Rate of Return*. Amsterdam: North-Holland, 1963.
   A booklet based on one of Solow's lectures delivered at the F. de Vrier Foundation in The Netherlands. It clearly highlights the salient feature of neoclassical capital theory without using too much mathematics. Suitable for both undergraduate students and professional economists.

_____. *Growth Theory: An Exposition*. Oxford, England: Oxford University Press, 1970.

Based on a lecture given by Solow, who won the Nobel Prize for his pioneering work in growth theory. Without using much mathematics, this short booklet focuses on one-sector growth models and discusses their policy implications. Appropriate for undergraduates and economists.

_____. "Technical Change and Aggregate Production Function," *Review of Economics and Statistics* 39 (August, 1957): 13-32.

One of numerous articles in the 1950's and early 1960's that argued that technology was the missing element in most neoclassical thinking on growth. Solow pioneered the distinction between embodied and disembodied capital.

Sombart, Werner. *The Quintessence of Capitalism: A Study of the History and Psychology of the Modern Business Man*. New York: Howard Fertig, 1967.

Combines history, religion, psychology, statistics, and philosophy to give a living picture of the modern businessperson in capitalist society. Sombart finds the explanation of modern economic organization in the spirit of the modern businessperson, and he traces the development of that spirit across wide ranges of space and time.

Sommers, Albert T. *The U.S. Economy Demystified*. Lexington, Mass.: Lexington Books, 1985.

A simple, readable description of the national income and product accounts. Explains the concepts of real and nominal GNPs as part of the complex economic system in which consumers live, work, save, and invest and provides a framework in which the reader can insert information about the real and nominal GNPs. One of the few books to discuss changes in the real money supply.

Sowell, Thomas. *Classical Economics Reconsidered*. Princeton, N.J.: Princeton University Press, 1974.

A brief (152-page) but excellent survey of the key propositions and implications of the classical school of economics. The author discusses classical economics both as a social philosophy and as a method of technical analysis. Suitable for college students.

Spencer, Milton H. *Contemporary Economics*. 7th ed. New York: Worth, 1990.

Consumer surplus is presented in a modern setting to assist one in understanding the concept. It must be recognized that the topic is closely linked to utility analysis of consumer demand. Margin concepts are also explained. The more probing reader may find the illustrations challenging.

Sraffa, Piero. *Production of Commodities by Means of Commodities.* Cambridge, England: Cambridge University Press, 1960.
The fundamental work in which Sraffa introduced his model. Although it does not use mathematics, it is a difficult work and is probably best approached after the other items listed. Written in a very compressed style. No political or social applications of the system are discussed.

Starr, Philip C. *Economics: Principles in Action.* Belmont, Calif.: Wadsworth, 1988.
Starr presents economic principles in a traditional format but with analytical illustrations which might be too difficult for the general reader. Nevertheless, he presents a clear statement of the link between microeconomics and macroeconomics. Also contains a good glossary of economic terms.

Steedman, Ian. *Marx After Sraffa.* London: New Left Books, 1978.
This book probably did more than any other to popularize Piero Sraffa's model. Supports a reconstruction of Marxism using Sraffa and vigorously rejects the labor theory of value. The book is also a key work on the rise of analytic Marxism.

Steindl, Josef. *Maturity and Stagnation in American Capitalism.* New York: Monthly Review Press, 1976.
A serious and technically competent Marxian analysis of the Great Depression in the United States in the 1930's, with a rigorous analytical framework and careful use of extensive statistical data. It was originally published in 1952, when growth rather than stagnation was more apparent. This book lays bare what Karl Marx called capitalism's "laws of motion" and is recognized as one of the most original and important contributions to the study of monopoly capitalism. According to Steindl, the function of competition is the elimination or prevention of excess capacity, which leads to a lower rate of profit and a tendency toward stagnation. Oligopoly leads to an increase in profit margins and a fall in effective demand. Steindl's stagnation thesis has become more relevant since 1970.

Stigler, George J. "The Economics of Information." *Journal of Political Economy* 69, no. 3 (1961): 213-225.
The classic article on the importance of information, the antithesis of uncertainty, with application to search theory.

_____ . *Essays in the History of Economics.* Chicago: University of Chicago Press, 1965.
Contains two of the best historical synopses of demand theory and empirical demand studies, respectively, in Stigler's "The Development of Utility Theory" (chapter 5) and "The Early History of Empirical Studies of Consumer Behavior" (chapter 7). Given their readability and insight, these writings should be the first that are consulted by the novice.

_____ . "Notes on the History of the Giffen Paradox." *Journal of Political Economy* 55 (April, 1947): 152-156.
An excellent summary of the first fifty years' history of the Giffen paradox. Examines all the evidence available, including Giffen's writings, and draws the conclusion that there is very little evidence that Giffen goods exist.

_____ . "Perfect Competition, Historically Contemplated." In *Essays in the History of Economics.* Chicago: University of Chicago Press, 1961.
A somewhat more difficult survey by a Nobel Prize winner in economics. Traces the ambiguities and difficulties in the definition of competition from the time of Adam Smith. The evolution to the present rigorous definition is described. A classic essay, and the general reader who is familiar with introductory economics should be able to follow the argument.

_____ . *Production and Distribution Theories.* New York: Macmillan, 1946.
A careful analysis of the main approaches to price and wage determination by a Nobel laureate. The neo-Ricardian school is not covered, but particularly valuable is Stigler's discussion of the controversy between John Bates Clark and Frank H. Knight. The latter questioned Clark's derivation of the justice of capitalism from the theory of marginal productivity.

_____ . *Production and Distribution Theories: The Formative Period.* New York: Macmillan, 1941.

Developed from Stigler's Ph.D. thesis, this critical survey chronicles the development of the marginal productivity theory and its relationship to a cohesive theory of distribution. The coverage spans the work of ten primary economists from 1870 to 1895.

_____. *The Theory of Price*. 4th ed. New York: Macmillan, 1987. Sums up the case for and against the existence of Giffen goods, and offers additional argument as evidence against their existence. A very readable and intuitive treatment of the relationship between production and costs is found in chapters 7 through 10. Stigler has contributed in an integral way to modern economists' perceptions of supply. Costs, externalities, and supply are discussed; the market supply for a factor of production, such as labor, also is examined.

Stokey, Edith, and Richard Zeckhauser. *A Primer for Policy Analysis*. New York: W. W. Norton, 1982.
Written from the perspective of decision analysis and mathematical techniques. Places cost-benefit analysis in that perspective, as well as providing a simple introduction to many of the mathematical techniques used by economists.

Strachey, John. *The Nature of Capitalist Crisis*. New York: Covici, Friede, 1935.
A distinctly pro-Marxist tract which sets out to explain how the capitalist world created the conditions that led to the Great Depression of the 1930's. Offers Marxist solutions, based heavily on the content of Marx's major work, *Das Kapital* (1867; *Capital*, 1886).

Survey of Current Business. 1920-
A monthly publication from the Bureau of Economic Analysis of the Department of Commerce that contains recent estimates of the real and nominal GNPs and other national income and product accounts items, as well as related articles on national income accounting.

Susskind, Charles. *Understanding Technology*. Baltimore: The Johns Hopkins University Press, 1973.
Still a very fundamental and simple but comprehensive account of the topic. It covers the history of technology as well as its relationship to ideologies, values, and social and ethical problems. Barely but attractively illustrated. Informative indexes.

Sweezy, Paul. *The Theory of Capitalist Development*. Oxford, England: Oxford University Press, 1941.

A definitive examination of the schools of Marxist thought. The author was a leading U.S. Marxist and well schooled in modern economic theory. This classic has not been challenged or even approached by any later study.

Tawney, Richard H. *Equality.* 1931. Reprint. London: Unwin Books, 1964.
Not only highlights the historical and institutional factors that play an important role in distribution but also presents a candid, and convincing, argument as to the normative aspects and implications of questions of distribution.

Temin, Peter. *Lessons from the Great Depression.* Cambridge, Mass.: MIT Press, 1989.
In these three lectures delivered at Oxford University, Temin looks at the international causes of the Great Depression. The attempt to restore the international gold standard and the continuation of deflationary thinking behind the gold standard are prime suspects.

Thomas, Robert Paul. *Microeconomic Applications: Understanding the American Economy.* Belmont, Calif.: Wadsworth, 1981.
Presents microeconomic issues in a simple and concise style which the general reader will understand. Avoids the use of graphical analysis, and the examples that are used are clear and direct. The key points at the end of each chapter provide good highlights.

Thurow, Lester C. *Dangerous Currents: The State of Economics.* New York: Random House, 1984.
Offers a good review of macroeconomic theory and a critical analysis on the policies at work from a Keynesian point of view. Well written and suitable for a general audience.

_____ . *Generating Inequality.* New York: Basic Books, 1971.
An outstanding empirical and theoretical investigation into income distribution in the U.S. economy. Highly recommended for anyone who wants to go beyond mere theory.

Tinbergen, Jan. *Economic Policy.* Amsterdam: North-Holland, 1956.
A classic book on the principles and design of economic policy and the evolving aims-means structure.

_____ . *On the Theory of Economic Policy*. Amsterdam: North-Holland, 1970.

This short book (78 pages) is the first generally available systematic discussion of economic policy using the targets and instruments approach. It was originally published in 1952. The theory is illustrated with numerical examples from actual experiences in planning at the Netherlands Central Planning Office. Although the book is reasonably self-contained, some mathematical sophistication is helpful.

Titmuss, R. M. *The Gift Relationship, from Human Blood to Social Policy*. New York: Vintage Books, 1972.

Titmuss's vision of the role of social policy in shaping a better community was neither a reformist, a social democratic, nor an old Tory kind. Instead he developed in this book a kind of Durkheimian conception of social policy as an instrument of social solidarity and moral regulation. He argues that orthodox economic analysis places undue emphasis upon a social psychology of self-interested action, thus denying the human capacity for other-oriented action He concludes with a strong preference for the voluntary blood donor system of Great Britain over the market-based system of the United States.

Tobin, James. *Policies for Prosperity: Essays in a Keynesian Mode*. Edited by P. M. Jackson. Cambridge, Mass.: MIT Press, 1987.

Contains forty-three essays written by the 1981 Nobel laureate in economics, which are addressed to a nonacademic audience. The essays present the theory and practice of Keynesian economics and discuss alternative macroeconomic models and their implications for policymakers. Very well written.

Toffler, Alvin. *The Third Wave*. New York: William Morrow, 1980.

Known as a futurist, Toffler explains his theory concerning humankind's evolutionary "waves of technology" and explores the human potential in the business world of the twenty-first century and beyond.

Tool, Marc R. *An Institutionalist Guide to Economics and Public Policy*. Armonk, N.Y.: M. E. Sharpe, 1984.

This edited volume contains essays by more than a dozen well-known institutionalists. Although a few discuss economic policy as a conceptual issue, most examine specific policy areas. Topics include inflation and unemployment, economic security and welfare, labor-market policies, environmental protection, industrial policy, government regulation, agriculture, trade, and economic development.

Trescott, Paul B. "Ideology and Inflation." *Acta Monetaria* 3 (1979): 17-26.
An elementary survey of cost-push doctrines with criticism based on economic theory and statistical data. Argues that cost-push theory is faulty and tends to extend burdensome government controls.

_____. "Patinkin and the *Real* Real-Balance Effect." In *Perspectives on the History of Economic Thought*, edited by Donald A. Walker, vol. 2. Brookfield, Vt.: Gower, 1989.
Surveys the treatment of real balance effects by various economists, stressing the differences between the wealth-based version and the disequilibrium version.

Tsiang, S. C. "Keynes's Demand for Liquidity, Robertson's Loanable Funds Theory, and Friedman's Monetarism." *Quarterly Journal of Economics* 94 (May, 1980): 467.
A critical analysis of liquidity preference theory, which argues that it is identical to the classical loanable funds theory. While this is a difficult article, it is an important alternative to Keynesian theory.

Tsuru, Shigeto. *The Economic Development of Modern Japan: The Selected Essays of Shigeto Tsuru*. Vol. 2. Aldershot, England: Edward Elgar, 1995.
A collection of essays by Japan's foremost economist, including "Has Capitalism Changed?," which was published in 1961 as a small book. Tsuru studied under Joseph Schumpeter at Harvard University before World War II and is thoroughly at home in both Marxist and Keynesian paradigms.

_____. *Japan's Capitalism: Creative Defeat and Beyond*. Cambridge, England: Cambridge University Press, 1993.
A look at the recovery process in Japan after World War II. Tsuru emphasizes the active role of the Japanese government in encouraging the continuing success that followed. He analyzes the welfare significance of Japan's money-oriented affluence and the emergence of a distinctive "corporate capitalism" based on an unbalanced expansion of the internal surplus in firms. He concludes that the successes have led to a new set of intractable problems.

Tufte, Edward R. *Political Control of the Economy*. Princeton, N.J.: Princeton University Press, 1978.

This brief, readable study presents evidence that there has been a macroeconomic political business cycle in the United States and other Western countries, with demand stimulation often occurring a short time before elections.

Turner, Marjorie S. *Joan Robinson and the Americans*. Armonk, N.Y.: M. E. Sharpe, 1989.

Joan Robinson used to say that, because she could not do mathematics, she had to think. Even without mathematics, most of Robinson's writings are rough going for those who are not professional economists. This book provides a clear, understandable introduction to the life and works of this important post-Keynesian theorist, as well as a sense of the differences between neoclassical economists and the post-Keynesians.

United States. President. *Economic Report of the President*. Washington, D.C.: Government Printing Office, 1980-1990.

Presents the perspective that the structure of the U.S. economy is sound, based primarily on data and statistics of economic growth. The conclusion is that the American economy is developing and basically healthy. This conservative predilection embodying mainstream economic theory denies U.S. long-term economic decline and crisis and negates the need for changes in structure, especially that of social organization.

U.S. Bureau of Economic Analysis. *GNP: An Overview of Source Data and Estimating Methods*. Methodology Paper Series MP-4. Washington, D.C.: Government Printing Office, 1989.

A simple presentation of the methodology of the estimation of the national product and income accounts. Provides a detailed presentation of the sources of data and estimating methods that are used in preparing real and nominal estimates of all income-side and product-side components of the gross national product.

Van Raaij, W. Fred, Gery M. van Veldhoven, and Karl-Erik Wärneryd, eds. *Handbook of Economic Psychology*. Boston: Kluwer Academic Publishers, 1988.

A collection of readings reviewing the contributions of psychologists to understanding economic behavior, including consumer behavior, business behavior, tax evasion, unemployment, and energy conservation. The strong psychological perspective taken by the book and the emphasis on psychological models makes it perhaps more suitable for students in psychology than for students in economics.

Van Winden, Frans A. A. M. "The Economic Theory of Political Decision-Making: A Survey of Perspective." In *Public Choice*, edited by Julien van den Broeck. Dordrecht, The Netherlands: Kluwer Academic Publishers, 1988.

A brief but remarkably lucid exposition of the premises of public choice theory and its major areas of application. Van Winden is balanced and judicious regarding the contributions made by public choice theory as well as the "limitations and shortcomings of the present state of the art." This paper should be the first resort of the beginning student looking for an accessible entrée into public choice theory.

Varian, Hal R. *Microeconomic Analysis*. 2d ed. New York: W. W. Norton, 1984.

A popular graduate text that covers consumer theory, demand functions, estimation, and duality. Provides a link between the intermediate college microeconomic theory presentation of cost and the formal duality literature. Discusses equity and fairness, as well as wealth equity and income equity. Gives an outstanding presentation of the relationship between cost and production functions. Assumes some familiarity with calculus.

Veblen, Thorstein. *The Place of Science in Modern Civilization and Other Essays*. New York: Augustus M. Kelley, 1919.

This volume contains many of Veblen's important essays, including penetrating insights into the development of economic theory as well as many of Veblen's own original contributions to economic analysis. Of particular importance is the three-part essay entitled "The Preconceptions of Economic Science."

_____. *The Theory of the Leisure Class*. New York: New American Library, 1953.

An original and entertaining analysis of the changing patterns of spending and consumption at higher levels of income.

Veseth, Michael. *Introductory Macroeconomics*. 2d ed. Orlando, Fla.: Academic Press, 1984.

Although this work deals with the big issues in the economy, the author takes time to present an exciting approach concerning demand within the context of market behavior. The presentation of reasons for changes in demand is interesting and should be quite stimulating and clear for the beginner.

Viner, Jacob T. "Cost Curves and Supply Curves." *Zeitschrift fur Nationalokonomie* 3 (1931): 23-46. Reprinted in *American Economic Association Readings in Price Theory*, edited by George J. Stigler and Kenneth E. Boulding. Chicago: Richard D. Irwin, 1952.
The classic reference on the derivation of supply curves from cost curves.

Von Neumann, John. "A Model of General Equilibrium." *Review of Economic Studies* 13 (1945): 1-9.
A very mathematical and abstract article by one of the most important contributors to time preference theory.

Von Neumann, John, and Oskar Morgenstern. *The Theory of Games and Economic Behavior*. 2d ed. Princeton, N.J.: Princeton University Press, 1947.
Even though von Neumann's language is obtuse at times, this book is still the logical starting point for anyone interested in modern game theory. His mathematical illustrations may be impenetrable for the average reader but will be useful to more advanced students. The classic statement of game theory in application to economics.

Vygodski, V. S. *The Story of a Great Discovery: How Karl Marx Wrote "Capital."* Translated by Christopher S. V. Salt. Turnbridge Wells, Abacus Press, 1974.
A translation from the original Russian. Vygodski's essay is representative of mid-twentieth century Marxist estimates of the importance of Marx's original theories.

Walras, Léon. *Elements of Pure Economics*. Translated by William Jaffé. London: Allen & Unwin, 1954.
"[S]o far as pure theory is concerned, Walras," Joseph Schumpeter says, "is in my opinion the greatest of all economists." Walras' prose is difficult, but Jaffé's commentary helps greatly to clarify Walras' meaning.

Walsh, Vivian, and Harvey Gram. *Classical and Neoclassical Theories of General Equilibrium: Historical Origins and Mathematical Structure*. New York: Oxford University Press, 1980.

The title nicely sums up what this book does. Its main strength is its attention to classical (structural) general equilibrium theories, typically ignored by most.

Walters, A. A. *An Introduction to Econometrics*. New York: W. W. Norton, 1970.

A good first book in econometrics. Although it is not designed for the layperson, it is not overly technical.

_____. "A Survey of Cost and Production Functions." *Econometrica* 31 (1963): 1-66.

The definitive article on production functions. Walters begins with the theoretical basis for the set-theoretic approach to production, continues on to functional specifications, covers the production-cost relationship, and critiques the existing econometric literature. He presents a comparison of previous empirical studies and concludes with an extensive reference compilation.

Walton, Clarence, ed. *Inflation and National Survival*. New York: Academy of Political Science, 1979.

In a little more than two hundred pages, eighteen authorities present divergent views on inflation theory and policy. Results are both readable and intellectually respectable. Contains Henry Wallich's proposal for tax-based incomes policy.

Ward, Benjamin N. *The Socialist Economy: A Study of Organizational Alternatives*. New York: Random House, 1967.

Part 2 deals with classical Stalinism and command economies, although there is some technical and mathematical material that requires some background in economics and mathematics.

Warner, Kenneth E. *Cost-Benefit and Cost-Effectiveness Analysis in Health Care: Principles, Practice, and Potential*. Ann Arbor, Mich.: Health Administration Press, 1982.

Explains the basic concepts of cost-benefit analysis and cost-effectiveness analysis and explores their application to the analysis of public health projects.

Waud, Roger N. *Macroeconomics*. 4th ed. New York: Harper & Row, 1989.

An introductory macroeconomics textbook that contains a relatively simple description of the national income and product accounts, including a discussion on net national product and capital depreciation.

Weeks, John. *Capital and Exploitation.* London: Edward Arnold, 1981.
    Covers economic topics as they relate to exploitation and includes the
    analyses of prominent Marxist economists. Clear and to the point.

Weintraub, E. Roy. *General Equilibrium Analysis.* New York: Cambridge
University Press, 1985.
    One of the best introductions to general equilibrium theory. Among its
    many virtues are that it is concise and well written, and it does not use
    mathematics as a crutch for not explaining what the theory implies.
    Much of this book is written as an exchange between a group of
    students and a teacher. Chapter 1 sets out the formal framework of an
    Arrow-Debreu model under some simplifying assumptions. Through
    mock classroom discussions, many of the subtle points of general
    equilibrium modeling are explored.

Weitzman, Martin L. *The Share Economy.* Cambridge, Mass.: Harvard
University Press, 1984.
    This book argues, from a macroeconomic and mathematical-economic
    viewpoint, the advantages to a national economy of paying a large part
    of labor's share in income as a share of profits. It began the controversy
    on this score in the mid-1980's.

Weld, John. "Coase, Social Cost, and Stability: An Integrative Essay."
Natural Resources Journal 13 (October, 1973): 595-613.
    Weld looks at a case from the original Coase article from the perspec-
    tive of how important the legal specification of rights is to the case.
    Weld uses the simple examples of Coase so the article could be read
    by high school students or above.

Whitaker, J. K. "Alfred Marshall (1842-1924)." In *The New Palgrave: A
Dictionary of Economics,* edited by John Eatwell, Murray Milgate, and
Peter Newman. Vol. 3. New York: Stockton Press, 1987.
    Whitaker is perhaps the leading modern authority on Marshall and his
    works. In this remarkably detailed summary of Marshall and his
    contributions to the development of economic theory, there is some
    technical material, but most of the essay is understandable to those with
    little background in economics.

Wicksell, Knut. *Lectures on Political Economy.* Translated by E. Classen.
Vol. 2. London: Routledge & Kegan Paul, 1934.
    The most accessible work by the economist who originated the distinc-
    tion between the natural and market rate, fundamental to the develop-

ment of capital theory and instrumental in the creation of the influential Swedish school. Wicksell's use of the natural rate to explain business fluctuations resembles that of the Austrian model.

Wicksteed, Philip H. *The Common Sense of Political Economy*. London: Macmillan, 1910.
Contains one of the first clear statements of the concept of opportunity cost.

Williams, Eric. *Capitalism and Slavery*. New York: Capricorn Books, 1966.
Williams' thesis is that the profits from colonialism and slavery allowed the European industrial revolution to take place. A classical work in the Marxist tradition. Eschews economic theory, and, instead, relies upon a chronology, some data, and indignation. Nevertheless, it has had a substantial impact upon the noneconomic approach to colonialism; it has also been used to justify reparations to the descendants of some groups.

Williams, Raburn. *Inflation! Money, Jobs and Politicians*. Arlington Heights, Ill.: AHM Publishing, 1984.
Fairly light reading appropriate for a general audience. Begins with a discussion of seigniorage and the macroeconomic debate over the Phillips curve. The bulk of the book, however, is Williams' view of the evolution of the United States macroeconomy from 1965 to 1980 and the role played by government policies.

Williamson, Oliver E. *The Economic Institutions of Capitalism*. New York: Free Press, 1985.
The definitive work on transaction cost motives for vertical integration. Develops a mostly verbal theory of transaction cost economics that provides a clear description of the trade-offs between market exchange, contractual exchange, and vertical integration. For the general reader.

Wilson, George W. *Inflation: Causes, Consequences, and Cures*. Bloomington: Indiana University Press, 1982.
Clear survey of history and theory written for a lay audience. A good first read.

Wolf, Charles, Jr. "A Theory of 'Non-Market' Failure: Framework for Implementation Analysis." *Journal of Law and Economics* 21 (April, 1979): 3-10.

A condensed version appears in *The Public Interest* 55 (Spring, 1979): 114-133, and was reprinted in R. Haveman and J. Margolis, *Public Expenditure and Policy Analysis*, 3d ed. (Boston: Houghton Mifflin, 1983). This is an important work that presents an additional considera- tion when analyzing whether the public sector should intervene in a private market transaction even when "market failure" is perceived. Wolf argues that there are many tendencies in nonmarket organizations toward inefficiencies, because of the difficulty in measuring results and the existence of goals, rules, and procedures (internalities) that some- times cause organizational behavior that is incongruent with societal goals. He expands on this topic in *Markets and Governments: Choos- ing Between Imperfect Alternatives* (Cambridge, Mass.: MIT Press, 1988.)

Wolf, Richard D., and Stephen A. Resnick. *Economics: Marxian Versus Neoclassical*. Baltimore, Md.: The Johns Hopkins University Press, 1987.
A This book has a simple yet thorough coverage of both basic topics of neoclassical and Marxist economic theories as they are relevant to comparisons.

Wolff, Robert Paul. *In Defense of Anarchism*. New York: Harper & Row, 1970.
A very unusual book by a left-wing political philosopher. Wolff con- tends that, except for unanimity, every method of political decision making violates individual rights. He concludes that all governments are immoral. It is very important to note that Arrow's impossibility theorem forms the centerpiece of Wolff's argument.

Wolfson, Murray, and Vincent Buranelli. *In the Long Run We Are All Dead: A Macroeconomics Murder Mystery*. 2d ed. New York: St. Martin's Press, 1990.
A novel based on Keynes's famous quip that government cannot wait for the economy to correct by itself because, "in the long run we are all dead." Humorous and instructive as an introduction to Keynesian economics, the book sets forth the various pros and cons of activist policy.

Wood, John Cunningham, ed. *Karl Marx's Economics: Critical Assess- ments*. London: Croom Helm, 1988.
A multivolume work belonging to a series of edited works on major economic questions of worldwide importance. Its coverage of topics is very impressive, including literally hundreds of individual contribu-

tions, all brief and gauged for easy understanding by the educated reader, that are focused on the meaning of certain of Marx's writings, as well as criticism of other theorists' attempts to analyze Marx's theories.

Working, E. J. "What Do Statistical 'Demand Curves' Show?" *Quarterly Journal of Economics* 41 (1927): 212-235. Reprinted in *Readings in Price Theory*, edited by George J. Stigler and Kenneth E. Boulding. Chicago: Richard D. Irwin, 1952.

In one of the earliest articles that explains the identification problem, Working indicates the futility of deriving the demand relation from observed market prices and quantities without separately estimating the demand and supply functions.

Wright, David McCord. *The Keynesian System*. Bronx, N.Y.. Fordham University Press, 1962.

Concise and readable. Discusses the consumption function and the marginal propensity to consume, in a section aptly titled "The Keynesian Tool Box," and explains how the various parts of the system fit together.

Wykstra, Ronald A. *Education and the Economics of Human Capital*. New York: Collier-Macmillan, 1971.

A composition of articles in the economic literature including such authors as Theodore Schultz, Edward F. Denison, H. S. Houthakker, Gary S. Becker, and many others. There are three broad topics of interest: the role that education and the development of human capital play in economic growth; the returns to investment in education; and other important issues in the economics of education. Highly readable and appropriate for the specialist, nonspecialist, and even the noneconomist. A good introduction into the literature of human capital development. Contains an index.

Yeager, Leland. *Experiences with Stopping Inflation*. Washington, D.C.: American Enterprise Institute, 1981.

Presents histories of the drastic reductions of price inflations in a variety of contexts. Chapter 2 deals with the ending of six periods of hyperinflation.

_____. "Some Questions About Growth Economics." *American Economic Review* 4 (March, 1954): 55-63.

A basic, critical analysis of growth theory with a section on the ability of the Harrod-Domar model to be as mathematically precise as its originators imply.

Young, Allan A. "Increasing Returns and Economic Progress." In *Readings in Welfare Economics*, edited by Kenneth Arrow and Tibor Scitovsky. Homewood, Ill.: Richard D. Irwin, 1969.

A reprint of Young's classic 1928 article, presenting a strong argument for viewing Adam Smith's insights into scale economies in the broadest possible terms. Although short (thirteen pages), the article is not easy reading; nevertheless, it is quite worthwhile for its perspective on increasing returns as a key to understanding the dynamics of the development process.

Zamagni, Stefano. "Ricardo and Hayek Effects." *Oxford Economic Papers* supp. 36 (November, 1984): 135-151.

Zamagni strongly supports Hayek against Nicholas Kaldor's criticism. He emphasizes the importance of turnover time in the explanation of the effect. Hayek's account considers the businessperson's decision of how to invest. It deals with the time before the new techniques were brought into existence. Kaldor assumed, wrongly, that new machinery would be instantaneously available.

Zellner, Arnold. *An Introduction to Bayesian Inference in Econometrics*. New York: John Wiley & Sons, 1971.

A classic work and the most comprehensive introduction to Bayesian inference in econometrics. Discusses both the theory and its applications. Zellner provides several Fortran computer algorithms for applied work. Written at a sophisticated level, requiring a knowledge of calculus and linear algebra.

Zimbalist, Andrew, Howard J. Sherman, and Stuart Brown. *Comparing Economic Systems: A Political-Economic Approach*. 2d ed. New York: Harcourt Brace Jovanovich, 1988.

An examination of the economic systems of countries such as Japan, Sweden, the Soviet Union, China, Cuba, Hungary, and Yugoslavia up to 1987-1988, with a minimum of theory.

Monetary Theory and Practice

Aaron, Henry J., and Joseph A. Pechman, eds. *How Taxes Affect Economic Behavior*. Washington, D.C.: Brookings Institution, 1981.
Chapter 4, written by Robert Gordon and Burton Malkiel and entitled "Corporation Finance," discusses the effect of taxation, including the investment tax credit, upon corporate finance. They examine the efficiency implications of the 1981 tax structure and evaluate several tax-reform proposals.

Abken, Peter A. "Innovations in Modeling the Term Structure of Interest Rates." *Atlanta Economic Review* 39 (July/August, 1990): 38-43.
Written for the general reader. Summarizes the ongoing research into the forecasting of the term structure, especially the research over the period from 1975 to 1990. Emphasizes research using option contract risk measures and rational expectations assumptions. Includes a first-rate reference section at the end of the article.

Aguilar, Linda. "Still Toe to Toe: Banks and Nonbanks at the End of the 80's." *Economic Perspective* 13 (January/February, 1990): 12-23.
This article reviews how the distinctions between banks and nonbank intermediaries have blurred, as well as the resulting rise in nonbank competition which banks are facing. It is written as a nontechnical article for the financial community and includes tables and figures.

Altman, Edward I., ed. *Handbook of Financial Markets and Institutions*. 6th ed. New York: John Wiley & Sons, 1987.
A reference work for financial practitioners, but very clearly and concisely written and not overly technical. Section 13 addresses commercial banks, while section 15 looks at thrifts. Each section contains a description of history, assets and liabilities, and regulatory environment, as well as a discussion of major issues to be resolved. Both sections contain charts and a bibliography.

Anderson, L. C., and L. L. Jordan. "Monetary and Fiscal Actions: A Test of Their Importance in Economic Stabilization." *Review*, Federal Reserve Bank of St. Louis 50 (November, 1968): 11-24.
This 14-page statistical study could be regarded as the benchmark empirical work related to the resurgence of monetarism in the 1960's. Advanced-level macroeconomics and an understanding of statistical regression technique are necessary to appreciate this study.

Aronowitz, Stanley. *Working Class Hero: A New Strategy for Labor.* New York: Pilgrim Press, 1983.

A critique of American union history and current orientation by a well-known labor historian and former union official. Aronowitz describes how unique aspects of American unionism came about that now pose problems, and advocates changes in union strategy and orientation.

Auerbach, Robert D. *Money, Banking, and Financial Markets.* 3d ed. New York: Macmillan, 1988.

A good general text that includes references to government debt management and money creation. Chapter 15 is especially useful, as it describes the mechanics of central bank liability creation, which forms the base for the U.S. money supply. Chapter 7, "Commercial Banking," and appendix B, "History of Money and Banking in the United States to 1863," tie the U.S. experience to the English currency controversy. It is a very convenient first reading of the controversy, in the context of a money and banking book. One of the best discussions of the Bullionist controversy from the perspective of the U.S. banking experience.

Baer, Herbert, and Sue F. Gregorash, eds. *Toward Nationwide Banking: A Guide to the Issues.* Chicago: Federal Reserve Bank of Chicago, 1986.

Examines the trends, as well as the legal and economic frameworks, for nationwide banking. Empirical studies are included, and the banking industries of various countries are compared.

Baltensperger, Ernst. "Credit Rationing: Issues and Questions." *Journal of Money, Credit, and Banking* 10, no. 2 (1978): 170-183.

With the slowdown of economic growth of the late 1950's and early 1960's, the supply and rationing of loanable funds became an issue. The present work reviews, in terms that can be understood by the noneconomist, the research spawned by that era.

Baltensperger, Ernst, and Timothy M. Devinney. "Credit Rationing Theory: A Survey and Synthesis." *Journal of Institutional and Theoretical Economics* 141, no. 4 (1985): 475-502.

This is an update of the earlier work by Baltensperger. The most notable addition in this review is the application of the efficiency wage theory to credit markets. The essence of the theory is that the willingness to pay a high interest rate reflects the riskiness of a borrower. Only low-risk firms are able to obtain credit.

Barro, Robert J. "Are Government Bonds Net Wealth?" *Journal of Political Economy* 82 (November/December, 1974): 1095-1117.

This article requires graduate-level economics and mathematics to comprehend. It is cited as a reference here to indicate what is regarded as the definitive resurrection of the Ricardian equivalence theorem.

Benston, George J., ed. *Financial Services: The Changing Institutions and Government Policy.* Englewood Cliffs, N.J.: Prentice-Hall, 1983.

An excellent overview of the historical development of U.S. public policy toward banks, thrift institutions, and other financial institutions.

Benston, George J., and George G. Kaufman. "Understanding the Savings-and-Loan Debacle." *The Public Interest* 25 (Spring, 1990): 79-95.

Analyzes the causes of the savings and loan troubles. Claims that the response of the Congress and the regulators to the difficult situation led to the disastrous collapse of the industry. Suitable for the general reader.

Black, Tyrone, and Donnie Daniel. *Money and Banking.* 3d ed. Homewood, Ill.: Business Publications, 1988.

This undergraduate textbook is a good starting place. The money creation process is carefully explained with enough institutional background and economic analysis to make this explanation meaningful.

Blaug, Mark. *Economic Theory in Retrospect.* Homewood, Ill.: Richard D. Irwin, 1968.

Chapter 4, "Ricardo's System," contains a high-level interpretation of the Bullionist controversy. The following chapter, "Say's Law and Classical Monetary Theory," provides a setting for both the Bullionist and Antibullionist positions in the controversy.

Bloomfield, Arthur I. *Monetary Policy Under the International Gold Standard: 1880-1914.* New York: Federal Reserve Bank of New York, 1959.

An authoritative account of the way in which central banks manipulated the rules of the gold standard to protect nations' internal economies against price fluctuations, as transmitted through the balance of payments.

Board of Governors of the Federal Reserve System. *The Federal Reserve System: Purposes and Functions.* Washington, D.C.: Author, 1984.

This highly informative 120-page booklet may be obtained at no charge from the Federal Reserve. The topics covered include the structure and history of the Federal Reserve, monetary policy, the role of the Federal Reserve in the international sphere, and other functions and services that the Federal Reserve System performs. Written for the general public and high school students.

Bordo, Michael D. "The Lender of Last Resort: Alternative Views and Historical Experience." *Economic Review* (Federal Reserve Bank of Richmond, Virginia), January/February, 1990, 18-29.

A nontechnical article outlining the lender-of-last-resort function of central banks and arguing that this function, when applied to solvent banks, can prevent a banking panic.

Bosworth, Barry P., Andrew S. Carron, and Elizabeth H. Rhyne. *The Economics of Federal Credit Programs*. Washington, D.C.: Brookings Institution, 1987.

Analyzes federally chartered credit agencies covering housing and mortgage credit, small business lending, export-import finance, farm credit, and student loans.

Boulding, Kenneth E. *Macroeconomics*. Vol. 2 in *Economic Analysis*. New York: Harper & Row, 1966.

Although this is an old textbook, it probably contains the clearest and most complete exposition on liquidity preference available.

Bowden, Elbert V. *Money, Banking, and the Financial System*. St. Paul, Minn.: West, 1989.

Chapter 7 is devoted to the evolution of the thrift industry. A major part of chapter 8 is relevant to the topic, describing the deregulation of the 1980's and the S&L crisis. Although any money and banking textbook will provide useful information on thrifts, this one has more extensive coverage of the topic than most.

Broaddus, Alfred. *A Primer on the Fed*. Richmond, Va.: Federal Reserve Bank of Richmond, 1988.

A booklet, intended for the layperson, outlining the structure, functions, and monetary policy actions of the Federal Reserve System. One of the best short (74-page) nontechnical books on the Federal Reserve. Includes a bibliography.

Brue, Stanley L., and Campbell R. McConnell. *Macroeconomics: Principles, Problems, and Policies*. New York: McGraw-Hill, 1990.

Considered one of the best books on the principles level, explaining in detail how fiscal and monetary policies operate in the real world. The authors present sufficient examples and data to back up their theories. Illustrates the three alternatives of the Federal Reserve for affecting the money supply in the economy.

Cargill, Thomas F. *Money, the Financial System, and Monetary Policy.* 4th ed. Englewood Cliffs, N.J.: Prentice-Hall, 1991.
A money and banking textbook. In particular, chapters 11 through 14 provide clear discussions of the general principle and historical background of government regulation, major changes in financial regulation in 1979 and the 1980's, and an evaluation of the regulatory changes. Suitable for college students.

Cook, Timothy Q., and Timothy D. Rowe, eds. *Instruments of the Money Market.* 6th ed. Richmond, Va.: Federal Reserve Bank of Richmond, 1986.
A detailed description of money market instruments and their interest yields. Includes an examination of such instruments as certificates of deposit, Eurodollars, Treasury bills, commercial paper, and options on short-term interest rate futures. Includes a subject index.

Cooper, S. Kerry, and Donald R. Fraser. *The Financial Marketplace.* 3d ed. Reading, Mass.: Addison-Wesley, 1990.
Written for a college-level course on the U.S. financial system, this book is very readable. While it discusses much more than depository institutions, chapter 9 deals specifically with depositories. Chapters 1-5 put the topic in the context of the overall financial system, and chapters 12-14 discuss depository institution regulation and likely directions of change.

Cramp, A. B. "Liquidity." In *The New Palgrave: A Dictionary of Economics*, edited by John Eatwell, Murray Milgate, and Peter Newman. New York: W. W. Norton, 1989.
Cramp provides a thorough definition of liquidity.

Credit Union National Association. *Yearbook.* Madison, Wis.: Credit Union National Association, 1978-
CUNA provides a host of services to member credit unions and speaks for the credit union movement. CUNA's annual report reflects both the ideology of the movement and the current financial status of the Association.

Cunningham, Rosemary Thomas, and Thomas J. Cunningham. "Recent Views of Viewing the Real Rate of Interest." *Atlanta Economic Review* 39 (July/ August, 1990): 28-37.

A readable account of the theory of the real rate of interest which examines the influence of central banks.

Dalgaard, Bruce R. *Money, Financial Institutions, and Economic Activity.* Glenview, Ill.: Scott, Foresman, 1987.
A very readable textbook for college money and banking courses. Provides a sound overview of modern financial institutions. Many sections may be read even by those without technical training in economics. In addition, Dalgaard devotes several pages to a discussion of Gresham's law.

Davidson, Paul. *Money and the Real World.* London: Macmillan, 1978.
Davidson provides a post-Keynesian analysis of the roles that money and liquidity preference play in the economy. The discussion of the "marginal propensity to purchase bonds out of savings" is particularly interesting.

Degan, Robert A. *The American Monetary System.* Lexington, Mass.: D. C. Heath, 1987.
Chapter 4 of this book provides a concise summary of events and policies of the Great Depression. Contains an excellent nontechnical discussion of the major economic theory controversies arising from this period. Also covered elsewhere are the panic of 1907 and the depression of 1920-1921.

Dennis, William J., William C. Dunkelberg, and Jeffrey S. Van Hulle. *Small Business and Banks: The United States.* Washington, D.C.: NFIB Research and Education Foundation, 1988.
This monograph reviews the results of the fourth in a series of credit-availability surveys conducted by the National Federation of Independent Business. It is written expressly for the entrepreneur and layperson.

Dertouzos, Michael, Richard K. Lester, and Robert M. Solow. *Made in America.* Cambridge, Mass.: MIT Press, 1989.
This authoritative and prestigious MIT study concludes that monetary and fiscal policy are not enough to rejuvenate the American economy and that changes in values and social organization will be required. Especially noteworthy as Solow is a Nobel laureate of the mainstream thought. An emphasis on institutional adjustment and change in social organization from a liberal perspective, dealing with the industrial

policy debate. The contributions of Lester C. Thurow, Robert Reich, and the *Cuomo Commission Report* are reflected.

Dublin, Jack. *Credit Unions: Theory and Practice*. Detroit: Wayne State University Press, 1966.
This brief text provides a clear explanation of the operation of a credit union.

Dunkelberg, William C., and Jonathan A. Scott. *Credit, Banks, and Small Business: 1980-1984*. Washington, D.C.: NFIB Research and Education Foundation, 1985.
This monograph reviews the results of three biennial surveys of the relationships between lending institutions and small firms. By means of descriptive statistics, the authors assess the terms under which businesses are able to obtain credit.

Eckes, Alfred E., Jr. *A Search for Solvency: Bretton Woods and the International Monetary System, 1941-1971*. Austin: University of Texas Press, 1975.
Although a chapter briefly surveys the "Death of Bretton Woods," Eckes focuses upon the negotiations leading up to the 1944 agreement. He docs an excellent job of showing how the system was shaped by the conviction that the beggar-thy-neighbor trade policies of interwar years had played a major role in bringing on World War II, combined with memories of the pre-1914 gold standard. A weakness is that Eckes relies primarily on American sources and accordingly views matters primarily from the U.S. perspective.

Fabozzi, Frank J., and Frank G. Zarb, eds. *Handbook of Financial Markets: Securities, Options, and Futures*. 2d ed. Homewood, Ill.: Dow Jones-Irwin, 1986.
A survey for the interested lay reader of how the different money, credit, and capital markets operate.

Fabritius, M. Manfred, and William Borges. *Saving the Savings and Loan: The U.S. Thrift Industry and the Texas Experience, 1950-1988*. New York: Praeger, 1989.
Gives background on the savings and loan problem, and provides detailed information on the crises from 1979 to 1982 and from 1983 to 1988, particularly in regard to Texas thrift institutions. Puts the savings and loan problem in perspective. For general readers or specialists.

Federal Reserve Bank of Chicago. *Modern Money Mechanics*. Chicago: Author, 1982.

   A pamphlet, intended for the general public, which describes the mechanical process of money creation. Includes a concise description of the characteristics of money, as well as how the Federal Reserve System attempts to control it. Available free to the public.

Federal Reserve Bank of New York. *Funding and Liquidity: Recent Changes in Liquidity Management Practices at Commercial Banks and Securities Firms*. New York: Author, 1990.

   Provides a detailed examination of liquidity management practices at the level of an individual financial firm. Defines terms and explains concepts. Suitable for college students.

_____ . *Recent Trends in Commercial Bank Profitability: A Staff Study*. New York: Author, 1986.

   The best available study of the profitability of large money center banks (those in New York, for example) in the 1980's. A detailed study of the sources of bank earnings, and why bank profits have been adversely affected by interest-rate increases and inflationary pressures. Primarily for specialists.

Fisher, Irving. *The Purchasing Power of Money*. Rev. ed. New York: Macmillan, 1925.

   Although the institutional details are out of date, this pioneering work by one of America's most distinguished economists is still of great value and very readable. Puts money creation into the context of an international monetary system in ways which are becoming more relevant.

_____ . *Stable Money: A History of the Movement*. New York: Adelphi, 1934.

   Because of the "impracticability of index wages and index bonds," Fisher presents a proposal to regulate the value of money itself via an index approach.

_____ . *The Theory of Interest*. New York: Macmillan, 1930.

   Further develops the ideas that were first published in *Appreciation and Interest* (1896) and *The Rate of Interest* (1907). A commanding synthesis of theory and empirical analysis, with many original insights and clarifications. Much of contemporary monetary economics and finance is found in this classic, including continuous and discrete compounding, nominal versus real interest rates, high versus rising prices, and distributed lag effects.

Fitzgibbons, Athol. *Keynes's Vision: A New Political Economy.* New York: Oxford University Press, 1988.

Focuses on the thinking of John Maynard Keynes in economic and political matters, as well as his approach to economic policy. Written for noneconomists who are interested in Keynes's philosophical writings.

Flannery, Mark J., and Dwight M. Jaffee. *The Economic Implications of an Electronic Monetary Transfer System.* Lexington, Mass.: Lexington Books, 1973.

One of the earlier books on the electronic transfer of funds. Describes the nature of these types of transfers, discusses their broader implications, and speculates about the future course of this system. Chapter 2 includes an excellent description of various systems of exchange in historical perspective. Largely in nontechnical language.

Florida, Richard L., ed. *Housing and the New Financial Markets.* New Brunswick, N.J.: Center for Urban Policy Research. 1986.

This readings book has excellent coverage of how the mortgage market works and how it has been changed by deregulation. Part 5 (readings 12 through 15) and reading 9 are devoted entirely to thrift industry topics. In addition, most of the other twenty-one readings have relevant information on thrifts that can be located by referring to a thorough and well-organized index.

Friedman, Milton. *The Essence of Friedman.* Edited by Kurt Leude. Stanford, Calif.: Hoover Institution Press, 1987.

This collection of Friedman's writings contains major essays dealing with monetarism. Although "The Quantity Theory: A Restatement" requires some mathematical background, "The Supply of Money and Changes in Prices and Output" will be of interest to the general reader. Friedman clearly explains, in his logical style, the tenets of monetarism.

_____. "Monetary Policy: Theory and Practice." *Journal of Money, Credit, and Banking* 13 (February, 1982): 98-118.

Friedman, the leading monetarist of the twentieth century, presented this paper as a lecture in 1981. He examines the actual practices of monetary policy and gives the reasons for its frequent lack of success. Written with conviction and humor.

_____. "The Quantity Theory of Money: A Restatement." In *Studies in the Quantity Theory of Money*, edited by Milton Friedman. Chicago: University of Chicago Press, 1956.

This difficult article by a Nobel laureate in economics could be regarded as the definitive beginning of modern-day monetarism and the monetarist view that eventually deficit spending will crowd out an equal amount of private spending.

_____. "The Role of Monetary Policy." *American Economic Review* 58 (March, 1968): 1-17.

Develops the view that, in the long run, changes in the money supply cannot cause "real" economic magnitudes (notably unemployment and interest rates) to diverge from their "natural" values but will be reflected in the inflation rate. Though the ideas are sophisticated, the exposition is a model of lucidity.

_____. *Studies in the Quantity Theory of Money*. Chicago: University of Chicago Press, 1956.

A seminal work that lays out the modern quantity theory of money. The first chapter contains Friedman's famous restatement of the quantity theory, and the remaining chapters contain articles by other leading monetarists on empirical and theoretical issues supporting the quantity theory.

Friedman, Milton, and Anna J. Schwartz. *A Monetary History of the United States, 1867-1960*. Princeton, N.J.: Princeton University Press, 1963.

Written by two eminent economists (Friedman is a Nobel Prize winner), this book is a fascinating historical narrative of nearly a century of changes in the U.S. money stock. The history, development, and policies of the Federal Reserve System are examined in detail.

Galbraith, John Kenneth. *Money: Whence It Came, Where It Went*. Boston: Houghton Mifflin, 1975.

Popularly written by an economist and public servant, this liberal interpretation treats tax changes during the twentieth century in the context of expanding government responsibilities. Contains good notes and a full and excellent index. Makes for informative and thoughtful reading.

Garner, C. Alan. "The Yield Curve and Inflation Expectations." *Economic Review* 9 (September/October, 1987): 28-37.

A good choice for readers interested in the relationship between expected inflation and the term structure of interest rates. Well written, very readable, and contains no equations. Examines the various macroeconomic occurrences that can and do affect the yield curve, with particular emphasis on the 1980-1987 period.

Garrett, Garet, and Murray Rothbard. *The Great Depression and New Deal Monetary Policy*. San Francisco: Cato Institute, 1980.

The authors survey the impact, in international terms, of changing monetarist policies practiced by the United States both before and during the Great Depression.

Goldenweiser, E. A. *American Monetary Policy*. New York: McGraw-Hill, 1951.

An examination of Federal Reserve monetary policy from 1914 through 1950. An earlier and somewhat less critical view of the Federal Reserve. Includes an index and charts.

Gordon, Robert J., ed. *Milton Friedman's Monetary Framework*. Chicago: University of Chicago Press, 1974.

In less than 200 pages, this book presents a good simple statement by Milton Friedman of the essence of his monetary analysis and critical essays by a number of other leading monetary scholars.

Graddy, Duane B. *The Bank Holding Company Performance Controversy*. Washington, D.C.: University Press of America, 1979.

The historical development, growth, and regulation of bank holding companies are described in detail. The various nonbank activities of bank holding companies and their impact on the banking and financial sector are also examined. For a general audience.

Greenfield, Robert L., and Leland B. Yeager. "A Laissez-Faire Approach to Monetary Stability." *Journal of Money, Credit, and Banking* 14 (August, 1983): 302-315.

An almost futuristic presentation of a completely indexed payments system.

Greider, William. *Secrets of the Temple: How the Federal Reserve Runs the Country*. New York: Simon & Schuster, 1987.

An intriguing inside look at the workings of the nation's central bank. The rise of monetarism is viewed through its political overtones. The difficulty of controlling the money supply in an era of financial deregulation, and the failure of "fine-tuning" the money supply, are discussed in an informed and informal tone.

Harris, Lawrence. *Monetary Theory*. New York: McGraw-Hill, 1981.
Contains a good description of Walras' Law and its impact on monetary theory during the third quarter of the twentieth century. There are errors, however, in some of the equations contained in the book.

Harrison, William B. *Money, Financial Institutions, and the Economy*. Plano, Tex.: Business Publications, 1985.
Chapter 15 focuses on early monetary theory and the development of the quantity theory leading up to the Friedman model. Good historical background to the Keynesian innovations of the twentieth century. chapter 16 examines the classical model, of which the quantity theory forms one part.

Havrilesky, Thomas M., and Robert Schweitzer. *Contemporary Developments in Financial Institutions and Markets*. 2d ed. Arlington Heights, Ill.: Harlan Davidson, 1987.
Part 2 of this book of readings deals with issues that are relevant to the thrift industry. Of particular interest are "The Thrift Industry in Transition" by Patrick Mahoney and Alice White and "Recent Developments in the Credit Union Industry" by Douglas Pearce. Also, several readings (24 and 25) in Part 3 deal with recent developments in the mortgage market.

Hayes, Samuel L., III, and Philip M. Hubbard. *Investment Baking: A Tale of Three Cities*. Boston, Mass.: Harvard Business School Press, 1990.
The development of investment banking and financial markets in London, New York, and Tokyo.

Heinsohn, Gunnar, and Otto Steiger. "Private Property, Debts and Interest: Or, The Origin of Money and the Rise of Monetary Economies." *Studi Economici*, 21 (1983): 3.
Although this article may be difficult to find, it is the best analysis of the development of money as a means of financing deficit spending.

Henderson, James M., and Richard E. Quandt. *Microeconomic Theory: A Mathematical Approach*. New York: McGraw-Hill, 1980.
A close companion of virtually every economics graduate student. Chapter 9 deals with multimarket equilibrium and discusses Walras' law, but it does not carry the discussion very far into monetary theory.

Hirshleifer, Jack. *Investment, Interest, and Capital.* Englewood Cliffs, N.J.: Prentice-Hall, 1970.
Incorporates many of the breakthroughs in finance of the 1950's and 1960's into the analysis of interest and investment.

Hodgman, Donald R. *Commercial Bank Loan and Investment Policy.* Champaign, Ill.: Bureau of Economic and Business Research, University of Illinois, 1963.
In this seminal work, the author reviews the policy rules established by banks in the allocation of credit. Hodgman's central argument is that default risk limits the funds a lender will make available to the market at any interest rate. Contains extensive institutional information on the operation of a commercial bank.

Holzer, Henry Mark. *The Gold Clause.* New York: Books in Focus, 1980.
A review of the history and legal status of the gold clause.

Horvitz, Paul M., and Richard A. Ward. *Monetary Policy and the Financial System.* 6th ed. Englewood Cliffs, N.J.: Prentice-Hall, 1987.
Horvitz gives a thorough, yet nontechnical, description of financial intermediaries with emphasis on commercial banks while also including savings and loan associations, credit unions, and insurance companies. The different types of financial assets and liabilities are explained. Also contains a number of chapters devoted to a summary of monetary theory and monetary policy for those interested in the macroeconomic aspects of the financial system.

Humphrey, Thomas M. "The Real Bills Doctrine." *Economic Review* (Federal Reserve Bank of Richmond) 68 (September/October, 1982): 13-22.
A good, brief historical and theoretical summary of the real bills doctrine. The mathematical theory is completely relegated to footnotes, making the article accessible to advanced high school students.

Ibbotson, Roger G. *Stocks, Bonds, Bills, and Inflation.* Homewood, Ill.: Dow Jones-Irwin, 1989.
Contains extensive data and charts comparing historical interest rates and inflation. The data are useful for examining long-term trends in the relationship between interest rates and inflation. Suitable for the general reader.

Jeffee, Dwight D. *Credit Rationing and the Commercial Loan Market.* New York: John Wiley & Sons, 1971.

Synthesizes the credit-rationing theory of the 1950's and 1960's. Essential reading before going on to the work done in the 1980's on the relationship between interest rates and the quality of the loan applicant.

Jones, Frank J., and Benjamin Wolkowitz. "Determinants of Interest Rates." In *Handbook of Financial Markets*, edited by Frank J. Fabozzi and Frank G. Zarb. Homewood, Ill.: Dow Jones-Irwin, 1986.

This article provides a clear, concise discussion of the relationship among inflation, the real rate of interest, and nominal interest rates. The discussion of inflation and interest rates is integrated within a general discussion of the theory of interest rate determination. Although intended for finance practitioners, it is suitable for general readers.

Kahn, R. F. "Some Notes on Liquidity Preference." *The Manchester School of Economic and Social Studies* 22 (September, 1954): 229-257.

A classic article, presenting the Keynesian view of liquidity preference, that is fairly accessible to the nonspecialist.

Kane, Edward J. *The S&L Insurance Mess: How Did It Happen?* Washington, D.C.: Urban Institute Press, 1989.

An excellent analysis of the S&L crisis written by one of the generally acknowledged experts in the field. Kane discusses in detail how regulators and the FSLIC provided wrong managerial incentives for the S&L industry, and why they were so slow to correct them. Although some topics are technical and difficult, Kane explains them with insight and clarity. He also brings a balanced perspective to the issue of blame: for an example of this, see the section at the beginning of chapter 3 entitled "Innocent Versus Guilty Mistakes."

Kaufman, Henry. *Interest Rates, the Markets, and the New Financial World*. New York: Random House, 1986.

An analysis of the far-reaching changes which have taken place in financial markets. Kaufman, a well-known Wall Street economist, analyzes the main influences which have caused interest rates to fluctuate much more than used to be the case. Requires some analytic skill, but the effort is well worth it.

Kenen, Peter B. *Financing, Adjustment, and the International Monetary Fund*. Washington, D.C.: Brookings Institution, 1986.

This general study of IMF operations since 1947 gives special attention to the implications of post-1960's borrowing by the IMF to expand its lending resources.

Kettl, Donald. *Leadership at the Fed.* New Haven, Conn.: Yale University Press, 1986.
Focuses on the individuals who have exercised power at the Federal Reserve. Kettl argues that the Federal Reserve's power has been dependent of the leadership of its chairmen.

Keynes, John Maynard. "Alternative Theories of the Rate of Interest." *Economic Journal* 47 (June, 1937): 241.
Keynes's clearest attempt to distinguish his liquidity preference theory of the rate of interest from the old classical loanable funds view.

_____. *The General Theory of Employment, Interest, and Money.* London: Macmillan, 1936.
The original statement of the theory of liquidity preference is presented in seemingly simple terms. Unfortunately, Keynes often smoothed over difficulties, making his ideas seem simpler than they really were. Suitable for college students.

_____. *Tract on Monetary Reform.* London: Macmillan, 1923.
This most readable of Keynes's technical books is outstanding for its analysis of inflation and the way in which it relates the money creation process to systems of exchange-rate management.

Klein, John J. *Money and the Economy.* 6th ed. New York: Harcourt Brace Jovanovich, 1986.
A 560-page text written for a college-level course in money and banking. Describes financial institutions as well as monetary theory and policy. Suitable for the general reader. Includes author and subject indexes, references, figures, and tables.

Klein, Robert J. *The Money Book of Money.* Boston: Little, Brown, 1987.
A personal financial planner designed for the noneconomist and published by Klein and the editors of *Money Magazine.* Covers personal goals, retirement planning, estate planning, divorce settlements, child care, and a host of other interesting issues. Also covers investing and saving, including stocks, bonds, and real estate. Finally, the book examines issues regarding income tax, bank dealings, and insurance. An index is provided.

Krooss, Herman E., and Martin R. Blyn. *A History of Financial Interme-diaries*. New York: Random House, 1971.

Provides a history of financial intermediaries in the United States through 1970, including, but not limited to, depository institutions. The history is treated in chronological order rather than by institution type. The book is dry but easily understood by the general reader.

Kuttner, Robert. *The Economic Illusion*. Boston: Houghton Mifflin, 1984.

A stimulating and iconoclastic critique of the "conventional wisdom" on the relationship between equality and economic growth by *Business Week* and National Public Radio commentator Kuttner. A wide range of topics includes an extensive discussion of the role that trade unions play in the capitalist democracies, contrasting American and European unions.

Laidler, David E. *The Demand for Money*. 2d ed. New York: Dun-Donnelly, 1977.

A fairly brief (182-page) exhaustive survey of what is known about the demand for money. Although it is somewhat dated, especially in terms of more recent empirical findings, it is highly useful in that it is accessible to undergraduate majors in economics.

Lehmann, Michael B. *The Dow Jones-Irwin Guide to Using the Wall Street Journal*. 3d. ed. Homewood, Ill.: Down Jones-Irwin, 1990.

This outstanding book integrates economics, financial markets, and investments. Lehmann explains how monetary and fiscal policies are used to influence business cycles and investment behavior. Very well written, concise, and well suited for the lay reader. Highly recom-mended.

Litan, Robert E. *What Should Banks Do?* Washington, D.C.: Brookings Institution, 1987.

Addresses the issues concerning the legal segmentation between banks and other financial institutions. What may happen to bank operations when the financial product-line restrictions are relaxed? The benefits and risks of financial product deregulation are examined.

Luckett, Dudley G. *Money and Banking*. 3d ed. New York: McGraw-Hill, 1984.

Emphasizing the institutional aspects of international finance, this text investigates the history of changes in the regulatory structure of the banking industry. The material is directed at undergraduate readers.

McCallum, Bennett. *Monetary Economics: Theory and Policy*. New York: Macmillan, 1989.

A condensed graduate-level textbook. Money supply and demand are introduced in chapters 1 through 4, and much of the remainder of the book deals with the elements in the adjustment process—prices, output, interest rates, and the foreign exchange rate. Contains extended discussion of inflation in chapters 6, 7, and 8. Summarizes recent developments in the economic theory of inflation.

McConnell, Campbell R. *Economics*. New York: McGraw-Hill, 1987.

Part 3 provides a complete understanding of the money and banking system in the United States, detailing the creation of money and its role in economic expansion. Part 4 continues the look at the economics of expansion and its application. Intended for beginning college students in economics or finance, but is very readable for the nonspecialist.

McCulloch, J. Huston. *Money and Inflation: A Monetarist View*. 2d ed. New York: Academic Press, 1982.

This hundred-page paperback is designed to give college students an introduction to the analysis of inflation. Cost-push arguments are examined and criticized in chapter 3.

McEachern, William A. *Economics: A Contemporary Introduction*. Cincinnati: South-Western, 1988.

Chapter 13 of this book provides a superb analysis of assets and liabilities, especially those of depository institutions. McEachern explains the concepts of money, near moneys, and liquidity. Through simplified balance-sheet illustrations, the reader is made aware of the different assets and liabilities that banks have to manage as well as how they relate to the money supply.

McInerny, Ralph, and Evan Oppenheimer, eds. *Savings and Loan*. New York: Macmillan, 1990.

Gives the reader an in-depth look at the S&L industry through the 1980's. One topic of concern is the future of the industry, whether the S&Ls become obsolete or should the industry be saved. Well written and organized in a logical fashion.

Madura, Jeff. *Financial Markets and Institutions*. St. Paul, Minn.: West, 1989.

Written as a textbook for an undergraduate course in financial institutions, the text should be accessible to the nonspecialist. Chapters 15-17 focus on banks, while chapter 21 discusses S&Ls and savings banks and chapter 22 looks at credit unions. Contains charts, graphs, and some references.

Maisel, Sherman J. *Managing the Dollar*. New York: W. W. Norton, 1973.
A delightful and realistic paperback book written by a former member of the Federal Reserve Board. Recounts his experiences and reflections on the operations of the Federal Reserve. A nonmonetarist perspective. Includes an index.

Malkiel, Burton G. *A Random Walk down Wall Street*. 4th ed. New York: W. W. Norton, 1985.
A very readable discussion of recent research on the stock market. Suitable for undergraduates.

_____. *The Term Structure of Interest Rates*. Princeton, N.J.: Princeton University Press, 1966.
This important book details the major theories about the term structure in a way that is fairly readable, although not simple. Most difficult passages can be skipped, however, with no loss of continuity. Also summarizes the empirical work done by Malkiel and others who have tested the explanatory theories. This work is usually cited as a prime reference in term structure articles and research publications.

Mayer, Thomas, James Duesenberry, and Robert Aliber. *Money, Banking, and the Economy*. New York: W. W. Norton, 1990.
One of several available college textbooks written for undergraduate money and banking courses, this book has a strong focus on policy and the role of the Federal Reserve. Contains a clear and concise chapter that is devoted to the topic of central banking and the structure of the Federal Reserve. Contains a useful and informative discussion of monetarism, the quantity theory, and the implementation of monetary policy.

Melton, William C. *Inside the Fed: Making Monetary Policy*. Homewood, Ill.: Dow Jones-Irwin, 1984.
Intended for the general reader, this book describes how monetary policy is planned and carried out. Emphasis is placed on the Volcker years, but there is some discussion of monetary policy history. The book contains a glossary, and there is an excellent appendix on open-market operations.

Meltzer, Allan H. "The Demand for Money: The Evidence from the Time Series." *Journal of Political Economy* 71 (June, 1963): 219-246.

A good example of the kind of empirical study that found a stable demand function for money that was explained largely by income and interest rates. Intermediate macroeconomics and an understanding of statistical regression analysis are required to follow the study.

Melvin, Donald J., Raymond N. Davis, and Gerald C. Fischer. *Credit Unions and the Credit Union Industry.* New York: New York Institute of Finance, 1977.

A readable but somewhat dated description of credit unions and the credit union movement in the United States.

Meulendyke, Ann-Marie. *U.S. Monetary Policy and Financial Markets.* New York: Federal Reserve Bank of New York, 1989.

Meulendyke is a manager and senior economist assigned to the Federal Reserve Bank of New York's trading desk, where open market operations take place. Examines the evolution of U.S. monetary policy and practices. Includes charts.

Miles, Marc A. *Beyond Monetarism: Finding the Road to Stable Money.* New York: Basic Books, 1984.

An insightful critique of monetarism from a supply-side economist. Written with the general reader in mind, Miles's discussion traces the ascendancy of monetarism in the policy arena and examines the flaws that make a constant monetary growth rule bad economic policy. Instead, Miles advocates price rules for monetary policy.

Miller, Roger LeRoy, and Robert W. Pulsinelli. *Modern Money and Banking.* 2d ed. New York: McGraw-Hill, 1989.

An excellent textbook, designed for college students but accessible to others. Chapter 9, "Regulation of Depository Institutions," gives a good summary of U.S. banking legislation through the 1980's, including a summary of the Depository Institutions Deregulation and Monetary Control Act of 1980. The discussions of American banking history (chapters 12 and 13), the origins of banking (chapter 4), and the 1980's problems of both savings and loans and banks (chapter 10) should prove enlightening to the interested layperson.

Mises, Ludwig von. *The Theory of Money and Credit.* Translated by H. E. Batson. London: Jonathan Cape, 1934.

This work first appeared in German in 1912 and is the fundamental Austrian work on monetary theory. It employs Wicksellian insights extensively and introduces the concept of forced savings. The notion of the natural rate of interest is basic to the book's fundamental aim: the integration of monetary theory with price theory.

Mishkin, Frederic S. *The Economics of Money, Banking, and Financial Markets*. Glenview, Ill.: Scott, Foresman, 1989.

A best-selling introductory level money and banking textbook. Written in clear prose, with few equations (mostly relegated to appendices). Includes a short, succinct chapter on risk and the term structure of interest rates, as well as a case study of yield curve movements during the 1980-1988 period. Explains in detail, with the use of diagrammatic analysis, how money supply affects the appreciation and depreciation of currencies. The author also points out other important market factors that have a direct influence on the value of currencies.

Monetary Policy in the 1990s. Kansas City: Federal Reserve Bank of Kansas City, 1989.

Combines analyses by practitioners and economists on domestic and international aspects of monetary policy. In particular, Benjamin Friedman's contribution "Changing Effects of Monetary Policy on Real Economic Activity" analyzes the difficulties which monetary policy has encountered in dealing with changes in the U.S. economy in the 1980's, such as increasing private indebtedness and a more competitive banking environment.

Moore, Geoffrey H. *Business Cycles, Inflation, and Forecasting*. 2d ed. National Bureau of Economic Research Studies in Business Cycles 24. Cambridge, Mass.: Ballinger, 1983.

A comprehensive guide to the historical behavior of the business cycle in the United States. Explains the relationship between the business cycle and unemployment, and the business cycle and inflation. Suitable for undergraduates.

Mott, Tracy. "Towards a Post-Keynesian Formulation of Liquidity Preference." *Journal of Post Keynesian Economics* 8, no. 2 (1985-1986): 222.

An extension of John Maynard Keynes's theory of liquidity preference, tying liquidity preference to profit expectations of firms.

Nadler, Paul S. *Commercial Banking in the Economy*. New York: Random House, 1986.

A useful and straightforward discussion of the process of managing loans and deposits by commercial bankers. Includes a discussion of the new role of thrift institutions, with interesting insights into the changes of the 1970's and 1980's. Recommended for general readers.

Niehans, Jurg. "Metzler, Wealth and Macroeconomics: A Review." *Journal of Economic Literature* 16 (March, 1978): 84-95.
A technical but readable criticism of the kind of real balance effect which emphasizes money as a component of wealth. Niehans stresses that the disequilibrium approach is more plausible and more powerful.

Ornstein, Franklin. *Savings Banking: An Industry in Change.* Reston, Va.: Reston, 1985.
Devoted solely to describing the operations of savings and loan associations and mutual savings banks. The history and development of these thrifts are covered in chapter 1. The remaining chapters provide a detailed description of such topics as regulatory procedures, chartering and branching procedures, and operations functions prior to the Financial Institutions Reform, Recovery, and Enforcement Act of 1989.

Parkin, Michael. *Economics.* Reading, Mass.: Addison-Wesley, 1990.
Chapter 17 describes the structure of capital markets in the United States, including both the demand for and supply of capital. Parkin distinguishes financial assets from real assets. Using a flow diagram, he illustrates clearly how households, firms, and financial intermediaries interact with one another to translate savings into investments in capital markets. A balance sheet for the United States helps the reader to appreciate the size of U.S. capital markets and to understand the relative role played by households, firms, and financial intermediaries.

Patinkin, Don. *Money, Interest, and Prices.* New York: Harper & Row, 1965.
Patinkin attempts to collect the microeconomic (that is, the static rational) decision activity of individuals into a coherent explanation of macroeconomic behavior. He does this with limited success, but no one has done better. It is, however, instructive to go over just how Patinkin goes about this task.

Payer, Cheryl. *The Debt Trap: The International Monetary Fund and the Third World.* New York: Monthly Review Press, 1974.

The authors labels the International Monetary Fund as "the most powerful supranational government in the world today" and accuses it of interfering in the internal affairs of borrowing countries. She also attacks foreign aid as a means of perpetuating dependence.

Pigou, A. C. "The Value of Money." *Quarterly Journal of Economics* 31 (November, 1917): 38-65.

This article expanded the work of Alfred Marshall into an early formal analysis of the relation between money demand, velocity, and total spending in the economy. Intermediate macroeconomics and some algebra are required to follow the argument.

Pizzo, Stephen, Mary Fricker, and Paul Muolo. *Inside Job: The Looting of America's Savings and Loans*. New York: McGraw-Hill, 1989.

The three investigative reporters who wrote this book emphasize fraudulent, unethical, and unsavory behavior of S&L management during the 1980's. They also do a good job of describing the shortcomings of government regulation of the industry. The reader should be warned to keep all this in perspective, however, as even without these abuses and illegal activities, the S&L industry would still have had high failure rates. Nevertheless, these activities, the S&L industry would still have had high failure rates. Nevertheless, these activities were important contributing factors to the S&L crisis, particularly in the case of government regulatory failure.

Poole, William. *Money and the Economy: A Monetarist View*. Reading: Mass.: Addison-Wesley, 1978.

As its title indicates, this book explores monetarism. Nevertheless, it contains a fairly lengthy discussion of hyperinflation and is very readable.

Powell, Jim. *The Gnomes of Tokyo*. Rev. ed. New York: American Management Association, 1989.

From the personal perspective of a group of leading Japanese executives, this text shows how world financial and industrial markets are linked.

Pugh, Olin S., and F. Jerry Ingram. *Credit Unions: A Movement Becomes an Industry*. Reston, Va.: Reston, 1984.

One of the few books available that is devoted solely to the topic of credit unions. The subjects that are covered include history and development, organization and structure, regulation, and a detailed explanation of management issues. The final chapter analyzes the future growth prospects of the industry, given the important legislative changes of the early 1980's.

Quinn, Brian Scott. *The New Euromarkets.* New York: John Wiley & Sons, 1975.
This book includes a description of dollar- and other currency-denominated Eurobonds.

Ritter, Lawrence S., and William L. Silber. *Principles of Money, Banking, and Financial Markets.* 6th ed. New York: Basic Books, 1989.
A money and banking textbook. Chapters 7 and 8 of this very readable book contain a detailed discussion about the basic operation of a bank and the banking industry in general.

Robertson, Dennis Holme. *Money.* 1922. Reprint. Cambridge, England: Cambridge University Press, 1961.
A charming classic in economics. Develops the theory of the value of money in nonmathematical terms. The chapters are headed by quotations from Lewis Carroll's *Alice's Adventures in Wonderland* (1865) and *Through the Looking-Glass and What Alice Found There* (1871).

Rose, Peter S. *The Changing Structure of American Banking.* New York: Columbia University Press, 1987.
Rose examines the structural changes of American banking in the post-World War II era. The impact of those structural changes on bank performance is evaluated. Chapter 10 reviews the competition between banks and other depository institutions. Although the author reviews much academic research, the book is still accessible to the general reader. The book has an extensive bibliography, an index, and scattered tables.

_____. *Money and Capital Markets.* Plano, Tex.: Business Publications, 1986.
One of the better texts in the money and banking area of economics. Contains a very complete section on interest rates and security prices, including a good chapter on the term structure and inflation. Also includes an extensive list of references at the end of the chapter. Very good for readers who are interested in using the term structure of interest rates for forecasting purposes.

Rose, Peter S., and Donald R. Fraser. *Financial Institutions.* Dallas, Tex.: Business Publications, 1980.

A comprehensive textbook on the management of financial institutions. Includes complete descriptions and analyses of all major types of financial markets and institutions.

Roussakis, Emmanuel N. *Commercial Banking in an Era of Deregulation.* New York: Praeger, 1989.

A highly readable and well-written book for the specialist, the nonspecialist, and the noneconomist. Begins with a review of the U.S. banking system from a historical perspective and proceeds to issues in the 1980's. Covers topics regarding the management of a bank, its sources and uses of funds, the objectives of portfolio management, and a variety of other issues. Provides an index.

Sardello, Robert J., and Randolph Severson. *Money and the Soul of the World.* Dallas: Pegasus Foundation, 1983.

A very different view of the power of money in which the authors delve into the psychology of a monetary system.

Selgin, George A. *The Theory of Free Banking.* Totowa, N.J.: Rowman & Littlefield, 1988.

A superb presentation of the theoretical case for free banking. There is some discussion of historical examples, but the overwhelming concern attempts to demonstrate the viability—even the superiority—of free banking. Particularly notable is the fact that Selgin builds his case for free banking almost entirely without recourse to either mathematics or statistics.

Shaw, W. A. *The History of Currency, 1252 to 1896.* Reprint. New York: Augustus M. Kelley, 1967.

Originally published in 1896, this work exclusively studies the minting of coins by various Western nations, with a wealth of data for anyone interested in monetary history. Those investigating Gresham's law should pay particular attention to the tables that record the annual market fluctuations in the exchange rate between gold and silver for the period 1687 to 1893.

Siegel, Barry N., ed. *Money in Crisis: The Federal Reserve, the Economy, and Monetary Reform.* San Francisco: Pacific Institute for Public Policy Research, 1984.

A collection of essays by prominent monetary economists. The topics range from a statistical test of a well-known theory of business cycles, a review of Federal Reserve performance since 1945, and a history of the gold standard (1821 to 1971), to an argument for free banking and a survey of the Great Depression. Highly recommended.

Sims, Christopher A. "Money, Income, and Causality." *American Economic Review* 62 (September, 1972): 540-552.

In this article, Sims shows how a certain form of bivariate time series analysis can be used to indicate whether the correlation between two time series is the result of the first causing the second, the second causing the first, or the two causing each other.

Smith, Adam. *An Inquiry into the Nature and Causes of the Wealth of Nations.* 1776. Reprint. New York: Modern Library, 1937.

An especially valuable reference for the description and policy implications of minting practices and the extraction of seigniorage under early commodity money standards. Relevant passages are scattered throughout. See especially book 2, chapter 2; book 3, chapter 6 (on seigniorage); and book 5.

Smith, Gary. *Money, Banking, and Financial Intermediation.* Lexington, Mass.: D. C. Heath, 1991.

An intermediate money and banking text. Examines financial intermediation and the economy, the role of money in economic activity in a special international section, financial markets in a section on default risk, and interest-rate risk. Also contains sections on financial futures and options, loans, the stock market, risk models, the role of intermediation in the economy, the regulation of the financial system, monetary policy, aggregate supply, inflation, and the IS-LM model. The text is appropriate for the nonspecialist and the noneconomist. A glossary and an index are provided.

Solmon, Lewis C. *Economics.* 2d ed. Reading, Mass.: Addison-Wesley, 1976.

This self-study text provides an introductory look at the importance of money and lending in the economy in chapter 13 and at commercial banks in chapter 14. Both units follow the text with several good examples and questions for readers to test their skills. The student who is unfamiliar with economics will find this text a refreshingly understandable overview of many interesting topics.

Solomon, Robert. *The International Monetary System, 1945-1976: An Insider's View.* New York: Harper & Row, 1977.

Although presenting a succinct summary of the Bretton Woods agreement and its implementation, this work has as its major focus the efforts, beginning in the early 1960's, to remedy the defects that were becoming evident in the system and then to rebuild viable international monetary arrangements after its collapse. In writing this account, Solomon draws upon his participation in many of those efforts as senior staff economist in the international field for the United States Federal Reserve Board.

Sorkin, Alan L. *Monetary and Fiscal Policy and Business Cycles in the Modern Era.* Lexington, Mass.: D. C. Heath, 1988.

In the chapter on monetary policy, Sorkin explains in depth the relationship between the level of interest rates and exchange rates in the economy. He also illustrates such relationships by using real-life examples. This book, highly informative and well written, is highly recommended for those interested in learning about the relationship between fiscal policy and exchange rates.

Spellman, Lewis J. *The Depository Firm and Industry.* New York: Academic Press, 1982.

An advanced text that examines financial institutions and their role in the economy. Begins with a good historical perspective of depository firms and institutions from the 1800's to the Banking Act of 1980. Examines the economic theory of the financial firm in detail, alternative goals of the firm (including deposit rather than profit maximization), the effects of disintermediation on the financial firm, the difficulties of deposit ceilings, and empirical studies of implicit deposit rates and average production costs. Also discusses the role of capital accumulation in the financial system, financial policy, and the aggregate economy and an aggregate growth model with a financial-sector emphasis. Primarily for the specialist, but the nonspecialist will also find many of the topics interesting. Each chapter has a good bibliography. Also contains an index.

Stigum, Marcia. *The Money Market.* Rev. ed. Homewood, Ill.: Dow Jones-Irwin, 1983.

One of the most comprehensive and detailed guides to U.S. financial markets, including Eurodollar markets. Written for the lay reader who has no prior special knowledge of financial markets.

Studenski, Paul, and Herman E. Krooss. *Financial History of the United States*. New York: McGraw-Hill, 1952.
Still the standard.

Taggert, Robert A. "Secular Trends in the Financing of Corporations." In *Corporate Capital Structures in the United States*, edited by Benjamin M. Friedman. Chicago: University of Chicago Press, 1985.
A description of trends concerning the choices made by corporations in arranging financing in stock and credit markets.

Temin, Peter. *Did Monetary Forces Cause the Great Depression?* New York: W. W. Norton, 1976.
A rebuttal to Milton Friedman's view that poor monetary policy caused the Great Depression. Temin finds that a sharp drop in consumption preceded the Depression. There was a tendency for productive capacity to outrun effective demand as real wages increased more slowly than productivity in the 1920's.

Tew, Brian. *International Monetary Cooperation, 1945-70*. 10th ed. London: Hutchinson, 1970.
In the broadest of the histories listed here, Tew considers not only the IMF in a global setting but also its relative impact on individual countries' (primarily Great Britain's) internal financial policies.

Thornton, Henry. *An Enquiry into the Nature and Effects of the Paper Credit of Great Britain*. London: Allen & Unwin, 1939. Reprint. Fairfield, N.J.: Augustus M. Kelley, 1978.
Thornton's book, written in 1802, was perhaps the best book on monetary theory of the nineteenth century. Unfortunately, it is poorly organized and at times difficult to read.

Timberlake, Richard H., Jr. *The Origins of Central Banking in the United States*. Cambridge, Mass.: Harvard University Press, 1978.
An excellent historical work focusing on the period from 1840 to the establishment of the Federal Reserve System in 1914. Concludes that central banking is an opportunistic response to banking problems, including the banking crises of the late nineteenth century, not a natural evolution, and that the private bank clearinghouses of the nineteenth century performed all the essential functions of a central bank.

Tobin, James. "Liquidity Preference as a Behavior Towards Risk." *Review of Economic Studies* 25 (February, 1958): 65-86.

This rigorous work by a Nobel laureate in economics develops the first application of formal portfolio theory to examining the speculative motive for holding money.

Trescott, Paul B. *Money, Banking, and Economic Welfare.* New York: McGraw-Hill, 1960.
A standard treatment of money and banking that provides a balanced account of currency and money issues.

Tsiang, S. C. "Keynes's Demand for Liquidity, Robertson's Loanable Funds Theory, and Friedman's Monetarism." *Quarterly Journal of Economics* 94 (May, 1980): 467.
A critical analysis of liquidity preference theory, which argues that it is identical to the classical loanable funds theory. Although this is a difficult article, it is an important alternative to Keynesian theory.

United States. President. *Economic Report of the President.* Washington, D.C.: Government Printing Office.
This book is published annually and provides the administration's view on the state of the economy and the interaction and effectiveness of both monetary and fiscal policy. A wealth of statistical material on trends in prices, output, employment, and wages is included in an appendix. Written for a general audience.

U.S. Board of Governors of the Federal Reserve System. "The Depository Institution Deregulation and Monetary Control Act of 1980." *Federal Reserve Bulletin* 65 (June, 1980): 44-54.
This is a nontechnical summary of this most important act, not the act itself. The most relevant parts for the present context are Titles I and II, although the reader should absorb the entire reading, if only to get an idea of the complexities of modern banking legislation and to understand that the Banking/Currency debate is only part of the story.

_____ . *The Federal Reserve System: Its Purposes and Functions.* Washington, D.C.: Author, 1985.
A comprehensive yet succinct description of the Federal Reserve System and its activities which is intended for the general public. Chapter 2 reviews monetary policy and the measurement of the various official versions of the money supply. Available free to the public.

Valentine, Lloyd M. *Business Cycles and Forecasting.* 7th ed. Cincinnati: South-Western, 1986.

Contains a description of the historical behavior of U.S. business cycles, summarizes major business cycle theories, and provides a technical guide to forecasting business cycles. The first three parts of the book are less demanding; the section on forecasting assumes some statistical knowledge.

Van Horne, James C. *Financial Market Rates and Flows* 2d ed. Englewood Cliffs, N.J.: Prentice-Hall, 1984.

Provides a detailed discussion of the relationship between nominal and real rates of interest, as well as how interest rates are determined. Directed at those who are familiar with the basics on interest rates and desire a more rigorous theoretical treatment of the subject. Suitable for college students.

Viner, Jacob. *Studies in the Theory of International Trade.* London: Allen & Unwin, 1955.

Chapters 3 and 4, "The Bullionist Controversies," are especially pertinent in this standard reference for both the history and theory of the events of the controversy.

Watts, Tim J. *Nonbank Banks: Regulating Credit Unions, Savings and Loans, and Other Thrift Institutions.* Monticello, Ill.: Vance Bibliographies, 1989.

Helps readers distinguish the differences among thrift institutions. Provides an in-depth examination of the rules and regulations with which each financial institution must abide. Well organized and provides the reader with an extensive knowledge of thrift regulatory practices.

Wells, Paul. "A Post Keynesian View of Liquidity Preference and the Demand for Money." *Journal of Post Keynesian Economics* 5, no. 4 (1983): 523.

A clear exposition of the Keynesian approach to liquidity preference, which expands on John Maynard Keynes's original formulation to take account of recent financial innovations.

White, Lawrence H. *Free Banking in Britain: Theory, Experience, and Debate, 1800-1845.* New York: Cambridge University Press, 1984.

A controversial and influential work. The author not only presents a strong theoretical case for free banking but also provides considerable detail regarding both Scottish free banking (1765-1845) and the nineteenth century British debates on free banking versus central banking. There is some use of calculus, but that section can be omitted without loss to the nontechnical reader.

Wilcox, James A. *Current Readings on Money, Banking, and Financial Markets*. Glenview, Ill.: Scott, Foresman/Little, Brown Higher Education, 1990.

A book of thirty-eight readings and journal articles that are designed for both the specialist and nonspecialist. Covers banking deregulation, the savings and loan crisis, the role of deposit insurance in bank failures, a cashless society in the future, the international debt crisis, banking reform, discretionary monetary policy, interstate bank failures, and a variety of other issues. Some articles are very readable for the noneconomist and others are not. Presents a good view of the literature.

Willett, Thomas D., ed. *Political Business Cycles: The Political Economy of Money, Inflation, and Unemployment*. Durham, N.C.: Duke University Press, 1988.

Mostly monetarist in approach, this book nevertheless will be useful to those who prefer the Keynesian view. The degree of difficulty varies from article to article.

Woerherde, Walter J. *The Savings and Loan Industry: Current Problems and Possible Solutions*. Westport, Conn.: Quorum Books, 1984.

Woerherde is one of the first to point out the problems that developed in the S&L industry in the early 1980's. He gives numerous solutions to these problems and prophetically warns that if steps are not quickly taken, the industry will face a financial crisis.

Yeager, Leland. *International Monetary Relations: Theory, History, and Policy*. 2d ed. New York: Harper & Row, 1976.

An excellent text on the principal international issues centering on money. Gives keen and well-researched insights into the gold and gold-exchange standards. The presentation is widely accessible.

Fiscal Theory and Practice

Aaron, Henry. *The Value-Added Tax: Lessons from Europe*. Washington, D.C.: Brookings Institution, 1981.

Provides an excellent overview of the way in which value-added taxation has been implemented in European countries—the principal adopters of the tax.

Aaron, Henry, and Michael Boskin, eds. *Economics of Taxation.* Washington, D.C.: Brookings Institution, 1980.
A book of about twenty essays on taxation topics collected from various publications. Contributors include Michael Boskin, Martin Feldstein, Richard Musgrave, and others. Includes both advanced and introductory-level articles. The essay entitled "Total U.S. Taxes and Their Effect on the Distribution of Income," by Benjamin Okner, is an excellent first choice.

Aaron, Henry J., and Harvey Galper. *Assessing Tax Reform.* Washington, D.C.: Brookings Institution, 1985.
Examines various proposals for federal tax reform. Focuses on federal personal and corporate income tax and examines the possibility of a federal sales or value-added tax. Presents a clear and objective assessment of difficult issues relevant to designing and maintaining a fair, efficient, and administrable tax system. Relatively nontechnical; both specialists and nonspecialists can benefit. Index.

Adams, James R. *Secrets of the Tax Revolt.* San Diego: Harcourt Brace Jovanovich, 1984.
An excellent discussion of the theoretical underpinnings of the 1980's antitax revolt, including the Laffer effect.

Advisory Commission on Intergovernmental Relations. *Local Revenue Diversification: Local Sales Taxes.* Washington, D.C.: Author, 1989.
Argues that while the property tax is the mainstay of local governments, it has been under strain. Examines the merits of resorting to other taxes, such as sales taxation. Argues for a balanced local tax structure. Contains a bibliography.

_____. *Significant Features of Fiscal Federalism.* Vols. 1-2. Washington, D.C.: Author, 1989.
These volumes are the best source of tax data for federal, state, and local governments. They provide information on tax rates, tax revenues, and interstate comparisons. Published annually.

Aronson, J. R., and John L. Hilley. *Financing State and Local Governments.* 4th ed. Washington, D.C.: Brookings Institution, 1986.

This book describes and analyzes fiscal systems of state and local governments in the United States. Chapter 6 deals with business taxes, including various forms of corporate income taxes in use by the states. An interesting topic covered here is the apportionment of tax liability of multistate corporations among the several states.

Auerbach, Alan J. "Corporate Taxation in the United States." *Brookings Papers on Economic Activity* 13 (1983): 451-513.
An excellent discussion of the effects of the corporate income tax, including some original research by the author. Not a comprehensive discussion, but focuses on several aspects: the nonneutrality of the tax between equipment and structures, the nonneutrality among industries, and the effects on incentives to invest, including the combined effects of accelerated depreciation and the investment tax credit.

Ballard, Charles L., John B. Shoven, and John Whalley. "The Total Welfare Cost of the United States Tax System: A General Equilibrium Approach." *National Tax Journal* 38 (June, 1985): 125-140.
Provides estimates of the efficiency gains that might be realized by a switch from an income- and profit-based tax system to a consumption-type value-added tax.

Beck, Morris. *Government Spending: Trends and Issues.* New York: Praeger, 1981.
Describes the trend and growing role of the government sector in the industrialized economies, including the United States and European countries. Detailed analysis on the effects of government spending, the transfer payment system, and taxation on the federal, state, and local levels. Many tables, figures, and a bibliography are included. Provides useful information for college and high school students.

Bingham, Richard D., Brett Hawkins, and F. Ted Hebert. *The Politics of Raising State and Local Revenue.* New York: Praeger, 1978.
Provides a good overview of the linkage between politics and economics at the state and local level. Also addresses the issue of federal aid to state and local units of government.

Blinder, Alan S. *Economic Policy and the Great Stagflation.* New York: Academic Press, 1979.
A perceptive history lesson and in-depth analysis of governmental economic policy in the 1970's. Carefully discusses the dilemma of

policy-making in that period and the effects of inappropriate policy decisions. This concise and well-written book is suitable for the general public. Illustrated with figures and economic data.

Blinder, Alan S., and Robert M. Solow. "Analytical Foundations of Fiscal Policy." In *The Economics of Public Finance*, edited by Alan S. Blinder et al. Washington, D.C.: Brookings Institution, 1974.
This chapter contains an overview of the theory of fiscal policy.

Blum, Walter J., and Harry Kalven, Jr. *The Uneasy Case for Progressive Taxation.* 1953. 5th impression. Chicago: University of Chicago Press, 1966.
A classic on the subject. A solid, honest, and objective assessment of a perennially explosive subject. Discusses progressive taxation from legal-constitutional and economic as well as ethical perspectives. Excellent for a general readership as well as specialists. Author and subject indexes.

Boaz, David, ed. *Assessing the Reagan Years.* New York: Cato Institute, 1988.
This 430-page book provides a good guide to the development of government fiscal policies in the 1980's. Reviews of the Reagan Administration's economic programs on taxation, spending, and transfer payment policies are given by various contributors, including Malcolm Forbes, Jr., and Robert W. Crandall. Suitable for a general audience.

Break, George, and Joseph A. Pechman. *Federal Tax Reform: The Impossible Dream?* Washington, D.C.: Brookings Institution, 1975.
Among many other proposed reforms, this book considers the effects of reforming the investment tax credit from three viewpoints: a laissez-faire approach, a social engineering approach, and a pragmatic fiscal approach.

Browning, Edgar K., and William R. Johnson. *The Distribution of the Tax Burden.* Washington, D.C.: American Enterprise Institute, 1979.
Disputes the conclusions of the John Pechman and Benjamin Okner studies, which argued that the overall tax system was basically proportional (except at the very top and bottom). Also, includes cash and in-kind transfers in measuring effective rates. Concludes that the

overall tax system is progressive. Nonspecialists and others may benefit. No index.

Burkhead, Jesse, and Jerry Miner. *Public Expenditure*. Chicago: Aldine, 1971.
Covers government spending from many points of view but emphasizes operational analysis. For this reason, this book places cost-benefit analysis in the general context of government spending and budgeting.

Carson, Robert B. *What Economists Know: An Economic Policy Primer for the 1990s and Beyond*. New York: St. Martin's Press, 1990.
Contains interesting and well-written historical background on macroeconomics, especially chapters 3 and 4, which deal with the development of Keynesian theory and the eventual weakening of the fiscal policy agenda as new concerns captured the attention of macroeconomists.

Clotfelter, Charles. *Federal Tax Policy and Charitable Giving*. Chicago: University of Chicago Press, 1985.
A masterful summary and synthesis of the many empirical studies which estimate the effect of tax deductions on personal giving. Clotfelter also reports on and extends the smaller literature on tax effects on bequests, corporate donations, volunteer effort, and foundations. All conclusions are accessible to the general reader, but some sections on methodology are for specialists.

Cnossen, Sijbren, and C. Sandford. *Taxing Consumption*. Paris: Organization for Economic Cooperation and Development, 1988.
Provides a comparative review of consumption tax systems and main policy issues. Coverage extends across countries and includes detailed discussion of relevant issues relating to general and selective sales taxes, as well as value-added taxes. Also examines international and interjurisdictional issues. Somewhat technical, printed in a typeface that is difficult to read, but specialists and nonspecialists can benefit. Contains a selective annotated bibliography.

Commerce Clearing House. *U.S. Master Tax Guide*. 74th ed. Chicago: Author, 1989.
This tax guide is published annually, providing an excellent one-volume source of information on U.S. personal and corporate income taxes. With approximately six hundred pages of tax information, well

indexed paragraph-by-paragraph, it is a comprehensive source of specific tax information useful in preparation of returns.

Due, John F., and John L. Mikesell. *Sales Taxation: State and Local Structure and Administration.* Baltimore: The Johns Hopkins University Press, 1983.

A classic: perhaps the best, most comprehensive, relatively nontechnical coverage. Provides historical details and covers such topics as sales tax exclusions and exemptions, taxation of services, sales tax administration, sales tax delinquency, sales tax audit programs, use taxation, and local government sales taxation. Specialists and general readers can benefit. Contains a selected bibliography and an index.

Feige, Edgar L., ed. *The Underground Economies: Tax Evasion and Information Distortion.* New York: Cambridge University Press, 1989.

A collection of papers discussing the meaning, measurement, and implications of the underground economy. A number of papers focus on the information problems that are created for public policy by the existence of the underground economy. Includes studies of the underground economy, in particular, the developed economies of both capitalist and communist countries.

Feldstein, Martin. *Capital Taxation.* Cambridge, Mass.: Harvard University Press, 1983.

The book deals with the major effects of taxation on saving, portfolio choice, business investment, and economic growth. The level is intermediate. Feldstein includes several charts, but not too many equations. Contains an excellent list of references for further study. The last chapter is also very good, although very rigorous, concerning inflation, income taxes, and interest rates.

Fink, Richard H., ed. *Supply-Side Economics.* Frederick, Md.: University Publications of America, 1982.

A compilation of readings on the supply-side school argument and criticism of it.

Fisher, Ronald C. *State and Local Public Finance.* Glenview, Ill.: Scott, Foresman, 1988.

This text has good coverage of general information on tax rates and taxation along with exceptional information on specific state and local tax policy issues.

Friedman, Benjamin. *Day of Reckoning: The Consequence of American Economic Policy Under Reagan and After*. New York: Random House, 1988.

Friedman is well-known for his economics of government policy. This 323-page book focuses on the major developments of fiscal policies in the 1980's—the economic background and consequences on interest rates, foreign exchange, public debts, and foreign loans. The problems of policy-making in the 1980's and beyond are carefully discussed. A well-written book suitable for a general reader.

Friedman, Milton, and Rose Friedman *Free to Choose: A Personal Statement*. New York: Avon Brooks, 1980.

Two distinguished economists place the increased fiscal and monetary roles of modern states in a conservative perspective. Popularly written and provocative, but well based factually. Particularly good, if brief, on specific tax systems. Contains few illustrative materials and end-notes, but an excellent index.

Ghazanfar, S. M. "Equity Effects and Revenue Potential of Sales Taxation of Services: Some Empirical Findings." *Public Finance Quarterly* 3 (April, 1975): 163-189.

Examines the effects of adding various combinations of consumer services in Idaho's sales tax base, which, like most other states in the country, is commodities-oriented. Overall progressivity-regressivity indexes are computed. Concludes that judicious inclusion of services in the base enhances revenues as well as reduces regressivity. Contains a bibliography.

Gold, Steven D., ed. *The Unfinished Agenda for State Tax Reform*. Denver: National Conference of State Legislatures, 1988.

Fourteen papers, most presented at a conference in October, 1987, focus on tax reforms by the states in 1987 and the neglected issues relevant to the 1990's. Discusses the meaning of balance in state-local tax systems; principles of a high-quality revenue system; state tax expenditure budgets; models of state income tax reform; the Florida experience on sales tax of services; tax relief for low-income groups; and the virtues of a state value-added tax. Excellent for the general reader, academicians, and policymakers. Contains an index.

Gordon, Robert J. *Macroeconomics*. 5th ed. Boston: Little, Brown, 1990.

A classic intermediate textbook by a Keynesian economist. Provides a thorough development of macroeconomic theory with many diagrams and supporting statistical evidence. Gordon concludes that discretionary fiscal policy is effective but infeasible in the U.S. institutional setting.

Gordon, Roger, and Burton Malkiel. "Corporation Finance." In *How Taxes Affect Economic Behavior*, edited by Henry J. Aaron and Joseph A. Pechman. Washington, D.C.: Brookings Institution, 1981.
This chapter discusses the effect of taxation on corporate finance. The authors examine the efficiency implications of the 1981 tax structure and evaluate several tax-reform proposals.

Hailstones, Thomas J. *A Guide to Supply-Side Economics*. Richmond, Va.: Robert F. Dame, 1982.
Places the Laffer effect in the context of supply-side economics, and traces the historical development of the basic tenets of the supply-side view.

Hansen, Bent. *The Economic Theory of Fiscal Policy*. Cambridge, Mass.: Harvard University Press, 1958.
One of the seminal works in fiscal policy. Part 1 contains Hansen's original general theory of policy. The book, translated from Swedish, is intended for the specialist but can be read by the general reader with some mathematical background.

Haveman, Robert, and Julius Margolis, eds. *Public Expenditure and Policy Analysis*. 2d ed. New York: Rand McNally, 1977.
Contains articles covering most of the controverted aspects of cost-benefit analysis as well as a number of actual analyses of specific public programs. Most of the articles are written in language that the average educated layperson can understand. Together with the book's introduction, they offer a good overview of public economics and cost-benefit analysis.

Heller, Walter. "Fiscal Policies for Underdeveloped Economies." In *Papers and Proceedings of the Conference on Agricultural Taxation and Economic Development*, edited by H. P. Wald. Cambridge, Mass.: Harvard University Press, 1954.
This paper summarizes some of the problems encountered by developing countries in the conduct of fiscal policies, especially regarding taxes. Requires no economics background. Still relevant despite its date of publication.

_____ . *New Dimensions of Political Economy.* Cambridge, Mass.: Harvard University Press, 1966.

Contains material presented in the Godkin lectures at Harvard by the former chairman of President John F. Kennedy's Council of Economic Advisers. He reveals his own plans for revenue sharing, which were eventually enacted during the Nixon Administration. Heller celebrates the virtues of fiscal policy, the triumph of Keynesian thinking in the New Economics of the early 1960's, and the advent of modern welfare capitalism. He also discusses the problems of educating politicians.

Johnson, Harry G. "Is Inflation the Price of Rapid Development, or a Retarding Factor?" *Malayan Economic Review 11* (April, 1966): 12-15.

This article reviews the arguments for and against using inflation as an engine of growth. A relatively nontechnical article.

Kahn, C. Harry. "The Place of Consumption and Net-Worth Taxation in the Federal Tax Structure." In *Broad-Based Taxes: New Options and Sources*, edited by Richard Musgrave. Baltimore: The Johns Hopkins University Press, 1973.

Gives an exceptionally clear explanation of the two arguments for the superiority of consumption to income as a tax base. Kahn argues for a tax on net worth as a way of capturing additional income.

Kaldor, Nicholas. *An Expenditure Tax.* London: Allen & Unwin, 1955.

The classic exposition of the concept of the personal expenditure tax, this very readable book considers the relationship of expenditure taxation to taxable capacity and examines the effects upon saving, risk taking, growth, and the incentive to work.

Keynes, John Maynard. *The General Theory of Employment, Interest, and Money.* New York: Harcourt Brace Jovanovich, 1936.

The theoretical justification for activist fiscal policy and the death knell for the neoclassical quantity theory. Keynesian analysis dominated macroeconomic policy-making in the twentieth century, and this book is the bible with which generations of scholars debated and analyzed. This work does not actually use the IS-LM framework, however, although the book was the basis for its creation and use.

King, Mervyn A., and Don Fullerton. *The Taxation of Income from Capital.* Chicago: University of Chicago Press, 1984.

A comparative study, sponsored by the National Bureau of Economic Research, of the taxation of capital income in Great Britain, Sweden,

(West) Germany, and the United States. The types of investment tax credits or grants in each of these countries is covered in detail. In addition to information on the corporate income taxes in these countries, other aspects of capital taxation are discussed, such as taxation of dividends and wealth and the treatment of capital gains.

Laffer, Arthur, and Jan P. Seymour, eds. *The Economics of the Tax Revolt: A Reader.* New York: Harcourt Brace Jovanovich, 1979.

A collection of essays, selected by Laffer himself, that discuss the Laffer effect and other aspects of the antitax revolt of the 1980's.

Lee, Dwight R., ed. *Taxation and the Deficit Economy: Fiscal Policy and Capital Formation in the United States.* San Francisco: Pacific Research Institute for Public Policy, 1986.

Contributed articles explore various aspects of the American economic and political system as they affect investment. Several authors discuss the Laffer effect.

Leftwich, Richard, and Ansel Sharp. *Economics of Social Issues.* 7th ed. Cincinnati: South-Western, 1989.

This book approaches basic economics from the perspective of examining the underlying economic analysis of important issues such as pollution, crime, and education subsidies. Written in very clear and understandable prose, including few mathematical equations. The chapters on government revenue and fiscal policy are recommended.

Lockard, Duane. *The Politics of State and Local Government.* 3d ed. New York: Macmillan, 1983.

Provides a simplified explanation of state and local politics, emphasizing fiscal matters. Treats the question of how voting can influence public-sector economic action.

McClure, Charles E., Jr. *Must Corporate Income Be Taxed Twice?* Washington, D.C.: Brookings Institution, 1979.

A report on a conference sponsored by the Brookings Institution, this book is a brief for the integration of the corporate income tax and the personal income tax. Arguments both for and against integration are presented clearly, without bias. Foreign experience is reviewed, and the administrative feasibility of integration is explored.

Michigan Department of Treasury. Taxation and Economic Policy Office. *Analysis of the Michigan Single Business Tax.* Lansing: Michigan Department of Treasury, 1985.

This publication provides a good practical guide to analyzing the way the only value-added tax in the United States works.

Musgrave, Richard A., and Peggy B. Musgrave. *Public Finance in Theory and Practice.* 5th ed. New York: McGraw-Hill, 1989.
This text is the traditional bible of public finance, including theory and applications of taxation and government expenditure programs as well.

Okun, Arthur M. *The Political Economy of Prosperity.* New York: W. W. Norton, 1970.
This well-written book presents a background study on economic policy-making in clear, understandable terms. Okun expressed a more realistic view of Keynesian policy than that generally held in the 1960's. The topics include consensus, controversy, and implementation in the political arena. Suitable for a general audience.

Pechman, Joseph A. *Federal Tax Policy.* 5th ed. Washington, D.C.: Brookings Institution, 1987.
This encyclopedic reference book on U.S. tax policy contains a nontechnical presentation of fiscal policy and very detailed appendices on the history of the tax code, the economic analysis of taxation, and tables of related macroeconomic statistics. Pechman chronicles the slowness with which Congress has implemented tax policy changes.

_____. *The Rich, the Poor, and the Taxes They Pay.* Boulder, Colo.: Westview Press, 1986.
A collection of articles published over the previous twenty years by one of the most prominent public-finance scholars of recent times (he died in 1989). Discusses various issues—comprehensive income taxation, major structural issues in tax design, negative income taxation, social security, and the like. Argues that the tax system has become less progressive over the two decades covered by the study. Advocates base-broadening and greater progressivity. Well written and relatively nontechnical. Intended for the general reader; specialists may also benefit. Bibliography, index.

_____. *Tax Reform: The Rich and the Poor.* 2d ed. Washington, D.C.: Brookings Institution, 1989.
Chapter 12 provides an excellent short summary of the value-added tax that is based on Pechman's work and on his testimony before congressional hearings on the adoption of a VAT.

_____ , ed. *What Should Be Taxed, Income or Expenditure?* Washington, D.C.: Brookings Institution, 1980.

An examination both for and against the concept of an expenditure tax by a number of scholars. Especially noteworthy are the chapters by David Bradford, "The Case for a Personal Consumption Tax"; William Andrews, "A Supplemental Personal Expenditure Tax"; and Michael Graetz, "Expenditure Tax Design." Bradford argues that both equity and efficiency considerations favor the consumption base, as this base results in a fairer distribution of burden and less distortion in the use of resources. Andrews considers the use of an expenditure tax to supplement the income tax, which amounts to the double taxation of consumption. Graetz, in great detail, examines virtually every aspect of the implementation of an expenditure tax, concentrating on those features and problems that are peculiar to the expenditure tax, as opposed to those that are shared by both expenditure and income taxes.

_____ . *Who Paid the Taxes, 1966-85?* Washington, D.C.: Brookings Institution, 1985.

Examines the burden distribution of all major taxes (as well as transfers) at the three levels of government in the United States: federal, state, and local. A sequel to the 1974 study (with Benjamin Okner), which concluded that for 1966 the tax system as a whole was roughly proportional. Similar conclusions for 1970, 1975, 1980, and 1985. Excellent. Nonspecialists may benefit. Bibliography, index.

Peterson, Wallace C. *Income, Employment, and Economic Growth.* 6th ed. New York: W. W. Norton, 1988.

Chapters 7 and 15 are written in a very readable and accessible manner. They serve as an excellent introduction to policy questions and the economic context in which changes in the tax structure were used in order to spur the economy or counteract inflation. Numerous references are provided for further study on each of the tax changes that is mentioned.

Powell, Walter W., ed. *The Nonprofit Sector: A Research Handbook.* New Haven, Conn.: Yale University Press, 1987.

Commissioned survey papers from a variety of disciplines. Topics include history, economic and political theories, tax treatment, government-nonprofit partnerships, measuring performance, leadership, the non-profit role in the culture, neighborhood, health care, social service, education, advocacy industries, sources of support, and comparative perspectives. Authoritative and accessible.

Rose-Ackerman, Susan, ed. *The Economics of Nonprofit Institutions: Studies in Structure and Policy.* New York: Oxford University Press, 1986. Reprints many of the classic articles from technical journals on the economics of the nonprofit sector, with a few new ones. Includes the papers of Burton A. Weisbrod, Henry Hansmann, Avner Ben-Ner, and Rose-Ackerman on contract failure, government failure, and fund-raising, as well as papers on tax policy, grants, and entrepreneurship.

Rosen, Harvey S. *Public Finance.* 2d ed. Homewood, Ill.: Richard D. Irwin, 1988.
    This excellent modern public finance text contains a very good treatment of the value-added tax in chapter 20 that considers various taxes on consumption.

Samuelson, Paul A., and William D. Nordhaus. *Economics.* 13th ed. New York: McGraw-Hill, 1989.
    A Nobel laureate as well as a nationally known economist and a great writer, Samuelson once served as an academic consultant to the Federal Reserve Board and economic adviser to President John F. Kennedy. This book is especially strong in fiscal policy and is one of the best-sellers in the market. Although some of the sentences and definitions of terms may be difficult to comprehend, those who appreciate the applications of theories in diagrams will find this text appealing.

Schiff, Jerald. *Charitable Giving and Government Policy: An Economic Analysis.* New York: Greenwood Press, 1990.
    A theoretical and empirical analysis of the effects of government spending and tax policies on donations, volunteering, and organizational behavior. Although it is based upon a sophisticated technical analysis, mathematics has been segregated to appendices; thus, the decision is largely accessible to the general reader.

Slitor, Richard. "Administrative Aspects of Expenditure Taxation." In *Broad-Based Taxes: New Options and Sources,* edited by Richard Musgrave. Baltimore: The Johns Hopkins University Press, 1973.
    A thorough and concise examination of the administrative feasibility of an expenditure tax. The concept of expenditures is covered, as well as a detailed treatment of various problem areas. The key features of the 1942 U.S. Treasury proposal are treated in an appendix.

Smith, Adam. *An Inquiry into the Nature and Causes of the Wealth of Nations.* 1776. New York: Random House, 1937.

This is Smith's 1776 classic, with a modern introduction, notes, marginal summary, and an enlarged index. Contains Smith's tax canon.

Stein, Herbert. *The Fiscal Revolution in America*. Chicago: University of Chicago Press, 1969.

Stein chronicles the history of the Keynesian revolution in the United States, from Herbert Hoover's tax hike through the tax cut of 1964. The discussion is nontechnical and readable. Although it focuses on discretionary policy, it also discusses the evolution of automatic stabilizers.

_____. *Presidential Economics: The Making of Economic Policy from Roosevelt to Reagan and Beyond*. New York: Simon & Schuster, 1988.

Stein makes the subject of economic writing understandable to the general public. This 450-page book integrates the development of economic theory with the history of policy-making. A careful overview of fiscal policies in practice from the Great Depression of the 1930's to the Reagan Administration. Figures and data on major economic indexes from 1930 to 1982.

Stiglitz, Joseph E. *Economics of the Public Sector*. 2d ed. New York: W. W. Norton, 1988.

A modern undergraduate text which teaches both tax and expenditure sides of public finance. Provides a very good historical background on the U.S. tax system, as well as excellent treatment of both tax theory and policy issues.

Summers, Lawrence H., ed. *Tax Policy and the Economy*. Cambridge, Mass.: National Bureau of Economic Research, 1989.

Five conference papers provide information and analysis relevant to tax policy, presenting perspectives on current and future issues. Topics are budget deficits, tax incentives, burden distribution, and inflation, as well as venture capital and capital gains taxation. Also discussed are incentive effects of the corporate alternative minimum tax, and the Japanese tax reform and the effective tax rate on Japanese corporate investments. Intended for specialists. No index.

Tanzi, Vito. *Taxation, Inflation, and Interest Rates*. Washington, D.C.: International Monetary Fund, 1984.

A collection of articles on the interplay of inflation and taxes with evidence from several nations. The papers that are presented are in the style of journal articles and would only be appropriate for advanced undergraduate and graduate students.

Thurow, Lester. *Dangerous Currents: The State of Economics.* New York: Random House, 1984.
Offers a good review on macroeconomic theory and critical analysis on the policies at work. Well written and suitable for a general audience.

United States. President. *Economic Report of the President.* Washington, D.C.: Government Printing Office.
An annual publication that provides the administration's view on the state of the economy and the interaction and effectiveness of both monetary and fiscal policy. Contains statistical material on trends in prices, output, employment, and wages in an appendix. Written for a general audience.

_____ . *Economic Report of the President.* Washington, D.C.: Government Printing Office, 1962.
This report contains the original arguments of the Kennedy Administration in favor of an investment tax credit to stimulate investment.

_____ . *Economic Report of the President.* Washington, D.C.: Government Printing Office, 1963.
A very readable elementary explanation of the current state of the economy in 1963 and an analysis of the problems that inhibited economic performance. Includes the rationale for the 1964 tax cut, a rudimentary presentation of the multiplier process, and the estimated effects of the tax cut. Economic reports in succeeding years may be referred to for similar analysis, policy prescriptions, and the results of tax policies as they were intended to influence consumption.

U.S. Congress. Congressional Budget Office. *The Changing Distribution of Federal Taxes: 1975-1990.* Washington, D.C.: Government Printing Office, 1987.
Measures changes in the distribution of major federal taxes (combined and separately) for three representative years: 1977, 1984, and 1988. Concludes that between 1977 and 1984, federal taxes became less progressive, but between 1984 and 1988, the distribution of taxes (subsequent to the 1986 Tax Reform Act) became more progressive but less than in 1977. Numerous tables on tax-burden distribution by income levels. Well written; any interested reader can benefit. No index.

_____ . *Federal Taxation of Tobacco, Alcoholic Beverages, and Motor Fuels.* Washington, D.C.: Government Printing Office, 1990.
Covers discussion in the late 1980's relating to the expansion of federal excise taxation in the United States. Provides evidence of the declining role of such taxation in the federal tax system as well as the overall U.S. tax structures. Argues that the regressivity issue is less relevant because of changes in consumption patterns across income classes. Provides extensive statistical information. Well written; specialists and nonspecialists can benefit.

U.S. Department of Treasury. *Tax Reform for Fairness, Simplicity, and Economic Growth.* Washington, D.C.: Government Printing Office, 1984.
This report provides a comprehensive view of transforming the U.S. tax system. Includes a discussion of value-added taxes.

Valentine, Lloyd M., and Daniel Ellis. *Business Cycles and Forecasting.*
Presents a concise discussion of fiscal policy within the context of other programs for achieving economic growth and stability. The presentation is nonmathematical. One weakness is that legislative changes of the 1980's, such as the Gramm-Rudman-Hollings Act, are not given sufficient emphasis.

Wanniski, Jude. *The Way the World Works: How Economies Fail and Succeed.* New York: Basic Books, 1978.
The book that did the most to popularize the Laffer curve and show how it related to other tenets of supply-side economics.

Watts, Gary, and Frank Masters, eds. *Property Taxation.* Washington, D.C.: National Education Association, 1985.
This short (eighteen-page) booklet is well written and easy to read. Briefly covers the development of property taxes, court decisions, limitations, and how inflation affects property tax revenue.

Weintraub, Sidney. "TIP as an Inflation Suppressant." In *Our Stagflation Malaise: Ending Inflation and Unemployment.* Westport, Conn.: Quorum Books, 1981.
Weintraub's book is rather uneven, but his chapter on tax-based incomes policies (TIP) is outstanding. It discusses the advantages of TIP over other anti-inflationary policies, different possible variants of TIP, and the potential problems with implementing a TIP.

Weisbrod, Burton A. *The Nonprofit Economy*. Cambridge, Mass.: Harvard University Press, 1988.
   Further development of many of the theories discussed in this article, written in a clear and thought-provoking manner. Considers the general theme of what institutional forms are appropriate for what roles. Presents evidence from many sources on whether nonprofits are more trustworthy than for-profits. Considers tax policy, fund-raising regulation, and the unfair competition debate.

Young, Dennis. *If Not for Profit, for What?* Lexington, Mass.: Lexington Books, 1983.
   A fine summary of the literature on the sector, followed by a development of Young's theory of entrepreneurial sorting. Organizational behavior is largely determined by the personalities and competencies of entrepreneurs. In turn, the nondistribution constraint and tax and regulatory policies determine which types of entrepreneurs will locate in each sector. Very accessible.

Public Finance

Adams, Henry C. *Public Debts*. New York: D. Appleton, 1893.
   A classic in public finance; discusses the relationship between national government borrowing and the cycle of war and peace, and the much different, development-oriented borrowing by local government.

Anderson, Gary M. "The U.S. Federal Deficit and National Debt: A Political and Economic History." In *Deficits*, edited by James M. Buchanan, Charles K. Rowley, and Robert D. Tollison. New York: Basil Blackwell, 1987.
   Presents a brief survey of how the national debt has grown over time.

Ando, Albert, E. Cary Brown, and Ann F. Friedlaender, eds. *Studies in Economic Stabilization*. Washington, D.C.: Brookings Institution, 1968.
   Although somewhat dated, this collection of papers is the most detailed examination of built-in stabilizers available. In the light of proposals to institute a nationwide value-added tax, its study of the stabilizing characteristics of this tax remains valuable. The book is, however, technical, with equations and econometric analysis.

Aronson, J. R., and John L. Hilley. *Financing State and Local Governments*. 4th ed. Washington, D.C.: Brookings Institution, 1986.

Describes and analyzes fiscal systems of state and local governments in the United States. Chapter 6 deals with business taxes, including various forms of corporate income taxes used by states and the various tax credits and investment incentives. An interesting topic covered here is the apportionment of tax liability of multistate corporations among the several states.

Auletta, Ken. *The Streets Were Paved with Gold.* New York: Random House, 1979.
A very readable account of New York's fiscal crisis. A reporter looks at the various explanations which were offered to explain how New York came close to bankruptcy and provides an analysis of the merits and faults of each. Provides useful insights into a complex problem for readers without much economics or financial training.

Baumol, William J., and Alan S. Blinder. *Economics, Principles, and Policy.* New York: Harcourt Brace Jovanovich, 1988.
This elementary text defines the terms of central bank debt monetization and provides a typical discussion of its macroeconomic effects with the IS-LM model. Also included is a discussion of the "true" burden of the debt.

Bennett, James T., and Thomas J. DiLorenzo. *Underground Government: The Off-Budget Public Sector.* Washington, D.C.: Cato Institute, 1983.
One of the early and more complete analyses of off-budget borrowing and use of credit guarantees. Considers the history of the usage at both the federal and the subnational levels, and offers some explanations why such activities might be more politically acceptable than other government operations.

Bernheim, B. Douglas. "A Neoclassical Perspective on Budget Deficits." *Journal of Economic Perspectives* 3 (Spring, 1989): 55-72.
This article is a good representative presentation of the modern-day classical view of crowding out. Advanced macroeconomics is required.

_____ . "Ricardian Equivalence: An Evaluation of Theory and Evidence." In *NBER Macroeconomics Annual*, edited by Stanley Fischer. Cambridge, Mass.: MIT Press, 1987.
A comprehensive review of Ricardian equivalence and the public debt controversy. Although this essay is aimed at a professional audience, it is accessible to the general reader.

Bierman, Harold, Jr. *Implementing Capital Budgeting Techniques*. Cambridge, Mass.: Ballinger, 1988.

> Describes working managers' perceived problems of implementing capital budgeting decision-making techniques. Surveys the capital budgeting literature dealing with these problems and suggests methods of coping with them. The book attempts to link academic capital budgeting literature with the current interests of business managers. Contains an extensive bibliography of capital budgeting literature in professional journals for each major topic.

Buchanan, James M. *The Public Finances*. 3d ed. Homewood, Ill.: Richard D. Irwin, 1970.

> Chapter 4 of this classic, but somewhat dated, text contains a good nontechnical explanation of public goods.

Buchanan, James M., Charles K. Rowley, and Robert D. Tollison, eds. *Deficits*. New York: Basil Blackwell, 1987.

> A well-rounded and accessible discussion of deficits. This collection of essays by well-known and respected economists examines historical, theoretical, and political issues surrounding this topic.

Cagan, Phillip, ed. *The Economy in Deficit*. Washington, D.C.: American Enterprise Institute, 1985.

> This 300-page-plus volume contains a range of articles by noted economists covering various aspects of deficits, channels of crowding out, and the politics of deficits. Some of the articles require advanced economics, some require statistics, and some do not.

Cebula, Richard J. *The Deficit Problem in Perspective*. Lexington, Mass.: Lexington Books, 1987.

> This compact work (105 pages) devotes two chapters to the theoretical and empirical aspects of crowding out. The book contains a large number of references to all aspects of the crowding-out process. An intermediate level of undergraduate macroeconomics and a knowledge of statistical regression analysis are required to follow the discussion.

Courant, Paul N., and Edward M. Gramlich. *Federal Budget Deficits: America's Great Consumption Binge*. Englewood Cliffs, N.J.: Prentice-Hall, 1986.

> A very short and accessible work on the 1980's deficits. It gives some background in macroeconomics and discusses various solutions, both economic and political.

Debt, Financial Stability, and Public Policy: A Symposium. Kansas City: Federal Reserve Bank of Kansas City, 1986.

Contains the papers and critical commentary that were presented at the symposium, which brought together leading economists, Federal Reserve officials, and executives from government, financial institutions, and businesses. The topics include both U.S. debt and the international debt crisis. Includes some technical graphs and tables.

Eisner, Robert. *How Real Is the Federal Deficit?* New York: Free Press, 1986.

In this fairly brief book (240 pages), Eisner argues and presents calculations in support of his view that when adjusted for inflation, the government deficits of the 1980's in particular turn out to be essentially trivial. Eisner also presents statistical evidence in support of his contention that deficit spending produces a crowding-in effect on investment and total spending in the economy. The book contains much data and number crunching; some of it can be followed with a knowledge of basic economics, but a good bit of it requires advanced economics and statistics.

Fink, Richard H., and Jack C. High, eds. *A Nation in Debt: Economists Debate the Federal Budget Deficit.* Frederick, Md.: University Publications of America, 1987.

A good overview of the issue of deficit financing. As a collection of essays, it examines impacts of debt financing as well as inflationary effects of deficits.

Foley, Duncan. "Resource Allocation and the Public Sector." *Yale Economic Essays* 7, no. 1 (1967): 45-98.

In this piece, Foley gave equity the technical meaning that has proliferated in the economics literature. The context of equity's appearance involved the financing of public goods.

Friedman, Benjamin. "Crowding Out or Crowding In? Economic Consequences of Financing Government Deficits." *Brookings Papers on Economic Activity* 3 (1978): 593-654.

The classic analysis of the conditions under which crowding out, or crowding in (its opposite), is likely to occur. AJlthough it is fairly technical, the nonspecialist should be able to understand the important points made by Friedman.

_____ . *The Day of Reckoning: The Consequences of American Economic Policy Under Reagan and After.* New York: Random House, 1988.

A fascinating, if unflattering, look at the Reagan Administration. This rather lengthy work (333 pages), written for a general audience, argues vigorously that deficits and the national debt do impose a burden on future generations. There is no specific discussion of crowding out as such; however, throughout the book there are many references to data that imply one type of crowding-out effect or another. Friedman argues that the accumulated government debt will lead to lower living standards in the United States.

Friedman, Milton, and Anna J. Schwartz. *A Monetary History of the United States, 1867-1960.* Princeton, N.J.: Princeton University Press, 1963.

An excellent source of information on all depressions since the Civil War, including those in the 1870's, the 1890's, and 1920-1921. Chapter 7 (published separately by the same company as *The Great Contraction, 1929-1933*) is the foundation for the monetarist interpretation of this period. Emphasis is placed on the importance of banking developments and Federal Reserve Board policy as causal forces.

Gaertner, Wulf, and Alois Wenig, eds. *The Economics of the Shadow Economy.* New York: Springer-Verlag, 1985.

A collection of papers on the underground economy drawn from an international conference. Discusses the definition and measurement of the underground economy, its relationship with the regular economy, the factors underlying participation in the underground economy, and the effect of government policies. Both theoretical and empirical studies are included. Some of the papers are relatively technical, but most are written in a form quite accessible to a general academic audience.

Gilmour, John. *Reconcilable Differences?: Congress, the Budget Process, and the Deficit.* Berkeley: University of California Press, 1990.

An authoritative critique of the United States congressional budget process, emphasizing the "reconciliation" phase. Picks up the history of 1966 and carries the account through the implementation of the Gramm-Rudman-Hollings Act. An index provides access to a wealth of concrete details.

Heilbroner, Robert, and Peter Bernstein. *The Debt and the Deficit: False Alarms/Real Possibilities.* New York: W. W. Norton, 1989.
A generally accessible and fairly brief (144-page) primer written for a general audience on the broad topic of deficits, national debt, and the notion of a burden on future generations. Two chapters are devoted to a discussion of interest-rate-induced crowding out. A number of simple data examples are used to illustrate the author's arguments.

Hirsch, Werner Z., and Anthony M. Rufolo. *Public Finance and Expenditure in a Federal System.* San Diego: Harcourt Brace Jovanovich, 1990.
A general text on public finance with chapters on debt finance as well as the impact of debt on the creation of fiscal problems.

Ippolito, Dennis S. *Hidden Spending: The Politics of Federal Credit Programs.* Chapel Hill: University of North Carolina Press, 1984.
An extensive discussion of the use of credit by the federal government: direct lending, credit guarantees, and off-budget borrowing and lending.

Jimenez, Emmanuel. *Pricing Policy in the Social Sectors: Cost Recovery for Education and Health in Developing Countries.* Baltimore: The Johns Hopkins University Press, 1987.
An interesting discussion of the possible uses of pricing to allocate social services in the developing countries.

Johansen, Leif. *Public Economics.* Skokie, Ill.: Rand McNally, 1965.
Originally published in Norwegian, this excellent book, though old, is still one of the clearest and most accessible descriptions of the problems and techniques of economic policy. Chapter 2 includes a general discussion of targets and instruments which, while abstract, presents succinctly the main findings of the theory.

Journal of Economic Perspectives 3 (Spring, 1989).
A special issue that presents a number of professional articles devoted to the subject of deficits. It is easily accessible and covers an interesting array of topics.

Loque, Dennis E., ed. *Handbook of Modern Finance.* Boston: Warren, Gorham and Lamont, 1984.
Chapters 7 and 8 cover the long-term bond market and state and local government finance.

Mattera, Philip. *Off the Books: The Rise of the Underground Economy.*
New York: St. Martin's Press, 1985.
   A concise, provocative, and very readable treatment of the underground economy. Attempts to show the relationship between the underground economy and changes in the larger economy and argues that
   the underground economy has both exploitative and liberating aspects,
   which present difficult dilemmas for policymakers. Suitable for the
   general reader.

Matzer, John, Jr., ed. *Capital Financing Strategies for Local Governments.* Washington, D.C.: International city Management Association,
1983.
   A fairly comprehensive presentation of major financing techniques
   used by local governments. Includes descriptions of different methods
   and their uses as well as some discussion of the marketing of municipal
   debt.

Meyer, Laurence H., ed. *The Economic Consequences of Government
Deficits.* Boston: Kluwer-Nijhoff, 1983.
   This collection of essays, by various authors, examines a variety of
   possible negative effects of government deficit spending. Some of
   these essays are appropriate for the nonspecialist.

Minarik, Joseph. *Making America's Budget Policy: From the 1980s to the
1990s.* Armonk, N.Y.: M. E. Sharpe, 1990.
   Overviews the making of United States budget policy in the 1980's,
   describing the budget-policy environment and analyzing the economic
   and political issues implicated by budget reform. Assesses the short-
   term risks that are associated with the nation's reliance on foreign
   credit. Contains a preface by Senator Bill Bradley of New Jersey.

Musgrave, Richard A. *The Theory of Public Finance.* New York:
McGraw-Hill, 1959.
   A distinguished contribution to the subject, although a difficult book
   for beginners. Although taxation is treated throughout, chapters 1, 5,
   8, 10, and 11 are especially pertinent. The notes are full, and there is
   an excellent index of names and subjects that aids selective reading.
   Required reading for serious students.

Musgrave, Richard, and Peggy Musgrave. *Public Finance in Theory and
Practice.* 5th ed. New York: McGraw-Hill, 1989.

The dean of public finance theory, Richard Musgrave, and his wife provide an economic rationale for government intervention when externalities are present, and for intergovernmental grants to address interjurisdictional externalities that are present in a federal system such as that of the United States. Particularly useful are chapter 17 on taxation effects on capacity output and part 7 on fiscal policy and stabilization.

Mushkin, Selma J., ed. *Public Prices for Public Products.* Washington, D.C.: Urban Institute, 1972.
Perhaps the most complete set of readings on the topic in existence. A few of the articles may be difficult for the nonspecialist, but most are easy to follow.

Ott, David J., and Attiat F. Ott. *Federal Budget Policy.* 3d ed. Washington, D.C.: Brookings Institution, 1977.
Written for the general reader, this is a readable description of fiscal policy with a good discussion of automatic stabilizers, the natural deficit, and crowding out. Includes useful, though dated, statistics and charts.

Parkin, Michael. *Economics.* Reading, Mass.: Addison-Wesley, 1990.
Dedicates at least one chapter to the study of how capital (money) markets work. A discussion of the flows of money and the methods by which investments are generated and promote economic growth is handled nicely through the use of flow diagrams. Provides a good training ground for those interested in developing a working knowledge of the interactions between households, firms, and the government in the financial capital market.

Peterson, John E., and Wesley C. Hough. *Creative Capital Financing for State and Local Governments.* Chicago: Municipal Finance Officers Association, 1983.
This book was compiled when creative financing was a popular topic, and some of the techniques have been rendered obsolete by changes in the tax laws. Nevertheless, it provides a good introduction to some of the more creative options available for public-sector borrowing.

Rosen, Harvey S. *Public Finance.* 2d ed. Homewood, Ill.: Richard D. Irwin, 1988.

One of the best available textbooks on public finance. Well written with few equations or statistics. Contains a good discussion of Gramm-Rudman and inflationary distortions.

Santow, Leonard Jay. *The Budget Deficit: The Causes, the Costs, the Outlook.* New York: New York Institute of Finance, 1988.
   Provides basic knowledge of budget realities in a readily accessible question-and-answer format. Traces the massive increase in the United States budget deficit from 1974 to 1986, explaining its timing, causes, and costs, and even assessing blame. Each of the fifty questions are answered within one to ten pages. Quantitatively based.

Stabile, Donald R., and Jeffrey A. Cantor. *The Public Debt of the United States: An Historical Perspective, 1775-1988.* New York: Praeger, 1991.
   This 220-page volume presents a comprehensive history of the U.S. national debt and reviews the methods that the government has used to manage and administer it. The authors describe the impact of wars, recessions, and macroeconomic policy on the growth of the debt and trace how government debt policy was linked to the evolution of the banking system. Suitable for a general readership and contains tables, an index, and a bibliography.

Stiglitz, Joseph E. *Economics of the Public Sector.* 2d ed. New York: W. W. Norton, 1989.
   A textbook in public finance by one of the economists working on the frontiers of the subject. Part 1 explains why some economic activities are undertaken collectively. Chapter 5 deals with public goods and publicly provided private goods. There is some technical economic analysis, but most of the argument is clear and accessible to noneconomists.

Swann, Dennis. *The Economics of the Common Market.* 6th ed. New York: Penguin Books, 1988.
   A leading British economist looks at the actual mechanism of the European marketplace, considering tariffs, monetary integration, and the major economic policies of the European Economic Community in agriculture, energy, transport, regional development, and society.

Tanzi, Vito, ed. *The Underground Economy in the United States and Abroad.* Lexington, Mass.: Lexington Books, 1982.

A collection of papers which includes a number of important papers previously published elsewhere. Focuses largely on different methodologies for measuring the underground economy. Includes studies of the underground economy in a number of countries.

United States. Executive Office of the President. Office of Management and Budget. *Special Analyses: Budget of the United States Government.* Washington, D.C.: Government Printing Office, 1972-
This document, published annually, has a section entitled "Borrowing and Debt" and one entitled "Federal Credit Programs," which offer extensive analysis and current data on each of these topics.

United States. President. *The Economic Report of the President.* Washington, D.C.: Government Printing Office. 1947-
This annual report, prepared by the Council of Economic Advisors, normally discusses the government's budget of the previous year and predicts the budget deficit (surplus) of the coming year. An extensive appendix contains more than a hundred pages of economic data, including several pages devoted to the budgets of the federal, state, and local governments of the United States.

U.S. Office of Management and Budget. *Budget of the United States Government.* Washington, D.C.: Government Printing Office, 1982.
Surveys expenditures, taxes, and deficits, giving a good indication of the size and complexity of the U.S. budget.

Van Horne, James C. *Financial Market Rates and Flows.* Englewood Cliffs, N.J.: Prentice-Hall, 1978.
An analysis of the determination and relationships between various interest rates, and their connections with the flow of funds.

Wildavsky, Aaron. *The Politics of the Budgetary Process.* Boston: Little, Brown, 1964.
A classic examination of the linkage between politics and budgetary policy. It provides several examples of how constituent interests are translated into economic policy through the federal budget process. Suitable for college-level readers.

INTERNATIONAL ASPECTS

International Trade

Adams, John, ed. *The Contemporary International Economy: A Reader.* 2d ed. New York: St. Martin's Press, 1985.

Discusses a series of articles by several authors and treats specific areas of international trade. The problems experienced by countries involved in trade are examined carefully to aid the reader in understanding the implications of policies enacted. Significant trade agreements are presented and analyzed in a thought-provoking way.

Alexandrides, Costas G., and Barbara L. Bowers. *Countertrade: Practices, Strategies, and Tactics.* New York: John Wiley & Sons, 1987.

One of the best books on countertrade. In clear, understandable terms, it explains the basic principles and practices for organizing, financing, and executing countertrade effectively in international business operations. This book is different from other books on countertrade because it integrates countertrade with international trade and business.

Andersen, Torben Juul. *Currency and Interest Rate Hedging: A User's Guide to Options, Futures, Swaps, and Forward Contracts.* New York: New York Institute of Finance, 1987.

Provides a good introduction to the entire range of protection against the risk of currency fluctuations. Easy to read with comprehensive examples.

Anikin, Andre. *Gold: The Yellow Devil.* New York: International Publishers, 1983.

Anikin's analysis of the reasons why gold has ceased to be the basis of monetary systems is particularly interesting because it is an example of creative thinking under difficult political conditions. Originally written in 1978, the book reflects the problems posed by the Organization of Petroleum Exporting Countries and significant supply-side inflation. Anikin believes that there is little doubt that the future evolution of the monetary system will be linked with gold in some way. Anikin discusses the French valuation of gold reserves at market prices, which were ten times as high as the value used by the United States for its gold reserves. Anikin recognizes that higher interest rates can limit the rise in the price of gold but fails to anticipate Paul Volcker's anti-inflation policies.

Appleyard, Reginald T., ed. *International Migration Today.* Vols. 1-2. Paris: United Nations Educational, Scientific, and Cultural Organization, 1988.

Both volumes are collections of papers written on international migration. Volume 1 explores the migration trends of the major regions of the world, as well as the evolution of these flows. Volume 2 discusses issues of migration in detail. This collection is written for the general public, particularly those interested in migration history and public policy.

Axtell, Roger. *The Do's and Taboo's of International Trade.* New York: John Wiley & Sons, 1989.

A simple primer on the mechanics of international trade that is especially useful to someone interested in actually engaging in trade. Designed for the lay reader and is not a theoretical treatment of the subject.

Bahmani-Oskooee, Mohsen. "Deterioration in the Terms of Trade Improves the Balance of Payments Even If Not the Trade Balance: Some Evidence from LDCs." *Quarterly Review of Economics and Business* 30 (Autumn, 1990): 3.

Bahmani-Oskooee provides a theoretical scenario for devaluation as a policy tool in providing assistance in balance of payments improvement. His scenario includes the notion of the impact of devaluation on terms of trade. Examples are drawn from four Third World countries over a period of ten years to support his hypothesis.

Balance of Payments Statistics, 1979-

Published monthly and annually, this journal contains BOP statistics for International Monetary Fund (IMF) member countries (about 140 countries). The monthly issues contain aggregate annual data and, where available, monthly, quarterly, or semiannual data. The yearbook is published in two volumes. The first volume contains national aggregate and disaggregate data; the second contains fifty-five tables that present regional area and world totals of BOP components. The monetary unit that is used is the IMF Special Drawing Rights (SDR).

Baldwin, Robert E. *Nontariff Distortions of International Trade.* Washington, D.C.: Brookings Institution, 1970.
> Although dated, this book offers a clear, detailed introduction to the array of import restrictions that ten years later was seen as an integral part of the new protectionism. Suitable for advanced college students.

_____. *Trade Policy in a Changing World.* Chicago: University of Chicago Press, 1989.
> A collection of essays on U.S. trade policy and U.S. approaches to negotiations on the General Agreement on Tariffs and Trade (GATT). Baldwin reviews U.S. trade policy since World War II, the theoretical basis for the policies that were adopted, the economics of the GATT, the employment effects and negotiating techniques of multilateral trade negotiations, current policy issues, and trade strategies. Suitable for students.

Batra, Raveendra N. *The Pure Theory of International Trade Under Uncertainty.* London: Macmillan, 1975.
> Batra extends trade theory by incorporating uncertainty into the standard Heckscher-Ohlin trade model. Some exposure to international trade theory is presumed.

Bhagwati, Jagdish. *Protectionism.* Cambridge, Mass.: MIT Press, 1988.
> This 147-page book is a collection of lectures delivered by one of the foremost experts on international trade policies and practices. Includes analyses of the evolution of free trade practices and the General Agreement on Tariffs and Trade, as well as important current economic issues such as voluntary export restraints. Suitable for college students.

Bigman, David, and Teizo Taya, eds. *Floating Exchange Rates and the State of World Trade and Payments.* Cambridge, Mass.: Ballinger, 1984.
> A set of technical essays considering the role of central banks and capital controls in the process of the adjustment of exchange rates toward equilibrium. The essays analyze and draw on the actual history of exchange-rate movements in their analysis of various theories.

Bloomfield, Arthur I. *Monetary Policy Under the International Gold Standard: 1880-1914.* New York: Federal Reserve Bank of New York, 1959.
> An authoritative account of the way in which central banks manipulated the rules of the gold standard to protect nations' internal economies against price fluctuations, as transmitted through the balance of

payments. Best suited to specialists or economics majors at the under-graduate level and above.

Bonker, Don. *America's Trade Crisis: The Making of the U.S. Trade Deficit.* Boston: Houghton Mifflin, 1988.
A concrete, well-written account of the United States trade deficit, authored by Congressman Bonker of the state of Washington. Features a comprehensive glossary of technical terms, documentary notes, and suggested readings. A knowledgeable introduction, written by a congressional insider.

Bordo, Michael, and Anna J. Schwartz, eds. *A Retrospective on the Classical Gold Standard.* Chicago: University of Chicago Press, 1984.
A fairly advanced collection of scholarship on the gold standard experience in the nineteenth and twentieth centuries. Articles take both a broad theoretical approach to the gold standard and a country-specific, case-study approach. Although addressed primarily to the specialist, the book is readable by most undergraduates.

Brooks, S., K. Cuthbertson, and David G. Mayes. *The Exchange Rate Environment.* London: Croom Helm, 1986.
Provides a good foundation for a serious understanding of various models of foreign exchange interaction. Despite its use of algebra as a basis of communicating ideas, this well-written text allows the diligent reader to grasp its concepts. As the book was written in Great Britain, its examples refer to the pound sterling rather than the dollar and may confuse an American reader at first.

Brown, Brendan. *The Forward Market in Foreign Exchange.* New York: St. Martin's Press, 1983.
The book is a simple and easy-to-read study of arbitrage, speculation, broker-dealer, and market-making operations in foreign currencies. There are many examples of currency arbitrage, and very few graphs or equations are included. Highly recommended as an introductory volume in the study of currency arbitrage, the book also includes sections on forward and swap contracts.

Camps, Miriam, and William Diebold, Jr. *The New Multilateralism.* New York: Council on Foreign Relations, 1986.
An analysis of issues in the world trading system. Various questions that the General Agreements on Tariffs and Trade must consider in

order to deal with the trade problems of the present and future are also discussed. Accessible to a general audience.

Carbaugh, Robert J. *International Economics.* 3d ed. Belmont, Calif.: Wadsworth, 1989.

An introductory-level textbook that provides a formal and systematic discussion of international trade theories. Also contains numerous descriptive data, and an introductory analysis of trade policies and the financial aspects of world trade.

Carson, Robert B. *Macroeconomic Issues Today.* New York: St. Martin's Press, 1987.

An excellent comparison of conservative, liberal, and radical views on international finance and trade. Seven other issues are also included to round out this well-written, 211-page book. The radical argument on American overseas investment is particularly useful as a comparison to more conventional textbook approaches.

Carvounis, Chris. *The United States Trade Deficit of the 1980s: Origins, Meanings, and Policy Responses.* New York: Quorum Books, 1987.

This 190-page analysis hinges on a sustained contrast of the monetarist and the structuralist explanations of chronic United States trade deficits. Within this analytic framework, separate chapters are devoted to the origins of the deficit, its meanings, and appropriate policy responses.

Caves, Richard E., and Ronald W. Jones. *World Trade and Payments.* Boston: Little, Brown, 1986.

This international trade text covers the reciprocal demand (offer curve) theory, the Marshall-Lerner condition, and other important applications of partial equilibrium analysis in international trade theory.

Chacoliades, Miltiades. *Principles of International Economics: Theory and Empirical Evidence.* 3d ed. New York: McGraw-Hill, 1990.

Chapter 2 describes the concept of absolute advantage and gives a concise illustration. Chapter 12 explains the principles and issues of the balance of payments. Chapter 15 deals with the relationship between the balance of trade and national income, covering topics such as surpluses, deficits, and terms of trade. Written clearly enough for the general reader.

Cline, William, ed. *Trade Policy in the 1980s.* Washington, D.C.: Institute for International Economics, 1983.

The twenty-two articles in this volume offer a detailed assessment of the international trade issues. The book contains overviews and detailed sectoral analyses of import restrictions. Suitable for college students.

Conybeare, John A. C. *Trade Wars: The Theory and Practice of International Commercial Rivalry*. New York: Columbia University Press, 1987.
Focuses on trade wars as factors influencing regional development. Looks at six different historical trade policy incidents and assesses their implications. Although narrow in scope, this book is appropriate for the general reader.

Csikos-Nagy, Bela, and David G. Young, eds. *East-West Economic Relations in the Changing Global Environment*. New York: St. Martin's Press, 1986.
A selection of articles originating from the proceedings held by the International Economic Association. East-West barter and trade in general are examined in some detail: economic interaction, institutional framework, energy trade, technological cooperation, financial cooperation, and comparative trade advantage. Written for those informed about trade, the book also has interesting viewpoints and is a good source for term papers. Recommended audience: junior or senior college students.

Danielsen, Albert L. *The Evolution of OPEC*. New York: Harcourt Brace Jovanovich, 1982.
A case study of the workings of the Organization of Petroleum Exporting Countries (OPEC) cartel. Shows how collusion can be profitable.

Davis, Lance E., and Robert A. Huttenback. *Mammon and the Pursuit of Empire*. Cambridge, England: Cambridge University Press, 1986.
The best study on the costs and benefits to Great Britain of its Empire from the mid-nineteenth century to World War I. The authors use primary and other sources to support their claim that the British Empire was a substantial net drain on the resources of the United Kingdom.

Dernburg, Thomas F. *Global Macroeconomics*. New York: Harper & Row, 1989.
Chapter 10 provides a description of the monetary approach to the balance of payments under fixed and flexible exchange rates. Chapter 11 explains the asset market approach. Chapters 13 and 14 provide

excellent descriptions of the historical development of the international monetary system from the gold standard to 1989.

Destler, I. M. *American Trade Politics: System Under Stress.* Washington, D.C.: Institute for International Economics, 1986.
This book focuses on the political dynamics of U.S. trade policy. Also offers a detailed appendix on antidumping and countervailing duty actions. Suitable for college students.

Dornbusch, Rudiger. "Purchasing Power Parity." In *The New Palgrave: A Dictionary of Economics*, edited by John Eatwell, Murray Milgate, and Peter Newman. New York: Macmillan, 1987.
A survey article on the advantages and disadvantages of purchasing power parity.

Eichengreen, Barry, ed. *The Gold Standard in Theory and History.* New York: Methuen, 1985.
An excellent collection of some of the most important works (in the form of excerpts and articles) on the gold standard experience across time. The book can be read from the undergraduate level on up.

Elderkin, Kenton W., and Warren E. Norquist. *Creative Countertrade: A Guide to Doing Business Worldwide.* Cambridge, Mass.: Ballinger, 1987.
Designed for the international trading firm executive, this 221-page overview sketches the traditional forms of countertrade, outlines the basic steps that are involved in different types of transactions, examines the different parties that are involved, analyzes the reasons for resistance to countertrade, and proposes "creative countertrade" strategies, ending with a forecast for the future. Although addressed to potential practitioners, this clear, concise, and well-organized text is well suited to nonspecialists.

Ellsworth, Paul T., and J. Clark Leith. *The International Economy.* New York: Macmillan, 1987.
Presents mercantilist theories and their applications to economic policy and practice in an excellent narrative. The first edition provides more historical data than the later editions. The information is well documented and is reported in a manner that will interest the reader. The shortcomings of the mercantilist system are also noted.

Emmanuel, Arghiri. *Unequal Exchange: A Study of the Imperialism of Trade.* Translated by Brian Pearce. New York: Monthly Review Press, 1972.

A well-known critique of the traditional North-South specialization and trade patterns. It discusses the role of the terms of trade in transmitting inequality, which the author argues arises from an "unequal exchange" between the North and the South. Recommended for college students.

Ethier, Wilfred J. *Modern International Economics.* 2d ed. New York: W. W. Norton, 1987.

This book provides two very exciting and informative chapters on the political implications of policy decisions in international trade. The issues of tariffs and other barriers to free trade are examined. Cited cases are excellent examples of how decisions affect a country and its citizens.

Faust, Jon. "U.S. Foreign Indebtedness: Are We Investing What We Borrow?" *Economic Review* (July/August, 1989): 3-19.

An excellent article which in simple terms explains historical trends in the U.S. net external position and analyzes the link between foreign capital inflows and investment in the United States during the 1980's.

Fisher, Bart S., and Kathleen M. Harte, eds. *Barter in the World Economy.* New York: Praeger, 1985.

This book grew out of a workshop seminar conducted at Georgetown University School of Foreign Service and is a selection of articles that describe the mechanics of barter, barter scenarios, and problems associated with barter domestically and internationally. This book is not very technical and is suitable for a general audience; high school and college students will find it an excellent reference.

Francis, Dick. *The Countertrade Handbook.* New York: Quorum Books, 1987.

Provides a good introduction to the actual practice of countertrade. The discussion covers topics such as documentation, countertrade insurance, and the countertrade service industry. Illustrated with many figures.

Friman, H. Richard. *Patchwork Protectionism: Textile Trade Policy in the United States, Japan, and West Germany.* Ithaca, N.Y.: Cornell University Press, 1990.

Offers a comparative analysis of the political dynamics that lead developed countries to adopt different types of import restrictions.

Illustrates these dynamics in the textile sector. Suitable for advanced college students.

Gardner, Richard N. *Sterling-Dollar Diplomacy: The Origin and Prospects of Our International Economic Order*. Rev. ed. New York: McGraw-Hill, 1969.

The 1956 edition of this work, here reprinted, traces the rise and fall of Anglo-American cooperation on international trade and monetary policies between 1941 and 1950, focusing upon negotiation of the Bretton Woods agreement, the Anglo-American Loan Agreement of 1945, and the proposed charter for an international trade organization in the fall of 1950. A new, 95-page introduction titled "Sterling-Dollar Diplomacy: A Twenty-five Year Perspective" combines a judicious assessment of the achievements of the Bretton Woods system with an astute analysis of its failings.

General Agreement on Tariffs and Trade. *Basic Instruments and Selected Documents* 1 (1953).

The main volumes contain the texts of various agreements in force. The annual supplements include decisions, conclusions, and reports presented to the contracting parties of the GATT during the previous period. Suitable for a general audience.

Gershman, Michael. *Smarter Barter: A Guide for Corporations, Professionals, and Small Business*. New York: Viking Press, 1986.

Gershman explains the basics of barter and how U.S. companies barter in order to solve specific business problems. The reader will find numerous examples related to the media and the travel industry, as well as the Internal Revenue Service. Suitable for a general audience.

Glickman, Norman J., and Douglas P. Woodward. *The New Competitors*. New York: Basic Books, 1989.

A broad-ranging book on the implications for American business of foreign investment in the United States. It is written in an easy-to-read, popular style that more than makes up for the relative lack of hard macroeconomic data. An excellent source of information for the beginning student.

Graham, Edward M., and Paul R. Krugman. *Foreign Direct Investment in the United States*. Washington, D.C.: Institute for International Economics, 1989.

An economic treatise outlining the arguments for the maintenance of traditional open policies toward foreign investment in the United States. The evaluation of the national security consequences of foreign investment is excellent, and the bibliography contains many valuable references for the reader interested in government policy toward foreign investment.

Gray, Peter H. *International Economic Problems and Policies.* New York: St. Martin's Press, 1987.
Gray develops the offer curve from the presentation of a table, what he calls a commonsense approach.

Gregory, Paul R., and Roy J. Ruffin. *Basic Economics.* Glenview, Ill.: Scott, Foresman, 1989.
Explains the relationship between money supply and exchange rates very well, incorporating both the fixed-rate system and flexible-rate system into the analysis. Accessible to readers without a strong background in economics.

Grimwade, Nigel. *International Trade: New Patterns of Trade, Production, and Investment.* New York: Routledge, Chapman & Hall, 1989.
A well-written and readable book that contains a clear discussion of trade theory and trade history. In addition, the book incorporates clear discussions of highly relevant issues such as the rise of multinational firms, problems of adjusting to a freer trade environment, trade in services, and new and emerging forms of international economic involvement.

Guttmann, Robert. *How Credit-Money Shapes the Economy: The United States in a Global System.* Armonk, N.Y.: M. E. Sharpe, 1994.
A pathbreaking critique of contemporary international monetary policy building on the works of John Maynard Keynes and Karl Marx. Guttmann criticizes the monetarist biases of the Maastricht Treaty , especially the early deregulation of capital movements within the European Economic Community. Guttmann develops a plan for a truly supranational form of credit-money, building on Keynes's Bancor Plan.

Handbook of International Trade and Development Statistics. New York: United Nations, 1967-
This yearbook is published annually by the United Nations. Part 5 of each yearbook presents balance of payment summaries for developed

and developing countries and territories by region, economic grouping, and country. Compared with a similar International Monetary Fund publication (*International Financial Statistics*), this publication is more concise and will be more useful to readers who do not need heavily detailed information.

Hazlitt, Henry. *From Bretton Woods to World Inflation: A Study of Causes and Consequences*. Chicago: Regnery Gateway, 1984.

This volume consists of twenty-three editorials that Hazlitt wrote for *The New York Times* on the Bretton Woods conference at the time, a summary of his misgivings published in *The American Scholar* (Winter, 1944/1945), and five later pieces. An adherent of the gold standard (as distinct from the Bretton Woods gold exchange standard), Hazlitt was and remains a harsh critic of the arrangement. The crux of his indictment is that Bretton Woods "institutionalized" inflation.

Heckscher, Eli. "The Effect of Foreign Trade on the Distribution of Income." In *Readings in the Theory of International Trade*, edited by Howard S. Ellis and Lloyd A. Metzler. Philadelphia: Blakiston, 1949.

Suitable for college students. The original statement of the Heckscher-Ohlin results.

Heywood, John. *Using the Futures, Forwards, and Options Markets*. London: A & C Black, 1984.

This short book covers all of the aspects of the foreign currency futures market. Contains many examples and makes an excellent reference book, but is a little terse. Every line is meaningful, and a close reading will facilitate understanding. Well organized with an extensive table of contents and a comprehensive glossary.

Hilf, Meinhard, Francis G. Jacobs, and Ernst-Ulrich Petersmann. *The European Community and GATT*. Deventer, The Netherlands: Kluwer, 1986.

A collection of papers presented in the two conferences held in 1984. The volume deals with the common idea of the application of the rules of the General Agreement on Tariffs and Trade (GATT). Included are selected GATT documents. Suitable for a general audience.

Holmes, Alan R. *The New York Foreign Exchange Market*. New York: Federal Reserve Bank of New York, 1960.

An excellent institutional description of the balance of payments in its relation to the working of the foreign-exchange market.

Howitt, Arnold. *Managing Federalism: Studies in Intergovernmental Relations.* Washington, D.C.: CQ Press, 1984.

A good introduction to the political side of regional development. Emphasizes governmental cooperation using a case-study approach.

Hufbauer, Gary Clyde, and Joanna Shelton-Erb. *Subsidies in International Trade.* Washington, D.C.: Institute for International Economics, 1984.

This text covers a variety of issues in international trade. Provides a large amount of detail but is not easy reading for beginners in this field. Recommended for graduate students.

International Financial Statistics. Washington, D.C.: International Monetary Fund. 1979-

A convenient source (published monthly) for information on the flow of capital into and out of most countries in the world.

International Monetary Fund. *Annual Report on Exchange Arrangements and Exchange Restrictions.* Washington, D.C.: Author, 1979-

This report is a useful reference for identifying trade practices by country. In addition to information on monetary exchange arrangements and restrictions, it provides information on quotas and other trade restrictions, tariffs, other taxes, and licensing. Information is provided alphabetically by country for all IMF member countries.

Iversen, Carl. *Aspects of the Theory of International Capital Movements.* Copenhagen: Levin and Munkgaard, 1935. Reprint. New York: Augustus M. Kelley, 1967.

A classic text on the subject in the literary, nonmathematical style of its day.

James, Estelle, ed. *The Nonprofit Sector in International Perspective: Studies in Comparative Culture and Policy.* New York: Oxford University Press, 1989.

A collection of fifteen papers (three by James), which test the generality of the theories of the nonprofit sector by comparing the experiences in different countries. All of the papers are accessible to the general reader, but some have technical sections. The long introduction, which summarizes each paper and relates it to existing theories, is superior.

Johnson, Omotunde E. G. "Currency Depreciation and Export Expansion." *Finance and Development* 24 (March, 1987): 1.

This article takes the issue of devaluation through the process of implementation as a part of a larger policy package. There is an effort to demonstrate the requirements on the part of the policy administrators for managing the devaluation within the framework of the planning model. The issue of the impact of protectionist trade barriers in developed countries on the devaluation response is also treated.

Kenen, Peter B. *The International Economy.* 2d ed. Englewood Cliffs, N.J.: Prentice-Hall, 1989.

An intermediate-level textbook in which the idea of the offer curve is developed rather early, on page 29.

Kennedy, Charles R. *Political Risk Management.* New York: Quorum Books, 1987.

Reports on the political risk management practices of the United States' multinational banks and industrial corporations. Describes how various companies assess and manage political risk. The Middle East and Persian Gulf examples are excellent, as are the insights into the General Motors political risk assessment methods. This book is most valuable for the reader with a basic understanding of international business and a good understanding of current events.

Keynes, John Maynard. "The German Transfer Problem." In *Readings in the Theory of International Trade.* Philadelphia: Blakeston, 1950.

The Keynes paper (originally published in 1929), together with the article by Ohlin, cited below, is the classic confrontation on the matter of the real effect of capital transfer, the results of which depend upon the Marshall-Lerner condition.

Kindleberger, Charles P. *Marshall Plan Days.* Winchester, Mass.: Allen & Unwin, 1987.

A case study of the first major regional development effort on an international scale. Well written, but also highly theoretical and difficult to read. Provides a good historical account of the Marshall Plan's intentions and outcomes.

King, Philip. *International Economics and International Economic Policy: A Reader.* New York: McGraw-Hill, 1990.

One of the best collections of essays treating the problems, policies, decisions, and implications of international trade policy. Covers the late 1980's and early 1990's, as well as the concerns of policymakers.

The problems of trade experienced by developing countries are highlighted with those of developed ones.

Korner, Peter, Gero Maass, Thomas Siebold, and Rainer Tetzlaff. *The IMF and the Debt Crisis*. Translated by Paul Knight. Atlantic Highlands, N.J.: Humanities Press, 1986.

This overview of International Monetary Fund (IMF) policies and procedures is quite critical in its assessment of wealthy countries' domination of monetary relationships not despite, but often because of, the IMF.

Korth, Christopher M. *International Countertrade*. New York: Quorum Books, 1987.

The chapters of this book are based on the presentations that were given at a conference at the University of South Carolina. The discussion is directed to those who are already familiar with the basics and want more detail regarding current countertrade practices in various parts of the world and in different industries. Suitable for college students.

Kraus, Willy, and Wilfried Lutkenhorst. *The Economic Development of the Pacific Basin*. New York: St. Martin's Press, 1986.

The first chapter provides an introduction to the basic problems of current international trade policy and the General Agreement on Tariffs and Trade (GATT) framework of rules and also argues that the concept of a globally valid trade policy has entered a fundamental crisis. Accessible to a general audience.

Krauss, Melvyn. "Recent Developments in Customs Union Theory: An Interpretive Survey." *Journal of Economic Literature* 10 (June, 1972): 413-446.

A survey of books and journal articles emphasizing the two forces of trade creation and trade diversion.

Kreinin, Mordechai E. *International Economics: A Policy Approach*. New York: Harcourt Brace Jovanovich, 1987.

Chapter 6 provides an easily understood description of the adjustment processes to balance of payments disequilibriums. Pages 108-113 concentrate on the specie-flow mechanism. Chapter 12 presents a nongraphical discussion of the Heckscher-Ohlin trade model. The book as a whole covers a wide variety of theoretical and factual topics in international trade and finance.

Krueger, Anne O. *Exchange Rate Determination.* Cambridge, England: Cambridge University Press, 1983.
A survey of the literature of exchange-rate determination. Chapter 4 discusses the monetary approach to the balance of payments.

Krugman, Paul. "Is Free Trade Passé?" *The Journal of Economic Perspectives* 1 (Fall, 1987): 131-144.
A very readable professional economist's journal, *Economic Perspectives* provides articles on a variety of topics of concern to nonspecialists. Krugman's article offers a description of some of the extensions in international trade theory.

_____. "What Do Undergraduates Need to Know About Trade?" *American Economic Review*, (May, 1993): 23-26.
A succinct critique of such pundits as Lester Thurow, Ira Magaziner, and Robert Reich, and of what Krugman calls "pop internationalism." Students should regard trade as a production process that transforms exports into imports. Imports, not exports, are the fruits of international trade. Krugman criticizes industrial policy in general.

Krugman, Paul R., and Maurice Obstfeld. *International Economics: Theory and Practice.* Boston: Scott, Foresman, 1988.
While covering theories of international trade and finance in a comprehensive fashion, this text considers in detail the involvement of central banks in setting and influencing the rates of exchange. Chapter 4 provides a description of the Heckscher-Ohlin model to those familiar with basic algebra. Pages 84-86 are a description of some of the results of tests of the validity of the H-O model. Chapter 10 (specifically pages 229-236) provides an easily readable description of import substitution and export promotion.

Lal, Deepak. *The Poverty of Development Economics.* London: Institute of Economic Affairs, 1983.
Chapters 1 and 2 offer a point-by-point condemnation of interventionist policies in foreign trade.

Lenin, V. I. *Imperialism: The Highest Stage of Capitalism.* New York: International Publishers, 1916.
Lenin searches for the causes of the outbreak of World War I. He uses much of J. A. Hobson's research to buttress his argument that the advanced capitalist countries were looking for outlets for their surplus

to stave off the falling rate of profit. Lenin saw the struggle for foreign markets as leading to war.

Lerner, A. P. "The Diagrammatical Representation of Cost Conditions in International Trade." *Economica* 7 (1932): 346-356.

This is apparently the paper that added Lerner's name to the appellation "Marshall-Lerner." Also see Lerner's paper "The Symmetry Between Import and Export Taxes" (*Economica*, n.s. 4 1936), pages 308-313.

Levey, Marc M., ed. *Foreign Investment in the United States*. New York: John Wiley & Sons, 1989.

This book is intended for the person who wishes to do research on the legal and tax issues associated with direct foreign investment in the United States. It is difficult, technical reading, but its 766-page length makes it a rich source of comprehensive, detailed information.

Levi, Maurice. *International Finance: Financial Management and the International Economy*. New York: McGraw-Hill, 1983.

This reference explains in depth, with extensive use of diagrams, the effects of both fiscal and monetary policies on exchange rates in financial markets around the world. Quite technical in its presentation of concepts and thus not suitable for high school students.

Lewis, W. Arthur. *The Evolution of the International Economic Order*. Princeton, N.J.: Princeton University Press, 1978.

In Lewis' view, before economies reach their "turning point," the existence of surplus labor acts as an anchor on wages. The turning point is reached when all labor is "absorbed," or employed in production. After the turning point, wages can increase, reflecting productivity growth. Prior to the turning point, something like Thomas Robert Malthus' "iron law of wages" prevails.

Lindblom, Charles E. *Politics and Markets: The World's Political-Economic Systems*. New York: Basic Books, 1977.

An excellent overview of the interactions between political and economic systems.

Lo, N. Chi. "Curing the U.S. Trade Deficit." *Canadian Business Review* 17 (Winter, 1990): 4.

Lo shows the application of several theoretical approaches to the mid-1980's dollar crisis. Clearly illustrates how the effects of popular proposals would impact the U.S. economy. Lo presents his findings in a useful policy analysis approach.

Long, Oliver. *Law and Its Limitations in the GATT Multilateral Trade System.* Dordrecht, The Netherlands: Martinus Nijhoff, 1985.
   As a former director-general of the General Agreement on Tariffs and Trade (GATT), Long addresses the questions of what the GATT is, what it does, and how it functions, including the legal aspects and the negotiating process of the system. For general readers.

MacBean, A. I., and P. N. Snowden. *International Institutions in Trade and Finance.* London: Allen & Unwin, 1981.
   Chapter 8 includes a discussion of expansion of the European Economic Community from six members to nine. The relative importance of trade creation and trade diversion is considered.

McConnell, Campbell R. *Economics.* 11th ed. New York: McGraw-Hill, 1987.
   A highly popular introductory-level economics book that is especially readable. Part 7 covers four chapters on international economic issues.

MacEwan, Arthur. *Debt and Disorder: International Economic Instability and U.S. Imperial Decline.* New York: Monthly Review Press, 1990.
   A narrative of international debt and disorder from 1970 to 1990, identifying factors that disrupted the international financial system. Analyzes Third World reliance on foreign capital, and demonstrates close ties between the United States trade deficit and foreign debt. Concludes with a two-chapter examination of the political questions that are implied by foreign debt.

McKinnon, Ronald I. "Monetary and Exchange Rate Policies for International Financial Stability: A Proposal." *Journal of Economic Perspectives* 2 (Winter, 1988): 83-103.
   A proposal advocating the use of purchasing power parity to determine a permissible range for the exchange rates between the United States, West Germany, and Japan.

Magdoff, Harry. *The Age of Imperialism: The Economics of Foreign Policy.* New York: Monthly Review Press, 1969.
   An outstanding description of the U.S. economic empire. This is indispensable reading for anyone uncomfortable with the distortions about the world economy dispensed by neoclassical economists. Claims that the U.S. economy is extracting a surplus from the Third World.

Marshall, Alfred. "The Pure Theory of Foreign Trade." In *London School of Economics Reprints*. London: London School of Economics, 1930.
   The original derivation of the relevant propositions and conclusions. Very readable; contains original diagrams.

Meade, J. E. *The Balance of Payments*. Vol. 1 in *Theory of International Economic Policy*. London: Oxford University Press, 1951.
   A painstaking presentation of the economic theoretical context in which analysis of capital flows takes place.

Meese, Richard. "Currency Fluctuations in the Post-Bretton Woods Era." *The Journal of Economic Perspectives* 4 (Winter, 1990): 117-134.
   From a journal which provides summary articles for nonspecialists. This article is a slightly technical description of the asset market approach and the various empirical tests that have been used on it.

Meier, Gerald M. *International Economics*. New York: Oxford University Press, 1980.
   Part 1 contains a detailed discussion of the gains from specialization in trade. The material is suitable for students, although a little technical for the general reader.

Meyer, Stephen A. "The U.S. as a Debtor Country: Causes, Prospects, and Policy Implications." In *The International Financial Reader*, edited by Robert W. Kolb. Miami, Fla.: Kolb, 1990.
   This article emphasizes the role of saving-investment imbalance in the surge of U.S. net external indebtedness during the 1980's. Also emphasized are the differences in external positions of the United States and developing-country debtors and the prospects for a turnaround in U.S. external position. Suitable for college students and the general reader.

Miller, Elisa B. "An Excursion for Today's Teachers of Comparative Advantage." *Challenge* 28 (March/April, 1980): 64.
   This is a short application of the principle of comparative advantage. It is suitable for beginning students.

Mirow, Kurt Rudolf, and Harry Maurer. *Webs of Power: International Cartels and the World Economy*. Boston: Houghton Mifflin, 1982.
   Describes the patterns of collusion among the international corporations that set the prices of chemicals, electrical machinery, ocean shipping, petroleum, steel, synthetic fibers, and uranium. A well-documented, stylistically sophisticated account of multinational corpora-

tions operating in contravention of domestic and international laws. Useful to economists and informative to general readers.

Mowery, David C., ed. *International Collaborative Ventures in U.S. Manufacturing*. Cambridge, Mass.: Ballinger, 1988.
A collection of essays exploring the reasons for and benefits from international joint ventures. It is useful in comparing joint ventures to direct foreign investment which is associated with foreign ownership and control. Most of the examples come from the automobile industry.

Mundell, Robert. *Man and Economics: The Science of Choice*. New York: McGraw-Hill, 1968.
This small book is easy and pleasurable to read. Written by an eminent international economist for a general audience, it is full of anecdotes and trivia that illustrate and entertain. The determination of value, or market price, is well developed. Highly recommended.

Officer, Lawrence. *Purchasing Power Parity and Exchange Rates: Theory, Evidence, and Relevance*. Greenwich, Conn.: JAI Press, 1982.
An extensive survey of the theoretical and empirical literature on purchasing power parity.

Ohlin, Bertil. *Interregional and International Trade*. Cambridge, Mass.: Harvard University Press, 1933.
Contains an elaboration of Eli Heckscher's earlier work on the factor proportions model. Suitable for college students.

_____ . "The Reparation Problem, a Discussion." In *Readings in the Theory of International Trade*, edited by Howard S. Ellis. Philadelphia: Blakeston, 1949.
The companion paper to John Maynard Keynes's "The German Transfer Problem," contained in the same volume. The Marshall-Lerner condition is implicit in the analysis.

Ott, Mark. "Is America Being Sold Out?" In *The International Financial Reader*, edited by Robert W. Kolb. Miami, Fla.: Kolb, 1990.
A good attempt to deal with some widespread misconceptions about the direct foreign investment in the United States. Ott discusses the benefits of this component of foreign inflows to the U.S. economy and puts its size in perspective.

Pierre, Andrew J., ed. *A High Technology Gap? Europe, America, and Japan*. New York: Council on Foreign Relations, 1987.

Technological gaps can be the basis for a comparative advantage in world markets. This book clearly discusses an important issue, technological competition among the world's largest economies.

Pool, John Charles, and Stephen C. Stamos. *The ABCs of International Finance*. Lexington, Mass.: D. C. Heath, 1987.
Examines international trade and its links with international finance, focusing on issues of international monetary flows.

Porter, Michael E. *The Competitive Advantage of Nations*. New York: Free Press, 1990.
Porter offers excellent analysis and insight into the world of multinational corporations and focuses on their global strategies. Considered to be a major reference work on the study of international business.

Prebisch, Raúl. "Dependence, Development, and Interdependence." In *The State of Development Economics: Progress and Perspectives*, edited by Gustav T. Ranis and T. Paul Schultz. Oxford, England: Basil Blackwell, 1988.
This article provides some interesting insights into how Prebisch assesses his contributions to economic theory and policy. Together with the comments on it by Jagdish Bhagwati which follow, the two articles give the reader a good sense of the debate between Prebisch and the mainstream of economic theory. Suitable for undergraduates, but best understood by those with some prior understanding of the debate.

Robinson, Richard D., ed. *Direct Foreign Investment*. New York: Praeger, 1987.
A comprehensive collection of essays which addresses government policy toward foreign investment. Regional experiences in Southeast Asia, Latin America, Europe, and Japan; the policies of multinational corporations; and cost-benefit analysis focusing on developing countries are included. This book presumes a basic understanding of international finance and trade.

Salvatore, Dominick. *International Economics*. 3d ed. New York: Macmillan, 1990.
This widely used textbook should be fairly accessible, and its exposition of offer curves, as used in trade theory, is readily understandable.

_____ , ed. *The New Protectionist Threat to World Welfare*. New York: North-Holland, 1987.

Twenty-six articles discuss the causes and effects of the new protectionism. The selections include detailed discussions of import restrictions used by developed and developing countries. Suitable for college students.

Samuelson, Paul A. "The Transfer Problem and Transport Costs: The Terms of Trade When Impediments are Absent." *Economic Journal* 62 (June, 1952): 278-304.

A comprehensive analysis of the problem, with the conclusion that there is no prior way to tell how a transfer payment will affect the terms of trade.

Schaffer, Matt. *Winning the Countertrade War.* New York: John Wiley & Sons, 1988.

This book is an excellent source on countertrade, is written in a clear style and contains many examples of barter and countertrade. Must reading for novices in the field with good examples of complex issues simply presented. Recommended for all audiences.

Scholl, Russell B. "International Investment Position: Component Detail for 1989." In *Survey of Current Business.* Washington, D.C.: Department of Commerce, 1990.

This article provides detailed discussion of individual components of the United States' total foreign assets and liabilities and the methods used for their valuations. It also includes data on each component over the period 1975-1989.

Schott, Jeffrey J., ed. *Completing the Uruguay Round: A Results-Oriented Approach to the GATT Trade Negotiations.* Washington, D.C.: Institute for International Economics, 1990.

A collection of papers on the desirable outcome of trade negotiations in the Uruguay Round of the General Agreement on Tariffs and Trade (GATT). Each area under negotiation is covered, including safeguards, textiles, subsidies, antidumping, agriculture, trade in services, investment, intellectual property rights, and dispute settlement.

Schott, J. J., and M. G. Smith, eds. *The Canadian U.S. Free Trade Agreement: The Global Impact.* Washington, D.C.: Institute for International Economics, 1988.

Discusses various effects of the 1988 free trade agreement on Canada, the United States, and other countries.

Schydlowsky, Daniel M. "A Policymaker's Guide to Comparative Advantage." *World Development* 12 (April, 1984): 439-450.
A slightly technical, although certainly readable, description of the day-to-day applications of comparative advantage.

Simmonds, Kenneth R., and Brian H. W. Hill, eds. *Law and Practice Under the GATT.* New York: Oceana, 1989.
This periodically updated volume is a collection of selected GATT (General Agreement on Tariffs and Trade) documents and commentaries which present the basic constitutive and interpretative texts of the system, along with materials on the outcome and implementation of various rounds of negotiations. Accessible to a general audience.

Sommers, Albert T. *The U.S. Economy Demystified.* Lexington, Mass.: Lexington Books, 1985.
An interesting and short (129-page) explanation of the national economic accounting system. It includes easy-to-read descriptions of the balance of payments and its components. The analysis of the limitations of economic statistics is useful for students of foreign investment.

Sparos, John. *Inequalizing Trade?* Oxford, England: Clarendon Press, 1983.
One of the most authoritative works on the subject of terms of trade. A novel feature of this monograph is its estimations of the factorial terms of trade, establishing a link between them and trade-induced inequalization. Recommended for advanced college students, but the general reader may benefit from nontechnical sections and tables presenting historical data on the terms-of-trade measures.

Spero, Joan Edelman. *The Politics of International Economic Relations.* New York: St. Martin's Press, 1990.
Although concerned with the interaction between politics and economics in international relations, several chapters offer a detailed discussion of the dynamics of import restriction. Suitable for advanced high school and college students.

Stern, Robert M., ed. *U.S. Trade Policies in a Changing World Economy.* Cambridge, Mass.: MIT Press, 1987.
This book is a 437-page collection of essays by notable economists on a range of trade policy issues confronting the United States. Topics discussed include protectionism, trade wars, and negotiation procedures of the General Agreement on Tariffs and Trade.

Survey of Current Business, 1979-
    Published quarterly and annually, by the U.S. Department of Commerce's Bureau of Economic Analysis, this publication contains estimates and analyses of U.S. economic activities. The section entitled "U.S. International Transactions" provides aggregate and disaggregate entries of current balance of payments items, such as the current account balance and the merchandise trade balance. The Department of Commerce also releases monthly trade balance figures to the press.

Swann, Dennis. *The Economics of the Common Market.* 6th ed. New York: Penguin Books, 1988.
    A leading British economist looks at the actual mechanism of the European marketplace, considering tariffs, monetary integration, and the major economic policies of the European Economic Community in agriculture, energy, transport, regional development, and society.

Takayama, A., and R. K. Anderson. "Devaluation, The Specie Flow Mechanism, and the Steady State." *Review of Economic Studies* 44 (June, 1977): 347-361.
    In this rather technical but very understandable paper, Anderson and Takayama completely track the relation between the gold standard and the exchange-rate equilibrium. Extensive use of the Marshall-Lerner stability condition is made. A classic on the "monetary" model of balance of payments adjustment.

Thornton, Henry. *An Enquiry into the Nature and Effects of the Paper Credit of Great Britain.* 1811. Reprint. London: George Allen & Unwin, 1939.
    For the reader who is interested in the history of the subject, both Joseph Schumpeter and Jacob Viner credit Thornton with most of the original thought on the monetary approach to the balance of payments.

Todaro, Michael P. *Economic Development in the Third World.* 3d ed. New York: Longman, 1985.
    Chapter 12 offers an excellent description of the Ricardian and Heckscher-Ohlin trade theories, with emphasis on their roles in the growth of the poorest countries in the world.

Tolchin, Martin, and Susan Tolchin. *Buying into America.* New York: Random House, 1988.
    This book, written for popular audiences, provides an interesting contrast to free market economic views, raising concerns over the

depth and magnitude of foreign investment in the United States. Well written, but contains more anecdotal material than comprehensive data.

Triffin, Robert. *Gold and the Dollar Crisis.* New Haven, Conn.: Yale University Press, 1960.
A perceptive (even prophetic) analysis of the fatal weakness in the Bretton Woods system. If, on one hand, the world continued to depend upon U.S. deficits for the growth of reserves, U.S. reserve liabilities would increase so much relative to the nation's assets that instability would result because official holders of dollars would begin to fear possible devaluation of the dollar. If, on the other hand, the U.S. deficits were eliminated, the loss of this source of reserve growth would depress world trade and economic activity. Efforts to implement Triffin's recommendation of empowering the International Monetary Fund to meet liquidity needs proved too little, too late.

United Nations. Conference on Trade and Development. *Trade and Development Report.* New York: United Nations. 1981-
In addition to reviewing the year's trade and development issues, each annual report contains a thorough discussion of a different aspect of international trade, economics, finance, or development. The 1984 report provides an excellent discussion of the establishment and evolution of the General Agreement on Tariffs and Trade and of the development of nontariff trade barriers. The report defends preferential treatment for developing countries. Suitable for college students.

United States. President. *Economic Report of the President.* Washington, D.C.: Government Printing Office. 1947-
The tables in this annual publication are a handy source for figures on the net capital flow into and out of the United States. Any noteworthy developments are discussed in the text.

_____ . *Economic Report of the President.* Washington, D.C.: Government Printing Office, 1989.
This part of the 1989 report discusses recent changes in U.S. net external position, problems in measuring it, and domestic policy implications of U.S. net external indebtedness.

_____ . *Economic Report of the President.* Washington, D.C.: Government Printing Office, 1990.

This part of the 1990 report focuses on the investment-saving gap in the United States, the role of net foreign capital inflows in closing this gap, and the factors influencing domestic saving and investment.

U.S. Department of the Treasury. Customs Service. *Importing into the United States*. Washington, D.C.: Government Printing Office, 1989.

This 90-page manual is designed for businesspeople who import products into the United States. It provides detailed information on import regulations, documentation, and procedures, including information on tariffs and quotas. All items subject to quotas are listed. There are also brief, simple explanations of trade agreements in which the United States participates, such as the Generalized System of Preferences.

Verzariu, Pompiliu. *Countertrade, Barter, and Offsets: New Strategies for Profit in International Trade*. New York: McGraw-Hill, 1985.

Intended to acquaint private-sector company executives and public officials with basic information about the practice of countertrade. Readers with an interest in the legal aspects of countertrade can find examples of countertrade contracts in the appendices.

Viner, Jacob. *The Customs Union Issue*. New York: Carnegie Endowment for International Peace, 1953.

A classic study of the concept of customs unions prior to the formation of the European Economic Community.

_____. *Studies in the Theory of International Trade*. London: Allen & Unwin, 1937.

Chapters 3 and 4, "The Bullionist Controversies," and chapter 5 "English Currency Controversies, 1825-1865," provide the most important and accessible work on this topic for the general reader. The text uses the Bullion Report and other original sources to render an accurate, interesting, and readable history of the entire controversy to 1865. Viner narrates and criticizes the insights and errors of the great figures in the epoch: David Ricardo, Henry Thornton, Thomas Robert Malthus, and many others.

Walker, Townsend. *A Guide for Using the Foreign Exchange Market*. New York: John Wiley & Sons, 1981.

One of the easier books to read on foreign exchange markets. Contains many worked examples, a series of problems with responses, and an analysis of the responses. Written to educate the corporate treasurer, and examples are designed to emphasize investment and risk minimization.

Weil, Gordon L., ed. *A Handbook on the European Economic Commission.* New York: Praeger, 1965.

A concise compilation of the basic EEC documents. Excerpts of documents have been included relating to every major aspect of the EEC. An extensive bibliography of EEC documents and publications is included. Suitable for students.

Weisweiller, Rudi. *Introduction of Foreign Exchange.* Dover, N.H.: Woodhead-Faulkner, 1983.

A somewhat condensed version of Weisweiller's earlier book, *Foreign Exchange.* Offers a basic account of foreign exchange trading, including a description of covered interest arbitrage, illustrated with examples. Includes a brief bibliography at the end of the book. Aimed primarily at a business audience, the book is not overly technical.

Welt, Leo G. B. *Trade Without Money: Barter and Countertrade.* New York: Harcourt Brace Jovanovich, 1984.

An excellent review of barter and countertrade with a great amount of detail presented in a logical and efficient manner. Easy to read and a very good source for term papers or reports. Recommended for all audiences.

Williamson, John. "International Capital Flows." In *The New Palgrave: A Dictionary of Economics*, edited by John Eatwell, Murray Milgate, and Peter Newman. New York: Stockton Press, 1987.

A more technical, advanced presentation of the subject.

_____. *The Open Economy and the World Economy.* New York: Basic Books, 1983.

Chapter 1 provides a historical description of the expansion of international trade over the past two hundred years. The second and third chapters offer a slightly technical, but very thorough, description of comparative advantage and the Heckscher-Ohlin model.

World Bank. *World Development Report.* New York: Oxford University Press, 1988.

An annual publication by the World Bank containing data on the terms of trade and other trade-related indicators for more than 120 developed and developing countries.

Yarbrough, Beth V., and Robert M. Yarbrough. *The World Economy: Trade and Finance.* New York: Dryden Press, 1988.

This detailed, 666-page introduction to the world economy provides discussions of economic theory with examples and cases. There is an extensive discussion of tariffs in chapter 7 and of quotas and voluntary export restraints in chapter 8. Although there is a heavy emphasis on mathematical equations, overall the book is written clearly enough for persons without a background in economics. Suitable for college students.

Yeager, Leland. *International Monetary Relations: Theory, History, and Policy.* 2d ed. New York: Harper & Row, 1976.

An excellent text on the principal international issues centering on money. Gives keen and well-researched insights into the gold and gold-exchange standards. The presentation is widely accessible.

Growth and Development

Adas, Michael. *Machines as the Measure of Men: Science, Technology, and Ideologies of Western Dominance.* Ithaca, N.Y.: Cornell University Press, 1989.

An outstandingly well-researched account whose special interest lies in its treatment of the reactions of non-Western societies, such as those of Africa and China, to Western inventions. Scantily illustrated but generously annotated.

Agarwala, A. N. and S. P. Singh, eds. *The Economics of Underdevelopment.* New York: Oxford University Press, 1963.

This book, although outdated, provides an excellent overview of the early thought on underdeveloped countries within classical growth theory. Papers by all the major economists who set the foundation for the theory of underdevelopment are included.

Arndt, H. W. *Economic Development: The History of an Idea.* Chicago: University of Chicago Press, 1987.

The various phases of evolution of the ideas and theories of economic development are described—the initial outgrowth from reactive nationalism; the period of emphasis on growth per se; the evolution of theories on employment, poverty alleviation, and basic needs provision; and the radical critiques of Right and Left.

Bauer, Peter. *Dissent on Development*. Cambridge, Mass.: Harvard University Press, 1972.
A very useful portrayal of the activities of development economists. Bauer places this specialty within the wider context of economics as a whole. He is particularly illuminating on the place of state regulation in economic growth. His own perspective is that of an unabashed classical liberal, and his wide knowledge of the literature provides an excellent guide to further study.

Bhagwati, Jagdish, and T. N. Srinivasan. "Trade Policy and Development." In *Dependence and Interdependence*, edited by Gene Grossman. Oxford, England: Basil Blackwell, 1985.
This article (chapter 6 of the book) provides a slightly technical description of the issues surrounding import substitution and export promotion, with emphasis on empirical tests of growth rates of countries following these alternative growth policies.

Bird, Graham, ed. *Third World Debt: The Search for a Solution*. Brookfield, Vt.: Gower, 1989.
A series of papers contributed to an international conference held by the economics department at the University of Surrey in England. Although the attempt was to keep the book nontechnical, the reading level is high, designed for academics, students, practitioners, and policymakers. Includes an index and a particularly interesting and amusing chapter entitled "Beware of Debtspeak."

Biswas, Margaret, and Per Pinstrup-Anderses, eds. *Nutrition and Development*. New York: Oxford University Press, 1985.
This collection of articles by eminent development experts argues that there is a direct correlation between nutrition and poverty and that only long-run accelerated economic development based on sustainable patterns of growth and relevant education can eliminate malnutrition.

Boeke, J. H. *Economics and Economic Policy of Dual Societies*. Homewood, Ill.: Richard D. Irwin, 1953.
This book, with more a sociological than economic approach, popularized the concept of dualism. Offers a good understanding of the broad nature of a dual economy.

Brinkman, Richard L. *Cultural Economics*. Portland, Oreg.: Hapi Press, 1981.

Cultural economics represents a theory and conception of the economic process in the framework of culture evolution. A primary emphasis of this study, using a holistic and interdisciplinary methodology, concerns the conceptual distinction between economic growth and economic development.

Browne, Stephen. *Foreign Aid in Practice*. New York: New York University Press, 1990.

Without taking a philosophical position, this book provides a comprehensive introduction to aid, its origins and history, its forms and conditions, its basic rationale, the ways it functions, and the impediments to its better functioning. Provides an unbiased introduction to the world of foreign aid and is a good book to read before delving into the heated debates surrounding this issue.

Bulmer-Thomas, Victor. *Input-Output Analysis in Developing Countries: Sources, Methods, and Applications*. New York: John Wiley & Sons, 1982.

Focuses on input-output applications in developing countries. Offers a thorough discussion of difficult empirical issues that arise in preparing transactions tables and in applying input-output analysis.

Cabral, Amilcar. *Revolution in Guinea: An African People's Struggle*. London: Stage 1, 1969.

A book by one of the most original of Africa's socialist thinkers and political activists and a leading influence on Third World political thought. Describes the struggle for independence from Portuguese colonialism and offers a realistic and self-critical assessment of the nature of revolutionary struggle in the Third World.

Campos, Roberto de Oliveira. "Economic Development and Inflation with Special Reference to Latin America." In *OECD: Development Plans and Programs*. Paris: OECD Development Centre, 1964.

This article discusses two views of inflation—structuralism and monetarism—in the context of the Latin American region. Serves as a good backdrop to the discussions on inflation and economic development.

Cassen, Robert. *Does Aid Work?* Oxford, England: Clarendon Press, 1986.

This study, commissioned by the Joint Ministerial Committee of the Boards of Governors of the World Bank and International Monetary Fund, attempts to measure the effectiveness of aid in terms of the objectives commonly set, including growth and poverty alleviation.

The book concludes that aid has had some very positive impacts and also makes recommendations for improving the role of aid within the current donor-recipient structure.

Chenery, Hollis, and T. N. Srinivasan, eds. *Handbook of Development Economics*. 2 vols. New York: Elsevier Science, 1989.

A sourcebook on development economics which discusses foreign aid within its economic and political context and the role it plays in theories of development. Contains articles from both the neoclassical and structural schools and is intellectually balanced.

Chilcote, Ronald H. *Theories of Development and Underdevelopment*. Boulder, Colo.: Westview Press, 1984.

This work is a review of leftist radical perspectives by a political scientist. It examines theories of development and underdevelopment by Karl Marx, Vladimir Ilyich Lenin, and Leon Trotsky, as well as of the evolution from them of the theories of Paul A. Baran and the Marxist and non-Marxist proponents of dependency.

Clower, Robert, et al. *Growth Without Development*. Evanston, Ill.: Northwestern University Press, 1966.

Uses Liberia as a case study in arguing that the economic growth in primary commodities produced by foreign concessions was not accompanied by structural or institutional change.

Crosby, Alfred W. *Ecological Imperialism*. Cambridge, England: Cambridge University Press, 1986.

An account of the biological/epidemiological consequences of colonialism, the book gives a general history with a novel approach: the relationships of biology to history. Crosby's account of the biological impact of colonialism is very readable and thought provoking.

DeGregori, Thomas R., ed. *Development Economics: Theory, Practice, and Prospects*. Boston: Kluwer, 1989.

Contains a series of chapters that present recent key issues of development. The chapter by Peter Cashel-Cordo discusses the role of external assistance in causing and relieving debt. The chapter and commentary by Dilmus James and Randal Thompson discuss technology transfer and the role of aid projects.

Di Marco, Luis Eugenio, ed. *International Economics and Development: Essays in Honor of Raúl Prebisch*. New York: Academic Press, 1972.

The introduction to this volume of essays, "The Evolution of Prebisch's Economic Thought," is a valuable guide to the influence of Prebisch's ideas on economic theory and policy. Suitable for a nonspecialist audience.

Dornbusch, Rudiger, and Stanley Fischer. *Macroeconomics*. 5th ed. New York: McGraw-Hill, 1990.
    Chapter 6 provides an excellent discussion of the balance of payments and foreign exchange regimes. Chapter 20 offers a description of the monetary approach to the balance of payments.

Fei, John, and Gustav Ranis. *Development of the Labour Surplus Economy: Theory and Policy*. Homewood, Ill.: Richard D. Irwin, 1964.
    One of the more rigorous and comprehensive theories on economic development in the dual economy. Requires some effort but is worthwhile. The process of development described in the book is not very different from Arthur Lewis' model, but it is more thorough. Criticisms of Lewis' model apply here as well.

Galbraith, John Kenneth. *The Nature of Mass Poverty*. Cambridge, Mass.: Harvard University Press, 1979.
    This work examines poverty in the developing world. It explains how the mass poverty of less developed nations differs from the poverty experienced by developed nations, and provides some policy solutions. This book is accessible to all readers and is written with the style and wit that have made Galbraith famous. One minor gap in the book is that it addresses only rural poverty in the less developed world and thus ignores urban poverty.

George, Susan. *A Fate Worse than Debt*. New York: Grove Press, 1988.
    An excellent source for the nonspecialist, this book includes coverage of the problem of developing-country debt, its background, and possible solutions. Also includes case studies of specific countries and areas with problems of debt. The writing style is engaging, with numerous anecdotes. Includes an index and a bibliography.

Gillis, Malcolm, Dwight H. Perkins, Michael Roemer, and Donald R. Snodgrass. *Economics of Development*. 2d ed. New York: W. W. Norton, 1987.
    Chapters 16 and 17 offer detailed descriptions of import substitution and export promotion, with emphasis on the theoretical underpinnings as well as the empirical effects of each strategy.

Goode, Richard. *Government Finance in Developing Countries.* Washington, D.C.: Brookings Institution, 1984.

Examines a variety of issues in fiscal policy that confront developing countries, including the development of a national budget, the size and effects of expenditures, and the role of foreign and domestic borrowing. Goode emphasizes the need to consider administrative capacity when evaluating the suitability of fiscal measures in developing countries.

Griffin, Keith. *Alternative Strategies for Economic Development.* New York: St. Martin's Press, 1989.

The study examines the growth record of a sample of nineteen countries from Asia, Africa, and Latin America. In describing alternative paths to development, it classifies them into six strategies, which are discussed analytically as well as through country experiences.

Haberler, G. "Terms of Trade and Development." In *Economic Development for Latin America*, edited by Howard S. Ellis. London: Macmillan, 1961.

A good source (pages 275-297) for some early criticisms of the Prebisch-Singer hypothesis.

Heller, Walter. "Fiscal Policies for Underdeveloped Economies." In *Papers and Proceedings of the Conference on Agricultural Taxation and Economic Development*, edited by H. P. Wald. Cambridge, Mass.: Harvard University Press, 1954.

This paper summarizes some of the problems encountered by developing countries in the conduct of fiscal policies, especially regarding taxes. Requires no economics background. Still relevant despite its date of publication.

Hellinger, Stephen, Douglas Hellinger, and Fred M. O'Regan. *Aid for Just Development.* Boulder, Colo.: Lynne Rienner, 1988.

Reviews the evolution of foreign aid and the causes of its failure and proposes a new system within which aid can be better employed for developmental, not political, impact. Espouses a growing point-of-view that aid should be the work of nongovernmental organizations that focus on humanitarian and economic, not political objectives.

Higgins, Benjamin. "The Dualistic Theory of Underdeveloped Areas." *Economic Development and Cultural Change* 4 (January, 1956): 99-115.

Readers who read J. H. Boeke's *Economics and Economic Policy of Dual Societies* above must read this article for a balanced view. Some parts of the book are a critique of Boeke's concept of dualism. It is well written and easy to follow.

_____ . *Economic Development*. Rev. ed. New York: W. W. Norton, 1968.

A basic college undergraduate text in economic development and growth. The indexed references to Harrod-Domar are good and reasonably elementary.

Higgins, Benjamin, and Jean Downing Higgins. *Economic Development of a Small Planet*. New York: W. W. Norton, 1979.

A much abbreviated and updated version of the classic text *Economic Development*, by Benjamin Higgins, which dominated the classroom in the 1960's. Basic issues of development theory, strategy, and planning as they evolved into the late 1970's are carefully summarized and illustrated with numerous case studies.

Hirschman, Albert O. "The Political Economy of Import-Substituting Industrialization in Latin America." *The Quarterly Journal of Economics* 82 (February, 1968): 1-32.

A seminal article on the problems inherent in following import-substitution policies.

Hogendorn, Jan S. *Economic Development*. New York: Harper & Row, 1987.

In a large part of chapter 12, the author presents an excellent critical review of the theoretical arguments and empirical evidence on the terms of trade in a manner suitable for readers with little or no background.

Holt, Robert, and John E. Turner. *The Political Basis of Economic Development*. Princeton, N.J.: Van Nostrand, 1966.

An exploratory study in comparative political analysis written for laypersons. Of particular interest are chapters 3 and 4, dealing in part with France's former governmental structures and procedures, as well as with its historical methods of searching for and attaining its economic goals. Colbertism and French mercantilism are interestingly placed in appropriate perspective against developments elsewhere. Chapter 7 poses provocative and relevant hypotheses about persisting limitations on governments' economic powers. A bibliography of published works is extensive and is arranged by countries. No illustrations; the index is adequate.

Hudec, Robert E. *Developing Countries in the GATT Legal System.* Brookfield, Vt.: Gower, 1988.

Traces the development of the General Agreement on Tariffs and Trade (GATT), with emphasis on the position of the developing countries. Hudec makes the argument that developing countries would benefit more from parity of obligations (mutual trade concessions with the industrial countries) than from one-sided, or preferential, tariff concessions. Suitable for students.

Jimenez, Emmanuel. *Pricing Policy in the Social Sectors: Cost Recovery for Education and Health in Developing Countries.* Baltimore: The Johns Hopkins University Press, 1987.

An interesting discussion of the possible uses of pricing to allocate social services in the developing countries.

Jones, Hywel G. *An Introduction to Modern Theories of Economic Growth.* New York: McGraw-Hill, 1976.

Jones presents the systems of equations that several well-known schools of thought have used to model economic growth. Included are the Harrod-Domar model, the neoclassical one-sector model, and the neoclassical two-sector model, as well as a discussion of economic growth and welfare.

Kanbur, Ravi. "North-South Relations." In *The New Palgrave Economic Development,* edited by John Eatwell, Murray Milgate, and Peter Newman. New York: W. W. Norton, 1989.

An essay on the various issues of developing-country and developed-country relations, including trade, international investment, and international debt. Although written at a relatively high level, the discussion is readable by the layperson. Includes a bibliography.

Kilby, Peter, ed. *Entrepreneurship and Economic Development.* New York: Free Press, 1971.

Selections include the principal sociological and psychological theories of entrepreneurial supply, as well as Third World case studies and policy analyses that pertain to these theories. The first essay makes the case for a modified constitutive function for the entrepreneur in late-developing economies.

Lewis, Arthur. "Economic Development with Unlimited Supplies of Labour." *Manchester School of Economics and Social Studies* 22 (May, 1954): 105-138.

One of the more important seminal articles on development in the dual economy. Assumes that the reader has some basic knowledge of economics. Well written, with easy-to-follow diagrams. After reading this article, one would benefit from consulting Gerald Meier's "A Critique of Boeke's Dualistic Theory."

Lichtensztejn, Samuel, and Monica Baer. *Fondo Monetario Internacional y Banco Mundial [The International Monetary Fund and the World Bank]*. San José, Costa Rica: Editorial Nueva Sociedad, 1986.

This comprehensive study of the two agencies created after the Bretton Woods conference is valuable not only for its perspective on less developed countries' views on the IMF but also for the many statistical tables it provides.

Lister, Marjorie. *The Economic Community and the Developing World*. Brookfield, Vt.: Gower, 1988.

Deals with the relationship between the EEC and the sixty-six developing countries in Africa, the Caribbean, and the Pacific (ACP). Analyzes the role of the Lome Convention (1975) in constructing a new international economic order. The Lome convention was intended to be a model of North-South relations. Examines the obstacles for ACP unity and for the implementation of the Lome Convention proposals. Suitable for students.

Love, Joseph. "Raúl Prebisch and the Origins of the Doctrine of Unequal Exchange." *Latin American Research Review*, 15, no. 3 (1980): 45-72.

Love examines the question of how and why Prebisch formulated his initial thesis, arguing that his ideas were highly developed several years prior to the publication of his treatise in 1950. Although written by a historian for an academic audience, this article is accessible to a college student audience.

Meier, Gerald. "A Critique of Boeke's Dualistic Theory." In *Leading Issues in Economic Development*. 2d ed. Oxford, England: Oxford University Press, 1970.

On pages 128-138, Meir provides a good critique of J. H. Boeke's observations about the dual economy and some of the generalizations at which he arrived.

_____ . *Emerging from Poverty: The Economics That Really Matters.* New York: Oxford University Press, 1984.
One of the United States' leading development economists provides an outline of the history of the institutions, efforts, and achievements in the development of poor nations. Provides a useful and accessible survey of pre-1945 and post-1945 development economics.

_____ . *The International Economics of Development.* New York: Harper & Row, 1968.
A major work that applies the neoclassical static theory (at best comparative statics) of comparative advantage. Analysis, concept, and theory are those of economic growth. Although the policy derived from the theory may be conducive to economic growth, the less developed world, however, needs economic development.

_____ . *Leading Issues in Economic Development.* 5th ed. New York: Oxford University Press, 1989.
This prominent, almost standard text on development discusses undeveloped and underdeveloped countries from the point of view of traditional growth theory.

_____ . "Mobilizing Domestic Resources." In *Leading Issues in Economic Development.* 3d ed. New York: Oxford University Press, 1976.
This section provides an integrated view of fiscal and monetary policies in the process of economic development. Meier has carefully selected various articles in order to present a balanced view of the issues. Suitable for the general reader.

Mosley, Paul. *Foreign Aid: Its Defense and Reform.* Lexington: University Press of Kentucky, 1987.
Examines the various economic and political justifications for aid and evaluates the evidence regarding the actual impact of aid, concluding with a case for the defense and reform of aid within the establishment perspective.

Pearson, Lester, et al. *Partners in Development: Report of the Commission on International Development.* New York: Praeger, 1969.
The first annex contains an exhaustive summary of the diverse structures and the major economic characteristics of developing countries.

Perroux, François. *A New Concept of Development.* Paris: UNESCO, 1983.

French economist Perroux is an internationally recognized economist who has written much about the conceptual distinction between growth and development.

Portes, Alejandro, Manuel Castells, and Lauren A. Benton, eds. *The Informal Economy: Studies in Advanced and Less Developed Countries.* Baltimore: The Johns Hopkins University Press, 1989.

A collection of papers reviewing existing literature on informal economies, presenting findings from a number of cities and countries, and analyzing implications for public policy. With a number of field studies, this book provides one of the most detailed pictures available of the nature and range of informal economic activities in a variety of settings. Also discusses their role in the restructuring of capitalist economies.

Prebisch, Raúl. *The Economic Development of Latin America and Its Principal Problems.* New York: United Nations, 1950.

This book presents the original exposition of Prebisch's ideas. It is worth reading if only to see how much subtler his ideas are than would appear from reading exclusively secondary sources. A nontechnical presentation which is accessible to a general audience.

Psacharopoulos, George, Jee-Peng Lee, and Emmanuel Jiminez. *Financing Education in Developing Countries.* Washington, D.C.: World Bank, 1986.

This 67-page study illustrates the budgetary restrictions in Third World countries within which the educational system must be financed. Written for an informed audience of nonspecialists, the study outlines options for public policy and enlivens them throughout with examples in separate text.

Reynolds, Lloyd G. *Economic Growth in the Third World: 1850-1980.* New Haven, Conn.: Yale University Press, 1985.

Reynolds identifies certain preconditions that are necessary for sustained economic growth, including national unification, continuity of government, external peace, and internal order. In addition, the rate of economic growth in developing countries is recognized as especially dependent on whether there is worldwide economic expansion and trade.

Riddell, Roger C. *Foreign Aid Reconsidered*. Baltimore: The Johns Hopkins University Press, 1987.

Analyzes the fundamental ethical and theoretical questions raised in the aid debate and systematically evaluates the arguments of those in favor of official aid and those from the right and the left who are critical of such interventions.

Rondinelli, Dennis A. *Development Administration and U.S. Foreign Aid Policy*. Boulder, Colo.: Lynne Rienner, 1987.

The author examines how foreign aid has been managed in the United States, the changing approaches to its administration since the 1940's, and how its management has created distortions in its objectives. This author is one in a large group of aid critics stating that the management of foreign aid has responded to bureaucratic donor agency demands instead of to the evolutionary nature of the development process.

Roth, Gabriel. *The Private Provision of Public Services in Developing Countries*. New York: Oxford University Press, 1987.

Features dozens of examples of public functions that are being provided by the private sector at competitive prices. The thrust of Roth's work stresses the need for the expansion and cultivation of the private sector as a means of efficient resource mobilization and sustainable economic development.

Samuelson, Paul A. *Economics*. New York: McGraw-Hill, 1989.

A pace-setting, mainstream textbook of many editions that dominates the post-World War II era and helps to integrate Keynesian economics in the mold of the "neoclassical synthesis." Although Nobel laureate Samuelson introduced the basic verities of economics to many college students, he also taught that growth was essentially the conceptual equivalent to economic development. Sets the boundaries of the teaching of economics in its mainstream manifestations as basically a study of the statistics of economic growth.

Sheridan, Richard B. "The Wealth of Jamaica in the Eighteenth Century." *Economic History Review* 18 (1965): 292-311.

A good example of a noneconomic study of colonialism. Sheridan argues that Jamaica and, by implication, the British West Indies were very profitable for the British. He does this by measuring the net capitalized value of assets in Jamaica, while assuming (implicitly) no opportunity cost for capital or costs that the British had to pay, such as higher prices for sugar and military expenses. Presents a good picture of the debate on colonialism.

Singer, Hans W. "The Distribution of Gains Between Investing and Borrowing Countries." *American Economic Review* 40 (May, 1950): 473-485.

The article presents Singer's version of the declining terms of trade thesis. It is interesting to note that Singer's analysis is not identical with that of Raúl Prebisch, placing greater emphasis on the slower rate of growth of demand for primary products than for manufactured goods, rather than on differences in market structure. In addition, the declining terms of trade argument is only one of a number of arguments that Singer marshals against the specialization of developing countries in the export of food and raw materials. Suitable for nonspecialists.

Szentes, Tomas. *The Political Economy of Underdevelopment*. Budapest: Akademiai Kiado, 1971.

The author advised the government in Tanzania in the 1960's before writing this insightful book.

Thomas, Robert P. "A Quantitative Approach to the Study of the Effects of British Imperial Policy on Colonial Welfare: Some Preliminary Findings." *Journal of Economic History* 25 (1965): 615-638.

This study initiated the economic investigations into the burdens of being a colony. Thomas looked for economic origins in the American Revolutionary War and did not find them. Using simple economic theory and biasing all estimates in favor of the hypothesis that the American colonies were being economically exploited, he finds that the net cost of being a colony was less than one-half of 1 percent of colonial income. The study is a landmark in assessing the economic costs and benefits of being a colony; it is easily accessible to the nonspecialist.

_____ . "The Sugar Colonies of the Old Empire: Profit or Loss for Great Britain." *Economic History Review* 21 (1968): 30-45.

This is a critique of Richard B. Sheridan's thesis concerning the profitability to the British of their West Indian colonies in the eighteenth century. One of the first economic studies of colonialism. Treatment of the subject is clear and understandable to nonspecialist readers. This article and Sheridan's will give the reader an insight to the economist's critique of colonialism.

Todaro, Michael. *Economic Development in the Third World*. New York: Longman, 1989.
Todaro duly notes the distinction between traditional or mainstream economics and development economics. It is the latter which concerns "rapid structural and institutional transformations of entire societies in a manner that will most efficiently bring the fruits of economic progress to the broadest segments of their populations." The view is that economies constitute social systems and consequently there is "the need to go beyond simple economics." This book also serves as a good introduction to the literature and the contributions of not only Kuznets but also other economists dealing with concepts and theories of structural and development analysis.

United Nations. Conference on Trade and Development. *The Least Developed Countries: 1988 Report*. New York: United Nations, 1989.
This annual publication contains statistical information on the forty-two LDCs and highlights issues of the efficiency of resource use and allocation, women's role in development, policies regarding production sectors, social development, transport and communications, measures to improve the institutional capabilities in LDCs, and the world of international support.

_____. *Trade and Development Report*. New York: United Nations. 1981-
In addition to reviewing the year's trade and development issues, each annual report contains a thorough discussion of a different aspect of international trade, economics, finance, or development. The 1984 report provides an excellent discussion of the establishment and evolution of the General Agreement on Tariffs and Trade and of the development of nontariff trade barriers. The report defends preferential treatment for developing countries. Suitable for college students.

United Nations. Department of Economic Affairs. *Structure and Growth of Selected African Economies*. New York: Author, 1958.
Discusses the nature and characteristics of dualism in Africa. The prototypes of dual economies are very instructive. Perhaps the easiest to read of all the articles on dual economies.

Walton, Gary M., and Hugh Rockoff. *History of the American Economy*. 6th ed. Orlando, Fla.: Harcourt Brace Jovanovich, 1990.
A textbook on U.S. economic history. Chapters 2-6 are devoted to colonial history and contain the most complete, succinct description

and analysis of the American colonial economy. Bibliographic listings at the end of each chapter are an adequate introduction to more specialized literature.

Watkins, Alfred J. *The Practice of Urban Economics*. Beverly Hills, Calif.: Sage Publications, 1980.
Urban economics is very close to the economics of development, and this book puts both into perspective. Provides an excellent outline of the developmental process.

Wilber, Charles K. *The Political Economy of Development and Underdevelopment*. 2d ed. New York: Random House, 1979.
Contains articles from traditional economics and the political economy school which challenge the characterization of developing countries by their per-capita gross national product and assert that development should be concerned with the reduction of poverty, unemployment, and inequality.

Willoughby, Kelvin W. *Technology Choice: A Critique of the Appropriate Technology Movement*. Boulder, Colo.: Westview Press, 1990.
Deals with the type of capital goods that are appropriate for both developing nations and developed nations. Examines the roots of the appropriate technology movement and builds on the work of Ernst Friedrich Schumacher and others. Carefully explores the various definitions and meanings of appropriate technology used in the literature in order to come up with a workable definition of the topic. Covers the use of appropriate technology separately in the "South" (Third World), the North (First World), and the world as an integrated whole. Also examines new international trends in the movement and criticisms of the movement. Contains an index.

Woods, Alan. *Development and the National Interest: U.S. Economic Assistance into the Twenty-first Century*. Washington, D.C.: Government Printing Office, 1989.
An excellent report authored by the administrator of the Agency for International Development. Outlines the various international regional development efforts that have taken place throughout the world. Quite suitable for the general reader.

World Bank. *Social Indicators of Development, 1989*. Baltimore: The Johns Hopkins University Press, 1989.

This annual publication includes social statistics on the developing countries, such as human resources, natural resources, income and poverty, expenditure, and investment in human capital.

_____. *Trends in Developing Economies*. Washington, D.C.: Author, 1989.

This annual publication provides extensive information on developing countries on a country-by-country basis and provides the reader with a good overview on the major economic and social issues which the countries are dealing with.

_____. *World Development Report*. New York: Oxford University Press.

Each issue, published annually since 1987, typically contains fifty pages about the state of the world economy, eighty pages of macroeconomic data on some 130 countries, and one hundred pages about an international development topic that differs each year. Written for a general audience, the 1980, 1984, and 1990 issues in particular contain invaluable information on human capital investment in the Third World.

_____. *World Tables*. 6th ed. Baltimore: The Johns Hopkins University Press, 1989-1990.

This annual report includes detailed statistical information on developing countries which allows them to be compared with each other and the industrialized world on the basis of a number of criteria.

Wykstra, Ronald A. *Education and the Economics of Human Capital*. New York: Collier-Macmillan, 1971.

A composition of articles in the economic literature including such authors as Theodore Schultz, Edward F. Denison, H. S. Houthakker, Gary S. Becker, and many others. There are three broad topics of interest: the role that education and the development of human capital play in economic growth; the returns to investment in education; and other important issues in the economics of education. Highly readable and appropriate for the specialist, nonspecialist, and even the noneconomist. A good introduction into the literature of human capital development. Contains an index.

APPLICATIONS

Industrial Organization and Regulation

Abrahamsen, Martin A. *Cooperative Business Enterprise*. New York: McGraw-Hill, 1976.

This book presents an excellent overview of the cooperative form of business. For years, this text was the standard reference for college courses dealing with cooperatives. Though somewhat dated, it contains useful information on cooperatives including their development and operation.

Adams, Walter, ed. *The Structure of American Industry*. New York: Macmillan, 1990.

Treats the structure, conduct, and performance of eleven major U.S. industries. Valuable for the general reader or student interested in relating monopoly/competition theory to actual industries. The concluding discussion on public policy summarizes the controversy over large firm size and antitrust enforcement from the viewpoint emphasizing social costs of market power.

Armstrong, Christopher, and H. V. Nelles. *Monopoly's Moment: The Organization and Regulation of Canadian Utilities, 1830-1930*. Philadelphia: Temple University Press, 1986.

Furnishes a well-written comparison to the better-known story in the United States. Focused on utility regulation, the book does not deal very much with other businesses regulated in Canada.

Arnold, Thurman W. *The Folklore of Capitalism*. New Haven, Conn.: Yale University Press, 1937.

An examination of the hidden assumptions and values in capitalist society, as expressed in common language and modes of behavior. Views on the relation between government and the economy are dated, but observations on the deep structure of capitalist society remain valid.

Bain, Joe. *Industrial Organization*. New York: John Wiley & Sons, 1959.
The original book concerning industrial organization. Gives a good
historic background on the subject.

Baldwin, William L. *Market Power, Competition, and Antitrust Policy.*
Homewood, Ill.: Richard D. Irwin, 1987.
A lengthy but accessible and largely nonmathematical discussion of
the legal and institutional aspects of monopolies, including the detec-
tion of monopoly power and the enforcement of antitrust policies. Also
contains examples of how the concept of monopoly power is inherent
in other market structures.

Berg, Sanford V., and John Tschirhart. *Natural Monopoly Regulation:
Principles and Practice.* Cambridge, England: Cambridge University
Press, 1988.
A survey of the basic microeconomic theory underlying natural monopoly, optimal pricing, rate-of-return constraints, technological
change, alternatives to conventional regulation, and deregulation. Suitable for readers with some background in formal microeconomics.

Berle, Adolf A., and Gardiner Means. *The Modern Corporation and
Private Property.* Chicago: University of Chicago Press, 1968.
A classic treatment of the evolution of modern property arrangements
in industrial society, and of the importance of the modern corporation,
both as a form of property and as an owner of property.

Blackstone, Erwin A., and Joseph P. Fuhr, Jr. "The Economics of Public
Utility Regulation: A Review Article." *Atlantic Economic Journal* 17
(June, 1989): 68-73.
Provides a good overview of the issues and practices concerning public
utility pricing.

Blair, Roger D., and David L. Kaserman. *Antitrust Economics.* Homewood, Ill.: Richard D. Irwin, 1985.
Provides an extensive analysis of explicit collusive agreements to fix
prices, as well as briefer treatments of the tacit collusion to fix prices,
the collusion to divide markets, and the collusion among customers to
boycott particular sellers.

_____ . *The Law and Economics of Vertical Integration and
Control.* New York: Academic Press, 1983.
This book provides an overview of the owner-control approach to
vertical integration, and it uses this theory to examine many of the more

important antitrust decisions regarding vertical integration. The anti-trust discussion in this book is suitable for the general reader, but a background in microeconomics is helpful for understanding the authors' development of the theory.

Bonbright, James C., Albert L. Danielsen, and David R. Kamerschen. *Principles of Public Utility Rates*. Arlington, Va.: Public Utilities Reports, 1988.

Examines the various topics concerning public utility pricing. This book uses no graphs and few mathematical equations; it can easily be understood.

Bork, Robert H. *The Antitrust Paradox: A Policy at War with Itself*. New York: Basic Books, 1978.

Bork is a persuasive spokesman for the Chicago School of antitrust. This thought-provoking book provides original and insightful critiques of a large number of antitrust decisions. Although addressed primarily to those with a background in antitrust, most sections are readily accessible to the nonspecialist.

Breit, William, and Kenneth G. Elzinga. *The Antitrust Casebook: Milestones in Economic Regulation*. 2d ed. Chicago: Dryden Press, 1989.

A collection of the most important collusion cases that have been decided by the U.S. Supreme Court since the passage of the Sherman Antitrust Act in 1890. Contains brief excerpts from many of the landmark judicial opinions in antitrust. Although the language used by the judges can make for difficult reading, with a little perseverance most readers will find the opinions fascinating reading. Excellent introductory passages by the editors help to place the cases in perspective.

Breyer, Stephen. *Regulation and Its Reform*. Cambridge, Mass.: Harvard University Press, 1982.

Provides the theoretical underpinnings of and case studies for the deregulation movement. Breyer worked closely with Senator Edward M. Kennedy to bring about deregulation of the airline industry in the late 1970's.

Brozen, Yale, ed. *The Competitive Economy*. Morristown, N.J.: General Learning Press, 1975.

Brozen has edited a fine book of selected readings in imperfect competition, regulation, antitrust, and some applications of antitrust law with contributions from Kenneth J. Arrow, Arthur Laffer, Joseph Schumpeter, George J. Stigler, J. Fred Weston, and others. Excellent for nonspecialists or college students.

Bunting, Robert L. *Employer Concentration in Local Labor Markets.* Chapel Hill: University of North Carolina Press, 1962.

This 180-page academic study is dated but still represents the most careful study available on the extent of monopsony in the United States. The study (using county-level data for the year 1948) found that monopsony, as indexed by various measures of employer concentration, was not a widespread problem in the United States.

Calvani, Terry, and John Siegfried, eds. *Economic Analysis and Antitrust Law.* 2d ed. Boston: Little, Brown, 1988.

An excellent collection of readings that includes articles accessible to a general audience as well as relatively advanced work. Each of the articles is written by a leading figure in antitrust analysis. The book succeeds in covering a wide range of topics in a balanced and objective manner. The editors conclude each section with an extensive set of bibliographic notes.

Canner, Glenn B., and James T. Fergus. "The Economic Effects of Proposed Ceilings on Credit Card Interest Rates." *Federal Reserve Bulletin* 72 (January, 1987): 1-13.

Examines the possible effects of price ceilings on the profitability of credit cards, the use and repayment patterns, and the possible adjustments by card issuers and consumers. Gives a good analysis of the consequences that can result from price ceilings.

Carlton, Dennis W., and Jeffrey M. Perloff. *Modern Industrial Organization.* Glenview, Ill,: Scott, Foresman, 1990.

An excellent example of detecting cartels through auctions data is presented on pages 213-217. See pages 280-286 for an introduction to Nash equilibrium. Recommended for all readers.

Caves, Richard. *American Industry: Structure, Conduct, Performance.* 6th ed. Englewood Cliffs, N.J.: Prentice-Hall, 1987.

Provides a compact (124-page) overview of the structure-conduct-performance model of markets, the mainstream framework for analyzing nonmonopoly markets in which firms have market power. Easily accessible to readers having only an introductory exposure to economics, providing an excellent introduction to entry barriers, collusion, cartels, mergers to monopoly, natural monopoly, patents, market efficiency, and the social consequences of monopoly power.

Chandler, Alfred D. *The Visible Hand.* Cambridge, Mass.: Belknap Press, 1977.
  Provides a valuable historical perspective on the development of business enterprises in the United States, including the rise of the corporate form of business organization and its impact on companies. Particularly noteworthy is the discussion of professional management as a response to the corporation. A bibliography and references are included.

Clarkson, Kenneth W., and Roger Miller. *Industrial Organization.* New York: McGraw-Hill, 1982.
  Provides a good introduction to industrial organization, economic theory, evidence, and public policy, with examples of antitrust cases. Includes numerous graphs, tables, and charts. Excellent for college students as well as nonspecialists.

Clarkson, Kenneth W., Roger LeRoy Miller, Gaylord A. Jentz, and Frank B. Cross. *West's Business Law: Text, Cases, and Legal Environment.* 1980. 2d ed. St. Paul, Minn.: West, 1989.
  Written and designed for the serious legal student; an excellent legal research text. Cases, forms, appendices, a glossary, and ethics sections are included.

Crew, Michael A., and Paul R. Kleindorfer. *The Economics of Public Utility Regulation.* Cambridge, Mass.: MIT Press, 1986.
  An excellent and readable survey combining the economic theory of regulation with a historical overview, comparisons of different methods of regulation, and applications to electricity, telecommunications, natural gas, and water. Two chapters deal exclusively with peak-load pricing. Also contains a chapter on efficiency and equity. Topics can be understood in the absence of the book's mathematical equations.

Cunningham, James P. *The Competition Law of the EEC: A Practical Guide.* London: Koran Page, 1973.
  Intended for businesspeople and lawyers, this book is nevertheless a very interesting look at the complexity of the laws regulating business affairs within the European Economic Community (EEC). Individual cases are discussed in addition to the general presentation of EEC legislation and the workings of the Community's legal system.

Denzau, Arthur T. *Made in America: The 1981 Japanese Automobile Cartel*. St. Louis: Center for the Study of American Business, Washington University, 1986.

This succinct, data-based work of scholarship concludes that the Japanese automobile cartel handsomely benefits Japanese firms at the expense of American car buyers.

Derthick, Martha, and Paul J. Quirk. *The Politics of Deregulation*. Washington, D.C.: Brookings Institution, 1985.

The authors downplay the notion that economic self-interests mostly motivate politics. Covering the airline, trucking, and telecommunications industries, the authors argue instead that, even though industry interests opposed deregulation, they failed because the new economic thinking, the abilities of politicians to use publicity to bolster their positions, and new legal doctrines worked against continuation and extension of regulation. While a useful study, it ignores too much the effects of technological and economic change over time on regulation.

Dertouzos, Michael, Richard Lester, Robert Solow, and the MIT Commission on Industrial Productivity. *Made in America: Regaining the Productive Edge*. Cambridge, Mass.: MIT Press, 1989.

An important and thorough investigation of international competitiveness. Includes recommendations for change aimed at regaining the competitive edge in world markets, as well as case studies of eight major industries in the United States, ranging from textiles to semiconductors.

Disner, Eliot G. *Antitrust for Business: Questions and Answers*. New York: Federal Legal Publications, 1989.

An interesting 125-page guide to the antitrust laws intended for a general business audience. Leads the reader through sixty-four commonly asked antitrust questions and their answers. An excellent guide for those wishing to identify or avoid antitrust violations in everyday business situations.

Dolan, E. G., and D. E. Lindsey. *Microeconomics*. Chicago: Dryden Press, 1988.

This text, like many other economics textbooks, contains useful passages on subsidies. Chapters 3 and 5 provide good examples of subsidies, as well as their effects on demand and supply. Recommended for college students.

Dugger, William M. *Corporate Hegemony*. Westport, Conn.: Greenwood Press, 1989.

This institutionalist analysis explains how corporations influence the entire culture of the United States. Dugger argues that corporate values and beliefs are replacing those of the school, family, community, and other social institutions. Includes an excellent, detailed (eight-page) bibliographical essay on the corporation and its role in capitalist society.

Dunkelberg, William C., and Jonathan A. Scott. *Credit, Banks, and Small Business: 1980-1984*. Washington, D.C.: NFIB Research and Education Foundation, 1985.

This monograph reviews the results of three biennial surveys of the relationships between lending institutions and small firms. By means of descriptive statistics, the authors assess the terms under which businesses are able to obtain credit.

Friedman, James W. *Oligopoly and the Theory of Games*. Amsterdam: North-Holland, 1977.

Presents traditional models of oligopolistic behavior (such as the kinked demand curve model, the collusion model, and the leader-follower model).

Fromm, Gary, ed. *Studies in Public Regulation*. Cambridge, Mass.: MIT Press, 1981.

To understand why regulating well is difficult, see Paul Joskow and Roger Noll's "Regulation in Theory and Practice: An Overview." Comments by Alfred Kahn and George J. Stigler and a concluding chapter by Sam Peltzman on developments in regulatory economics are also recommended.

Fuller, John Grant. *The Gentlemen Conspirators: The Story of the Price-Fixers in the Electrical Industry*. New York: Grove Press, 1962.

Fuller documents how large firms in the electrical equipment industry colluded to set prices during the 1950's. Examines how the collusive agreement originated, operated, and was finally discovered by a Tennessee newspaper reporter.

Galbraith, John Kenneth. *The New Industrial State*. Boston: Houghton Mifflin, 1967.

Contains the best nontechnical view of the firm from a post-Keynesian perspective. Galbraith argues that the business firm, as postulated by traditional economic theory, no longer exists. Galbraith's famous wit and style is in full force here. Accessible to all audiences.

Gerritse, Ronald, ed. *Producer Subsidies*. London: Pinter, 1990.
Contains nine articles that analyze issues of theory and application with respect to subsidies. An excellent source for term papers. Recommended for college students.

Goldschmid, Harvey J., H. Michael Mann, and J. Fred Weston, eds. *Industrial Concentration: The New Learning*. Boston: Little, Brown, 1974.
Confronts traditional industrial organization economists with those who believe that profits in concentrated industries reflect economies of scale. The papers by Leonard W. Weiss and Harold Demsetz are particularly helpful.

Goldston, Eli, Herbert C. Morton, and G. Neal Ryland, eds. *The American Business Corporation: New Perspectives on Profit and Purpose*. Cambridge, Mass.: MIT Press, 1972.
This collection of essays on the subject of the American corporation is in two parts. Part 1 consists of eleven articles primarily by academics and is more objective, avoiding judgments on the record of business. The essays in part 2 were written by representatives of business, government, and journalism, and tend to display their respective points of view more clearly. In total, the two parts offer a stimulating discussion of some of the most troubling issues surrounding the modern American corporation.

Gray, Earle. *The Great Uranium Cartel*. Toronto: McClelland and Stewart, 1982.
A detailed history of the international uranium cartel, which was secretly formed in 1972 to control supply and increase price. The specialized bibliography features separate sections compiling relevant judicial proceedings, legislative hearings, diplomatic notes, books, and articles.

Green, Mark J., Beverly C. Moore, Jr., and Bruce Wasserstein. *The Closed Enterprise System: Ralph Nader's Study Group Report on Antitrust Enforcement*. New York: Grossman, 1972.
An extremely critical look at the enforcement of those statutes that prohibit the acquisition and exercise of monopoly power. The high degree of criticism handicaps the usefulness of the economic analysis,

but the volume does present a thorough description of the various federal agencies that are responsible for antitrust enforcement.

Greer, Douglas F. *Business, Government, and Society.* Englewood Cliffs, N.J.: Prentice-Hall, 1987.
Examines the various pricing behaviors of specific regulated industries. Well written, with few mathematical equations and graphs.

_____. *Industrial Organization and Public Policy.* 2d ed. New York: Macmillan, 1984.
A very readable overview of industrial organization, from perfect competition to monopoly, including industry studies and both early and later antitrust cases. Good discussion of advertising, business strategy, and technological change. Suitable for college students.

Gugliotta, Guy, and Jeff Leen. *Kings of Cocaine: Inside the Medellin Cartel, an Astonishing True Story of Murder, Money, and International Corruption.* New York: Simon & Schuster, 1989.
Records the historical development of the Colombian cartel of cocaine barons. This heavily researched, 391-page book brings together from many sources a wealth of factual details, including revealing photographs of cartel personnel engaged in operations.

Gujarati, Dadomar N. *Government and Business.* New York: McGraw-Hill, 1984.
Chapter 4 contains a good, yet brief, discussion on subsidies. Many examples are given in a simple, clear style. Suitable for undergraduates.

Gwartney, James D., and Richard E. Wagner, eds. *Public Choice and Constitutional Economics.* Political Economy and Public Policy 6. Greenwich, Conn.: JAI Press, 1988.
A collection of papers by adherents of public choice theory who favor strict constitutional limitations to control the self-aggrandizing tendencies of politicians and bureaucrats. The shared thesis is that the framers of the U.S. Constitution had farsightedly imposed such limitations but that those protections of individual economic liberty have been eroded by recent Supreme Court decisions, resulting in a dangerous overgrowth of governmental power.

Hanke, Steve H., ed. *Prospects for Privatization.* New York: Academy of Political Science, 1987.

Contains essays, written by specialists, covering a wide spectrum of issues, from the methods of privatization to the case against privatization. This volume represents one of the best readings on the subject for a general audience.

Harberger, Arnold C. "Monopoly and Resource Allocation." In *Microeconomics: Selected Readings*, edited by Edwin Mansfield. New York: W. W. Norton, 1971.

Harberger is the most often-quoted authority on the losses to society owing to allocative inefficiency. This paper is not highly technical, and there is very little use of mathematics, but it does not read easily. Some of the empirical results are highly quotable.

Hay, Donald A., and Derek J. Morris. *Industrial Economics: Theory and Evidence*. Oxford, England: Oxford University Press, 1979.

This undergraduate text offers a European perspective of issues in industrial organization. This view of the impact of conglomerate mergers on the marketplace differs somewhat from the American view.

Holloway, Steven Kendall. *The Aluminum Multinationals and the Bauxite Cartel*. New York: St. Martin's Press, 1988.

Discusses in detail various candidate definitions of "cartel" and presents a model for predicting company response to government cartels. Focuses on the international cartels in aluminum and in bauxite, the mineral used to produce aluminum.

Holmes, Thomas J. "The Effects of Third-Degree Price Discrimination in Oligopoly." *American Economic Review* 79 (March, 1989): 244-250.

A mathematical analysis of third-degree price discrimination under the industry structure of oligopoly. Using a duopoly model of a differentiated-products industry, the article shows what gives rise to discrimination between markets. A knowledge of advanced mathematics is necessary.

Ireland, Norman J. *Product Differentiation and Nonprice Competition*. Oxford, England: Basil Blackwell, 1987.

A technical book, good for advanced research on product differentiation. Recommended for senior college students and those attending graduate school.

Johnson, Leland L. "Behavior of the Firm Under Regulatory Constraint: A Reassessment." *American Economic Review* 63 (May, 1973): 90-97.

This article examines what had happened in the ten years after the original article on the Averch-Johnson effect, clarifying the theory and examining some of the empirical evidence.

Judd, Richard J., William T. Greenwood, and Fred W. Becker, eds. *Small Business in a Regulated Economy: Issues and Policy Implications.* New York: Quorum Books, 1988.

While most discussions of regulation of business focus on large corporations, this collection of essays focuses on the issue of the relation between small business and government regulatory policy. Some articles include statistics and some technical analysis, but most can be understood without specialized technical knowledge and deal with issues of vital importance to small businesses.

Kahn, Alfred E. *The Economics of Regulation.* 2 vols. New York: John Wiley & Sons, 1970-1971.

Volume 1 analyzes the reasons for and the theories of regulation. Volume 2 discusses the principles and institutions of regulation. Kahn describes complicated economic theories in terms clearly accessible to the general reader. These volumes reflect the intellectual connections between regulation and deregulation and formed the basis for Kahn's application of deregulation while chair of the Civil Aeronautics Board in the late 1970's.

Kalt, Joseph P. *The Economics and Politics of Oil Price Regulation: Federal Policy in the Post-Embargo Era.* Cambridge, Mass.: MIT Press, 1981.

An excellent analysis of the effects of price controls on the American energy market, wrapped in an analytical framework as much concerned with normative as positive economics. Extensive documentation and a lengthy bibliography are included.

Kefauver, Estes. *In a Few Hands: Monopoly Power in America.* New York: Pantheon Books, 1965.

This volume presents the late senator's analysis of the degree of monopoly power in a number of U.S. industries. While the information is not current, this work is of particular interest because of Kefauver's role in drafting one of the nation's more recent and most powerful pieces of antitrust legislation—the Celler-Kefauver Act (1950).

Koch, James V. *Industrial Organization and Prices.* 2d ed. Englewood Cliffs, N.J.: Prentice-Hall, 1980.

A college textbook on industrial organization. Chapter 13, "Oligopolistic Behavior and Pricing: Applied Topics," deals with various aspects of price discrimination, such as definition and conditions for discrimination. The three degrees of price discrimination are also illustrated using several examples.

Kwoka, John E., Jr., and Lawrence J. White, eds. *The Antitrust Revolution*. Glenwood, Ill.: Scott, Foresman, 1989.

Contains insightful, detailed analyses on a wide range of major antitrust cases. Case studies illustrate actual practices in the evaluation of mergers and joint ventures in the petroleum industry, automobile manufacturing, the soft drink market, and the airline industry.

Lane, Marc J. *Legal Handbook for Small Business*. Rev. ed. New York: American Management Association, 1989.

A practical, nuts-and-bolts guide for owners and managers of small businesses, including a discussion of the merits of incorporation and limited liability. Each section contains concrete information, such as names and addresses of government agencies, and specific laws that apply to specific situations.

Lerner, Abba P. "The Concept of Monopoly and the Measurement of Monopoly Power." In *Readings in Microeconomics*, edited by William Brett and Harold Hochman. New York: Holt, Rinehart and Winston, 1968.

Lerner provides a thorough and well-written discussion of monopoly pricing, the losses that are attributable to monopoly, and the measures of economic power. Portions of this essay may be difficult for some readers. For the most part, however, it is accessible to the reader who has some limited familiarity with economics.

Lipsey, Richard G., Peter O. Steiner, and Douglas Purvis. *Economics*. 8th ed. New York: Harper & Row, 1987.

This basic economics textbook gives an excellent, concise discussion of rationing, price controls, and black markets (pages 100-102). Similar discussions can be found in other editions of the textbook or in virtually any basic economics text.

Low, Richard E. *Modern Economic Organization*. Homewood, Ill.: Richard D. Irwin, 1970.

Chapter 7 provides a rather detailed and readable understanding of entry barriers and provides good examples. All the major issues dealing with market power, concentration, and product differentiation are covered quite well.

McCraw, Thomas K. *Prophets of Regulation: Charles Francis Adams, Louis D. Brandeis, James M. Landis, Alfred E. Kahn.* Cambridge, Mass.: The Belknap Press of Harvard Press, 1984.

Using a creative biographical approach, McCraw introduces the reader to the reasons for, the thinking about, and the changes in regulatory policy in the United States. Awarded the Pulitzer Prize in History, this book is based on copious research, furnishes the broader reform context in which regulation and deregulation materialized, and is the most accessible work to the general reader listed in this bibliography.

Machlup, Fritz. *The Political Economy of Monopoly: Business, Labor, and Government Policies.* Baltimore: The Johns Hopkins University Press, 1952.

In order to make "complicated things intelligible to the general reader," Machlup provides a comprehensive, detailed treatment of monopoly and government policies toward monopoly. On topics where controversy exists, he provides both sides of the argument, often with the purpose of undermining one side. Maintains an interesting tone throughout.

McLean, Iain. *Public Choice: An Introduction.* Oxford, England: Basil Blackwell, 1987.

One of the best overall introductions to the basic principles and major applications of public choice theory for the nonspecialist. McLean has a knack for presenting complex and abstruse concepts in layperson's language, and he is scrupulous about not intruding his own political and philosophical biases. Whereas most public choice analysts rely heavily upon the United States for evidence, McLean draws upon British experience as well for evaluating different hypotheses.

Magaziner, Ira C., and Robert B. Reich. *Minding America's Business: The Decline and Rise of the American Economy.* New York: Random House, 1982.

A clear, easy-to-understand description of how other nations are prospering with the help of industrial policies. In contrast, the U.S. economy deteriorates because of its refusal to adopt such a policy. Although it lacks a theoretical justification for industrial policies, this book (by writers who later advised the Bill Clinton Administration) remains the best introduction around to industrial policy.

Mancuso, Joseph R. *Mancuso's Small Business Resource Guide*. Englewood Cliffs, N.J.: Prentice-Hall, 1988.

Contains a brief overview of partnerships, proprietorships, and corporate structures as they apply to the development of small business. Also contains extensive lists of organizations and reference material that would be useful to an individual who is considering a business's organizational structure. Entirely geared toward small business and is most useful as a "how-to" guide, rather than as a reference for more general purposes.

Massel, Mark S. *Competition and Monopoly*. Washington, D.C.: Brookings Institution, 1962.

Addresses the process of determining and maintaining the appropriate degree of competition from the perspective of the diverse and often conflicting goals that underlie actual policy formation. The interrelationship between law and economics in antitrust policy is emphasized. Written for both the general reader and the professional.

Miller, Roger LeRoy, Daniel M. Benjamin, and Douglass C. North. *The Economics of Public Issues*. New York: Harper & Row, 1990.

An easy-to-read book presenting applications of basic economic principles. Contains an analysis of how rent controls have resulted in the deterioration of apartments. Suitable for a general audience.

Mueller, Willard F. *A Primer on Monopoly and Competition*. New York: Random House, 1970.

Written by a well-known expert on the issues of market power and market concentration, this book is intended for the novice. The issue of barriers to entry is treated in a straightforward and readable manner. Concentration can be placed on chapters 3, 5, and 6, which deal most directly with this issue. Intended to be an introduction to market power issues, this book is very understandable for the nonspecialist.

Nader, Ralph, Mark Green, and Joel Seligman. *Taming the Giant Corporation*. New York: W. W. Norton, 1976.

This study of the large corporation takes a generally critical perspective, focusing on the adverse effects of large American corporations and how they have been able to erode the rule of law and ethical precepts. Those who disagree with this perspective will resist the conclusions of these authors, but they are presented persuasively and backed with objective statistics, not simply with rhetoric.

National Cooperative Business Association. *Cooperative Business in the United States*. Washington, D.C.: Author, 1985.
   A very basic description of cooperative principles. Examples of different types of cooperative activities are presented.

Noll, Roger C. "Major League Sports." In *The Structure of American Industry*, edited by Walter Adams. 6th ed. New York: Macmillan, 1982.
   The team sports business, because of its operating rules and a special legal status that effectively limits economic competition in the industry, provides a good opportunity to study monopsony in the making. This article provides a good, generally accessible discussion of the market structure for players and the nature of the so-called reserve clause that leads to the existence of monopsony.

North, Douglass C., and Roger L. Miller. *The Economics of Public Issues*. New York: Harper & Row, 1980.
   Devotes a chapter to wage and price controls. Provides a solid examination of the issues that concern price ceilings and the problems that can result.

Ottosen, Garry K. *Monopoly Power*. Salt Lake City, Utah: Crossroads Research Institute, 1990.
   This monograph provides an excellent and very readable introduction to monopoly power. Part 1 focuses on numerical measurements of monopoly power and how they are used by the antitrust authorities. Part 2 examines the extent of current and historical monopoly power in the U.S. economy, incorporating views from across the political spectrum. The more difficult mathematical exposition is relegated to the appendices.

Perry, Martin K. "Vertical Integration." In *Handbook of Industrial Organization*, edited by Richard Schmalensee and Robert D. Willig, Amsterdam: North-Holland, 1989.
   Accessible to the reader with some background in microeconomics, this work contains a thorough summary of the owner-control motivations for vertical integration and also describes applications to particular industries and public policy. An up-to-date bibliography of aca-

demic contributions should be especially useful to the more advanced student.

Piotrowski, Roman. *Cartels and Trusts: Their Origin and Historical Development from the Economic and Legal Aspects.* London: George Allen & Unwin, 1933.

The classical work on the origin and historical development of cartels, written in a highly learned but very readable style. Recounts the history of cartels in ancient Phoenicia, India, Greece, and Rome; throughout the medieval period; and in Europe from the Renaissance to the nineteenth century.

Plott, Charles R. "Industrial Organization Theory and Experimental Economics." *Journal of Economic Literature* 20, no. 1 (1982): 485-527.

An excellent introduction to how experimental economics can be used to test theories in industrial organization. Includes analyses of several classic experimental works in industrial organization.

Porter, Michael E. *Competitive Strategy: Techniques for Analyzing Industries and Competitors.* New York: Free Press, 1980.

Porter is a full professor at the Harvard Business School and is a widely quoted authority on corporate organization and strategic management. His books are very informative and are a "must read" for the serious economics student. See especially the chapters on strategies toward buyers and suppliers, and the chapter on the strategic analysis of vertical integration. Porter provides a nice discussion of how the businessperson might examine his or her rivals as well as his or her own decisions to integrate vertically.

Posner, Richard A. *Antitrust Law: An Economic Perspective.* Chicago: University of Chicago Press, 1976.

Posner is a judge on the U.S. Court of Appeals and a leading member of the Chicago School. Although the book assumes no background in economics on the part of its reader, it is somewhat difficult to read. Nevertheless, the effort is well worth it: Posner's arguments for overhauling U.S. antitrust laws and policy are compelling, and the work remains one of the definitive statements of the Chicago School's view of antitrust.

Posner, Richard A., and Frank H. Easterbrook. *Antitrust: Cases, Economic Notes, and Other Materials.* St. Paul, Minn.: West, 1981.

The definitive antitrust casebook, this work contains more than one thousand pages of excerpts, questions, comments, and analyses. Touches on every area of antitrust law and so is an excellent reference book for serious students of antitrust. A supplement updating the book through 1984 is available.

Ramanadham, Venkata V. *Public Enterprise: From Evaluation to Privatization.* London: Frank Cass, 1987.

Ramanadham builds upon solid analytical foundations to provide a conceptual framework for evaluation of the performance of both public and private enterprises. Although the book draws upon global experience for illustrative purposes, studies are too technical and they do not present a coherent analysis.

Reagan, Michael D. "Health Care Rationing: What Does It Mean?" *New England Journal of Medicine* 319 (October 27, 1988): 1149-1151.

This article serves as an excellent introduction to the basic issues of rationing medical services. Also included is an extensive list of references on the topic.

Robinson, E. A. G. *Monopoly.* New York: Pitman, 1948.

Part of the Cambridge Economic Handbooks series, this book is recommended to the general reader or student who wants a short but comprehensive treatment of monopoly. Includes price-output determination, welfare effects, how monopoly is established, the relationship of monopoly to industrial efficiency and stability, and the legal treatment of monopoly.

Robinson, Joan. *The Economics of Imperfect Competition.* 2d ed. London: Macmillan, 1969.

Robinson initiates the analysis of imperfect competition by giving a penetrating, and somewhat critical, presentation of the standard supply theory. Especially relevant are chapters 6, 7, 9, and 10. This sets the stage for noncompetitive market analysis in which the supply curve, by the usual construction, is not well defined.

Rottenberg, Simon. "The Baseball Players' Labor Market." *Journal of Political Economy* 64 (June, 1956): 242-258.

While dated, this is a generally readable and still interesting discussion on the organization of the professional baseball industry, the economics of the reserve clause, and the existence of monopsonistic exploitation.

Roy, Ewell P. *Cooperatives: Development, Principles, and Management.* 4th ed. Danville, Ill.: Interstate Printers & Publishers, 1981.
One of the most comprehensive texts on cooperatives. Provides excellent examples of consumer cooperatives as well as agricultural cooperatives. The historical evolution of cooperatives along with their taxation, management, and financing are covered in some depth.

Salop, Steven C., Lawrence J. White, Franklin M. Fisher, and Richard Schmalensee. "Horizontal Mergers and Antitrust." *Journal of Economic Perspectives* 1 (1987): 3-54.
A highly readable debate among leading industrial organization economists on merger policy, market definition, concentration indexes, and the Department of Justice's merger guidelines.

Samuelson, Paul A., and William D. Nordhaus haus, William D., and Paul A. Samuelson. *Economics.* 12th ed. New York: McGraw-Hill, 1985.
This textbook is among the best-written and best-received college-level introductory texts. Chapter 23, "Imperfect Competition: Monopoly and Regulation," develops the theory of the profit-maximizing monopolist with graphical and numerical examples. Also included is a discussion of natural monopoly and its regulation, data on concentration and scale economies in several important U.S. industries, and a brief discussion of the inefficiencies of monopoly markets.

Scherer, F. M. *Industrial Market Structure and Economic Performance.* 2d ed. Skokie, Ill.: Rand McNally, 1980.
Chapter 11 of this college textbook describes standard theoretical cases and types of price discrimination found in practice. The implications of discrimination for economic welfare are also discussed. The chapter on the structure of U.S. industry examines the extent of vertical integration in the U.S. economy, and the chapter on buyer power and vertical pricing relationships provides an accessible review of the theory.

Scherer, F. M., and David Ross. *Industrial Market Structure and Economic Performance.* Boston: Houghton Mifflin, 1990.
Probably the most comprehensive book on industrial organization. The perspective includes market structure and economic performance in Europe and other countries. Contains an extensive chapter on product differentiation and many examples with a great amount of detail.

Footnotes on antitrust cases and other studies sometimes take half a page. Excellent for graduate students.

Schmalensee, Richard, and Robert Willig. *Handbook of Industrial Organization*. Vol. 1. New York: North-Holland, 1989.
   Chapter 7 by Alex Jacquemin and Margaret E. Slade reviews collusion and horizontal mergers. Also contains chapters by John C. Panzar on industry structure, Bengt Holmstrom and Jean Tirole on the theory of the firm, Oliver E. Williamson on contracting, Martin Perry on vertical integration, and Carl Shapiro on oligopoly.

Scully, Gerald W. "Pay and Performance in Major League Baseball." *American Economic Review* 63 (December, 1974): 915-930.
   This study requires advanced-level economics and statistics to comprehend. It is of interest to the general reader to get a sense of what is involved in trying to measure a player's marginal revenue product. This estimate is then compared to the player's contract salary to estimate the dollar amount by which the player has been exploited.

Sharp, Ansel, Charles A. Register, and Richard H. Leftwich. *Economics of Social Issues*. 9th ed. Homewood, Ill.: Richard D. Irwin, 1990.
   Provides the reader with an excellent perspective on the economics of big business and monopoly power. Other topics are also discussed, including the history of airline regulation and deregulation as well as government control of prices, pollution, inflation, and poverty. Suitable for nonspecialists and college students.

Shepherd, William G. *The Economics of Industrial Organization*. 3d ed. Englewood Cliffs, N.J.: Prentice-Hall, 1990.
   A straightforward analysis of markets and the competition that takes place within them. Probably the most readily accessible book for the reader untrained in this area. Part 5 provides particularly important insights into the process of price fixing.

Sherman, Roger. *The Regulation of Monopoly*. Cambridge, England: Cambridge University Press, 1989.
   Covers much of the same material as other books, but with more emphasis on basic theory. Includes problems sets.

Shughart, William F., II. *The Organization of Industry*. Homewood, Ill.: Richard D. Irwin, 1990.
   A thorough, modern textbook accessible to readers with a year of college economics. Charts and algebra are employed, but the exposi-

tion is primarily verbal rather than mathematical. Chapters 3 and 4 explain the theory of the firm and review the structure of American industry. Chapter 6 covers the concepts of economies of scale, barriers to entry, and other factors influencing market structure in forty well-written pages. No bibliography, but extensive references are included in the footnotes.

Smith, Adam. *An Inquiry into the Nature and Causes of the Wealth of Nations*. 1776. Reprint. New York: Modern Library, 1937.
This classic work argues that merchants and manufacturers frequently collude in order to suppress competition in the marketplace.

Spulber, Nicolas. *Managing the American Economy from Roosevelt to Reagan*. Bloomington: Indiana University Press, 1989.
Examines the impact of major events on the way economists think about stabilization policy. Describes the setting in which the federal government assumed an interventionist role and how changing events generated new economic thinking and policies. Concludes that economists played a creative and successful role in this regard. Clearly written; well suited to nonspecialists. Index.

Stelzer, Irwin, and Howard Kitt. *Selected Antitrust Cases: Landmark Decisions*. Homewood, Ill.: Richard D. Irwin, 1986.
Contains concise, accessible excerpts of the court decisions that define antitrust and merger law. The legality of mergers depends on how courts interpret antitrust statutes and precedents regarding market definition, concentration criteria, and the relevance of potential entry.

Stigler, George J. *The Citizen and the State*. Chicago: University of Chicago Press, 1975.
Includes Stigler's seminal papers questioning the theoretical and empirical support underlying the "public interest" view of regulation. While subsequent research has developed and tested Stigler's "capture" theory, this remains its clearest presentation, by one of the few economists esteemed for the quality of his writing.

_____. *The Organization of Industry*. Homewood, Ill.: Richard D. Irwin, 1968.
This volume of reprints includes two short, classic articles directly relevant to this topic. Number 6, "Barriers to Entry, Economies of Scale, and Firm Size," clarifies the economic meaning of these terms, while number 7, "The Economies of Scale," lays out the author's

objections to the measurements of scale economies employed in studies of the type done by Pratten. Stigler also presents his preferred alternative for measuring economies of scale, the survivor principle, which infers scale effects from the time trend in firm sizes.

Stiglitz, Joseph E. *Economics of the Public Sector*. 2d ed. New York: W. W. Norton, 1988.
A leading college text on the government's role in the economy. Discusses why the government should intervene in the market economy and addresses causes of government failure. Suitable for college students.

Stocking, George W., and Myron W. Watkins. *Cartels in Action*. New York: Twentieth Century Fund, 1946.
An in-depth analysis of cartel formation and objectives, establishing important historical evidence as to when and why certain cartels have pursued price-fixing objectives.

_____. *Monopoly and Free Enterprise*. New York: Twentieth Century Fund, 1951.
Adds to the title topics an extensive theoretical and practical discussion of markets with few sellers. Antitrust law and major case histories are examined. The authors' view is that business conduct under laissez-faire promotes monopoly and therefore necessitates regulation. Accessible to the general reader and college student.

Storey, David J., ed. *The Small Firm: An International Survey*. New York: St. Martin's Press, 1983.
A broad survey of the nature and the role of the small firm. Separate essays discuss the small firm in the United States, Japan, the United Kingdom, Australia, the former Federal Republic of Germany, Sweden, Southeast Asia, and Africa. The thrust of the essays is to show that—not only in the developing or newly industrialized nations but also in the most advanced industrial nations—the small firm is the central unit of production and development.

Townsend, Harry. *Scale, Innovation, Merger, and Monopoly*. Oxford, England: Pergamon Press, 1968.
A short (101-page) book on these subjects. The first two chapters offer a simple, nonmathematical primer on the technical sources of scale economies and on the pecuniary advantages and disadvantages of large firms. The remaining seventy-five pages are devoted to topics related

to industrial concentration. The work includes an index but no bibliography.

U.S. Department of Justice, Antitrust Division. *U.S. Department of Justice Merger Guidelines*. Washington, D.C.: Government Printing Office, 1984.

The definitive statement of federal government policy toward horizontal mergers. Includes the conceptual criteria for market definition, the methods of measurement, the ease of entry, the efficiency and failing firm defenses, and HHI-based guidelines for antitrust action.

Varian, Hal R. *Intermediate Microeconomics*. New York: W. W. Norton, 1990.

Chapter 25 presents a rigorous development of monopoly pricing, as well as illustrations of the losses to efficiency that are attributable to such behavior. The analysis is both mathematical and graphical and should provide a good source for the individual who is interested in the mechanical aspects of monopolization. Still, large parts of the material are accessible to the individual who possesses an introductory level of economic education.

Vernon, Raymond, ed. *The Promise of Privatization*. New York: Council on Foreign Relations, 1988.

Intended to promote general understanding of the issues surrounding the privatization trend in the world: its promise and challenge. The collection of essays addresses the appropriateness of privatization programs in a number of different national settings with different political and economic structures. Country studies from Great Britain to Turkey attempt to shed light on the relationship between the causes of privatization programs and the developments likely to follow. Well suited to the general public as well as policymakers.

Waldman, Don E. *The Economics of Antitrust: Cases and Analysis*. Boston: Little, Brown, 1986.

A concise and very readable work, this book combines mainstream economic analysis with brief excerpts from a variety of antitrust decisions. In general, Waldman conveys a much less critical tone toward the antitrust laws than that found in the Bork or Posner books.

Weiss, Leonard W. *Case Studies in American Industry*. New York: John Wiley & Sons, 1979.

An examination of the various types of market structures using the case study approach. Also examines conduct and performance.

Wellisz, Stanislaw H. "Regulation of Natural Gas Pipeline Companies: An Economic Analysis." *Journal of Political Economy* 17 (February, 1963): 30-43.

This article, which appeared concurrently with the original Averch-Johnson article, examines, the overcapitalization issue concentrating on peak-load demand.

Wilson, James Q., ed. *The Politics of Regulation.* New York: Basic Books, 1980.

The essays in this book suggest in clear prose that regulation is as much as political phenomenon as an economic one. This work is cited often in studies of regulation and deregulation and is especially illuminating on the politics within regulatory commissions.

Labor Force and Population

Ashenfelter, Orley, and Albert Rees. *Discrimination in Labor Markets.* Princeton, N.J.: Princeton University Press, 1973.

A collection of articles covering race discrimination in education, neoclassical theories of discrimination, and unions and discrimination. It also contains a presentation by Ronald Oaxaca of his technique for empirically estimating the amount of labor market discrimination, for readers interested in the statistical side of this research. The article by Kenneth J. Arrow is a classic but may be too mathematical for those without some experience in microeconomics or a strong mathematical background.

Balliet, Lee. *Survey of Labor Relations.* 2d ed. Washington, D.C.: Bureau of National Affairs, 1987.

This 203-page book is remarkably thorough in its coverage of the development of unions and bargaining, the legal framework of bargaining, and contract negotiations and administration. Very accessible.

Bawden, D. Lee, and Felicity Skidmore, eds. *Rethinking Employment Policy.* Washington, D.C.: Urban Institute Press, 1989.

A series of papers by distinguished labor economists that were presented at the Urban Institute, a Washington think tank. Each paper focuses on possible policy solutions to unemployment. Although written primarily for a professional audience, the papers remain worthwhile to educated lay readers and undergraduate students.

Becker, Gary S. *The Economics of Discrimination.* Chicago: University of Chicago Press, 1957.
The first comprehensive book on the economics of discrimination. Becker developed almost all the neoclassical discrimination theories in use through the 1980's.

_____. *Human Capital: A Theoretical and Empirical Analysis with Special Reference to Education.* 2d ed. New York: Columbia University Press, 1975.
The classic work on human capital theory. Investigates the theoretical effects of on-the-job training and education on wages in great detail, as well as introducing, with simple mathematics, the concept of the rate of return on human capital. Presumes that productivity is a major determinant of wages. Although the presentation can be somewhat technical, the main points of the book are easily accessible to the lay reader.

Bergmann, Barbara R. *The Economic Emergence of Women.* New York: Basic Books, 1986.
Bergman, in quite accessible fashion, discusses the changes in the economic activities of women between the late 1800's and the 1980's. She includes excellent discussions of occupational segregation, comparable worth, and affirmative action. The bibliography makes this book an excellent starting place for further research, particularly in the area of sex discrimination.

Bernstein, Paul. *Workplace Democratization: Its Internal Dynamics.* Kent, Ohio: Kent State University Press, 1976.
This statistical study by a political scientist is one of the few to address the interaction of participation in profits and management in their impacts on productivity. An important study of American participatory enterprises, this book requires good knowledge of statistics.

Blau, Francine D., and Marianne Ferber. *The Economics of Women, Men, and Work.* Englewood Cliffs, N.J.: Prentice-Hall, 1986.
This 365-page book has two excellent chapters on women's labor supply. Contains discussions of how the labor force participation and hours of employment decisions are made; the trend in women's labor

force participation from the 1940's through the 1980's; the differences between black and white women's labor supply; and the effects on women's labor supply of nonmarket work and childbearing. Contains an index, tables, figures, and a bibliography.

Blinder, Alan S. *Hard Heads, Soft Hearts*. Reading, Mass.: Addison-Wesley, 1987.
Discusses the waste of resources that has resulted from unemployment. Suggests that economic policy exaggerates the perils of inflation and underestimates the virtues of low unemployment. President Bill Clinton appointed the author as deputy chairman of the Federal Reserve Board.

Bluestone, Barry, and Bennett Harrison. *The Deindustrialization of America*. New York: Basic Books, 1982.
The authors argue that, because U.S. business has focused on mergers and foreign investment rather than on production, cyclical and structural unemployment in the United States has increased. They then discuss numerous policy solutions. Many have quibbled with the analysis and policy assessments that are contained in this work; however, it remains a thought-provoking and compelling account of U.S. labor market problems at the end of the twentieth century.

Bogue, Donald J. *The Population of the United States: Historical Trends and the Future Projections*. New York: Free Press, 1985.
A comprehensive, statistically oriented analysis by one of American's top demographic scholars. For the advanced reader.

Borjas, George G., and Marta Tienda, eds. *Hispanics in the U.S. Economy*. Orlando, Fla.: Academic Press, 1985.
This collection of papers includes an opening section profiling various Hispanic groups. Following this are sections on earnings and labor supply, youth employment and school enrollment, occupational choices of women, migration, and case studies of immigrants to New York City. Some chapters are technical; most are suitable for advanced undergraduates.

Bornstein, Tim, and Ann Gosline, eds. *Labor and Employment Arbitration*. New York: Matthew Bender, 1990.
This three-volume series is the most complete treatise on arbitration. Covers every aspect of grievance and interest arbitration, with excel-

lent documentation of case citations. Contributing authors write chapters on their greatest area of expertise.

Borus, Michael E., ed. *Youth and the Labor Market*. Kalamazoo, Mich.: W. E. Upjohn Institute for Employment Research, 1984.

This collection provides a thorough survey of youth in the work force and represents an ideal starting point for one to become acquainted with the economic, demographic, and social characteristics of youth in the work force, which are presented in tables. Each article concentrates on a different aspect and supplies references.

Boserup, Ester. *Population and Technological Change*. Chicago: University of Chicago Press, 1981.

A major work by seminal author that argues that population growth has facilitated technological change in agriculture and allowed for more intensive use and greater food production. Attempts to demonstrate that land is not a fixed factor of production.

Boston, Thomas D. *Race, Class, and Conservatism*. Winchester, Mass.: Unwin Hyman, 1988.

This book aims to rebut the central propositions of neoconservative economists on the role of racial discrimination in black economic advancement. Not always convincing, the but good at laying out arguments of opponents. Suitable for a general audience.

Bowen, William G., and T. Aldrich Finnegan. *The Economics of Labor Force Participation*. Princeton, N.J.: Princeton University Press, 1969.

Three chapters are devoted to married women's labor supply and one to the labor supply of single women aged twenty-five to fifty-four. Examines the period from 1940 through 1960, particularly analyzing the effects of race, age, schooling, husband's employment status, and number and age of children on women's labor force participation. The level of writing and technicality is accessible to high school and college students as well as to the general reader. Contains 897 pages (181 pages devoted to women), tables, figures, and an index.

Braverman, Harry. *Labor and Monopoly Capital*. New York: Monthly Review Press, 1974.

The author views the outcome of labor economics as strongly influenced by the power of competing interest groups. He traces the origins of labor-management relations, the influence of technology upon work, and the changing composition of occupations within capitalist society.

Briggs, Vernon M., Jr., Walter Fogel, and Fred H. Schmidt. *The Chicano Worker.* Austin: University of Texas Press, 1977.

This 129-page book focuses on the experience of workers of Mexican heritage in the United States. Data on employment and income are presented and there is discussion of illegal immigration and other issues relevant to this worker group. Suitable for a general audience.

Brown, Charles. "Minimum Wage Laws: Are They Overrated?" *The Journal of Economic Perspectives* 2 (Summer, 1988): 133-145.

Brown provides an interesting and accessible critique of the economic consequences of the minimum wage. He lists the seminal articles on this topic in the reference section.

Brown, Charles, Curtis Gilroy, and Andrew Kohen. "The Effect of the Minimum Wage on Employment and Unemployment." *The Journal of Economic Literature* 20 (June, 1982): 487-528.

This extensive analysis includes numerous references, both technical and nontechnical, to the wide range of literature that deals with this topic.

Cain, Glen G. *Married Women in the Labor Force: An Economic Analysis.* Chicago: University of Chicago Press, 1966.

Using Bureau of the Census decennial census data, Cain examines women's labor force participation from 1900 to 1964, concentrating on the period from 1940 to 1964. Discusses the factors that influence married women's labor supply, such as family income, the wife's wage rate, other family members' wage rates, the value of the wife's unpaid home work time, the value of other family members' unpaid home work time, and the wife's preferences among market work, home work, and leisure. Contains 159 pages, an index, and tables.

Calabresi, Guido. *The Costs of Accidents: A Legal and Economic Analysis.* New Haven, Conn.: Yale University Press, 1970.

The first book-length attempt to apply economic methods to the study of a specific area of law, it is one of the "classics" in the law and economics literature. Calabresi is an academic lawyer speaking primarily to other academics. Nevertheless, the book is engaging and accessible.

Chamberlain, Neil W., Donald E. Cullen, and David Lewin. *The Labor Sector*. New York: McGraw-Hill, 1980.
A very comprehensive text on labor economics, intended for those uninitiated in economics. Includes discussions of the influence of labor unions, labor's political activity, discrimination, and equality.

Cherry, Robert. *Discrimination: Its Economic Impact on Blacks, Women, and Jews*. Lexington, Mass.: Lexington Books, 1989.
This 235-page book opens with a broad theoretical discussion of discrimination before turning in later chapters to specific issues involving blacks, women, and Jews. Theoretical views are distinguished by whether they are voiced by conservatives, liberals, or radicals. Topics covered include black youth employment problems, black-Jewish relations, and the impact of social welfare programs. Suitable for a general audience.

Clark, W. A. V. *Human Migration*. Beverly Hills, Calif.: Sage Publications, 1986.
A basic guide to migration, with an emphasis on economics and geography. Many definitions are provided, and descriptive data, pertaining to both internal and international migration, are analyzed. This book is written in simple language and is recommended to the general reader.

Cook, Alice H., Val R. Lorwin, and Arlene Kaplan Daniels, eds. *Women and Trade Unions in Eleven Industrialized Countries*. Philadelphia: Temple University Press, 1984.
This collection of essays examines one of the major issues of the contemporary labor environment, the changing composition of the work force, specifically the growing number of women workers. Deals with the variety of women's experiences with trade unions examining to what degree unions have come to recognize, influence, and integrate changes in women's status into their organizations.

Curtin, Philip D. *Death by Migration*. Cambridge, England: Cambridge University Press, 1989.
Curtin explains the success of European imperialism in the nineteenth century, and, by implication, its prior lack of success by focusing upon disease and epidemiology. In the early nineteenth century European troops in Africa had death rates approaching five hundred per thousand per year; by the turn of the century, rates were about six per thousand per year. The decline in death rates allowed European nations to

colonialize (colonies of conquest) Africa and Asia, areas which had previously been protected from European encroachment by their disease ecology. Gives an insight into the timing of the last great race for colonies.

Cyert, Richard M., and David C. Mowery, eds. *The Impact of Technological Change on Employment and Economic Growth.* Cambridge, Mass.: Ballinger, 1988.

A collection of papers by a panel of experts on technology and employment examining the effects of technological change on worker displacement, job creation and loss, the intersectoral flows of jobs and workers within the U.S. economy, skill requirements, and the distribution of incomes in the United States.

Danziger, Sheldon H., and Daniel H. Weinberg, eds. *Fighting Poverty: What Works and What Doesn't.* Cambridge, Mass.: Harvard University Press, 1986.

A collection of papers that were presented at a conference, but most are easily accessible to the nonspecialist. Several of the papers address methods to increase the earnings of the working poor or those not working and offer some history and evaluation of federal efforts.

Dilts, David A., and William J. Walsh. *Collective Bargaining and Impasse Resolution in the Public Sector.* New York: Quorum Books, 1988.

An excellent survey of the principles and practices of public-sector bargaining. Covers the processes of mediation, fact-finding, interest arbitration, and impasse resolution.

Dunlop, John T. *Dispute Resolution: Negotiation and Consensus Building.* Dover, Mass.: Auburn House, 1984.

Dunlop is a former U.S. secretary of labor, a founding father of industrial relations research. The volume covers all aspects of conflict resolution and importance of developing a social contract.

Easterlin, Richard A. *Birth and Fortune: The Impact of Numbers on Personal Welfare.* 2d ed. Chicago: University of Chicago Press, 1987.

A leading economic historian explores the way in which each individual is affected by the number of people who were born at the same time. Brief and written for the nonexpert audience. Predicted incorrectly that U.S. fertility rates would return to previous highs by 1995.

Eatwell, John. *What Happened to Britain?* Oxford: Oxford University Press, 1984.

A critical look at Margaret Thatcher's economic policy and the consequences for the Labour Party. Written by the chief organizer of *The New Palgrave*, who was an adviser to the Labour Party.

Edwards, Richard, Paolo Garonna, and Franz Toedtling. *Unions in Crisis and Beyond: Perspectives from Six Countries.* Dover, Mass.: Auburn House, 1986.
A collection of articles on the impact of changes in the world economy on unions in the United States and Western Europe. Concise, readable essays show how differences in union structure and strategy have led to varying degrees of success in coping with a less favorable climate.

Ehrenberg, Ronald G., and Robert S. Smith. "The Economics of Discrimination." In *Modern Labor Economics.* Glenview, Ill.: Scott, Foresman, 1988.
This chapter from an excellent labor economics text provides an overview of the subject of discrimination. The chapter provides data on earnings and incomes of minority groups, as well as a review of the various discrimination models.

Ehrlich, Paul R. *The Population Bomb.* 1968. Rev. ed. New York: Ballantine, 1971.
An extraordinarily influential modern presentation of the Malthusian theory that population growth is outpacing the world's ability to feed itself and rapidly diminishing the world's natural resources.

Elkouri, Frank, and Edna Aspen Elkouri. *How Arbitration Works.* 4th ed. Washington, D.C.: Bureau of National Affairs, 1985.
The universal standard for the practice of grievance arbitration. The handbook reference source for students, practicing arbitrators, and adversaries.

England, Paula, and George Farkas. *Households, Employment, and Gender: A Social, Economic, and Demographic View.* New York: Aldine, 1986.
This book, written by sociologists, is an attempt to blend the sociological and economic perspectives on gender issues, along with a large dose of demography. Reasonably successful in combining the best of the different disciplines, but does not sound particularly innovative or controversial. Written for the general reader.

Farley, Reynolds, and Walter R. Allen. *The Color Line and the Quality of Life in America.* New York: Russell Sage Foundation, 1987.

This 493-page book contains an extensive bibliography and useful historical data and statistics, mostly from the 1980 census, shown in understandable, readable form. Mostly about African Americans, but one chapter compares books about immigrants. Suitable for a general audience.

Fisher, Roger, and William Ury. *Getting to Yes: Negotiating Agreement Without Giving In.* New York: Penguin Books, 1981.
Designed for those that have no background in bargaining, this handbook for negotiating personal and professional disputes is very accessible and was a national best-seller.

Fleisher, Belton M., and Thomas J. Kniesner. *Labor Economics: Theory, Evidence, and Policy.* 3d ed. Englewood Cliffs: N.J.: Prentice-Hall, 1984.
An intermediate-level labor economics text that has one chapter on the analysis of monopsony; both theory and some empirical considerations are covered. Intermediate-level demand and supply economics would be helpful if not required in parts.

Flynn, Patricia M. *Facilitating Technological Change: The Human Resource Challenge.* Cambridge, Mass.: Ballinger, 1988.
On the basis of some two hundred microenterprise-level case studies detailed in an annotated bibliography, the book surveys how employers adjust to technical change. It develops the concept of skills-training life cycle—the human resource equivalent of the traditional product and technology life cycle—over the course of development of a technology.

Foner, Philip S. *The History of the Labor Movement in the United States.* 8 vols. New York: International Publishers, 1947-1989.
Foner is extremely proficient in detail and analysis. This multivolume set is very interesting reading for those who want to learn about history from the perspective of the working class.

Freeman, Richard B., and Harry J. Holzer. "Young Blacks and Jobs: What We Now Know." *The Public Interest* 78 (Winter, 1985): 18-31.
This accessible piece focuses on the youth group that suffers the most from youth unemployment—young blacks. The authors provide an analysis of the causes and consequences of the black youth labor market problem. This largely interdisciplinary discussion relates the employment problems of black youths to crime and other inner-city problems. Simple tables are used to present information.

Freeman, Richard B., and James L. Medoff. *What Do Unions Do?* New York: Basic Books, 1984.
This widely recognized and influential assessment of the role of unions in the United States interprets a major empirical research undertaking for the general reader. The study found that negative economic impacts of unions were outweighed by positive economic and social impacts.

_____. "The Youth Labor Market Problem in the United States: An Overview." In *The Youth Labor Market Problem: Its Nature, Causes, and Consequences*, edited by Richard B. Freeman and David A. Wise. Chicago: University of Chicago Press, 1982.
In a more technical work, Freeman and Medoff provide a most thorough analysis of the youth labor market problem. Although the article relies little on mathematics, the authors' discussion employs economic analysis that may be difficult for the uninitiated reader to follow. While references are provided, they may not be of great interest to those readers who are only interested in an overview of the subject matter.

Fuchs, Victor R. *Women's Quest for Economic Equality.* Cambridge, Mass.: Harvard University Press, 1988.
A highly readable 171-page presentation of relevant statistics and discussion of trends in the United States from 1960 to 1988. Fuchs stresses how the task of child rearing shapes womens' lives. For the general reader.

Galbraith, John Kenneth. *The Affluent Society.* Boston: Houghton Mifflin, 1958.
Written for nonspecialists, this provocative study sketches the chief characteristics of post-1950 wealthy America, including the character of the new leisure class. Galbraith is really exploring the early consequences of the applications of Keynesian economic programs in the United States. Contains few notes and a very helpful index.

Galenson, Walter. *A Primer on Employment and Wages.* New York: Vintage Books, 1966.
In clear, understandable language, this book explains the basic principles and practices of labor economics and labor market operations. The statistics are out of date, but that is easily remedied through use of current periodicals.

German, Julius G. *Labor Relations Law, Practice, and Policy.* Mineola, N.Y.: Foundation Press, 1978.

A classic summary of history, law, and court decisions to show the evolution and practice of contemporary government regulation of labor relations.

Gilpatrick, Eleanor C. *Structural Unemployment and Aggregate Demand.* Baltimore: The Johns Hopkins University Press, 1966.

Considers whether structural unemployment or lack of sufficient aggregate demand were primarily responsible for the persistently high unemployment rates in the United States from 1948-66. Gilpatrick demonstrates that both reasons for unemployment were important. The main strength of this book, from a contemporary perspective, is the method of analysis that is used to determine the causes of joblessness.

Greenwood, Michael J. *Migration and Economic Growth in the United States.* New York: Academic Press, 1981.

A comprehensive study of migration within the United States. Greenwood provides a thorough descriptive study of post-World War II migration behavior. Empirical analysis of models of migration and metropolitan growth are also included. This book is appropriate for college students.

Harrison, Bennett, and Barry Bluestone. *The Great U-Turn: Corporate Restructuring and the Polarizing of America.* New York: Basic Books, 1988.

By the authors of the most important book on deindustrialization, this text features a continuation of their outstanding research. Focuses more on the corporate sector and corporate restructuring and its implications for workers with jobs. The documentation of the declining wages in America during the 1970's and 1980's is outstanding.

Holley, William H., Jr., and Kenneth M. Jennings. *The Labor Relations Process.* 2d ed. Chicago: Dryden Press, 1984.

A very thorough text on the process of negotiating, administering, and applying a labor contract. The authors begin with the rights and responsibilities of both parties and continue with a discussion of the negotiation and administration of a contract. They discuss the possible outcomes of the bargaining process and how the contract influences different work environments. For the more ambitious reader.

Horowitz, Irving Louis, ed. *Power, Politics, and People.* New York: Oxford University Press, 1967.

A well-chosen collection of essays by sociologist C. Wright Mills, a critic of post-World War II America, which, despite original features, continues Thorstein Veblen's iconoclastic tradition. Excellent and informative concerning the old and new leisure classes. Contains notes, a full listing of Mills's provocative writings, and a good index.

Howland, Marie. *Plant Closings and Worker Displacement: The Regional Issues*. Kalamazoo, Mich.: W. E. Upjohn Institute, 1988.

Makes use of some of the best data available for the study of deindustrialization: the Dun's Market Identifiers file and the Current Population Survey supplement on displaced workers. Using these rich data sources, Howland explores the firm issues of plant closings, job dissolution, and regional profitability and the labor issue of the reemployment success of displaced workers.

Hughes, James J., and Richard Perlman. *The Economics of Unemployment*. New York: Cambridge University Press, 1984.

This study develops a comprehensive analysis of unemployment in the United States and Great Britain. The authors observe substantial differences in the measurement, explanation, and treatment of unemployment in the two countries. Presents a good synthesis of the literature on the economics of joblessness.

Jaynes, Gerald David, and Robin M. Williams, Jr., eds. *A Common Destiny: Blacks and American Society*. Washington, D.C.: National Academy Press, 1989.

A comprehensive report on the socioeconomic status of black Americans in the United States and changes since 1940. This 608-page book contains an extensive bibliography for each subject at the end of the corresponding chapter. Suitable for a general audience.

Jones, Derek C., and Jan Svejnar, eds. *Advances in the Economic Analysis of Participatory and Labor-Managed Firms*. 4 vols. Greenwich, Conn.: JAI Press, 1985-1990.

These volumes collect research papers on theory and evidence about labor participation in management, codetermination, and (especially in volume 3) profit sharing. Most require a good background in economic theory, statistics, or both.

_____. *Participatory and Self-Managed Firms: Evaluating Economic Performance*. Lexington, Mass.: D. C. Heath, 1982.

This volume is a collection of research papers on labor participation in management and on codetermination. Many of the papers contain evidence on the economic effectiveness of participatory enterprises, but most require a good background in economic theory, statistics, or both.

Keynes, John Maynard. *The General Theory of Employment, Interest, and Money.* New York: Harcourt, Brace, 1936.
This treatise effectively demolishes the classical theory of employment and income determination. Keynes demonstrates that cyclical unemployment may persist for some time in the absence of government programs to stimulate the economy.

Kleiner, Morris M., Robert A. McLean, and George F. Dreher. *Labor Markets and Resource Management.* Glenville, Ill.: Scott, Foresman, 1988.
This book, particularly chapters 2, 3, 14, and 15, provides a general overview of labor markets. Chapter 2 explains labor demand, labor supply, and wage rate determination from a theoretical standpoint and provides a rigorous treatment of the relationship between productivity and wages. Chapter 3 shows how wages are affected by human capital. Chapters 14 and 15 describe (if somewhat tediously) how human capital acquisition works in practice.

Kochan, Thomas A., and Harry C. Katz. *Collective Bargaining and Industrial Relations.* Homewood, Ill.: Richard D. Irwin, 1988.
A very thorough text on the nature of bargaining, the determination of bargaining structures, and the process of bargaining. Also includes some insights on objectives and strategies for bargaining.

Kochan, Thomas A., Harry C. Katz, and Robert B. McKersie. *The Transformation of American Industrial Relations.* New York: Basic Books, 1986.
The authors trace the development of the U.S. economy during the decade of 1975 to 1985. They explain the emergence of new industries and the demise of the basic infrastructure of the U.S. economy, examine these influences upon American workers, and explore some options for the future.

Kritz, Mary M., Charles B. Keely, and Silvano M. Tomasi, eds. *Global Trends in Migration.* New York: Center for Migration Studies, 1983.

A collection of research papers. Papers from the first section are written from economic, political, and social perspectives. Section 2 explores migration trends in different geographical regions of the world. Special issues concerning immigration assimilation are discussed in the last section. Appropriate for general readers as well as college students.

Krugman, Paul. *The Age of Diminished Expectations: U.S. Economic Policy in the 1990s.* Rev. ed. Cambridge, Mass.: MIT Press, 1994.
In the foreword, Paul Samuelson describes the book as a tour de force and Krugman as "the rising star of this century and the next." Krugman sees the U.S. economy as performing below expectations. He explains why more is not being done about the disappointing U.S. economy and concludes that necessary measures would be painful. The book ends with a discussion of prospects; he sees continued drift as the most likely outcome.

Larson, Simeon, and Bruce Nissen, eds. *Theories of the Labor Movement.* Detroit: Wayne State University Press, 1987.
An anthology of classic and contemporary writings on labor movement theory, designed for an undergraduate audience. Attempts to categorize labor theories on the basis of the overall social role each theory assigns to the labor movement. This approach provides a comparison of divergent views of the origins, development, and future of the labor movement.

Levin, Martin A., and Barbara Ferman. *The Political Hand: Policy Implementation and Youth Employment Programs.* New York: Pergamon Press, 1985.
Details how various forms of political pressure shaped the youth employment and training programs that emerged in the mid-1980's. Different perspectives are illustrated through a series of case studies.

Levitan, Sar, and Richard Belous. *More than Subsistence: Minimum Wages for the Working Poor.* Baltimore: The Johns Hopkins University Press, 1979.
A very readable, nontechnical survey of economic research on the minimum wage. Tends to be rather critical of the methodology and conclusions of the majority of such research.

Levitan, Sar A., Garth L. Mangum, and Ray Marshall. *Human Resources and Labor Markets.* 2d ed. New York: Harper & Row, 1976.

This comprehensive 631-page volume on manpower issues contains a sizable section on minority income and employment. The section begins with a clear description of the main economic theories of racial discrimination. Subsequent chapters cover black employment and income, Americans of Spanish origin, and Native Americans. Suitable for a general audience.

Lewis, G. J. *Human Migration*. New York: St. Martin's Press, 1982.
Lewis provides a thorough examination of internal migration in European nations as well as in the United States. Conceptual issues concerning migration and how they relate to the individual's decision to migrate are also investigated. Both spatial and temporal dimensions of migration are addressed. Suitable for undergraduate students.

Lloyd, Cynthia B., and Beth T. Niemi. *The Economics of Sex Differentials*. New York: Columbia University Press, 1979.
One chapter explains the theory of women's labor supply. Provides extensive coverage from 1947 to 1978, particularly of women's labor force participation, showing how these rates differ between men and women, white and nonwhite women, and people of different ages. Contains data on women's full-time and part-time employment and hours. Contains 355 pages, an index, a bibliography, tables, and figures.

Long, Larry. *Migration and Residential Mobility in the United States*. New York: Russell Sage Foundation, 1988.
Long provides a well-written descriptive analysis of trends in migration for the United States since 1940. Extensive use is made of U.S. census data. Emphasis is placed on different forms and patterns of geographic mobility. An extensive bibliography is provided. Written for those interested in quantitative studies of internal migration.

Malinvaud, Edmond. *The Theory of Unemployment Reconsidered*. 2d ed. Cambridge, Mass.: Basil Blackwell, 1985.
A short, nondoctrinaire treatment of macroeconomic policy in an economy which does not behave according to Say's Law in a strong sense and, hence, may be amendable to government demand policy action.

Marshall, Ray. "The Economics of Racial Discrimination: A Survey." *Journal of Economic Literature* 12 (September, 1974): 849-871.

This is the standard reference for economists for theoretical and empirical work on race discrimination. This lengthy survey article covers and analyzes the large body of work undertaken in the United States in the 1960's and early 1970's. Suitable for college students.

Menard, Scott W., and Elizabeth Moen. *Perspective on Population: An Introduction to Concepts and Issues*. New York: Oxford University Press, 1987.
A book of forty-seven readings designed for university students. The authors have classified them by their level of difficulty (about half are elementary). Excellently selected, and many items have bibliographies.

Miller, G. Tyler. *Living in the Environment*. 6th ed. Belmont, Calif.: Wadsworth, 1990.
In this university textbook, which is designed for an introductory course, chapters 7 and 8 are directly concerned with population. By implication, however, the entire book deals with the subject. Miller is strongly against population growth. Profusely illustrated and contains a good bibliography.

Montgomery, David. *Workers Control in America*. Cambridge, England: Cambridge University Press, 1979.
Analyzes the phenomenon of workers' struggle for control over their workplace from the Civil War through the New Deal. Discusses the relevance of this issue for contemporary unionism as the New Deal formula for resolving this central issue of labor-management relations appears to be breaking down.

Nadler, Leonard. *Developing Human Resources*. Houston: Gulf Publishing, 1970.
A nontechnical book that provides numerous examples of forms of on-the-job training and how it leads to greater productivity. A practical complement to Becker's theoretical concepts. 262 pages.

Nickerson, Jane Soames. *Homage to Malthus*. Port Washington, N.Y.: Kennikat Press, 1975.
In less than 150 pages, this readable study tells the important things about Thomas Malthus' life and work. For the general reader.

O'Kelly, Charlotte, and Larry S. Carney. *Women and Men in Society: Cross-Cultural Perspectives on Gender Stratification*. 2d ed. Belmont, Calif.: Wadsworth, 1986.

A very useful textbook discussing gender roles in a wide variety of modern and premodern societies. Provides a valuable worldview of sex segregation patterns and gives a picture of how anthropologists and sociologists approach the puzzle of sex segregation. For beginning undergraduates.

Okun, Arthur M. *Prices and Markets.* Washington, D.C.: Brookings Institution, 1981.

This study of the macroeconomic consequences of labor contracts influenced much subsequent research on profit sharing. Some knowledge of economic theory is required.

Oswald, Ruby. "Statement on U.S. Aims at the World Trade Ministers' Meeting: A Labor View." Reprinted in *The Contemporary International Economy: A Reader*, edited by John Adams. 2d ed. New York: St. Martin's Press, 1985.

This section consists of the introductory argument that trade liberalization costs jobs. Suitable for the general reader.

Paul, Ellen Frankel. *Equity and Gender: The Comparable Worth Debate.* New Brunswick, N.J.: Transaction, 1989.

This 143-page monograph is clear, concise introduction to the issue of comparable worth. Paul lays out the issues and explains why she is against the implementation of comparable-worth policies. Also provides a history of comparable-worth legislation up to 1989. For the general reader.

Pejovich, Svetozar, ed. *The Codetermination Movement in the West.* Lexington, Mass.: Lexington Books, 1978.

This volume collects research papers on codetermination. Most are quite critical of codetermination and pessimistic about its impact on economic performance, particularly on labor productivity; most are theoretical or historical rather than statistical in approach. Requires knowledge of economic theory.

Perlman, Richard. *The Economics of Education: Conceptual Problems and Policy Issues.* New York: McGraw-Hill, 1973.

Provides a thorough, nontechnical discussion of the costs and benefits (attributable, in part, to the effect of education on productivity and therefore on wages) of education, at the primary, secondary, and college levels. Also discusses how economic theory can be applied to show whether any particular course of study is worthwhile from an economic point of view.

Perry, Charles R., Bernard E. Anderson, Richard L. Rowan, and Herbert R. Northrop. *The Impact of Government Manpower Programs*. Philadelphia: University of Pennsylvania Press, 1975.
A thorough, detailed analysis of the manpower programs that were put into effect during the 1960's. Summarizes the main provisions of each manpower policy, surveys research on its impact, and provides an overall assessment of each program. This book will appeal most to those who enjoy facts and figures.

Peterson, Wallace C. *Income, Employment, and Economic Growth*. 4th ed. New York: W. W. Norton, 1978.
This volume presents an excellent discussion and comparison of the classical and Keynesian theories of employment. The discussion is basically nontechnical, with little use of mathematics. Well written.

Piore, Michael J., and Charles F. Sabel. *The Second Divide*. New York: Basic Books, 1984.
Claims that deterioration in economic performance (low productivity growth) results from limitations of the first "industrial divide," which was based on mass production. Relaunching growth requires a return to craft methods of production, enhanced by modern flexible equipment. Argues that "flexible specialization" means smaller, community-based firms whose success is based more on cooperation than on competition. Nontechnical.

Prasow, Paul, and Edward Peters. *Arbitration and Collective Bargaining: Conflict Resolution in Labor Relations*. New York: McGraw-Hill, 1970.
A practical discussion of the process of grievance arbitration. A balanced mix of analysis, philosophy, and pragmatism.

Pravda, Alex, and Blair A. Ruble, eds. *Trade Unions in Communist States*. Boston: Allen & Unwin, 1986.
An examination of trade unionism in communist states and the role unions play in the industrial relations and politics of their countries. The book sees these unions as having a dual role of protecting the interests of their members and promoting the productive needs of their societies. This dualism is compared with roles played by unions in Western industrialized countries.

Ragan, James F., Jr. "The Effect of a Legal Minimum Wage on the Pay and Employment of Teenage Students and Nonstudents." In *The Economics of Legal Minimum Wages*, edited by Simon Rottenberg. Washington, D.C.: American Enterprise Institute for Public Policy Research, 1981.
Ragan's work relies more heavily on mathematical and statistical tools for his explanation. It is accessible, however, to those readers who are versed in economic principles. Furthermore, this article is more narrowly focused, as it concentrates on teenagers. A complete bibliography is provided.

Rees, Albert. *The Economics of Work and Pay*. 2d ed. New York: Harper & Row, 1979.
A good text on labor economics that limits the use of technical analysis. There are a few places where a reader with no prior experience in economics might have trouble, but most of the material is readily understandable.

Reskin, Barbara F., ed. *Sex Segregation in the Work Place*. Washington, D.C.: National Academy Press, 1984.
A collection of articles on occupational segregation by many of the top economists working in the area. It focuses on three major themes: the extent and trends in occupational segregation theories of occupational segregation, and policies aimed at reducing sex segregation.

Rodgers, Harrell R., Jr. *Poor Women, Poor Families*. Armonk, N.Y.: M. E. Sharpe, 1986.
This book documents the rising number of female-headed families among the poor, and then discusses some consequences and possible cures. A flaw in this book is its failure to look into the causes of the rising incidence of female-headed families among the poor.

Rothbard, Murray N. *Man, Economy, and State*. 2 vols. New York: D. Van Nostrand, 1962.
A systematic presentation of economic principals. Rothbard offers a detailed defense of the marginalist approach against Keynesian objections. He claims that a depression need not be characterized by unemployment, as long as workers are willing to offer their services for reduced wages.

Rothschild, Donald P., Leroy S. Merrifield, and Harry T. Edwards. *Collective Bargaining and Labor Arbitration*. 2d ed. Indianapolis: Bobbs-Merrill, 1979.

This standard text for labor law emphasizes the arbitration process in labor relations. Also includes legal development of discrimination in collective bargaining.

Rothstein, Lawrence E. *Plant Closings: Power, Politics, and Workers.* Dover, Mass.: Auburn House, 1986.
Rothstein's research complements the work of Bennett Harrison, Barry Bluestone, and Marie Howland by concentrating on case studies of plant closings. Focusing on Youngstown, Ohio, and Longwy, Lorraine, Rothstein examines the role of legislation and local politics on plant closings.

Schor, Juliet. *The Overworked American.* New York: Basic Books, 1991.
Between 1969 and 1987, time on the job for the average American increased by 163 hours per year. Schor attributes this to the lower cost of management as a result of longer hours. Workers are also eager to improve or maintain their living standards. The consumerist treadmill and long-hour jobs have combined to form a cycle of "work and spend."

Shaikh, Anwar. "The Transformation from Marx to Sraffa." In *Ricardo, Marx, Sraffa*, edited by Ernest Mandel and Alan Freeman. London: Verso, 1984.
The centrality of labor in Marx's theory of value is established. The connection between value and money rates of profit is discussed, as is the determination of movements in relative prices by relative labor times. Empirical data are provided that support the validity of the labor theory of value as a price theory.

Simon, Julian L. *The Economics of Population Growth.* Princeton, N.J.: Princeton University Press, 1977.
A comprehensive scholarly analysis of all aspects of the economics of population. Simon is skeptical of much of the modern argument against population growth; an appendix presents "Common Objections to the Book's Conclusions and Some Simplified Rebuttals." The bibliography is thirty-six pages long. For the advanced reader.

Sowell, Thomas, ed. *Essays and Data on American Ethnic Groups.* Washington, D.C.: Urban Institute, 1978.
A series of articles that are intended for the general public and that compare the progress of different ethnic groups that have faced discrimination in the United States. Provides many interesting compari-

sons. See also, *Ethnic America: A History* (New York: Basic Books, 1981) by Sowell.

_____. *Markets and Minorities*. New York: Basic Books, 1981.
This 141-page book is intended for undergraduates familiar with elementary economics concepts. The discussion covers the experience of racial and ethnic minorities in America in various economic settings, including jobs, housing, treatment by government, and slavery. The overall focus is analytical, but interesting historical facts are found throughout the book.

Steinmann, Gunter. "Population, Resources, and Limits to Growth." In *Development Economics: Theory, Practice, and Prospects*, edited by Thomas R. DeGregori. Boston: Kluwer Academic Publishers, 1989.
Detailed scholarly analysis of natural resources and their relationship to population.

Sturmthal, Adolf, and James G. Scovine, eds. *The International Labor Movement in Transition*. Urbana: University of Illinois Press, 1973.
This collection of essays covers the evolution of labor movements in the United States, Europe, Japan, Africa, and South America. Highly readable essays focus on the relative importance of collective bargaining and political action in unions throughout the world.

Summers, Lawrence H. *Understanding Unemployment*. Cambridge, Mass.: MIT Press, 1990.
Provides empirical and novel evidence on the causes and consequences of unemployment, what new theories are needed to accommodate the facts, and how economic policy can remedy the situation.

Tregarthen, Timothy. "Critical Condition: Supply of Nurses Wearing Thin." *The Margin* 2 (October, 1987): 12-13.
This article in a popular British magazine examines the demand and supply forces that created the nursing shortage in the 1970's and 1980's. Suitable for a general audience.

United States. Minimum Wage Study Commission. *Report of the Minimum Wage Study Commission*. Washington, D.C.: Government Printing Office, 1981.
Includes discussions of the background and legislative history of the Fair Labor Standards Act, as well as evaluations of studies of the effects of changes in the minimum wage and public policy proposals, including the subminimum wage.

United States. President. *Employment and Training Report of the President*. Washington, D.C.: Government Printing Office, 1932-
The best source for data on employment and unemployment. Employment and wages by industry are reported, as well as employment and unemployment figures for various demographic groups. It should be remembered that official measures of unemployment do not correspond with ideal, theoretical measures.

U.S. Bureau of Economic Analysis. *Survey of Current Business*. Washington, D.C.: Government Printing Office, 1920-
This monthly periodical contains data on unemployment, unemployment rates, and many other economic indicators.

Vanek, Jaroslav. *The General Theory of Labor-Managed Market Economies*. Ithaca, N.Y.: Cornell University Press, 1970.
This large book set out a theory of labor-managed enterprises in the tradition of neoclassical economics, on which much subsequent research on labor-managed enterprises, codetermination, and profit sharing has drawn.

Veblen, Thorstein. *The Theory of the Leisure Class: An Economic Study of Institutions*. 1899. Reprint. New York: Macmillan, 1953.
A learned but thinly disguised assault on America's old leisure class that is carried off brilliantly. Required reading, but not easy. One either fully absorbs or rejects Veblen, but no one can dismiss his original insights. No notes, bibliography, or index, but the substance is both prolix and rich.

Wachtel, Howard. *Labor and the Economy*. 2d ed. San Diego: Harcourt Brace Jovanovich, 1988.
The treatment of wage legislation in chapter 23 is typical of what will be found in most textbooks in labor economics. Wachtel provides balanced discussions of both the theoretical and public policy issues.

Weeks, John R. *Population: An Introduction to Concepts and Issues*. Belmont, Calif.: Wadsworth, 1989.
A competent college-level textbook.

Weiner, Stuart E. "Enterprise Zones as a Means of Reducing Structural Unemployment." *Economic Review* 6 (March, 1984): 3-16.
This excellent short article provides a history of enterprise zones, an explanation of how they are supposed to reduce structural unemployment, and an assessment of this policy tool.

Welch, Finis. *Minimum Wages: Issues and Evidence.* Washington, D.C.: American Enterprise Institute, 1978.
This study presents a more favorable review of research dealing with the impacts of minimum wage legislation.

Wolfbein, Seymour L. *Employment, Unemployment, and Public Policy.* New York: Random House, 1965.
Describes in simple, easy-to-understand terms how unemployment is calculated, gives concrete examples of the different types of unemployment, and discusses how expansionary macroeconomic policies and manpower policies can remedy the problems of cyclical and structural unemployment. Unfortunately, the book is somewhat out of date. Nevertheless, it is the best simple and general introduction to unemployment and unemployment policy that is available.

Yates, Michael. *Labor Law Handbook.* Boston: South End Press, 1987.
A splendid reference for those who wish to understand the context of bargaining and the rules of the game. Eliminates the ambiguity of legal language, allowing the reader to understand the intent of the law.

Zack, Arnold M. *Grievance Arbitration.* Lexington, Mass.: Lexington Books, 1989.
A handbook for advocates to prepare and present arbitration cases. Uses case study to demonstrate the essential elements necessary in the appropriate decision-making process in grievance arbitration.

Welfare Economics

Aaron, Henry J., and William B. Schwartz. *The Painful Prescription.* Washington, D.C.: Brookings Institution, 1984.
Compares the functioning and results of the U.S. private market health care system with the British National Health Service, highlighting advantages and problems with both. Emphasis is on the problems of cost containment and access in health care.

Achenbaum, W. Andrew. *Social Security: Visions and Revisions.* New York: Cambridge University Press, 1986.
This three hundred-page book was written by a noted historian, with the goal of using lessons from the past and insights from the present to help public policymakers understand how Social Security has evolved

and what might be done to maintain its future viability. A superb book, it includes several bibliographic essays and maintains a calm neutrality.

Asch, Peter, and R. S. Seneca. *Government and the Marketplace*. Orlando, Fla.: Dryden Press, 1989.
Describes policies that have actually been implemented and comments on the effectiveness of these policies. In chapter 22, for example, the authors explain the theoretical underpinnings of the various antipollution policies that have been developed by economists.

Atkinson, A. B. *Social Justice and Public Policy*. Cambridge, Mass.: MIT Press, 1983.
This collection of essays includes Atkinson's classic article "On the Measurement of Inequality" (1970), along with an extended bibliography for 1970-1982, which includes a section on the Lorenz curve. Suitable for advanced undergraduates.

_____, ed. *Wealth, Income, and Inequality*. 2d ed. London: Oxford University Press, 1980.
This reader contains the classic articles in the area of economics of inequality. A section on the distribution of income contains several clear examples of Lorenz curves for Great Britain, The Netherlands, and West Germany, demonstrating curve comparisons across countries and time. Suitable for advanced undergraduates.

Auletta, Ken. *The Underclass*. New York: Random House, 1982.
Case studies of the ghetto poor by a New York City journalist. This book is very good when it describes why some people are poor and how difficult it is for them to escape poverty. The book is less satisfactory when it generalizes about the poor and about welfare policy from case studies.

Barth, Michael, George J. Carcagno, and John L. Palmer. *Toward an Effective Income Support System: Problems, Prospects, and Choices*. Madison: University of Wisconsin Institute for Research on Poverty, 1974.
Provides a systematic study of various income redistribution programs. The beginning essay by Irwin Garfinkel provides an excellent overview.

Berle, Adolf A. *The Twentieth Century Capitalist Revolution*. New York: Harcourt, Brace & World, 1954.

A classic in the field. The beginning point for studying the origins of the modern welfare state.

Bradley, Michael E. *Microeconomics*. 2d ed. Glenview, Ill.: Scott, Foresman, 1985.
Chapter 12 of this introductory text is one of the few treatments of welfare economics at the elementary level. There is some technical economic analysis, but all required analysis is introduced earlier in the text.

Buchanan, James, et al. *The Economics of Politics*. London: Institute of Economic Affairs, 1978.
Includes a superb nontechnical overview of public choice economics by Nobel laureate Buchanan, as well as a bibliography. Papers by other contributors explore market failure, the political business cycle, bureaucracy, and related topics.

Buchanan, James, and Gordon Tullock. *The Calculus of Consent*. Ann Arbor: University of Michigan, 1965.
A classic analysis by two founders of public choice analysis. Despite some technical material, much is written clearly for nonspecialists.

Burtless, Gary, ed. *Work, Health, and Income Among the Elderly*. Studies in Social Economics. Washington, D.C.: Brookings Institution, 1987
Deals with the effects of longer life spans on older people. Postulates that if people live much longer, then they should work longer, if they are able to. Examines issues of the work capacity of older people and whether some are forced to retire because of poor health. Suitable for undergraduates and graduate students.

Champagne, Anthony, and Edward J. Harpham, eds. *The Attack on the Welfare State*. Prospect Heights, Ill.: Waveland Press, 1984.
Ten separate articles are included in this anthology. Each article analyzes a different set of federal programs from a conservative perspective. Suitable for a general readership.

Cooper, Charles. *Economic Evaluation and the Environment*. Kent, England: Hodder & Stoughton, 1981.
Cooper looks at the economic approach to the evaluation of environmental damage. He also explains why it is difficult to measure the cost of this damage. Finally, he describes policies that will minimize damage, despite the problems of cost measurement.

Cooter, Robert, and Peter Rappoport. "Were the Ordinalists Wrong About Welfare Economics?" *Journal of Economic Literature* 22 (June, 1984): 507-530.

A literature review and synthesis that attempts to resuscitate a welfare function based on "material well-being" rather than individual utility functions.

Council on Environmental Quality. *Environmental Quality, Annual Report of the Council on Environmental Quality.* Washington, D.C.: Government Printing Office, 1979.

A report to the president containing statistics and a survey of air, water, toxic waste, noise, and other environmental policy issues likely to arise during the year.

Crandall, Robert. *Controlling Industrial Pollution.* Washington, D.C.: Brookings Institution, 1983.

Crandall describes U.S. antipollution policies as of 1983 and then comments on the effectiveness of each of these policies. He explains why some antipollution policies can seriously limit economic growth and describes policies that limit pollution while having a minimal impact on economic growth.

Crocker, Thomas, and A. J. Rogers. *Environmental Economics.* Hinsdale, Ill.: Dryden Press, 1971.

Crocker and Rogers describe the way in which the lack of well-defined property rights and the existence of the "free-rider problem" will lead to environmental disruption. They examine a number of solutions to the problem, including the pollution tax, direct controls, and the specification of low-pollution technology.

Dahl, Robert A., and Charles E. Lindblom. *Politics, Economics, and Welfare.* New York: Harper, 1953.

A political scientist and an economist collaborated on this comprehensive analysis which stresses such issues as control, organization behavior, and bargaining. Relatively advanced.

Danziger, Sheldon H., and Kent E. Portney, eds. *The Distributional Impacts of Public Policies.* New York: St. Martin's Press, 1988.

A very readable collection of papers that examine how government programs in the United States favor various income classes, geographic areas, interest groups, races, and genders.

Danziger, Sheldon H., and Daniel H. Weinberg, eds. *Fighting Poverty: What Works and What Doesn't.* Cambridge, Mass.: Harvard University Press, 1986.

Essays by both economists and noneconomists from a conference sponsored by the Department of Health and Human Services. The essays examine the causes of poverty and its potential cures. While the essays vary in quality and while some are rather technical, this book contains the thinking of many of the best social scientists who study poverty.

David, Otto A., and A. B. Whinston. "Welfare Economics and the Theory of Second Best." *Review of Economic Studies* 32 (January, 1965): 1-13.

A rather technical application of the theory of second best to some specific problems in economic welfare, and a discussion of some general rules implied by the special cases.

De Graaf, Janny. *Theoretical Welfare Economics.* Cambridge, England: Cambridge University Press, 1957.

A clear presentation of the fundamentals of welfare economics and ideal output theory. Somewhat dated.

Dobb, Maurice. *Welfare Economics and the Economics of Socialism.* Cambridge, England: Cambridge University Press, 1969.

A very good introduction and critique of welfare economics by one of the most prominent Western socialists. Part 1 is a very sound but dense introduction to the elements of welfare economics. The technical level of the material varies, but a sound background in intermediate microeconomics is strongly suggested.

Duncan, Greg. *Years of Poverty, Years of Plenty.* Ann Arbor: University of Michigan Press, 1984.

Looks at the movement into and out of the poverty population over time. Only indirectly addresses wage inequality, but provides a very useful perspective on the persistence of some types of income differences.

Easterlin, Richard A. "Does Economic Growth Improve the Human Lot? Some Empirical Evidence." In *Nations and Households in Economic Growth: Essays in Honor of Moses Abramovitz,* edited by Paul A. David and Melvin Reder. Stanford, Calif.: Stanford University Press, 1973.

A summary of how responses to various happiness surveys are related to the income levels of the respondents. The evidence presented in this selection has been widely cited as supporting the relative income hypothesis. Accessible to the noneconomist.

Ellwood, David T. *Poor Support: Poverty in the American Family*. New York: Basic Books, 1988. A readable, thoughtful account of poverty in the 1980's. Ellwood argues that poverty is no longer a single phenomenon with a single cause; rather, different types of families experience different sorts of poverty, and each sort of poverty requires a different solution.

Feiwel, George R., ed. *Arrow and the Foundations of the Theory of Economic Policy*. London: Macmillan, 1987.
An anthology that centers on modern welfare economic theory, including reformulations of Vilfredo Pareto's contributions.

Feldman, Allan M. "Welfare Economics." In *The New Palgrave: A Dictionary of Economics*, edited by John Eatwell, Murray Milgate, and Peter Newman. Vol. 4. London: Macmillan, 1987.
A very good brief survey of welfare economics and some areas of application. Parts are technically demanding, but the main arguments are understandable. Contains a useful brief bibliography.

Feldstein, Paul J. *Health Care Economics*. 3d ed. New York: John Wiley & Sons, 1988.
The standard text on the economics of health care, presenting in-depth analysis of the diverse medical markets and their interactions. Includes discussions of changes in the medical sector and in health policy. Clear exposition; helpful for readers to have some familiarity with economic concepts.

Flora, Peter, and Arnold J. Heidenheimer, eds. *The Development of Welfare States in Europe and America*. New Brunswick, N.J.: Transaction, 1981.
Offers an excellent analysis of its subject.

Foley, Duncan. "Resource Allocation and the Public Sector." *Yale Economic Essays* 7, no. 1 (1967): 45-98.
In this piece, Foley gave equity the technical meaning that has proliferated in the economics literature. The context of equity's appearance involved the financing of public goods.

Frech, H. E., III, ed. *Health Care in America: The Political Economy of Hospitals and Health Insurance*. San Francisco: Pacific Research Institute for Public Policy, 1988.

A collection of essays by noted authors in the fields of health economics and policy analysis. Essays are on a wide range of topics covering health care practices and alternative market-based approaches. Thorough and scholarly, but clear presentations.

Freeman, A. Myrick, III. *The Benefits of Environmental Improvement: Theory and Practice*. Baltimore: The Johns Hopkins University Press, 1979.

A fairly theoretical and technical survey of the many clever attempts to value environmental amenities. Covers contingent valuation, property value (hedonic) studies, the value of longevity, recreation benefits, and productivity benefits.

Fuchs, Victor R. *The Health Economy*. Cambridge, Mass.: Harvard University Press, 1986.

An analysis of health and medical care in a broad social, political, and economic context. Uses economics to clarify the basic questions of efficiency and equity in the provision of health care. Presents results of some empirical studies in a highly readable context.

Galbraith, John Kenneth. *Economics and the Public Purpose*. New York: New American Library, 1973.

Galbraith goes into some depth in his discussion of the theory of welfare economics. He deals with both the ideas of the distribution of wealth and income redistribution.

_____ . *The Nature of Mass Poverty*. Cambridge, Mass.: Harvard University Press, 1979.

This work examines poverty in the developing world. It explains how the mass poverty of less developed nations differs from the poverty experienced by developed nations, and provides some policy solutions. This book is accessible to all readers and is written with the style and wit that have made Galbraith famous. One minor gap in the book is that it addresses only rural poverty in the less developed world and thus ignores urban poverty.

_____ . *The New Industrial State*. Boston: Houghton Mifflin, 1967.

Galbraith is a noted economist and public servant whose very readable works have popularized important economic trends and issues. Here, Galbraith depicts the postindustrial environment in which the new leisure class emerged in the United States. Includes few notes and an excellent index.

Harrington, Michael. *The New American Poverty*. New York: Holt, Rinehart and Winston, 1984.

This work compares the poverty population in the early 1980's with the poverty population that existed in the early 1960's. While possessing neither the brilliance nor the impact of *The Other America*, this work provides a good description and analysis of the changing nature of poverty over a two-decade period.

_____. *The Other America*. New York: Macmillan, 1962.

This classic has been one of the most influential books of the twentieth century. More than anything else, this work inspired President Lyndon B. Johnson to declare his War on Poverty in 1964 and is responsible for much of the antipoverty legislation of the 1960's and early 1970's.

Haveman, Robert. "New Policy for the New Poverty." *Challenge* 31 (September/October, 1988): 27-36.

This nontechnical article reviews recent income redistribution efforts, outlines some important changes that have occurred in the nature of low-income families, and recommends some important changes in existing programs.

Heclo, Hugh, and Henik Madsen. *Politics and Policy in Sweden*. Philadelphia: Temple University Press, 1987.

An outstanding case study of the Western world's most highly developed welfare state.

Heidenheimer, Arnold J., Hugh Heclo, and Carolyn Teich Adams. *Comparative Public Policy: The Politics of Social Choice in America, Europe, and Japan*. New York: St. Martin's Press, 1990.

Although written for political science students, this book contains a wealth of detail concerning social welfare programs in the developed world. Also examines the economic and political trade-offs that are requires to establish and maintain the welfare state in the West.

Heilbrun, James. *Urban Economics and Public Policy*. 3d ed. New York: St. Martin's Press, 1987.

Provides an excellent survey of housing economics with an especially good discussion of housing policy issues, not just housing economics.

Hite, James, Hugh Macaulay, James Steppard, and Brian Yandle. *The Economics of Environmental Quality*. Washington, D.C.: American Enterprise Institute, 1972.

The authors demonstrate the way in which economic principles can be used in order to explain the existence of pollution. They also explain why the "free-rider problem" makes it difficult to measure the demand for environmental quality. Finally, they describe economic policies that will lead to pollution abatement.

Hurd, Michael D. "Research on the Elderly: Economic Status, Retirement, and Consumption and Saving." *Journal of Economic Literature* 28 (June, 1990): 565-637.

An excellent summary of economic research into the problems of aging by one of the major scholars in this field. The focus is on the important economic research, without a great deal of detail on specific programs. Suitable for college students.

Kamerman, Sheila B., and Alfred J. Kahn, eds. *Privatization and the Welfare State*. Princeton, N.J.: Princeton University Press, 1989.

The group if essays in part 1 discuss the meaning of the term "privatization" from a theoretical perspective and the main elements of a conceptual framework for the study of privatization. The essays in part 2 focus on empirical case studies assessing social welfare program impacts (a study of the relationship between privatization and efficiency, on one hand, and equity, on the other). A good primer for the college student who is interested in the subject.

Kneese, Allen V. *Measuring the Benefits of Clean Air and Water*. Washington, D.C.: Resources for the Future, 1984.

A survey of recent empirical studies that estimate the benefits of pollution control. Clear and nontechnical.

Lampman, Robert J. *Social Welfare Spending: Accounting for Changes from 1950 to 1978*. Orlando, Fla.: Academic Press, 1984.

An excellent book that traces the history of U.S. social welfare policy and discusses its success in a cost-benefit fashion. Introduces an accounting framework called secondary consumer income that is useful for analyzing the effect of government income redistribution schemes.

Lange, Oscar, and F. M. Taylor. *On the Economic Theory of Socialism*. Minneapolis: University of Minnesota Press, 1938.

Expresses Lange's long-lasting conviction that neoclassical economics, especially welfare economics, is best suited to serve as a foundation of a theory of a socialist economy. The chief purpose of his study was to disprove Von Mises' argument about the theoretical and practical infeasibility of economic calculus under socialism because of the absence of a genuine market (and a price) for capital. The Central Planning Board would be able to imitate the market, Lange argues. His postwar writing and experience in Poland produced a new look, including a restricted role of the Central Planning Board to areas where competition was weak.

Little, Jane Sneddon. "Medicaid." *New England Economic Review* 22 (March/April, 1991): 37.
A well-written analysis of the problems with the overall Medicaid program, including the large cost increases faced by state governments. The emphasis is on Massachusetts, but national data are also presented. Suitable for a general audience.

Mayo, Steven K. "Theory and Estimation in the Economics of Housing Demand." *Journal of Urban Economics* 10 (1981): 95-116.
A comprehensive survey of empirical studies of housing demand. Provides a summary of all the major studies and their estimates of the price and income elasticities of demand for housing.

Mencher, Samuel. *Poor Law to Poverty Program: Economic Security Policy in Britain and the United States*. Pittsburgh: University of Pittsburgh Press, 1967.
A historical look at social welfare which describes how major government programs were introduced in response to broad social and economic conditions.

Mincer, Jacob. *Schooling, Experience, and Earnings*. New York: National Bureau of Economic Research, 1974.
Together with Gary Becker's book, this 152-page study forms the basis of much work on the relation between education and earnings. It is fundamental and insightful reading, but the reader should be prepared to tackle more technical detail along the way.

Moon, Marilyn, ed. *Economic Transfers in the United States*. Chicago: University of Chicago Press, 1984.
An edited collection of papers at a relatively advanced level by economists that critically examine the measurement of transfer pay-

ments and their impact on the level and distribution of economic well-being.

Munnell, Alica H. "The Current Status of Our Social Welfare System." *New England Economic Review* 18 (July/August, 1987): 27-32.
Provides a description of the origins and evolution of the U.S. welfare system. Includes a comparison of various programs, as well as analysis of how political forces have shaped poverty programs. Suitable for high school and college students.

Murray, Charles. *Losing Ground: American Social Policy, 1950-1980.* New York: Basic Books, 1984.
A supply-side economist and sociologist looks at redistributive anti-poverty policies and argues that they make it profitable for the poor to have children and go on welfare. This book influenced President Ronald Reagan and was partly responsible for his attempts to reduce welfare spending. Although Murray overstates his case and his use of data is questionable throughout, the value of this book is its sensitivity to the potential negative effects of antipoverty policies.

Muth, Richard F. *Cities and Housing.* Chicago: University of Chicago Press, 1969.
The modern classic on housing and urban structure. Muth investigates the theory of housing and urban spatial form in the first part of the book. In the second part, he provides empirical tests of the models using data from Chicago.

Myers, Robert. *Social Security.* 3d ed. Homewood, Ill.: Richard D. Irwin, 1985.
Myers served as the chief actuary of the Social Security Administration for more than two decades and was executive director of the National Commission on Social Security Reform. The book provides a thorough factual description of social security programs in the United States. It is a valuable reference work with sixty-three detailed appendices.

Myrdal, Gunnar. *Beyond the Welfare State.* New Haven, Conn.: Yale University Press, 1960.
A critique of the welfare state that was written—significantly—during the period in which the welfare state was still expanding in the Western world.

North, Robert Carver. *The World That Could Be.* New York: W. W. Norton, 1976.

This excellent 149-page paperback identifies the danger of economic growth as an end rather than as a means. Noting Thomas More's assertion that the only true revolution is moral, argues that institutional reform is ineffective unless the new arrangement produces good men and good women who live Christian ethical values.

O'Connell, John F. *Welfare Economic Theory.* Boston: Auburn House, 1982.
A superb presentation of modern welfare economics, this book frames the place and importance of equity in the overall scheme. Very accessible; aimed at college students.

Olsen, Edgar O. "The Demand and Supply of Housing Service: A Critical Survey of the Empirical Literature." In *The Handbook of Regional and Urban Economics.* Vol. 2, edited by Edwin Mills. New York: Elsevier Science, 1987.
An excellent, critical review of the major empirical studies of both demand and supply elasticities.

Osberg, Lars. *Economic Inequality in the United States.* Armonk, N.Y.: M. E. Sharpe, 1984.
This 305-page book contains a useful discussion of the Lorenz curve and a comparison of various inequality measures. The book is nontechnical and is written to appeal to the general reader.

Pauly, Mark V. "Taxation, Health Insurance, and Market Failure in the Medical Economy." *Journal of Economic Literature* 24 (June, 1986): 629-676.
This article summarizes the literature on tax subsidies to health insurance and their effects on behavior in the medical care industry. Presents a good overview of trends in the economics of health care, with an extensive bibliography. Requires some understanding of basic economic concepts.

Pazner, Elisha A., and David Schmeidler. "A Difficulty in the Concept of Fairness." *Review of Economic Studies* 41 (1974): 441-443.
Proves that equitable allocations do not necessarily exist in the presence of production.

Phelps, Edmund S. "Recent Developments in Welfare Economics: Justice and Equity." In *Frontiers of Quantitative Economics*, edited by Michael Intriligator. Vol. 3B. New York: Elsevier, 1977.
A good survey of the work on distributive justice.

Phlips, Louis. *The Economics of Price Discrimination.* Cambridge, England: Cambridge University Press, 1983.

A comprehensive overview of the subject. The book explores the topic in the framework of a private economy with profit-maximizing firms bringing together all three strands of the discussion: the welfare theoretic, the regulatory, and the industrial organization contributions. Most materials are suitable for nonspecialists. Others require a knowledge of algebra and geometry.

Pigou, A. C. *The Economics of Welfare.* 4th ed. London: Macmillan, 1932.

This work, along with that of Joan Robinson, represents the definitive starting point for the analysis of labor market monopsony and the notion of wage and employment exploitation of workers. Pigou distinguishes "social cost" from "private cost" and "social benefit" from "private benefit." He proposes that governments tax producers in order to eliminate an excess of social cost over private cost and subsidize consumers in order to eliminate an excess of social benefit over private benefit. Requires graduate-level economics but is developed without any use of graphs or mathematics in the text proper. Recommended for specialists and college students.

Portney, Paul R., ed. *Public Policies for Environmental Protection.* Washington, D.C.: Resources for the Future, 1990.

Each chapter surveys recent policy developments and the prospects for improvement using economic theory. Chapters cover the history of federal regulation, air pollution policy, water pollution policy, hazardous wastes, toxic substances policy, monitoring and enforcement, and future direction. Highly recommended.

Reisman, David, Nathan Glazer, and Reuel Denney. *The Lonely Crowd.* Garden City, N.Y.: Doubleday, 1953.

An influential sociological study that interprets changes in American character and personality after 1945, including the makeup of the leisure class. The thesis is that prewar Americans tended to be "inner-directed," which was not true subsequently as a democratized society gave cues to individual behavior. Popularly written. Includes few notes and a modest index.

Rejda, George. *Social Insurance and Economic Security.* 3d ed. Englewood Cliffs, N.J.: Prentice-Hall, 1988.

A fine undergraduate textbook on social insurance which devotes more than half its pages to Social Security. In clear, understandable terms, it explains the basic principles of social insurance and examines the governmental programs to attack economic insecurity. Coverage is very thorough.

Russell, Louise B. *Medicare's New Hospital Payment System: Is It Working?* Washington, D.C.: Brookings Institution, 1989.
Looks at actual attempts to control costs in the largest U.S. government health program, Medicare. In spite of successful efforts to control costs, they continue to climb. The book is an excellent discussion of cost controls and is suitable for a general audience.

Savas, Emanuel S. *Privatization: The Key to Better Government.* Chatham, N.J.: Chatham House, 1987.
A must-read book on the topic. Takes a critical look at the proper role of government and considers the appropriate boundary between the roles of the public and the private sectors and between government responsibilities and private initiative. Savas concentrates on the provision of various services (such as road construction, city buses, and solid-waste disposal) that have demonstrated advantages of private delivery arrangements over publicly provided alternatives.

Sawers, Larry, and William Tabb, eds. *Sunbelt/Snowbelt.* New York: Oxford University Press, 1984.
A collection of sixteen papers dealing with urban growth. Many side issues are addressed in these papers.

Schultze, Charles L. *The Public Use of the Private Interest.* Washington, D.C.: Brookings Institution, 1977.
A long essay, addressed to policymakers, on the benefits of using economic incentives rather than command and control techniques for solving environmental problems. Includes many examples from the history of regulation.

Schulz, James H. *The Economics of Aging.* 4th ed. Dover, Mass.: Auburn House, 1988.
The standard textbook on the economics of aging. Minimizes economic jargon and deals with every important issue. Suitable for general audiences. A good starting point for anyone who is interested in this field.

Schwarz, John E. *America's Hidden Success: A Reassessment of Public Policy from Kennedy to Reagan.* Rev. ed. New York: W. W. Norton, 1988.

Written for a general readership. Provides an assessment of twenty-five years of American economic policy from 1960 to 1985. Raises a number of questions concerning various income redistribution programs in the light of changing economic conditions.

Scitovsky, Tibor. *The Joyless Economy: An Enquiry into Human Satisfaction and Consumer Dissatisfaction.* New York: Oxford University Press, 1976.
An innovative book that attempts to bring together evidence from psychology and economics in such a way as to enhance the understanding of the driving forces of human satisfaction. The section most relevant to the relative income hypothesis, however, is quite similar to the discussion found in the Easterlin selection.

Sen, Amartya. *Collective Choice and Social Welfare.* San Francisco: Holden-Day, 1970.
An articulate and imaginative, if somewhat technical, exposition of modern welfare theory.

Shafer, Thomas W. *Urban Growth and Economics.* Reston, Va.: Reston, 1977.
This book focuses on the economic forces that determine the location and size of cities.

Slottje, Daniel J. *The Structure of Earnings and the Measurement of Income Inequality in the U.S.* Amsterdam: North-Holland, 1989.
This technical monograph contains a full mathematical treatment of the Lorenz curve for those who are curious to see a formal statement of its properties. Also contains a comprehensive comparison of various measures of inequality using U.S. data from 1976 to 1985. Suitable for advanced undergraduates.

Snider, Delbert A. *Economic Myth and Reality.* Englewood Cliffs, N.J.: Prentice-Hall, 1965.
Provides an elementary view of various approaches to economic theory and policy. Deals with the idea of income redistribution in a very understandable way, but not all economists are likely to agree with the conclusions that are drawn here.

Stiglitz, Joseph E. *Economics of the Public Sector.* New York: W. W. Norton, 1986.

Chapter 3 is a good brief introduction to the basic propositions of welfare economics. The book also contains numerous applications of welfare economics to questions of government expenditures and taxes. A lucid overview of welfare criteria covering the issues raised by social welfare functions.

Stoline, Anne, and Jonathan P. Weiner. *The New Medical Marketplace: A Physician's Guide to the Health Care Revolution.* Baltimore: The Johns Hopkins University Press, 1988.

Designed to clarify the social and economic forces behind the health care revolution, this book gives a clear, concise view of the changing medical scene. Good glossary of acronyms and terms, and lengthy bibliography.

Struyk, Raymond J., and Marc Bendick, Jr. *Housing Vouchers for the Poor: Lessons from a National Experiment.* Washington, D.C.: Urban Institute Press, 1981.

This volume is a comprehensive report on the large-scale national experiment that used vouchers to assist the poor in obtaining better housing. Both demand-side and supply-side policies are explored using a voucher approach.

Sugden, Robert. *The Political Economy of Public Choice: An Introduction to Welfare Economics.* Oxford, England: Martin Robertson, 1981.

Sugden has two major aims. One is to present social choice theory in "plain English" to counterbalance what he sees as its tendency to become overly mathematical and incomprehensible to many observers. He is no more than partially successful in this ambition. His second aim is to go beyond simply a survey of the existing literature to write a synthesis; accordingly, he does not shy from expressing controversial personal normative judgments.

Sullivan, Arthur M. *Urban Economics.* Homewood, Ill.: Richard D. Irwin, 1990.

The most modern text available in urban economics. Presents a very good introduction to both housing economics and housing policy.

Taubman, Paul. *Income Distribution and Redistribution.* Reading, Mass.: Addison-Wesley, 1978.

A good, short (110-page) introduction to the topic of income inequality with useful illustrations of Lorenz curves. For beginning undergraduates.

Tinbergen, Jan, and Dietrich Fischer. *Warfare and Welfare: Integrating Security Policy into Socio-Economic Policy*. New York: St. Martin's Press, 1987.

An interesting application of the targets and instruments framework to a broader socioeconomic policy issue and problem: war and peace. The authors set for themselves the problem of determining, achieving, and managing an optimal structure for world society. At 181 pages, the development is compact and uses only occasional mathematics. It was written as a contribution to Peace Year 1986 and is dedicated to Olaf Palme.

Tullock, Gordon. *The Economics of Wealth and Poverty*. New York: New York University Press, 1986.

A critical look at government economic transfers. Instead of viewing transfers as a means to alleviate poverty, this book argues that most transfers serve the interests of the middle class and the political bureaucracy.

United States. President. *Economic Report of the President*. Washington, D.C.: Government Printing Office, 1985.

Chapter 4, "Health Status and Medical Care," and chapter 5, "Economic Status of the Elderly," provide a broad overview of important issues in the economics of aging. Suitable for the general reader.

U.S. Social Security Administration. *Social Security Bulletin*. Washington, D.C.: Government Printing Office, 1938-

The official monthly publication of the Social Security Administration, very accessible. It includes regular articles and statistical tables which update the operations of the system and explore issues such as the health and economic status of the elderly, experiences of disabled workers, public attitudes toward Social Security, and recent legislation.

_____ . *Social Security Bulletin: Annual Statistical Supplement*. Washington, D.C.: Government Printing Office, 1955-

A comprehensive array of information about U.S. welfare and social insurance with data, charts, and tables. Narratives explain the historical development of major programs and highlight the legislative changes that affect benefits.

_____ . *Social Security Handbook*. 10th ed. Washington, D.C.: Government Printing Office, 1988.

Presents provisions of the Social Security Act as amended through December 31, 1988, and gives a detailed description of the programs under the act, how they operate, who is entitled to benefits, and how they are obtained. A useful reference. Issued biennially.

_____. *Social Security Programs Throughout the World.* Washington, D.C.: Government Printing Office, 1989.

Provides an exhaustive survey of old-age, disability, death, sickness and maternity, work injury, unemployment, and family allowance programs around the world. The bulk of the work is a series of tables that provide information on the coverage, benefits, and funding for the social security systems of more than 140 nations and territories.

Varian, Hal R. "Distributive Justice, Welfare Economics, and the Theory of Fairness." *Philosophy and Public Affairs* 4 (1975): 223-247.

In the most accessible article listed here, Varian puts into words, most effectively, the results contained in his 1974 article (below). Suitable for a general audience.

_____. "Equity, Envy, and Efficiency." *Journal of Economic Theory* 9 (1974): 63-91.

A very technical and elegant presentation of equity theory, in the context of both exchange economies and production economies. Start here if interested in formal proofs. Although rigorous, still readable.

_____. *Microeconomic Analysis.* 2d ed. New York: W. W. Norton, 1984.

Within the framework of a first-year graduate microeconomic text, Varian (pages 284-287) discusses equity and fairness, as well as wealth equity and income equity.

Waltman, Jerold L., and Donley T. Studlar, eds. *Political Economy: Public Policies in the United States and Britain.* Jackson: University Press of Mississippi, 1987.

An interesting assortment of essays on the topic by economists, historians, and political scientists. The focus is on the social welfare policies in the United States and Great Britain during the Thatcher and Reagan Administrations.

Warner, Kenneth E. *Cost-Benefit and Cost-Effectiveness Analysis in Health Care: Principles, Practice, and Potential.* Ann Arbor, Mich.: Health Administration Press, 1982.

Explains the basic concepts of cost-benefit analysis and cost-effectiveness analysis and explores their application to the analysis of public health projects.

Wise, David A. *Issues in the Economics of Aging*. Chicago: University of Chicago Press, 1990.
A National Bureau of Economic Research project report that includes papers on the health of the elderly, their housing, living arrangements, labor force participation, and wealth and poverty. Suitable for advanced undergraduates and graduate students.

Yarbrough, Beth V., and Robert M. Yarbrough. *The World Economy: Trade and Finance*. New York: Dryden Press, 1988.
Chapter 4, "Trade, Distribution, and Welfare," contains a discussion of the gains from specialization in trade according to comparative advantage and the welfare aspects of unrestricted trade. Although the authors rely heavily on mathematical equations, the narrative is clear enough for the general reader.

Agricultural and Resource Economics

Abelson, Philip H., and Allan L. Hammond, eds. *Materials: Renewable and Non-Renewable*. Washington, D.C.: American Association for the Advancement of Science, 1976.
An excellent compilation of articles that detail the role of technology in defining and creating the resources for modern economies.

Aydelotte, William O. "The Country Gentlemen and the Repeal of the Corn Laws." *English Historical Review* 82 (January, 1967): 47-60.
An extremely important article in which the author shows that despite the common assumption that the Corn Law vote was based on class, it was in fact much more strongly related to party affiliation and constituency than on any social or economic factor.

Bachman, Kenneth L., and Raymond P. Christensen. "The Economics of Farm Size." In *Agricultural Development and Economic Growth*, edited by Herman M. Southworth and Bruce F. Johnston. Ithaca, N.Y.: Cornell University Press, 1967.
A theoretical, but nontechnical, analysis of the relationship between farm size and the efficiency of production, which is an important issue in land reforms that alter farm size by redistributing land.

Barnett, Harold J., and Chandler Morse. *Scarcity and Growth: The Economics of Natural Resource Availability.* Baltimore: The Johns Hopkins University Press, 1963.

The single work that forced many economists and other thinkers to revise their perspectives on natural resources. Presents empirical evidence on the decreasing scarcity of natural resources.

Bohi, Douglas R. *Analyzing Demand Behavior: A Study of Energy Elasticities.* Baltimore: The Johns Hopkins University Press, 1981.

A somewhat technical but readable detailed analysis of demand for energy, including empirical estimates of price and income elasticities.

Bradley, Michael E. "Mill on Proprietorship, Productivity, and Population: A Theoretical Reappraisal." *History of Political Economy* 15 (Fall, 1983): 423-449.

A restatement and critique of John Stuart Mill's arguments on land reform and peasant proprietorship. Essentially a theoretical article, but the general arguments are fairly accessible.

Bradley, Michael E., and M. Gardner Clarkark, M. Gardner, and Michael E. Bradley. "Supervision and Efficiency in Soviet Agriculture." *Soviet Studies* 23 (1972): 465-473.

A brief economic critique of the efficiency of Soviet collective and state farms. The central argument is that the unique difficulties of supervision of large numbers of farmers in physically large units is a critical cause of the chronic inefficiency of the Soviet model of collective agriculture.

Cobia, David, ed. *Cooperatives in Agriculture.* Englewood Cliffs, N.J.: Prentice-Hall, 1989.

One of the most recent texts dealing with cooperative business organizations. The authors do a particularly good job of discussing general cooperative principles, cooperative finance, and cooperative management. Very readable for general audiences and quite practical for anyone involved in cooperative management, even though the emphasis is on agricultural cooperatives.

Cochrane, Willard W. *The Development of American Agriculture: A Historical Analysis.* Minneapolis: University of Minnesota Press, 1979.

Provides a good discussion of the historical development of agriculture in the United States and examines the major forces that have changed agricultural production. Important issues such as government involvement in agriculture, foreign trade of agricultural products, and the competitive struggle of farmers are discussed within their historical context. Implications for present and future agricultural policy decisions are explored.

Conant, Melvin A. *The Oil Factor in U.S. Foreign Policy, 1980-1990.* Lexington, Mass.: Lexington Books, 1982.
　　Much more concerned with the national security implications of oil than energy economics, this brief, 113-page book offers useful insights concerning the international context of energy policy-making in the United States.

Davis, David Howard. *Energy Politics.* New York: St. Martin's Press, 1982.
　　An excellent readable account of the history of energy policy-making in each fuel area, and the degree of regulation experienced by each area in the American political process.

DeGregori, Thomas R. *A Theory of Technology: Continuity and Change in Human Development.* Ames: Iowa State University Press, 1985.
　　Argues that natural resources are a function of technology. A comprehensive theory of the nature of technology is offered as a framework for defining resources and how they are created. DeGregori argues that, through technology, humankind has been able to produce sufficient food for adequate nutrition and the abeyance of famine. He claims that problems in this area derive not from know-how but rather from income distribution and the resultant patterns of demand.

Doll, John P., and Frank Orazem. *Production Economics: Theory with Applications.* 2d ed. New York: John Wiley & Sons, 1984.
　　Primarily a college text for students of agricultural economics. A brief section in Chapter 2 on the costs of production, however, can be helpful to the beginner. The mathematics can be set aside to a certain extent, while the examples provide a sound understanding of the decision process. Many less complicated examples also help the reader to grasp cost-of-production concepts.

Downey, W. David, and Steven P. Erickson. *Agribusiness Management.* New York: McGraw-Hill, 1987.
　　Contains several chapters that provide an excellent overview of managing a business firm that also are relevant to a partnership. The authors present a concise discussion of the advantages and disadvantages of

the different forms of business organization. The differences between general and limited partnerships are also explained. Very readable for general audiences and quite practical for anyone involved in management.

Dreze, Jean, and Amartya Sen. *Hunger and Public Action.* Oxford, England: Oxford University Press, 1991.

The authors argue that public action is required to fight against famine and hunger and that income indicators are irrelevant to these issues because government action can assure that all citizens of even the poorest society have enough to eat.

Ferguson, Roy C., II. *Managing For Profit in Commercial Agriculture.* Englewood Cliffs, N.J.: Prentice-Hall, 1990.

Provides an easily understandable review of the business and economic concepts that must be understood in order to manage a business. In addition, the many examples that are offered will help the novice understand these concepts.

Fitzgerald, E. V. K. "Land Reform." In *The New Palgrave: A Dictionary of Economics,* edited by John Eatwell, Murray Milgate, and Peter Newman. Vol. 3. London: Macmillan, 1987.

A brief summary of modern land reforms and their theoretical and ideological underpinnings. Contains a useful bibliography.

Fried, Edward R., and Charles L. Schultze, eds. *Higher Oil Prices and the World Economy: The Adjustment Problem.* Washington, D.C.: Brookings Institution, 1975.

Although only concerned with the first oil crisis, the book is worth reading for its detailed analysis of the relationship between higher oil prices and the subsequent, short-term recession in the industrial world. Peppered with useful charts and data, the book contains excellent chapters on the effect of the higher petroleum prices on the less-developed world and the capacity of the international financial system to respond to challenges. Schultze likens OPEC's actions in 1973 to the imposition of a huge excise tax on the U.S. economy.

Futrell, Gene A., ed. *Marketing for Farmers.* St. Louis: Doane Information Services, 1982.

A guide for farmers and livestock producers to the agricultural marketing environment, this book does a good job of showing how futures markets are integrated with other aspects of agricultural marketing through hedging. Many detailed examples are given for grain and livestock marketing strategies, most incorporating futures. Some discussion of fundamental and technical price analysis is included. Recommended to those in agriculture who wish to improve their marketing programs.

Gittinger, J. Price, Joanne Leslie, and Caroline Hoisington. *Food Policy: Integrating Supply, Distribution, and Consumption*. Baltimore: The Johns Hopkins University Press, 1987.

Contains articles on the various components of a broadly based food policy approach to the supply, distribution, and consumption of food.

Hann, Danny. *Government and North Sea Oil*. New York: St. Martin's Press, 1986.

Focusing on a narrow but important subject, this short book (175 pages with index and references) offers one of the best analyses of the political economy of developing North Sea oil. Both descriptive and prescriptive, it should not be overlooked in the vast amount of works to be found on the politics and economics of oil.

Hildreth, R. J., Kathryn Lipton, Kenneth Clayton, and Carol O'Connor, eds. *Agriculture and Rural Areas Approaching the Twenty-first Century*. Ames: Iowa State University Press, 1988.

Provides a broad overview of economic and sociological problems of contemporary American agriculture. Topics such as resource and environmental economics, the macroeconomics of agriculture, implications of technological innovations, and management problems of farms and agricultural firms are covered.

Hoover, Edgar M. *An Introduction to Regional Economics*. New York: Alfred A. Knopf, 1971.

A very good introduction to regional economics. Designed as an undergraduate text and covers most of the basic points of regional economics including transfer, costs, location patterns, land use, and a number of topics in urban economics.

Johnson, D. Gale, ed. *The Politics of Food: Producing and Distributing the World's Food Supply*. Chicago: Chicago Council on Foreign Relations, 1980.

A very useful analysis of the world food supply and the problems of distribution by a number of well-known economists, writing from a variety of points of view.

King, Russell. *Land Reform: The Italian Experience*. London: Butterworths, 1973.

A concise, but quite detailed, description and analysis of Italian land reforms. Chapter 1 is a very readable, nontechnical summary of the theoretical issues in land reform.

Kneese, Alan. "Environmental Pollution: Economics and Policy." *American Economic Review* 61 (May, 1971): 153-166.

Investigates the applicability of Coase's two-party situation. Kneese finds that, when there are many parties involved in an externality situation, Coase's theorem is less likely to be applicable. More difficult, but fine for undergraduates.

Lee, Warren F., Michael D. Boehlje, Aaron G. Nelson, and William G. Murray. *Agricultural Finance*. 8th ed. Ames: Iowa State University Press, 1988.

A reference book for the more advanced reader. The concepts of lending, annuities, and amortization, however, are presented very simplistically at the start of each section. The novice can fully understand these concepts and ignore the more rigorous mathematical proofs.

MacAvoy, Paul W. *Energy Policy: An Economic Analysis*. New York: W. W. Norton, 1983.

A standard college text for energy economics courses, MacAvoy's work offers a clear and concise analysis of the economics of the oil, gas, coal, and electrical power industries in the United States, and of the frequently counterproductive policies which were passed to regulate them following the oil crisis of 1973.

McBride, Glynn. *Agricultural Cooperatives*. Westport, Conn.: AVI, 1986.

Provides an excellent review of the economic and legislative basis for the formation of cooperatives. In addition to explaining why cooperatives are formed, this book provides a very practical yet thorough explanation of how cooperatives are managed and operated.

McConnell, Campbell R., and Stanley L. Brue. *Microeconomics*. New York: McGraw-Hill, 1990.

Chapter 22, "Rural Economics: The Farm Problem," covers some basic principles of agricultural economics. A brief history of the farm problem is presented, followed by a discussion of farm income. Next, the long-run and short-run farm problem is analyzed by use of supply and demand, followed by an analysis of farm policy. This chapter contains many interesting data and graphs.

McLaren, Digby, and Brian Skinner, eds. *Resources and World Development*. New York: John Wiley & Sons, 1987.

A large, comprehensive collection of articles on virtually every aspect of resources and what defines and creates them by outstanding authors in science, engineering, and economics.

Meier, Kenneth J. *Regulation, Politics, Bureaucracy, and Economics*. New York: St. Martin's Press, 1985.

Chapter 5, "Regulating Agriculture," provides a thorough, up-to-date introduction to the regulatory agriculture policy in the United States. The agricultural industry is discussed first, followed by coverage of the agricultural regulatory agencies, who are responsible for implementing policies such as price supports. Also provided is a history of the politics of agricultural regulation and policy.

Nerlove, Marc. *The Dynamics of Supply: Estimation of Farmers' Response to Price*. Baltimore: The John Hopkins University Press, 1958.

For those with an interest in applied analysis, Nerlove's classic study provides an econometric approach to supply.

Peirce, William Spangar. *Economics of the Energy Industries*. Belmont, Calif.: Wadsworth, 1986.

An excellent introduction to the economics of the various extractive energy industries (coal, oil, and gas) and energy conversion industries (electric utilities, nuclear power, and solar power) in the context of the market and the public policy environments in which they operate.

Raup, Philip M. "Land Reform and Agricultural Development." In *Agricultural Development and Economic Growth*, edited by Herman M. Southworth and Bruce F. Johnston, Ithaca, N.Y.: Cornell University Press, 1967.

A remarkably comprehensive one-chapter summary of the key economic, political, and cultural dimensions of land reforms in underdeveloped countries. Although some of the information is dated, it is an excellent introduction to the subject.

Rose, Adam, Brandt Stevens, and Gregg Davis. *Natural Resource Policy and Income Distribution*. Baltimore: The Johns Hopkins University Press, 1988.

Describes a social accounting matrix (SAM), one of the more recent extensions of the input-output model. This model is useful for studying the effects of economic changes on income distribution across categories of households. The book illustrates the flexibility of the input-output model and its usefulness in addressing a wide range of public policy issues.

Rosenbaum, Walter A. *Energy, Politics, and Public Policy*. Washington, D.C.: Congressional Quarterly Press, 1981.

A useful supplement to the Davis book, this work is not so much concerned with the history of energy policy-making in America as with the political dynamics involved in a policy arena crowded with resource, technological, and political constraints.

Sampson, Anthony. *The Seven Sisters: The Great Oil Companies and the World They Shaped*. New York: Bantam Books, 1975.

Provides the most readable account of the rise and fall of the major oil companies, and their success in controlling competition, price, and the availability of oil on the world market from the inter-war period to the 1960's. Later printings have a postscript chapter on the 1979 oil crisis.

Sanders, M. Elizabeth. *The Regulation of Natural Gas: Policy and Politics, 1938-1978*. Philadelphia: Temple University Press, 1982.

Weaving together a review of relevant economic theory and an analysis of the influence of sectional politics in the regulation of the American gas industry, this book provides an interesting account of the politics of policy-making in areas of resource scarcity.

Scheppach, Raymond C., and Everett M. Ehrlich, eds. *Energy-Policy Analysis and Congressional Action*. Lexington, Mass.: Lexington Books, 1982.

Analyzes energy policies implemented during the Carter Administration, with particular attention to the misconceptions underlying them and the gradual shift from policies based on security considerations to the quest for economically efficient energy programs.

Schultz, Theodore W. *Transforming Traditional Agriculture*. New Haven, Conn.: Yale University Press, 1964.

This brief book, although dated, remains one of the clearest statements of many of the economic issues that are involved in traditional agriculture. Although it contains little on land reform, chapter 8 deals with the critical issues surrounding farm size and efficiency.

Simon, Julian L., and Herman Kahn, eds. *The Resourceful Earth: A Response to Global 2000*. New York: Basil Blackwell, 1984.
    An optimistic rebuttal to the Global 2000 Report that argues that the world is not in dire straits and that human creativity can be applied to the environmental and resource challenges that lie ahead.

Stobaugh, Robert, and Daniel Yergin, eds. *Energy Future: Report of the Energy Project at the Harvard Business School*. Rev. ed. New York: Vintage Books, 1983.
    Still the most often cited study of U.S. energy options, with particular attention to the value of conservation, "the key energy source."

Timmer, C. Peter, Walter P. Falcon, and Scott R. Pearson. *Food Policy Analysis*. Baltimore: The Johns Hopkins University Press, 1983.
    An excellent introduction and overview of the area of food economics. The authors include comprehensive chapters on each major aspect of food policy analysis, including analyses of food consumption and nutrition, food production systems, marketing functions, markets, food price formation, and macroeconomic food policies.

Tugwell, Franklin. *The Energy Crisis and the American Political Economy: Politics and Markets in the Management of Natural Resources*. Stanford, Calif.: Stanford University Press, 1988.
    An interesting account of the effects of post-1973 energy policy-making on American society. Perhaps the best of the books on energy and American political economy published shortly before the 1990 oil crisis.

United States. Global 2000 Study. *The Global 2000 Report to the President: Entering the Twenty-first Century*. 3 vols. Washington, D.C.: Government Printing Office, 1980-1981.
    A pessimistic assessment of the possibility that available resources would sustain continued economic growth.

U.S. Department of Agriculture. *The Basic Mechanisms of U.S. Farm Policy: How They Work, with Examples and Illustrations*. Miscellaneous Publication 1479. Washington, D.C.: Economic Research Service, U.S. Department of Agriculture, 1990.
    This booklet is intended for a wide audience as an introduction to key concepts of government programs for agriculture. It is arranged to simulate an informal briefing, with each page containing illustrative material and notes to the reader.

Wolfe, Arthur D. *The Law on American Business Organizations: An Environmentalist Approach.* New York: John Wiley & Sons, 1984.

Provides a thorough review of the issues surrounding business organization and the related legal points. The bibliography is especially helpful. Though the tax information that is discussed is somewhat dated, it does provide the reader with background that will be helpful in further reading on this topic.

World Resources Institute Staff. *World Resources, 1990-1991.* New York: Oxford University Press, 1990.

An annual survey of the current state and prospects of the world's resources that is organized and presented from the perspective that resources are being threatened.

Zimmermann, Erich W. *World Resources and Industries: A Functional Appraisal of the Availability of Agricultural and Industrial Materials.* 1933. Rev. ed. New York: Harper and Brothers, 1951.

Though empirically out of date, this massive, scholarly work was definitive in its time and employs knowledge from such diverse sciences as geology, metallurgy, and economics to frame a comprehensive understanding of the characteristics of resources. The theoretical sections remain relevant to the understanding of natural resources.

Business Applications

Accounting Principles Board. *Basic Concepts and Accounting Principles Underlying Financial Statements of Business Enterprises.* Statement of Accounting Principles 4. New York: American Institute of Certified Public Accountants, 1970.

Designed for professional users but understandable to college-level students, this book describes the development of and range of functions of accountants.

Advertising Age. 1930-

This weekly publication is a wealth of information on current events in the advertising industry, as well as current advertising campaigns. Very readable and can be found in most libraries.

Aitken, Hugh, ed. *Explorations in Enterprise.* Cambridge, Mass.: Harvard University Press, 1965.

A masterful overview of the historical approach and the work of the Center for Entrepreneurial History. Includes representative work of all the major participants.

Allingham, Michael. *Theory of Markets*. New York: St. Martin's Press, 1990.

This 128-page book begins with a study of "Black Monday" in 1987, when stock values fell by more than 20 percent. Allingham then carefully explains how expectations about future events by market participants change the price behavior in both commodity and financial markets. An interesting book for both business and economic students.

Anderson, Ronald W. *The Industrial Organization of Futures Markets*. Lexington, Mass.: D. C. Heath, 1984.

A book which addresses itself to the shady side of futures markets and their possible abuses. Although much of the economics is advanced, the general reader should find the survey in chapter 1 useful.

Andrews, Kenneth R. *The Concept of Corporate Strategy*. Homewood, Ill.: Richard D. Irwin, 1980.

Provides a basic easy-to-read introduction to the organization and strategy of corporations. Offers insight into corporate roles, responsibilities, ethics, behavior, and management.

Auerbach, Robert D. *Financial Markets and Institutions*. New York: Collier Macmillan, 1983.

A text that is devoted to financial markets and the theory and application that are behind them. Excellent background reading for understanding the economics of general investments. Provides excellent charts, tables, and graphs and also contains a good glossary of terms.

Baker, H. Kent, Gail E. Farrelly, and Richard B. Edelman. "A Survey of Management Views on Dividend Policy." *Financial Management* 13 (Autumn, 1985): 78-84.

This article reports on a survey of managers' views on dividend policy. Although it is intended for financial specialists, it is also suitable for the general reader.

Baltzell, E. Digby. *The American Business Aristocracy*. New York: Collier Books, 1962.

A well-researched, original contribution by an able sociologist who specialized in studies of the American rich. This study concentrates on Philadelphia's business elite. Popularly written, the conclusions controvert Thorstein Veblen's thesis. Full notes, a few tables, a good bibliography, and a useful index are provided.

Bernstein, Jacob. *How the Futures Markets Work.* New York: New York Institute of Finance, 1989.

This work answers many questions about futures markets, as its basic approach appeals to the futures newcomer. The presentation on technical price analysis is especially good. Recommended for the general reader.

Besant, Lloyd, ed. *Chicago Trading Manual.* Chicago: Chicago Board of Trade, 1985.

A well-written discussion of modern commodity exchanges and operating rules, with a description of the commodities traded.

_____ , et al., eds. *Commodity Trading Manual.* Chicago: Chicago Board of Trade, 1983.

A must for anyone wishing to learn more about futures markets. Covers all aspects of futures trading: exchange operations, hedging, supply-demand factors affecting specific commodities, the basics of price forecasting, and futures industry regulation. Suitable for a general audience.

Bierman, Harold, Jr. *Implementing Capital Budgeting Techniques.* Cambridge, Mass.: Ballinger, 1988.

Describes working managers' perceived problems of implementing capital budgeting decision-making techniques. Surveys the capital budgeting literature dealing with these problems and suggests methods of coping with them. The book attempts to link academic capital budgeting literature with the current interests of business managers. Contains an extensive bibliography of capital budgeting literature in professional journals for each major topic.

Bierman, Harold, Jr., and Seymour Smidt. *The Capital Budgeting Decision: Economic Analysis of Investment Projects.* New York: Macmillan, 1988.

Gives a clear conception of how to evaluate investment proposals. Begins with an intuitive presentation that is a suitable introduction for managers at any level, who must understand the ideas that are involved in evaluating capital investments but who are not directly involved in preparing investment evaluations. Then this book elaborates on these basic principles with increasingly sophisticated and mathematically complex refinements for managers who actually analyze and evaluate investments.

Black, Fischer, and Myron Scholes. "The Pricing of Options and Corporate Liabilities." *Journal of Political Economy* 81 (May/June, 1973): 637-654.

This classic work introduced the Black-Scholes model for pricing options. The model is theoretically sound and has been subjected to extensive testing.

Black, Nelms. *How to Organize and Manage a Small Business.* Norman: University of Oklahoma Press, 1946.

A classic manual for the small business owner that describes all aspects of business structure, management, analysis, financing, cost control, sales, and research. While the managerial methods have evolved since the book's first appearance, the discussion of the foundations of business management remains relevant. In addition, this treatise provides an opportunity for the novice to understand the workings of these types of businesses.

Brealey, Richard A. *An Introduction to Risk and Return from Common Stocks.* Cambridge, Mass.: MIT Press, 1969.

A descriptive 150-page work written by a portfolio manager and intended for the professional investor or beginning student of the market. Assumes no prior knowledge of statistics and uses no mathematical formulas, relying instead on tables, examples, and an occasional graph to illustrate important concepts. Part 3 focuses on portfolio theory.

Brealey, Richard, and Stewart C. Myersyers, Stewart C., and Richard Brealey. *Principles of Corporate Finance.* 2d ed. New York: McGraw-Hill, 1984.

While this undergraduate text is a survey of issues in corporation finance, it does include discussions of mergers of various types. The discussion centers not only on the ways in which a merger can be consummated but also on the financial motivations for mergers.

Brentlinger, Marilyn E., and Judith M. Weiss. *The Ultimate Benefit Book: How to Raise $50,000-plus for Your Organization.* Cleveland: Octavia Press, 1987.
The primary focus of this book is a direct hands-on approach to fund-raising, including marketing, advertising, and operations. Case studies are also included.

Brigham, Eugene F. *Fundamentals of Financial Management.* New York: Dryden Press, 1989.
Presents the basics of the conceptual foundation of the capital budgeting process and presents detailed examples of the calculation process. This type of treatment will help a reader familiarize himself or herself with the basics before moving on to more comprehensive coverage of capital budgeting. Contains a bibliography of journal articles that deal with capital budgeting.

Brown, Douglas M. "The Restaurant and Fast Food Race: Who's Winning?" *Southern Economic Journal* 56 (April, 1990): 984-995.
This article provides a useful example of the way in which the relationship between time and supply elasticity is used in modern economic studies. Understandable by noneconomists who are familiar with basic economics vocabulary. College and university libraries are good sources for the journal.

Brumbaugh, Dan R. *Thrifts Under Siege: Restoring Order to American Banking.* Cambridge, Mass.: Ballinger, 1988.
Explores the thrift crisis and its dangers to the health of the financial community. Brumbaugh forcefully argues that regulations designed to shield weak thrifts from closure threaten the survival of well-managed institutions. Details the short- and long-term measures required to restore order to American banking.

Budd, Nicholas. "The Future of Commodity Indexed Financing." *Harvard Business Review* 61 (July/August, 1983): 44-46.
Discusses a number of options for indexed securities.

Cassady, Ralph, Jr. *Auctions and Auctioneering.* Berkeley: University of California Press, 1967.
An elegant piece of work on historical and institutional aspects of auctions. Very readable; recommended for all readers.

Chamberlain, Lawrence, and George W. Edwards. *The Principles of Bond Investment*. New York: Henry Holt, 1911.
The classic in bond analysis.

Childs, John F. *Encyclopedia of Long-Term Financing and Capital Management*. Englewood Cliffs, N.J.: Prentice-Hall, 1976.
A discussion of bonds and their alternatives from the perspective of the corporate borrower.

Chinloy, Peter. *Real Estate: Investment and Financial Strategy*. Boston: Kluwer Academic Publishers, 1988.
An advanced treatment of the financial and legal aspects of both the borrower and the lender in the mortgage market, with an especially good focus on the problems of conventional mortgages and the role of alternative mortgage design. Appropriate for advanced undergraduates and graduate students.

Clarkson, Kenneth W., Roger LeRoy Miller, Gaylord A. Jentz, and Frank B. Cross. *West's Business Law: Text, Cases, and Legal Environment*. 1980. 2d ed. St. Paul, Minn.: West, 1989.
A major legal and business reference work that is written and designed for the serious legal student and is an excellent legal research text. Cases, forms, appendices, a glossary, and ethics sections are included.

Cooper, Dale F., and C. B. Chapman. *Risk Analysis for Large Projects*. New York: John Wiley & Sons, 1987.
A comprehensive coverage of the evaluation and management of the risk associated with large projects. This 260-page book is a valuable reference for construction managers and those involved in assessing risk for projects involving large amounts of capital. The discussion presumes a knowledge of basic probability concepts. The bibliography is rich with application examples to include offshore drilling, underground construction, and nuclear power plant design.

Coopers & Lybrand. *A Guide to Financial Instruments*. London: Euromoney Publications, 1987.
A survey of contemporary financial instruments in the Eurobond market.

Coppock, Joseph D. *Economics of the Business Firm*. New York: McGraw-Hill, 1959.

The economic foundation of proprietorship is discussed, as well as firm goals, competition, profit maximization, economic analysis tools, and market structure.

Corley, Robert N., Peter J. Shedd, and Eric M. Holmes. *Fundamentals of Business Law.* 4th ed. Englewood Cliffs, N.J.: Prentice-Hall, 1986.
This large reference work appears at first glance to be rather imposing, but it is actually written in clear terms. Contract law, remedies, and terminology are explained in excellent detail. Recent legal cases are provided that offer real-world situations. The complete uniform commercial code, a glossary, and an index are provided.

Cox, John C., and Mark Rubinstein. *Options Markets.* Englewood Cliffs, N.J.: Prentice-Hall, 1985.
One of the original and best books on all aspects of options. It explains the basic principles of option valuation models. The book is theoretically rigorous and widely used.

Crane, Judson A., and Calvert Magruder. *Cases on the Law of Partnership and Other Unincorporated Business Associations.* 2d ed. Indianapolis: Bobbs-Merrill, 1951.
A comprehensive sourcebook on case law relating to partnerships, limited partnerships, limited partnership associations, unincorporated joint stock companies, and joint ventures. Couched in legal language that takes some getting used to, the discussion answers virtually any legal question regarding such business forms.

Daft, Richard L. *Organization Theory and Design.* 2d ed. St. Paul, Minn.: West, 1986.
Presents the broad scope of the business manager's responsibilities and the many information sources on which the manager may draw including accounting and economics.

Deal, Terrence E., and Allen A. Kennedy. *Corporate Cultures: The Rite and Rituals of Corporate Life.* Reading, Mass.: Addison-Wesley, 1982.
Offers insight into the philosophical backdrop to corporate organizations and provides valuable information on past, present, and future corporate standards for ethics, values, and belief systems.

Dearden, John, and John Shank. *Financial Accounting and Reporting.* Englewood Cliffs, N.J.: Prentice-Hall, 1975.
Provides an overview of financial accounting techniques and financial reporting. The mechanics of the accounting process are also covered.

The authors explain how financial accounting reports are prepared in order to communicate economic changes to a wide audience, especially to those interested in the profitability of a business.

Denenberg, Herbert S., Robert D. Eilers, G. Wright Hoffman, Chester A. Kline, Joseph J. Melone, and H. Wayne Snider. *Risk and Insurance.* Englewood Cliffs, N.J.: Prentice-Hall, 1964.
Written for the beginning student, this classic textbook provides a thorough introduction to the application of risk concepts in the insurance industry. The explanation of basic risk concepts is outstanding. The discussion of risk management has applications beyond the insurance industry and is particularly valuable for the general reader.

Dertouzos, Michael L., Richard K. Lester, and Robert M. Solow. *Made in America: Regaining the Productive Edge.* Cambridge, Mass.: MIT Press, 1989.
Based on more than six hundred interviews in eight manufacturing industries, this book reviews emerging technology, discusses outdated strategies, and makes recommendations for a more productive United States. Stresses the importance of product customization, flexible manufacturing, and innovation in production.

Diamond, Barbara, and Mark P. Kollar. *Twenty-Four-Hour Trading: The Global Network of Futures and Options Markets.* New York: John Wiley & Sons, 1989.
Global futures trading is the theme in this book, which discusses various futures markets around the world. A very good history of futures trading is provided, along with some interesting views toward the future (especially computerized trading). Contains a directory of futures exchanges.

Doerflinger, Thomas M., and Jack L. Rivkin. *Risk and Reward.* New York: Random House, 1987.
A popular work written for general audiences. This 320-page book tells the story of the role played by risk takers in the growth and development of the United States. Includes many examples from the experiences of well-known corporations, as well as policy recommendations to foster American economic competitiveness. The bibliography contains numerous examples of twentieth century venture capitalists.

Downey, W. David, and Steven P. Erickson. *Agribusiness Management.* New York: McGraw-Hill, 1987.

This book contains several chapters that provide an excellent overview of the management of assets and liabilities within a business firm. The authors' discussion of a firm's balance sheet presents a concise description of the different types of assets and liabilities, as well as techniques for analyzing the liquidity and profitability of the firm. Designed for the practicing manager but very readable for general audiences as well.

Drucker, Peter F. *Concept of the Corporation*. 1946. Reprint. New York: Harper & Row, 1983.
Still relevant for managers of corporations and partnerships, as it examines issues related to the structure, organization, power relationships, and social responsibilities of business firms. One of the first books written on management by a leading expert.

Fabozzi, Frank J. *Floating Rate Instruments*. Chicago: Probus, 1986.
A survey of variable-rate securities.

Fabozzi, Frank J., and Irving M. Pollack. *Fixed Income Securities*. Homewood, Ill.: Dow Jones-Irwin, 1983.
Designed as a complete and detailed collection of readings, more than one thousand pages in length. Chapters 1, 6, and 13 are most appropriate for a general background on the stock market. Graphs and charts are included.

_____ , eds. *The Handbook of Fixed Income Securities*. Homewood, Ill.: Dow Jones-Irwin, 1987.
Everything one would ever want to know about bonds and other fixed income securities, and more.

Fama, Eugene F. "Random Walks in Stock Market Prices." *The Financial Analysts Journal* 21 (September/October, 1965): 3-7. An excellent discussion of the random walk characteristic of common-stock prices.

Farmer, Robert A. *What You Should Know About Contracts*. New York: Arco, 1969.
This popular work is written and designed for the general reader. Providing many examples of different types of contracts, it includes both a glossary and an index.

Federal Reserve Bank of New York. *Funding and Liquidity: Recent Changes in Liquidity Management Practices at Commercial Banks and Securities Firms*. New York: Author, 1990.

Provides a detailed examination of liquidity management practices at the level of an individual financial firm. Defines terms and explains concepts. Suitable for college students.

Feiwel, George R. *Cost: The Various Meanings of the Concept.* Edmonton: University of Alberta, 1964.
Review of some of the basic cost concepts as viewed by the accountant and the economist.

Financial Accounting Standards Board. *Elements of Financial Statements.* Statement of Financial Accounting Concepts 6. Stamford, Conn.: FASB, 1985.
Discusses the components of financial reports and the concepts and definitions that are used by accountants and in financial reports. Designed mainly for professionals, but written to be understandable to college students.

——————. *Objectives of Financial Reporting by Business Enterprises.* Statement of Financial Accounting Concepts 1. Stamford, Conn.: FASB, 1978.
Designed for professional accountants, this book describes the purposes of financial reporting and the range of tasks that an accountant performs. Should be understandable to college students.

Fink, Robert E., and Robert B. Feduniak. *Futures Trading: Concepts and Strategies.* New York: New York Institute of Finance, 1988.
A unified book, the joint work of two authors and not a collection of articles, which is meant to serve as a text for an extended but entry-level course in futures trading.

Fuller, Russel J., and James L. Farrell. *Modern Investments and Security Analysis.* New York: McGraw-Hill, 1987.
A standard introductory business finance textbook introducing the concepts used in investment analysis.

Goss, B. A., and B. S. Yamey. *The Economics of Futures Trading.* New York: John Wiley & Sons, 1976.
As indicated by the title, this is a book for economists, rather than practitioners. Some chapters involve mathematics, but the introduction should be useful for everyone.

Graddy, Duane B., and Austin H. Spencer. *Managing Commercial Banks: Community, Regional, and Global.* Englewood Cliffs, N.J.: Prentice-Hall, 1990.

Concentrating on the long-run goal of maximizing stockholders' wealth, this text provides a comprehensive survey of commercial banking suitable to a range of readers.

Graham, Benjamin, David L. Dodd, Sidney Cottle, and Charles Tatham. *Security Analysis.* 4th ed. New York: McGraw-Hill, 1962.

A classic work in the area of valuing securities. Professional analysts continue to refer to this text. Quite readable and suitable for the general reader.

Granger, C. W. J. *Forecasting in Business and Economics.* 2d ed. Boston: Academic Press, 1989.

A good introduction to how to use indicators in making business decisions, particularly in chapter 7.

Grether, David M., and Peter Mieszkowski. "Determinants of Real Estate Values." *Journal of Urban Economics* 1 (1974): 127-145.

A good example of a hedonic study, which decomposes house prices into components of price determined by structural characteristics, neighborhood and lot characteristics, and community characteristics.

Gup, Benton E., and Charles O. Meiburg. *Cases in Bank Management.* New York: Macmillan, 1986.

The cases in this book are focused on the issues that affect every banker. Not only useful for students who specialize in banking but also helpful for depositors and those who want to borrow money from banks. Suitable for the general public.

Hagin, Robert L. *Modern Portfolio Theory.* Homewood, Ill.: Dow Jones-Irwin, 1979.

A descriptive work from the research director of a major investment banking firm. Provides considerably more background information than Richard A. Brealey's book, with few mathematical or statistical formulas. The book's 353 pages also include an extensive glossary of financial and statistical terms that even a more experienced analyst will find useful.

Harvard Business Review. 1922-

Contains articles on advertising and economics that bridge the academic and industrial communities. The articles address state-of-the-art thinking and are succinctly and clearly written. Can be found in most libraries.

Hirshleifer, Jack. *Investment, Interest, and Capital.* Englewood Cliffs, N.J.: Prentice-Hall, 1970.
Contains an integration of much of the classic theory on discounting and its application to analyzing the firm's investment decisions. Suitable for upper-division college students.

Holloran, Thomas, and Judson Bryn. "United Airlines Stationed Manpower Planning System." *Interfaces* 16 (January/February, 1986): 13-24.
Provides a good illustration of the recognition of a problem and the application of linear programming to solve it. Although some parts are mathematical, a sophisticated mathematical background is not necessary.

Howell, John C. *The Guide to Business Contracts.* New York: Hamilton Press, 1978.
One of the many legal textbooks in Harper Hamilton's Citizen's Law Library series Law for the Layman, this book offers clear and concise legal information for the nontechnical reader. Provides general information on contracts including the organization, financing, and commercial agreements relating to business operations. A basic reference book that includes a glossary.

Institutional Investor editors. *The Way It Was: An Oral History of Finance, 1967-1987.* New York: William Morrow, 1988.
A very entertaining book of interviews from past subjects of *Institutional Investor* magazine. The interviews are all quite short and easily read, ranging from two to eight pages in length. Especially pertinent to arbitrage are the articles by Alan Greenberg, Joseph Perella, and Bruce Wasserstein.

Jaffe, Austin J., and C. F. Sirmans. *Real Estate Investment Decision Making.* Englewood Cliffs, N.J.: Prentice-Hall, 1982.
An intermediate presentation of the financial and legal aspects of buying property. Appropriate for advanced undergraduates.

Jarrow, Robert A., and Andrew Rudd. *Option Pricing.* Homewood, Ill.: Dow Jones-Irwin, 1983.
Develops various stock option pricing formulas. Chapter 1 presents the general idea of option pricing for nonspecialists. The Monte Carlo method for the evaluation of option pricing is discussed for the general

audience in chapter 14. References for potential practitioners are also given.

Jones, Charles P. *Investments: Analysis and Management*. New York: John Wiley & Sons, 1985.

A comprehensive treatment of the field of investments including portfolio theory (chapters 19 through 21). An understanding of basic statistics is useful but not essential, as the material is descriptive. While some of his derivations are a little terse, Jones's explanation of the evolution of portfolio theory from Harry Markowitz to William Sharpe is particularly good.

Jordon, James V., Robert S. Mackay, and Eugene J. Moriarity. "The Regulation of Commodity-Linked Debt and Depository Instruments." In *The Handbook of Financial Engineering*, edited by C. W. Smith and C. W. Smithson. New York: Harper Business, 1990.

The present regulatory status of price-indexed and price-linked securities.

Joseph, Joel D., and Jeffrey Hiller. *Legal Agreements in Plain English*. New York: Contemporary Books, 1982.

Provides a good introduction to the actual design, structure, and use of contract documents. The discussion offers insight into the language and forms that are used in contract law. Very easy to read and understand and serves as a good reference guide.

Kahn, Sharon, and the Philip Lief Group. *101 Best Businesses to Start*. New York: Doubleday, 1988.

Designed for those seriously considering starting their own business, whether it be a sole proprietorship or a partnership. The authors identify the resources required and skills needed, and provide tips for success in 101 different business areas.

Kaufman, Perry J. *Handbook of Futures Markets, Commodity, Financial, Stock Index, and Options*. New York: John Wiley & Sons, 1984.

A collection of essays by many authors, this massive reference is long on technique and facts and somewhat short on economic perspective. The ideal source of historical and institutional detail on markets for practically every commodity.

Kemeny, John G., Arthur Schliefer, Jr., J. Laurie Snell, and Gerald L. Thompson. *Finite Mathematics with Business Applications*. 2d ed. Englewood Cliffs, N.J.: Prentice-Hall, 1972.

An excellent textbook containing formulas and examples related to the mathematics behind discounting. Suitable for college students.

Kirsner. Laura, and Lyn Taetzsch. *Practical Accounting for Small Businesses.* 2d ed. New York: Van Nostrand Reinhold, 1983.
A primer on management's need for an appropriate accounting system and practical ways to implement an accounting system for the small business. Persons planning to start a small business would find it extremely useful.

Kolb, Robert W. *Investments.* Glenview, Ill.: Scott, Foresman, 1986.
The many books on financial topics by Kolb share a common trait; they are written with exceptional clarity and easy-to-follow examples of complex topics. He is particularly knowledgeable about financial futures and options. Practical examples illustrate the international aspects of investing and portfolio theory.

Kotler, Philip. *Marketing Management.* Englewood Cliffs, N.J.: Prentice-Hall, 1988.
Kotler is one of the world's leading authorities on marketing. He discusses the role of advertising vis-à-vis the promotional and marketing mixes. Kotler is a readable writer who utilizes a wealth of examples.

Labuszewski, John W., and John E. Nyhoff. *Trading Options on Futures.* New York: John Wiley & Sons, 1988.
Strategies and concepts are carefully explained and illustrated using examples drawn from actual trading situations.

Lamb, Robert, and Stephen P. Rappaport. *Municipal Bonds.* 2d ed. New York: McGraw-Hill, 1987.
A very complete description of many types of municipal bonds and their uses. Offers a good description of terms and analysis of issues for those unfamiliar with bond markets in general.

Lasson, Kenneth. *Mousetraps and Muffling Cups: One Hundred Brilliant and Bizarre Patents.* New York: Arbor House, 1986.
A frequently humorous description of stillborn inventions, such as eyeglass wipers, but also of familiar devices such as the vacuum cleaner. The challenge of this work, written for the general public, is to make the reader guess why many inventions, all illustrated, never got off the ground.

Lerner, Eugene, and William T. Carleton. *A Theory of Financial Analysis.* New York: Harcourt, Brace & World, 1966.

Several chapters in this book discuss the basic tools for financial analysis. Another chapter provides an analytical framework for basic accounting principles.

Leuthold, Raymond M., Joan C. Junkus, and Jean E. Cordier. *The Theory and Practice of Futures Markets.* Lexington, Mass.: D. C. Heath, 1989.

A textbook with in-depth explanations of how the futures and options markets function. Parts of the book are somewhat theoretical in nature, which may prove cumbersome for some readers unfamiliar with economic theory. Other parts, especially the discussion of hedging basics and exchange operations, are very straightforward, with plenty of examples allowing novice and experienced professional alike to appreciate the workings of futures markets.

Levitt, Theodore. "Exploit the Product Life Cycle." In *Product Policy for Industrial Goods Companies.* Cambridge, Mass.: Harvard University Press, 1976.

Originally published in the November/December, 1965, issue of *Harvard Business Review*, this article presents an easy-to-read overview of the product cycle and then expands it to include the concept of market stretching. For the reader interested in product management, this publication provides a good collection of readable articles on the topic.

Levy, Haim, and Marshall Sarnat. *Capital Investment and Financial Decisions.* Englewood Cliffs, N.J.: Prentice-Hall, 1983.

A text on capital budgeting.

Light, J. O., and William L. White. *The Financial System.* Homewood, Ill.: Richard D. Irwin, 1979.

An institutional approach to financial markets and interest-rate determination.

Litzenberger, Robert H., and K. Ramaswamy. "The Effects of Dividends on Common Stock Prices: Tax Effects or Information Effects." *Journal of Finance* 36 (May, 1982): 429-443.

This article contains a short review of statistical studies of dividends and firm value. Suitable for college students with a statistics background.

Loque, Dennis E., ed. *Handbook of Modern Finance*. Boston: Warren, Gorham and Lamont, 1984.
>   Chapters 7 and 8 cover the long-term bond market and state and local government finance.

Lorie, James H., and Leonard J. Savage. "Three Problems in Rationing Capital." *Journal of Business* 28 (October, 1955): 229-239.
>   One of the first articles to analyze shortcomings of popular investment decision rules seriously.

McCulloch, J. Huston. "The Ban on Indexed Bonds, 1933-77." *American Economic Review* 69 (December, 1980): 1018-1021.
>   The economic and legal status of price-indexed bonds in the United States. See the comment and reply on this article in the *American Economic Review*'s June, 1982, issue.

McDonald, John. *The Game of Business*. Garden City, N.Y.: Doubleday, 1975.
>   McDonald's explanation of cooperative games is the most easily accessible to nonspecialists. Highly recommended.

Maginn, John L., and Donald L. Tuttle. *Managing Investment Portfolios*. Boston: Warren, Gorham & Lamont, 1983.
>   Although this book is a collection of excellent works, chapters 5 and 10 are the most relevant to a study of stock markets. Well written and concise, but lacks sufficient graphs or charts. Chapter 10 is of particular interest and is concerned with individual stock portfolio construction.

Maskowitz, Milton, Robert Levering, and Michael Katz. *Everybody's Business: A Guide to America's Leading Four Hundred Corporations*. Garden City, N.Y.: Doubleday, 1990.
>   Offers much insight into the internal operation, historical background, and sales and profits of America's largest corporations. Other data include the corporate ranking by industry, founding year, location of headquarters, corporate logo, and types of product lines. Anyone who needs to research a variety of topics concerning American business will find this book to be a tremendous asset, as well as very interesting to read.

Matatko, John, and David Stafford. *Key Developments in Personal Finance*. Oxford, England: Basil Blackwell, 1985.
>   Outlines developments in the consumer finance industry in Great Britain in the 1980's.

Meier, Robert C., William T. Newell, and Harold L. Pazer. *Simulation in Business and Economics.* Englewood Cliffs, N.J.: Prentice-Hall, 1969.

A very good explanation of the applications of Monte Carlo methods in economics and the generation of random numbers. Also discusses simulations in inventory, queuing, and forecasting problems in management science. Very accessible to the general audience.

Meigs, Robert F., and Walter B. Meigs. *Accounting: The Basis for Business Decisions.* 8th ed. New York: McGraw-Hill, 1990.

Provides a thorough introduction to accounting processes and applications. The discussion covers the accounting cycle and the preparation of statements.

Miller, David W., and Martin K. Starr. *Executive Decisions and Operations Research.* Englewood Cliffs, N.J.: Prentice-Hall, 1960.

Contains the classic explanations of the use of mathematical methods to assist in executive decision making. This 446-page book includes a lucid development of the payoff matrix concept used to integrate risk assessment into business decisions. Production, marketing, and personnel examples are included. Written for the student of business decisions.

Miller, Merton H. "Behavioral Rationality in Finance: The Case of Dividends." *Journal of Business* 58 (October, 1986): S451-S468.

Reviews the evidence from academic research on the effects of dividend policy on the value of the firm. Suitable for college students.

Miller, Merton H., and Franco Modigliani. "Dividend Policy, Growth, and the Valuation of Shares." *Journal of Business* 33 (October, 1961): 411-433.

This is the original article that presented the argument that in the absence of personal taxes, dividend policy does not affect firm value. Although technical in nature, this article is important for the intellectual foundations of much of the current literature on dividend policy.

Mills, C. Wright. *The Power Elite.* New York: Oxford University Press, 1959.

A stimulating book by a noted sociological observer of post-1945 American life and the reshaping of power and its uses and misuses by new elites, inclusive of the new leisure class. Although not slavishly devoted to Thorstein Veblen's form of critical analysis, it is in the

Veblenian tradition. Excellent notes replace a bibliography, and the index is helpful.

Moore, Carl L., and Robert K. Jaedicke. *Managerial Accounting.* 3d ed. Cincinnati: South-Western, 1972.
    Designed to explain the interpretation and use of accounting data by company managers. The first three chapters are useful in explaining financial statements and in discussing problem areas important to management.

Moriarty, Shane, and Carl P. Allen. *Cost Accounting.* 3d ed. New York: John Wiley & Sons, 1991.
    Provides an understanding of management needs for product cost information. Gives emphasis to the use of appropriate techniques for recording and analyzing such costs.

Morse, Wayne J., James R. Davis, and Al L. Hartgraves. *Management Accounting.* 3d ed. Reading, Mass.: Addison-Wesley, 1991.
    Designed to present management issues and the information required to make decisions relative to them. An excellent book that looks at the big picture but shows the details as well.

Naisbitt, John. *Megatrends 2000.* New York: William Morrow, 1990.
    This popular work offers some very strong and accurate predictions, based primarily on changes in technology, for the business world. Very interesting and easy to read.

Needles, Belverd E., Jr., Henry R. Anderson, and James C. Caldwell. *Principles of Accounting.* 4th ed. Boston, Mass.: Houghton Mifflin, 1990.
    A college-level introductory textbook designed for those with no previous experience in accounting. The first few chapters will introduce the concepts, measurement tools, and difficulties of accounting. Any similar introductory accounting text will serve the same purpose.

Neubert, Christopher, and Jack Withiam, Jr. *How to Handle Your Own Contracts.* New York: Drake, 1975.
    Neubert and Withiam do an excellent job of explaining the nature and function of contracts and providing a direct hands-on approach to the subject. Especially suited for people who are interested in starting their own businesses and/or doing work as independent contractors.

Nielsen, Waldemar A. *The Golden Donors: A New Anatomy of the Great Foundations.* New York: E. P. Dutton, 1985.

Offers a fascinating journey into the hearts and minds of the world's rich and influential philanthropic foundations. Provides insight into the inner workings of thirty-six of the largest foundations. An excellent research and reference guide.

O'Connell, Brian. *America's Voluntary Spirit.* New York: Foundation Center, 1983.

As the president of the Independent Sector, O'Connell spearheads a group that is a national coalition of voluntary organizations, foundations, and corporations. This book presents selected readings on a variety of nonprofit topics and provides a good general overview of the subject.

O'Neil, William J. *How to Make Money in Stocks.* New York: McGraw-Hill, 1991.

An excellent book for those interested in how to select stocks. A very well-prepared introduction to individual stock portfolio selection and management. Clear and very well written, with outstanding examples and graphs that apply the concepts.

O'Shaughnessy, John. *Competitive Marketing: A Strategic Approach.* Boston: Allen & Unwin, 1984.

Presents product differentiation from a marketing point of view. Contains a chapter on market segmentation where strategies relating to product differentiation are explained. Suitable for all audiences.

Ogilvy, David. *Confessions of an Advertising Man.* New York: Atheneum, 1987.

This short book focuses on how the advertising industry and its agencies operate. Full of the wisdom of a master of the field.

_____. *Ogilvy on Advertising.* New York: Crown, 1983.

Ogilvy, whose ideas influence most current advertising, delineates what works in advertising and addresses many philosophical issues. Fascinating gems from one of the industry's giants.

Osteryoung, Jerome S. *Capital Budgeting: Long-Term Asset Selection.* 2d ed. Columbus, Ohio: Grid, 1979.

Provides a comprehensive survey of all aspects of capital budgeting at an intermediate level. Appropriate for advanced undergraduate and graduate students and as a reference guide for business managers at all levels of management.

Ostheimer, Richard H. "Who Buys What?" *Journal of Marketing* 22 (January, 1958): 260-272.

Presents tabular findings of Ostheimer's study of the percentage division of total spending among major goods and services in the United States. Especially useful in providing a bibliography for further work using the U.S. government documents from the Bureau of Labor Statistics and Department of Commerce studies.

Peters, Tom, and Nancy Austin. *A Passion for Excellence.* New York: Warner Books, 1985.

This New York Times best-seller presents numerous case studies on how some businesses, both large and small, achieved and sustained success. Managers of all kinds of firms, including partnerships, can learn from the authors' inspiring tales of paying attention to details and pursuing a business dream.

Petersen, Harold Craig, and W. Cris Lewis. *Managerial Economics.* 2d ed. New York: Macmillan, 1990.

Chapter 8 surveys general, and some special, topics in cost theory from a managerial decision-making vantage point.

Porter, Sylvia. *Sylvia Porter's Money Book.* Garden City, N.Y.: Doubleday, 1975.

Covers the spectrum of consumer finance including spending, insurance, borrowing, and investing.

Pratten, Clifford. *Economies of Scale in Manufacturing Industry.* Cambridge, England: Cambridge University Press, 1971.

The most exhaustive empirical study of the extent of scale economies, Pratten's book covers twenty-five industries in the mid-1960's. Book 1 discusses sources of and measurement methods used for scale effects; book 2, the results of the industry studies; and book 3, conclusions and implications, including both technical and pecuniary economies of scale.

Rappaport, Alfred, ed. *Information for Decision Making: Quantitative and Behavioral Dimensions.* 2d ed. Englewood Cliffs, N.J.: Prentice-Hall, 1975.

This book provides the reader with a broad spectrum of information needs of the modern manager. It presents differing views of current issues regarding the type and amount of information required.

Reilly, Frank K. *Investments*. Chicago: Dryden Press, 1986.

An intermediate-level treatment of investment and portfolio theory that is oriented toward individuals who are preparing for a career in these fields. A mixture of descriptive material and theory is presented without excessive mathematics. An interesting feature is the inclusion of a number of profiles of scholars who have made significant contributions to the field.

Reilly, John W. *The Language of Real Estate*. 3d ed. Chicago: Real Estate Education, 1989.

A truly exceptional book. Clear, concise, and well-organized, it covers the entire spectrum of real estate terminology and related legal concepts, including contracts, corporations, and partnerships. Of special note are the many historical notations within the definitions. Anyone doing research in real estate, architecture, or construction should consult this book.

Reinhardt, U. E. "Break-Even Analysis for Lockheed's Tri-Star: An Application of Financial Theory." *Journal of Finance* 27 (September, 1973): 821-838.

This article illustrates the application of break-even analysis for decision making in the area of finance by using a case study of Lockheed.

Render, Barry, and Ralph M. Stair. *Quantitative Analysis for Management*. 3d ed. Boston: Allyn & Bacon, 1988.

This college-level text on quantitative methods includes a chapter on the assignment problem.

Ries, Al, and Jack Trout. *Positioning: The Battle for Your Mind*. New York: McGraw-Hill, 1981.

This readable book deals with the psychological aspects of advertising communications and is replete with examples of successful, and not so successful, ad campaigns. Ries and Trout's concept of positioning greatly influenced the current generation of advertising executives and advertisers.

Riggs, James L. *Engineering Economics*. 2d ed. New York: McGraw-Hill, 1982.

Contains a good discussion on multiple products and nonlinear break-even analysis in chapter 3. Particularly recommended for those readers who are interested in an advanced treatment of this subject.

Robinson, Newton Y. "The Acceleration Principle: Department Store Inventories, 1920-1956." *The American Economic Review* 48 (June, 1959): 30-35.

This study of the various factors believed to cause inventory investment found that the acceleration principle was easily the dominant explanation for department stores in the period mentioned.

Rose, Peter S. *Money and Capital Markets.* 3d ed. Homewood, Ill.: Richard D. Irwin, 1989.

Chapter 19, entitled "The Residential Mortgage Market," describes the historical, institutional, and legal environment behind the mortgage market. Also gives a brief description of alternative mortgages and ways in which banks can make their mortgages more liquid. This text is intended for undergraduates, but the descriptive approach of this chapter is accessible to a general audience.

Rosenau, Milton D., Jr. *Faster New Product Development.* New York: American Management Association, 1990.

An example of the use of product cycle in product planning. Shows how understanding the product cycle can lead to improved product strategies.

Ross, Marc. "Capital Budgeting Practices of Twelve Large Manufacturers." *Financial Management* 14 (Winter, 1986): 15-22.

A survey of modern capital budgeting techniques used in large corporations.

Rudelius, William, and W. Bruce Erickson. *An Introduction to Contemporary Business.* 4th ed. New York: Harcourt Brace Jovanovich, 1986.

Provides a solid introduction to the basics of business. Includes descriptions of business organizations, including the merits and problems of each. The nature of the text is general and would best meet the needs of individuals who are not familiar with business terminology and concepts.

Salvatore, Dominick. *Managerial Economics.* New York: McGraw-Hill, 1989.

Managerial economics involves the application of economic theory and its related tools of analysis to a variety of problem solving situations that face managers in both business firms and the public sector. This intermediate-level text devotes several chapters to developing both the theoretical framework and the statistical techniques for assessing the income effect on the demand for a product. Examples of measured income elasticities for different goods are given.

Samson, Danny. *Managerial Decision Analysis.* Homewood, Ill.: Richard D. Irwin, 1988.

A textbook designed for upper-division and graduate students. Readers interested in automated methods for risk assessment will find the discussion of computer analysis of decision trees to be comprehensive, clear, and concise. A large-scale investment analysis example is also included. A basic knowledge of statistics is presumed.

Simmitt, Jery, ed. *The Corporate 500: The Directory of Corporate Philanthropy.* 6th ed. San Francisco: Public Management Institute, 1987.

This massive (1200-page) reference work provides current and accurate information on corporate giving. Mergers and acquisitions, business profiles, corporate name changes, research, scholarships, sample grants, and related publications are included.

Sinkey, Joseph F., Jr. *Commercial Bank Financial Management in the Financial Services Industry.* 3d ed. New York: Macmillan, 1989.

Provides an in-depth and technical survey of financial management that is aimed at graduate students and those interested in commercial bank management.

Sirmans, C. F. *Real Estate Finance.* New York: McGraw-Hill, 1989.

The book describes itself as a "comprehensive coverage of real estate finance within a decision-making framework. Both the borrower's and lender's perspective are examined—making it of interest to students and readers of all backgrounds." This description is essentially accurate, especially because the book gives thorough discussions of both the legal environment and the financial analysis that are involved in buying property. Its presentation of the present value and other financial analysis is covered in a textbook style that might be difficult for the general reader.

Skousen, K. Fred, Harold Q. Langendorfer, and W. Steve Albrecht. *Principles of Accounting.* 2d ed. New York: Worth, 1983.

Written to convey the logic and usefulness of the accounting function in business, the authors have addressed the "whys" of the process, as well as the "hows." The text is clear and straightforward, and the numerical examples are easy to follow. Frequent summaries throughout each chapter help the reader keep track of new material as it is covered.

Smith, Charles B. *A Guide to Business Research.* Chicago: Nelson-Hall, 1981.

A complete guide to the mechanics of conducting research in the areas of business development, structure, and management. Provides a good checklist for anyone wishing to do business research for writing projects of examination of potential markets.

Smith, Jack L., Robert M. Keith, and William L. Stephens. *Accounting Principles.* 2d ed. New York: McGraw-Hill, 1983.

The authors have written on the assumption that the reader's exposure to business has been very limited. Short case histories appear throughout the book that have been drawn from such sources as *Fortune*, *Forbes*, *Harvard Business Review*, securities and exchange releases, and *The Wall Street Journal* and show how accounting principles function in the everyday world of business.

Solmon, Lewis C. *Economics: Topics for Self Study.* New York: Appleton-Century-Crofts, 1972.

Essentially a self-study text with an accompanying workbook, which also provides a brief text and extensive application question and answers. This text and workbook provide an excellent source for the beginner or a good reference tool for the more advanced reader. Chapters 2, 3, and 28 provide a diverse look at business decisions and how costs are incorporated into profit maximization assumptions.

Soloman, Lanny M., Richard J. Vargo, and Larry M. Walther. *Financial Accounting.* 2d ed. New York: John Wiley & Sons, 1989.

An introduction to the principles and practices of accounting that assumes no previous background in accounting.

Standard & Poor's Corporation. *Standard & Poor's Ratings Guide.* New York: McGraw-Hill, 1979.

How a rating agency rates bonds.

Stanton, William J. *Fundamentals of Marketing.* New York: McGraw-Hill, 1981.

A complete text of marketing concepts, ideas, and strategies. Provides a good step-by-step approach to the understanding of marketing and its impact on modern business development.

Stevenson, William J. *Introduction to Management Science*. Homewood,
Ill.: Richard D. Irwin, 1989.
  A textbook for a management science course that examines utility
  theory and Bayesian decision making.

Stigum, Marcia. *Money Market Calculations: Yields, Break-Evens, and
Arbitrage*. Homewood, Ill.: Dow Jones-Irwin, 1981.
  An excellent sourcebook for price and yield calculations necessary in
  financial market arbitrage transactions. The book is very clearly written. The formulas are easy to understand, and numerous examples are
  given. Of practical interest, the methods and equations are the ones
  most often used by actual financial market participants.

Stone, Merlin. *Product Planning: An Integrated Approach*. New York:
Macmillan Press, 1976.
  Introduces product planning from an economist's point of view and
  discusses it relative to product cycle theory and practice. Easy reading
  for the manager or student.

Taggert, Robert A. "Secular Trends in the Financing of Corporations." In
Corporate Capital Structures in the United States, edited by Benjamin M.
Friedman. Chicago: University of Chicago Press, 1985.
  A description of trends concerning the choices made by corporations
  in arranging financing in stock and credit markets.

Taylor, Bernard W. *Introduction to Management Science*. 3d ed. Boston:
Allyn & Bacon, 1990.
  Chapter 22 is on break-even analysis. It starts from simple explanation
  of terms and concepts and ends with nonlinear cost and revenue
  functions using calculus. Good reading for both beginners and advanced readers.

Teweles, Richard J., and Frank J. Jones. *The Futures Game*. 2d ed. New
York: McGraw-Hill, 1987.
  A popular, how-to book, full of practical advice and written by two
  eminent researchers.

Trachtman, Michael G. *What Every Executive Better Know About the
Law*. New York: Simon & Schuster, 1987.
  This 250-page book offers insight into contract law at the executive-
  management level. An excellent legal reference work not only for
  contracts but for other important legal areas as well. For the advanced
  reader.

Train, Kenneth. *Qualitative Choice Analysis: Theory, Econometrics, and an Application to Automobile Demand.* Cambridge, Mass.: MIT Press, 1986.

The early chapters, introducing the specification of qualitative response models, their estimation, hypothesis testing, and goodness of fit, are very clearly written. The book also has a very good chapter on generalized extreme value models. The second half of the book is a good exposition of the techniques as they are applied to automobile demand in California.

Udell, John G., and Gene R. Laczniak. *Marketing in an Age of Change: An Introduction.* New York: John Wiley & sons, 1981.

A marketing textbook. Chapter 11 provides a view to how life cycles are presented in an academic setting. Provides good references.

Van Horne, James C. *Financial Market Rates and Market Flows.* 2d ed. Englewood Cliffs, N.J.: Prentice-Hall, 1984.

Describes the valuation of bonds and demonstrates the inverse relationship between the price and interest rate of an individual bond. Suitable for motivated college students.

_____ . *Fundamentals of Financial Management.* 7th ed. Englewood Cliffs, N.J.: Prentice-Hall, 1989.

Chapter 18 contains a readable discussion of many of the salient issues related to dividend policy.

Vichas, Robert P. *Handbook of Financial Mathematics, Formulas, and Tables.* Englewood Cliffs, N.J.: Prentice-Hall, 1979.

Contains explanations of specific mathematical formulas that can be used for discounting. This volume also contains tables that can be used to determine discount factors for a wide variety of discount rates. Accessible to college students.

Wasson, Chester R. *Dynamic Competitive Strategy and Product Life Cycles.* St. Charles, Ill.: Challenge Books, 1974.

An in-depth book on product cycles. Covers both the behavioral aspects of the product cycle and the aspects of managing products over their life cycle. Contains good examples and is enjoyable to read.

Webb, Samuel C. *Managerial Economics.* Boston: Houghton Mifflin, 1976.

One of the few textbooks of applied microeconomics that discusses the importance to business interests of income elasticity of demand, along with several other types of elasticities.

Weiner, Stuart. "Why Are So Few Financial Assets Indexed to Inflation?" *Economic Review* 5 (May, 1983): 3-18.
Discusses why there are so few price-indexed securities.

Weingartner, H. Martin. "Capital Rationing: N Authors in Search of a Plot." *Journal of Finance* 31 (December, 1977): 1403-1431.
Presents a linear programming approach to capital budgeting.

Weston, J. Fred, and Eugene F. Brigham. *Essentials of Managerial Finance.* 9th ed. Chicago: Dryden Press, 1989.
One of the bibles in its field, this book presents the manager's perspective on nearly all aspects of managerial finance, including financial statements, financial analyses, and the management of assets and liabilities. In addition, the book explains how various tax policies may influence capital investment decisions. Designed primarily for use as a college text but should be quite readable for nonspecialists, too.

Whitmyer, Claude, Salli Rasberry, and Michael Phillips. *Running a One-Person Business.* Berkeley, Calif.: Ten Speed Press, 1988.
Covers many of the down-to-earth topics that any successful manager of a small business, sole proprietorship, or partnership should understand. The topics discussed include starting the business, bookkeeping, marketing, finance, and legal matters, and the support services that are required.

Wilhelm, Jochen. *Arbitrage Theory.* New York: Springer-Verlag, 1985.
A highly technical book, containing many equations, lemmas, and proofs, in the fashion of a mathematical treatise. Definitely not for introductory purposes. For readers with a taste for mathematics, however, the book serves well, essentially developing arbitrage pricing theory through a mathematical presentation. One of a series of published college lectures.

Wilkes, F. M. *Capital Budgeting Techniques.* New York: John Wiley & Sons, 1977.
An advanced treatment of capital budgeting techniques that introduces linear programming, integer linear problems, and nonlinear and stochastic problems into the investment selection process. Moderate

mathematical abilities are required. The book covers all aspects of the capital budgeting decision.

Wood, John H., and Norma L. Wood. *Financial Markets*. New York: Harcourt Brace Jovanovich, 1985.

A text designed for money market courses. Detailed descriptions of financial instruments are provided. Contains an excellent discussion of the relationships between interest rates, the yield to maturity, and financial markets in chapters 18, 19, and 20. Includes author and subject indexes, references, figures, and tables.

Wright, Paul K., and David A. Bourn. *Manufacturing Intelligence*. Reading, Mass.: Addison-Wesley, 1988.

Describes, in fairly nontechnical terms, the use of artificial intelligence techniques in capturing the know-how of skilled manufacturing craftspeople so that intelligent machines can make small batches of customized products without human intervention. Instead of being built into machines, as under the old hard automation, expertise can be written into control software. Because many operations such as metal cutting are not well understood scientifically, precise manufacturing requires mimicking the skills and decision-making processes of craftspeople.

QUANTITATIVE METHODS

Allen, R. G. D. *Mathematical Analysis for Economists*. London: Macmillan, 1938.

A classic text of the use of mathematics in economics. Allen begins with numbers and functions and ends with the calculus of variations. He also wrote *Mathematical Economics* (London: Macmillan, 1956).

Amemiya, Takeshi. "Qualitative Response Models: A Survey." *Journal of Economic Literature* 19 (December, 1981): 1483-1536.

This survey article was written for those who have a rudimentary knowledge of statistics but who do not have familiarity with discrete choice modeling. It is meant to introduce the reader to the issues in qualitative response models rather than explicate with mathematical rigor or explore new methods in statistics.

Anderson, David R., Dennis J. Sweeney, and Thomas A. Williams. *An Introduction to Management Science: Quantitative Approaches to Decision Making*. St. Paul, Minn.: West, 1988.

A textbook that is designed for a college course in quantitative methods. Contains a chapter that deals with Bayesian decision making and a chapter that deals with utility theory, applying both to management science.

_____ . *Statistics for Business and Economics*. St. Paul, Minn.: West, 1984.

A college textbook that is designed for a college course in statistics. Devotes several chapters to mean-variance techniques that compare two or more populations.

Anderson, Theodore W. *The Statistical Analysis of Time Series*. New York: John Wiley & Sons, 1971.

This reference is very complete, although it requires the reader to understand some basic linear algebra. Anderson introduces the techniques that can be used to estimate the spectrum, the gain, and the coherence and describes the technique used to estimate the joint spectrum of several time series. Also presents a number of applications and examples.

Arrow, Kenneth J., and Michael D. Intriligator, eds. *Handbook of Mathematical Economics.* 3 vols. Amsterdam: North-Holland, 1981-1986.
A veritable, and somewhat imposing, encyclopedia of mathematical economics. This set consists of essays written on the major themes by several prominent mathematical economists. Not for the novice.

Auerbach, Alan J. "The Index of Leading Indicators: 'Measure Without Theory' Thirty-five Years Later." *Review of Economics and Statistics* 64 (1982): 589-595.
This paper studies the ability of the leading indicators to predict the level of the gross national product. Somewhat technical.

Bacon, Robert. *A First Course in Econometric Theory.* Oxford, England: Oxford University Press, 1988.
A textbook on econometric methods and models, with emphasis on the applications and the use of models and on the methods of intermediate levels of difficulty. Assumes a knowledge of basic economics and mathematics.

Becker, William E., and Donald L. Harnett. *Business and Economic Statistics with Computer Applications.* Reading, Mass.: Addison-Wesley, 1987.
A good introduction to statistics, providing worked examples of each type of statistical problem. Comes with a user-friendly Microstat disk and a computer workbook, so the reader can conduct statistical tests. This combination of text and disk helps the reader acquire both a theoretical and a practical background.

Beckman, Barry A., and Tracy R. Tapscott. "Composite Indexes of Leading, Coincident, and Lagging Indicators." *Survey of Current Business* 67, no. 11 (1987): 24-28.
A good summary of how the composite indexes are computed.

Ben-Akiva, Moshe, and Steven R. Lerman. *Discrete Choice Analysis: Theory and Application to Travel Demand.* Cambridge, Mass.: MIT Press, 1985.
The early chapters of this book are devoted to some basic ideas in statistics and economics necessary for the untrained reader to follow the later material on model specification, hypothesis testing, and sampling. The authors address binary, multinomial, and multivariate discrete choice models.

Bergstrom, A. R., ed. *Statistical Inference in Continuous Time Economic Models*. Amsterdam: North-Holland, 1976.

Bergstrom presents ten research projects produced by five authors. Each project develops techniques that can be used to produce economic models consisting of a system of continuous-time stochastic equations. Readers will probably be most interested in chapter 10, in which a continuous-time stochastic model of the economy of Great Britain is created and then tested using real-world data.

Berndt, Ernst. *The Practice of Econometrics: Classic and Contemporary*. Reading, Mass.: Addison-Wesley, 1991.

An advanced undergraduate or beginning graduate text in applied econometrics. While the coverage is quite broad, the treatment of maximum likelihood in the context of specific examples, which the reader may duplicate, is very helpful.

Bierman, Harold, Charles P. Bonini, and Warren H. Hausman. *Quantitative Analysis for Business Decisions*. Homewood, Ill.: Richard D. Irwin, 1991.

A textbook that is designed for a college course in business-oriented quantitative methods and presents chapters on both Bayesian decision making and utility theory.

Box, George E. P., and Gwilym M. Jenkins. *Time Series Analysis: Forecasting and Control*. San Francisco: Holden-Day, 1970.

The best book on the Box-Jenkins technique of time series analysis, which involves the identification of trends within a time series. These trends, which include autoregressive, moving-average, and seasonal components, can be identified by examining the correlations of the elements of a time series with its past values, leaving a residual series that is truly random. Presupposes that the reader has advanced mathematical training.

Brems, Hans. *Quantitative Economic Theory: A Synthetic Approach*. New York: John Wiley & Sons, 1968.

Brems does a good job balancing his verbal explanation with his mathematical explanation of John von Neumann's numerical valuation of utility. Recommended for high school and college students.

Brennan, Michael J., and Thomas M. Carroll. *A Preface to Quantitative Economics and Econometrics*. 4th ed. Cincinnati: South-Western, 1987.

This 550-page text introduces the student to mathematical, statistical, and econometric methods and models in economics. A knowledge of basic economics, but no knowledge of college-level mathematics, is assumed.

Bressler, Barry. *A Unified Introduction to Mathematical Economics.* New York: Harper & Row, 1975.
This textbook provides a particularly thorough and approachable introduction to mathematical concepts of optima and to the underlying mathematical concepts and many applications.

Brightman, Harvey. *Statistics in Plain English.* Cincinnati: South-Western, 1986.
Provides an excellent introduction to basic statistical theory. The author keeps explanations as simple as possible. Exercises help the reader work through fundamental problems, and the workbook format gives the reader an opportunity to practice skills.

Bristol, James D. *An Introduction to Linear Programming.* Boston: D. C. Heath, 1963.
Designed for high school and beginning college students, this book relies on graphs and illustrations rather than algebra as an approach to explaining linear programming principles.

Brown, Robert Goodell. *Smoothing, Forecasting, and Prediction of Discrete Time Series.* Englewood Cliffs, N.J.: Prentice-Hall, 1963.
In this book, Brown presents the time series technique of exponential smoothing.

Buffa, Elwood S., and James S. Dyer. *Management Science/Operations Research: Model Formulation and Solutions Methods.* New York: John Wiley & Sons, 1977.
A standard college textbook on quantitative methods that covers Bayesian decision making and utility theory.

Burmeister, Edwin, and A. Rodney Dobell. *Mathematical Theories of Economic Growth.* New York: Macmillan, 1970.
A textbook that covers in detail descriptive neoclassical growth models, as well as optimal growth literature. Uses high-level mathematics and for this reason is appropriate for advanced undergraduates and specialists.

Chatfield, Christopher. *The Analysis of Time Series: An Introduction*. 4th ed. New York: Chapman and Hall, 1989.

Spectral analysis is presented in chapters 6 and 7. Chatfield defines the spectrum, provides examples, and presents the techniques currently used to estimate the spectrum. Also shows how to construct confidence intervals for the spectrum and discusses the advantages and disadvantages of spectral analysis.

Chiang, Alpha C. *Fundamental Methods of Mathematical Economics*. 3d ed. New York: McGraw-Hill, 1984.

A standard textbook of mathematical economics in most graduate and undergraduate programs in economics in the United States. Defines the range of mathematical modeling tools which modern economists are expected to know. A large and difficult, but rewarding, book.

Clower, Robert W., Philip E. Graves, and Robert L. Sexton. *Intermediate Microeconomics*. San Diego: Harcourt Brace Jovanovich, 1988.

The appendix to chapter 3 offers a good introduction to econometric models in the specific context of supply and demand.

Cowell, F. A. *Measuring Inequality*. Oxford, England: Philip Alan, 1977.

This monograph compares various methods of charting inequality and computing inequality measures. Too technical for the casual reader, but useful for practitioners who may need to calculate inequality measures.

Daellenbach, Hans G., and Earl J. Bell. *User's Guide to Linear Programming*. Englewood Cliffs, N.J.: Prentice-Hall, 1970.

Approaches linear programming from the perspective of a decision maker and focuses on recognizing problems and formulating linear programming models rather than on solving the models.

Dantzig, George B. *Linear Programming and Extensions*. Princeton, N.J.: Princeton University Press, 1963.

The classical reference to linear programming. It is mathematically sophisticated and not recommended for the nontechnical reader.

Dauten, Carl A., and Lloyd M. Valentine. *Business Cycles and Forecasting*. 5th ed. Cincinnati: South-Western, 1978.

Easy reading with good application to economic theory. Provides a good understanding of forecasting as it pertains to the economy, from an economic standpoint as opposed to the more technical approach adopted by most texts.

Diewert, W. E. "Applications of Duality Theory." In *Frontiers of Quantitative Economics*, edited by M. D. Intriligator and D. A. Kendrick. Vol. 2. New York: Elsevier, 1974.
    While not simplistic in its presentation, this thorough survey by one of the central contributors to the field gives a sound heuristic approach to the formal theory, as well as providing illuminating historical notes.

_____. "Duality Approaches to Microeconomic Theory." In *Handbook of Mathematical Economics*, edited by K. J. Arrow and M. D. Intriligator. Vol. 2. New York: Elsevier, 1982.
    Slightly more pedagogical than Diewert's 1974 piece, this article provides an excellent introduction to the general theory of duality. Includes an exhaustive reference list.

Dorfman, Robert, Paul A. Samuelson, and Robert M. Solow. *Linear Programming and Economic Analysis*. New York: McGraw-Hill, 1958.
    The classic reference on linear programming.

Dowling, Edward T. *Introduction to Mathematical Economics*. 2d ed. New York: McGraw-Hill, 1991.
    In this superb text/workbook, Dowling proves to be extremely strong in the area of the instruction of techniques. Covers calculus, linear algebra, difference and differential equations, and the calculus of variations. An excellent point of departure for beginners.

_____. *Mathematics for Economists*. New York: McGraw-Hill, 1980.
    A modern text giving a superb intuitive and formal presentation of linear programming and the associated duality. Very accessible.

Fels, Rendigs, and C. Elton Hinshaw. *Forecasting and Recognizing Business Cycle Turning Points*. New York: National Bureau of Economic Research, 1968.
    Compares performance in recognizing business cycle turning points between the National Bureau of Economic Research and the Federal Reserve Board. Suitable for a general audience.

Fisher, Irving. *The Making of Index Numbers: A Study of Their Varieties, Tests, and Reliability*. 2d ed. Boston: Houghton Mifflin, 1927.
    A classic study of economic index numbers. It is relatively easy to read and very informative.

_____. *The Purchasing Power of Money.* Rev. ed. New York: Augustus M. Kelley, 1963.
In chapter 13, Fisher presents his proposal for indexing debts.

Fishman, George S. *Spectral Methods in Economics.* Cambridge, Mass.: Harvard University Press, 1969.
Somewhat less technical than the other references included in this bibliography. Fishman explains the concept of the spectrum by using examples from economics and describes the techniques that are used to estimate it using several examples. Also presents the concepts of gain and coherence, with examples.

Fox, Karl A. *Intermediate Economic Statistics.* New York: John Wiley & Sons, 1968.
Chapter 5 of this text contains a lengthy discussion of price and quantity index numbers. Interesting and easy to read.

Freund, John E., Frank J. Williams, and Benjamin M. Perles. *Elementary Business Statistics.* Englewood Cliffs, N.J.: Prentice-Hall, 1988.
These authors understand and present clearly the relationship between regression and correlation analyses. They show how the correlation coefficient can be derived from a regression analysis. The authors present real-life situations in which regression or correlation analysis can be used to facilitate decision making.

Frumkin, Norman. *Guide to Economic Indicators.* Armonk, N.Y.: M. E. Sharpe, 1990.
This 242-page book is a comprehensive guide to a wide range of economic indicators released by government agencies, as well as private organizations. Frumkin makes the study of leads and lags understandable to the general public. Indicators are grouped in several topics: aggregate demand and supply, labor, inflation, finance, government, international, cyclical indicators, and economic well-being. Its format includes description, data sources, methodology, accuracy, and the significance of constructing the indicators. Tables and figures are included. Suitable for a general audience.

_____. *Tracking America's Economy.* Armonk, N.Y.: M. E. Sharpe, 1987.
Explains the use of leading and lagging economic indicators as tools to forecast the business cycle. Provides information on how to assess

the statements of economic analysts and politicians about the state of the economy. For the nonexpert.

Gandolfo, Giancarlo. *Qualitative Analysis and Econometric Estimation of Continuous Time Dynamic Models*. Amsterdam: North-Holland, 1981.
Gandolfo presents a general procedure which can be used to estimate the values taken on by any unknown coefficients (or parameters) appearing in a continuous-time stochastic model. These procedures are invaluable if one is to apply continuous-time stochastic techniques to real-world economies. In the last three chapters, Gandolfo shows how his procedures can be used to construct a disequilibrium model of exchange-rate adjustment.

Glenberg, Arthur M. *Learning from Data: An Introduction to Statistical Reasoning*. New York: Harcourt Brace Jovanovich, 1988.
Presents an interesting approach to the study of statistics. The author emphasizes the use of statistical techniques in decision making, not another cookbook of how-to's.

Gordon, Gilbert, Israel Pressman, and Sanford Cohn. *Quantitative Decision Making for Business*. Englewood Cliffs, N.J.: Prentice-Hall, 1990.
A business textbook on quantitative methods that contains chapters about Bayesian decision making and utility theory. Suitable for college students.

Granger, C. W. J., and Paul Newbold. *Forecasting Economic Time Series*. Belmont, Calif.: Lifetime Learning Publications, 1983.
A thorough, if demanding, survey of contemporary time series analysis techniques.

Greene, William H. *Econometric Analysis*. New York: Macmillan, 1990.
A graduate text in econometrics. Assumes knowledge of mathematical statistics and linear algebra. The presentation of the theory of maximum likelihood in econometrics is very good.

Griliches, Zvi, ed. *Price Indexes and Quality Changes*. Cambridge, Mass.: Harvard University Press, 1971.
A collection of essays on price indexes by several scholars. Chapters 1 and 3 deal with hedonic price indexes, a subject of importance when commodities are altered over the passage of time.

Gujarati, Damodar. *Basic Econometrics*. 2d ed. New York: McGraw-Hill, 1988.

A good introduction to econometrics, this textbook is suitable for advanced undergraduates and graduate students. Thoroughly covers econometric theory and offers many examples of "real world" applications. Presumes knowledge of statistical theory.

Hacche, Graham. *The Theory of Economic Growth: An Introduction.* New York: St. Martin's Press, 1979.
An introductory book on growth theories that limits the use of mathematics. Strong focus on discussion of technical change. Appropriate for undergraduate economics students.

Hair, Joseph F., Jr., R. Anderson, and R. Tatham. *Multivariate Data Analysis.* 2d ed. New York: Macmillan, 1987.
One of the more readable books in multivariate analysis. Provides an overall understanding of multivariate techniques, yet differs from other books in this field because the text portion is followed by articles explaining the most common applications.

Harmon, Harry H. *Modern Factor Analysis.* 3d ed. Chicago: University of Chicago Press, 1976.
Provides a detailed description of some of the most commonly used factor rotation techniques. Recommended for those who would like a more detailed discussion on the theory and practice of rotation techniques.

Heitzman, William R., and Frederick W. Mueller. *Statistics for Business and Economics.* Boston: Allyn & Bacon, 1980.
A standard statistics textbook that is designed for college students. Contains several chapters on mean-variance techniques.

Hestenes, Magnus. *Calculus of Variations and Optimal Control Theory.* New York: John Wiley & Sons, 1966.
This authoritative study of the mathematics of optima covers the methods most commonly used by economists in studying intertemporal optima, from the viewpoint of advanced mathematics. Excellent mathematical preparation is required of the student who approaches this book.

Hinkle, Dennis E., William Wiersma, and Stephen S. Jurs. *Applied Statistics for the Behavioral Sciences.* 2d ed. Boston: Houghton Mifflin, 1988.
The authors present an easy-to-understand account of correlation and regression analyses. Their book provides examples of the application

of correlation and regression techniques in other disciplines, such as psychology and education.

Hogg, Robert V., and Allen T. Craig. *Introduction to Mathematical Statistics.* 3d ed. New York: Macmillan, 1970.
A text in mathematical statistics for the advanced undergraduate. The treatment of maximum likelihood estimation is brief but comprehensible, limited to discussions of estimation of the first and second moments of simple univariate and multivariate distributions.

Hymans, Saul H. "On the Use of Leading Indicators to Predict Cyclical Turning Points." *Brookings Papers on Economic Activity* 2 (1973): 339-384.
A classic study.

Intriligator, Michael D. *Econometric Models: Techniques and Applications.* Englewood Cliffs, N.J.: Prentice-Hall, 1978.
Chapter 2 presents perhaps the best overall introduction to models in economics, stressing econometric models. The discussion assumes a knowledge of intermediate economic theory and mathematical analysis.

_____. *Mathematical Optimization and Economic Theory.* Englewood Cliffs, N.J.: Prentice-Hall, 1971.
A study of the methods of mathematical optimization, including intertemporal optima and Pareto optima, with their applications in economic theory. Probably best suited to the needs of graduate students in economics.

Johnson, A. C., Jr., Marvin B. Johnson, and R. C. Buse. *Econometrics: Basic and Applied.* New York: Macmillan, 1986.
Contains information on applied research. A knowledge of calculus will be useful to make use of this text, which could serve as a comprehensive textbook on the subject.

Jones, Hywel G. *An Introduction to Modern Theories of Economic Growth.* New York: McGraw-Hill, 1976.
Probably one of the few books on growth models that does not require calculus. Discusses the fundamental properties of various growth models supplemented and provides the historical background of the underlying theories.

Kendall, Maurice G., and Alan Stuart. *The Advanced Theory of Statistics.* 3 vols. New York: Hafner, 1969-1976.
A reference book for the student with advanced training in statistics and mathematics. The authors consider the application of maximum likelihood to many distributions in statistics.

Kennedy, Peter. *A Guide to Econometrics.* Cambridge, Mass.: MIT Press, 1984.
Essential for all econometrics students. It provides excellent intuitive explanations of the theory of econometrics using a minimum of mathematics. Appendices following each chapter quickly present the material in mathematical notation. Kennedy's book should be used as a companion text, as it does not provide examples of applications.

Kim, Kyun. *Equilibrium Business Cycle Theory in Historical Perspective.* Cambridge, England: Cambridge University Press, 1987.
Kim traces the historical development of econometric macroeconomic models, relating these models to their ability to explain business cycle phenomena such as inflation and unemployment. Discusses more recent approaches to macroeconomic econometrics. Some readers may find this book to be too technical.

Kmenta, Jan. *Elements of Econometrics.* New York: Macmillan, 1971.
In this classic econometrics text, Kmenta presents a rigorous review of statistical theory before delving into econometrics. This book is geared more toward the theory than the application of econometric techniques. Suitable for the advanced undergraduate with a solid math background and the graduate student.

Kravis, Irving B. "Comparative Studies of National Incomes and Prices." *Journal of Economic Literature* 22 (March, 1984): 1-39.
Kravis examines the issue of how to convert incomes that are expressed in each country's domestic currency into a common currency. He finds that the usual practice of using exchange rates tends to overstate differences in income per capita. A better conversion method uses indexes of each currency's purchasing power that are constructed from detailed price surveys that allow more direct comparison of purchasing power.

Lapin, Lawrence L. *Statistics for Modern Business Decisions.* New York: Harcourt Brace Jovanovich, 1982.

A textbook for a college business course that uses statistics. Chapters on mean-variance techniques are presented.

Levin, Richard I. *Statistics for Management*. Englewood Cliffs, N.J.: Prentice-Hall, 1987.

This text is representative of a series for management students that deals with statistics. Presents least squares in a relatively simple approach but does require some knowledge of algebra to comprehend. There are many such texts and the reader is encouraged to find the one with which he or she feels most comfortable.

Lindley, D. V. *Introduction to Probability and Statistics from a Bayesian Viewpoint*. Cambridge, England: Cambridge University Press, 1965.

A comprehensive introduction to probability and statistics. Requires some knowledge of calculus.

Lipsey, Robert E., and Irving B. Kravis. *Is the United States Really Falling Behind?* New York: Conference Board, 1987.

Lipsey and Kravis review the evidence concerning productivity in the United States and other countries, addressing issues such as measurement problems, trends, relative rankings, underlying causes, and policy options.

Lipsey, Robert E., and Helen Stone Tice, eds. *The Measurement of Saving, Investment, and Wealth*. National Bureau of Economic Research Conference on Research in Income and Wealth 52. Chicago: University of Chicago Press, 1989.

Part of a technical series which examines various aspects of the measurement of income and wealth. While this volume analyzes some of the problems encountered in measuring saving, it will appeal primarily to those interested in technical details.

Lorenz, M. O. "Methods of Measuring the Concentration of Wealth." *Publications of the American Statistical Association* 9 (June, 1905): 209-219.

This article first defined the Lorenz curve and is useful in showing the inferior methods of illustrating wealth distribution which preceded it. Suitable for the general reader.

Lovell, Michael C. *Macroeconomics: Measurement, Theory, and Policy*. New York: John Wiley & Sons, 1975.

Chapter 11 of this textbook contains several sections in which price indexes are discussed. There is a good appendix to this chapter that discusses both quantity and price indexes.

Maddala, G. S. *Limited-Dependent and Qualitative Variables in Econometrics*. Cambridge, England: Cambridge University Press, 1983.
This graduate-level text is the most thorough and comprehensive treatment of qualitative response models, as well as those models which deal with dependent variables that are either censored or truncated.

Mason, Robert D., and Douglas A. Lind. *Statistical Techniques in Business and Economics*. Homewood, Ill.: Richard D. Irwin, 1990.
A text that examines statistical techniques and contains several chapters on mean-variance analysis. Suitable for college students.

Metzger, Robert W. *Elementary Mathematical Programming*. New York: John Wiley & Sons, 1967.
An elementary description of several methods of mathematical programming. Designed for people in business and industry with a minimal mathematical background.

Moore, G. H. "The Analysis of Economic Indicators." *Scientific American* 232 (January, 1975): 17-23.
A good exposition by one of the leading proponents of the indicator approach.

Mulaik, Stanley A. *The Foundations of Factor Analysis*. New York: McGraw-Hill, 1972.
Very comprehensive, includes a brief history of factor analysis. Also included is a discussion on the difference between using factor analysis for exploratory rather than confirmatory purposes. In general, the approach used is mathematical and is fairly difficult to follow for nontechnical readers.

Nelson, Charles R. *Applied Time Series Analysis*. San Francisco: Holden-Day, 1973.
Perhaps the best, most accessible introduction to contemporary time series analysis.

Newman, Peter K. *Readings in Mathematical Economics*. 2 vols. Baltimore: The Johns Hopkins University Press, 1968.

A collection of papers that show the applicability of, and range of technique in, mathematical economics. Many of these papers remain definitive works in the field, though the level of difficulty is as varied as the techniques that are employed.

Overall, John E., and C. James Klett. *Applied Multivariate Analysis.* New York: McGraw-Hill, 1972.
Fairly advanced treatment of factor analytic approach. Although it is application oriented, the interested reader can find discussions on and detailed descriptions of factor rotation methods such as varimax, quartimax, and equimax.

Pearson, A. W., and K. Holden. *Mathematics for Economists.* London: David & Charles, 1975.
Provides the basic level of mathematics that is required for an understanding of least squares. Designed for those with a very limited mathematical background. Straightforward and helpful.

Pindyck, Robert S., and Daniel L. Rubinfield. *Econometric Models and Economic Forecasts.* New York: McGraw-Hill, 1981.
Another classic econometrics textbook. Provides a brief review of statistical theory and an extensive presentation of basic and advanced econometric techniques. Offers numerous examples of real-world applications. Suitable for the advanced undergraduate with a solid math background and the graduate student.

Plane, Donald R., and Edward B. Oppermann. *Business and Economic Statistics.* Plano, Tex.: Business Publications, 1981.
A textbook for a college statistics course that applies mean-variance techniques in several chapters.

Press, S. James. *Bayesian Statistics: Principles, Models, and Applications.* New York: John Wiley & Sons, 1989.
A well-written book that provides a lively introduction to Bayesian statistics. An especially valuable section contains a description of available Bayesian statistical computer programs and where they can be obtained.

Render, Barry, and Ralph M. Stair. *Quantitative Analysis for Management.* Boston: Allyn & Bacon, 1988.
This college-level text on quantitative methods includes four chapters on linear programming with illustrations, examples, and solved problems.

Schmookler, Jacob. *Invention and Economic Growth*. Cambridge, Mass.: Harvard University Press, 1966.

On the basis of extensive patent statistics, this noteworthy work, even though challenged in part, holds that while intellectual stimuli explain the overall course of inventive activity, only market demand can account for the timing and appearance of specific inventions.

Sheffrin, Steven M., David A. Wilton, and David M. Prescott. *Macroeconomics: Theory and Policy*. Oxford, England: Oxford University Press, 1987.

Develops a macroeconomic model for discussing various policy issues and analyzes recent developments in macroeconomic research and modeling. No mathematics beyond high school algebra is required.

Shell, Karl, ed. *Essays in the Theory of Optimal Economic Growth*. Cambridge, Mass.: MIT Press, 1967.

A collection of fifteen articles on optimal growth models. All the models use optimal control techniques to investigate various aspects of growth. Appropriate for specialists.

Silberberg, Eugene. *The Structure of Economics*. 2d ed. New York: McGraw-Hill, 1990.

A graduate text that presents the requisite mathematics, and then applies it to the theory of the firm, the theory of the consumer, general equilibrium analysis, and intertemporal optimization.

Sommers, Albert T., and Lucille R. Blau. *The U.S. Economy Demystified: What Major Economic Statistics Mean and Their Significance for Business*. Lexington, Mass.: Lexington Books, 1988.

For in-depth, nontechnical explanations of economic statistics, an excellent source. Recommended highly for all readers.

Spivey, W. Allen. *Linear Programming: An Introduction*. New York: Macmillan, 1964.

Provides a self-contained and reasonable introduction to linear programming and other mathematical programming topics. The exposition is somewhat mathematical and requires some background in algebra.

Stengel, Robert F. *Stochastic Optimal Control*. New York: Wiley-Interscience, 1986.

In chapters 1 through 3, Stengel presents an introduction to dynamic modeling. Chapter 4 presents the Kalman filter, which can be used first to estimate the structure of a system of continuous-time stochastic equations and then to forecast the future behavior of the system. Finally, chapters 5 and 6 show how an economist can model the impact of attempts to control the system of equations.

Stuvel, G. *The Index-Number Problem and Its Solution.* Basingstoke, England: Macmillan, 1989.
An up-to-date scholarly book on the classic index-number problem. Well written and easy to read.

Takayama, Akira. *Mathematical Economics.* 2d ed. Cambridge, England: Cambridge University Press, 1985.
Requiring a base in formal mathematical analysis, Takayama delivers an expansive coverage of the advances in mathematical economics since the 1950's. There is an emphasis on mathematical programming, general equilibrium analysis, and growth theory.

U.S. Bureau of Economic Analysis. *GNP: An Overview of Source Data and Estimating Methods.* Methodology Paper Series MP-4. Washington, D.C.: Government Printing Office, 1987.
A simple presentation of the methodology of the estimation of the national product and income accounts. Focuses on a detailed presentation of the sources of data and the estimating methods that are used in preparing estimates of all income-side and product-side components of the gross national product, including the net national product.

U.S. Bureau of Labor Statistics. *The Consumer Price Index: History and Techniques.* Bulletin 1517. Washington, D.C.: Government Printing Office, 1966.
Although dated, this publication describes the early development of the CPI in the United States.

_____ . *Handbook of Methods.* Bulletin 2285. Washington, D.C.: Government Printing Office, 1988.
This publication describes the process of measuring the Consumer Price Index in the United States.

U.S. Department of Commerce. *Survey of Current Business.* Washington, D.C.: Government Printing Office.
This monthly periodical contains data on 111 different indicators, as well as on the three composite indexes.

U.S. Department of Commerce. Bureau of the Census. *Current Population Reports. Series P-60, Consumer Income.* Washington, D.C.: Government Printing Office, 1976-
These reports, which are issued periodically, include statistical data and narrative descriptions of measures of income and income equality, as well as detailed analyses of the various aspects of these measures.

U.S. Department of Commerce. Bureau of Economic Analysis. *Handbook of Cyclical Indicators: A Supplement to the Business Conditions Digest.* Washington, D.C.: Government Printing Office, 1984.
This government document is one of the most comprehensive guides to the compilation and classification of the economic time series data that make up the leading, coincident, and lagging indexes. Also provides primary data sources and statistical methodology used by the Bureau of Economic Analysis. Historical data and figures are included. Valuable for individuals who are interested in in-depth study of economic indicators.

U.S. Department of Economics and Statistics, Organization for Economic Cooperation and Development. *Consumer Price Indices: Sources and Methods and Historical Statistics.* Paris: Organization for Economic Cooperation and Development, 1984.
Describes the basic structure of the CPIs of all the countries that belong to the Organization for Economic Cooperation and Development, which are most of the world's major developed countries.

Varian, Hal R. *Microeconomic Analysis.* 2d ed. New York: W. W. Norton, 1984.
A very readable first-year graduate microeconomics textbook. Varian gives an outstanding presentation of the relationship between cost and production functions. Assumes some familiarity with calculus.

Wallace, William H., and William E. Cullison. *Measuring Price Changes: A Study of Price Indexes.* Richmond, Va.: Federal Reserve Bank of Richmond, 1979.
Explains the construction of several widely used price indexes. Intended for the general reader.

Wan, Henri Y. *Economic Growth.* New York: Harcourt Brace Jovanovich, 1971.
A rigorous, highly mathematical treatment of various growth models. Incorporates graphical analyses to highlight the mathematical results

of the models discussed. Appropriate for advanced undergraduates and specialists.

Wonnacott, Thomas H., and Ronald J. Wonnacott. *Econometrics.* 2d ed. New York: John Wiley & Sons, 1979.

In this undergraduate text, the authors have a simple presentation of the principle of maximum likelihood as it applies to regression analysis. Their diagrams are particularly useful for obtaining an intuitive understanding of maximum likelihood estimation.

AUTHOR INDEX

AUTHOR INDEX

SUBJECT INDEX

419

SUBJECT INDEX

SUBJECT INDEX

Nonprofit institutions, 206
Nonprofit organizations, 103, 351
Nonprofit sector, 205, 210, 231
Normative economics, 58, 77
Normative theory, 16, 53
Nuclear power, 330
Nurses, 304
Nutrition, 247

Off-budget borrowing, 211, 215
Offer curves, 224, 229, 232, 239
Office of Price Administration, 27
Oil, 326-328, 331
Oligopoly, 61, 78, 80, 82, 150, 268, 271
On-the-job training, 57, 299
OPEC. *See* Organization of Petroleum Exporting Countries
Open market operations, 183
Operations research, 99, 349, 364
Opportunity cost, 16, 63, 116, 161
Options, 169, 336, 339-340, 344, 346
Organization of Petroleum Exporting Countries (OPEC), 220, 225

Pareto, Vilfredo, 1, 14
Pareto optimum, 81, 121
Partial equilibrium, 61, 125, 224
Peak-load pricing, 266, 284
Perestroika, 89
Permanent income hypothesis, 59, 84, 92, 95, 106, 128
Phillips curve, 49, 101, 128, 132-133, 161
Physiocrats, 5-6, 8, 10, 16
Pigou, A. C., 3
Political business cycles, 32, 47, 90, 126, 156, 194, 308
Pollution, 143, 203, 307, 309, 314, 329
Population, 122, 291, 299, 303, 305
Portfolio management, 188

Portfolio theory, 343, 345
Positional goods, 99
Positive economics, 77, 83, 112, 118
Positivism, 7, 53
Post-Keynesian economics, 4, 84, 104, 111, 156, 170, 184, 193, 268
Poverty, 86, 95, 122, 143-144, 250, 255, 260, 290, 302, 310-313, 315-316, 322
Prebisch, Raúl, 249, 254
Prebisch-Singer hypothesis, 251
Price controls, 21, 27, 30, 41-42, 87
Price discrimination, 42, 138, 271, 279, 318
Price elasticity, 60
Price elasticity of supply, 146
Price fixing, 268, 280, 282
Price indexes, 368, 377
Principal-agent problem, 98
Private property, 124
Privatization, 270, 283, 314, 319
Product differentiation, 271, 279, 351
Product life cycle, 347, 354, 357-358
Production possibilities curve, 70, 141
Production theory, 65, 79, 85
Productivity, 3, 54, 107, 299, 312, 372
Progressive taxation, 197
Property rights, 64, 86, 97, 309
Property tax, 6, 195, 209
Protectionism, 10, 222, 227, 232, 239, 241
Psychology, 320
Public choice, 55, 128, 157, 270, 274, 308
Public choice theory, 63, 91
Public debt, 200
Public goods, 51, 61, 129, 132, 141, 212-213, 218, 311
Public investment, 74
Public sector, 282, 290, 311, 320
Public utilities, 63, 263-264, 266

425